Paul Found in His Letters

For David & Carol
Enjoy finding Paul
George H Martin
10-27-24

Paul Found in His Letters

George H. Martin

Claremont Press

Paul Found in His Letters

©2022 Claremont Press
1325 N. College Ave
Claremont, CA 91711

ISBN 978-1-946230-28-7

Library of Congress Cataloging-in-Publication Data

Paul Found in His Letters / George H. Martin
  ix + 336 pp. 22 x 15 cm.
  Includes bibliographical references and index
  ISBN 978-1-946230-28-7

Table of Contents

Acknowledgements	vii
1. Introduction	1
2. Paul in Arabia	31
3. Paul: What Does Your Name Mean?	53
4. Paul Living God's Story	69
5. Paul Lost in the Crowd	87
6. Paul Sent to the Nations	109
7. Paul in Community	123
8. Paul Found in Letters Heard	139
9. Paul an Unmanly Man	157
10. Paul Slave of Christ	193
11. Paul in a Troubled World	219
12. Paul the Mystic	245
13. Paul's Watch	275
14. Paul and the Kingdom to Come	299
Bibliography	307
Author Index	335

Acknowledgements

This journey began in the Spring of 2010. I was at a meeting in the home of Tex Sample. (He had retired from the St. Paul School of Theology in Kansas City where he taught theology.) He was living in Phoenix at the time. On his desk was a copy of a book by Douglas Campbell with the title *The Deliverance of God: An Apocalyptic Re-Reading of Justification in Paul*. "What's with that book?", I asked Tex. "Best damn thing I've read in a long time!" he declared.

I bought a copy of that 1200-page book and started on my journey. You won't find much about "justification" here, but as I've noted this is more about the history of Paul and not another theology of Paul

Along the way I was blessed with some wonderful mentors and friends. A number of years back Walter Dunnett helped me with my Greek which made a great difference as I entered more deeply into my research into Paul. He also gave me some treasured books from his library. Sadly, Walter died in 2019. A few years before Richard Pervo passed away in 2017 we met on a few occasions. Scholars who know his work might see Richard looking over my shoulder in this book. A special word of thanks needs to be extended to Neil Elliott who was most helpful as I created a draft letter of the theme of the book as I sought a publisher. There were also so many Pauline scholars whom I met through email so often in the Covid years. You know who you are, and I hope you are aware of my gratitude for your support and encouragement.

Speaking of a publisher, I am most grateful that Claremont Press found me. I had simply sought out Tom Phillips who I knew was connected to the Claremont School of Theology to ask him some questions about his work on Paul. I did not know he was the editor. He had done some research on my work which was posted at the time on my website for friends to read. In our first conversation Tom asked me if I would submit my manuscript when it was completed for their consideration. As they say, "The rest is history." The book was accepted just as Tom stepped down from being its editor. I'm also grateful to Professor Andrew Schwartz, the editor at Claremont

Press, and his team who helped usher this work into print. My special thanks to Chris Crawford the copy editor. I am so pleased to be connected to the fine work of Claremont Press.

In the process of writing this book I met with many small groups of laity and clergy to find out what they knew about St. Paul. I would ask, "What do you like about Paul? What don't you like? What are the hardest parts of his letters to understand?" We had lively discussions. Their concerns, questions, and doubts about Paul stayed with me all through my research. They helped write this book.

After I started writing I was able to make some presentations based on my research. One Spring I was blessed to meet with the clergy in the Diocese of Northwest Texas. Thank you, Bishop Scott Mayer, for that invitation. I thank my Lutheran bishop, Tom Aitken, who invited me to speak to the retired clergy of the Northeast Minnesota Synod. Bishop Susan Brown Snook also welcomed me to offer a one-day seminar in 2019 in the Diocese of San Diego. I was blessed when the Assistant Rector of All Saints Episcopal Church in Atlanta, Andy Barnett, invited me to lead a Zoom class on Paul this past year.

One special memory of presenting this material took place at St. Stephens Episcopal Church in Edina, Minnesota. The lecture was advertised as "Finding the St. Paul You Never Knew." One person who came was seriously disappointed. She thought I was some kind of expert on St. Paul, Minnesota, and I would reveal secret places to see and visit in our sister city that she did not know about. Needless to say, I needed a different title for this book.

While writing I posted each chapter on my website for friends to read, but more importantly to give me feedback. Paul Schelin was the one who faithfully read every chapter and always saw mistakes and sometimes things that just didn't make any sense. Others included Dick Duling and Manny Fimbres, my son-in-law.

Another dear friend was Brother Glen Lewandowsky with the Brethren of the Holy Cross in Onamia Minnesota. Time and again when I needed a translation of something from Latin he helped me. I was also able to meet on a few occasions with members of his community.

As already noted, I have been so blessed with the many scholars who have shared their ideas, their papers, and most of all their encouragement to me in the process of my research and writing. In particular I am so grateful to those who were willing to write endorsements of my book. Three appear on the cover of the book from George Lyons, Arland Hultgren, and Caroline Osiek. There are also endorsements on my website (www.paulfound.org) from Glen Lewandowski and Tex Sample. The website will have additional resources related to my research and a way to respond with questions and comments.

I could not have done all the research behind this book without the resources of two seminary libraries. My thanks to Peter Watters, the librarian at Luther Seminary in St. Paul. I have no idea how many books I've borrowed over the years. I also had access to the library's internet resources. The other librarian who assisted me so many times was Mitzi Budde from Virginia Theological Seminary in Alexandria Virginia. There were innumerable articles and papers, often from obscure journals which Mitzi and her assistants always found for me.

There was one person who stepped into my life who helped my writing at the end of this process. It is Ruth Wood. My wife and I took a Viking River cruise in December 2019. There we met Ruth and Dave Wood and became instant friends. When I told Ruth about my book and she let me know about her academic career as an English professor I had met the person who would help me edit all my rough drafts of chapters. Countless hours, and innumerable emails led to the MS sent to Claremont Press, and then the massive re-write that brought the book down to a reasonable size. Ruth is the angel sent to me!

Most important are the loving and supporting members of my family. Our children (Kate, Sue, Tim and Mike) all grew up in the years when I was such a busy pastor, and now in my retirement they have offered me so much love and encouragement in my research and my writing. One person really is most special of all. We've been married ever since we were in college. Both of us were thinking I would really retire, but then I happened to begin my studies of Paul. It was my dear and loving wife who cheered me on and inspired me to see this book become a reality. It is to Caroline that I dedicate this book.

Chapter 1
Introduction

> "Because of the entrenched nature of the traditional paradigm, it is very difficult to see Paul with a new set of eyes."
> - Pamela Eisenbaum[1]

> "Too much of Paul's life is completely hidden from us... for any of us who have worked, or are working, in this field to be overconfident."
> - John Knox[2]

For almost 2,000 years people have been asking questions about St. Paul. One of the first could have been a prison guard charged with censoring outgoing letters from the prison in which he was being held. Four of the letters that bear Paul's name came from times when he was imprisoned: Ephesians, Colossians, Philippians, and Philemon.[3]

What did this guard think about Paul who mentioned the loyal women who worked beside him in his letter to the Philippians? Men in authority and power didn't consult with women or have them at their side during their work. Not in Caesar's world. Women as coworkers? It was totally at odds with the way most men in Rome saw themselves. The censor reading Paul's prison letter sent to the Philippians had to think the man is crazy. Paul had written that Euodia and Syntyche were his coworkers, and he said their names were written "... in the book of life" (Phil 4:3).

---

[1] Pamela Eisenbaum, *Paul Was Not a Christian: The Original Message of a Misunderstood Apostle* (New York: Harper Collins, 2009), 216.

[2] John Knox, "Chapters in a Life of Paul — A Response to Robert Jewett and Gerd Lüdemann ," in *Colloquy on New Testament Studies: A Time for Reappraisal and Fresh Approaches*, ed. Bruce Corley (Macon: Mercer University Press, 1984), 364.

[3] Credit for the way this book starts belongs to Elizabeth Tamez who wondered how the letter to the Phillipians could have possibly passed unnoticed by a prison censor. Elizabeth Tamez. "Author's Introduction to Philippians," in *Philippians, Colossians, Philemon*, ed. Elsa Maex et al. (Collegeville: Liturgical Press, 2016), 78.

Did this same guard happen to read Paul's shortest letter, the one sent to Philemon? If so, he must have surely wondered about Paul's sanity in using kinship language describing a slave[4] — Onesimus — as his own child. Paul wished that Philemon would receive Onesimus back not as a slave "…but more than a slave, a beloved brother" (Phlm 16). The world in which prison guards lived was *vertically shaped* in terms of power and authority. Clearly slaves could never be *the equal* of their owner. What a crazy idea Paul had! That a slave and his owner could somehow see each other as brothers?[5] My hypothetical guard charged with censoring prison letters had to be thinking Onesimus deserved death or at least a very severe beating at the hands of Philemon.

Romans, which is Paul's longest letter, was not sent from a jail cell, and is presumably the last one of his letters, but it would have been equally puzzling to any Roman in authority. Paul began that letter with the totally unexpected claim of being a "slave," calling himself a *slave of Christ*. (Rom. 1:1). The Greek word is *"doulos,"* which is sometimes *weakly* translated as "servant"[6] — a term in our world fitting with the concept of helping one another. Paul knew, however, that a slave wasn't free to serve. Slaves had no choice when asked to do something. They were always under orders. They were the possession (*just property*) of someone else. Paul's consistent reference to himself as a "slave" was not how he started out in life. Why on earth would any man or woman in that world willingly adopt that personal identity?

Even more puzzling to a man in 1st century Rome would have been the last chapter of Romans where we find the longest set of personal greetings found in any of Paul's letters. The chapter begins with Paul commending Phoebe who is "…a deacon[7] of the church at Cenchrae." (Rom 16:1). She holds an office of leadership! Next, Paul

---

[4] Often Onesimus has been described as a "runaway slave," but in Chapter 10 "Paul Slave of Christ," the argument is that he was *sent* to help Paul in prison.

[5] David Horrell notes that Paul's language implies "equal-regard"…that (in some sense) supervenes over their (former) relationship as owner and slave. David Horrell, *Solidarity and Difference: A Contemporary Reading of Paul's Ethics* (New York: Bloomsbury T & T Clark, 2016), 126.

[6] "Servant" is in the NRSV (New Revised Standard Version). Most of the well-known translations use the word "servant."

[7] The Greek word there is *diakonon*. It is the source for our word "deacon."

mentioned Prisca and Aquila. They are a couple to be sure, but why would Paul mention Prisca first?

There is a reference to another couple, Andronicus and Junia, who were in prison at one point with Paul. Then he added an astounding detail "...they are prominent among the apostles and they were in in Christ before I was" (Rom 16: 7). The reference to this couple obviously troubled some unnamed scribe, or maybe more than one, making a new copy of Romans in the centuries prior to the Renaissance. No one knows if it was intentional to turn Junia into Junias—the name of a man but beginning with translations starting in the 13th century the masculine name Junias frequently appears. Luther, for example, "opted for 'den Juniam', and continental translations have since then mostly followed this masculine interpretation."[8]

Junia had become Junias in many translations in the past 500 years.[9] *She* had been turned into a *he*! A few scribes, perhaps independently, with tattered copies of Romans may have decided Paul couldn't have meant that there was a woman who was an *ambassador* of Christ. But he did.

From Paul's letters, especially the seven certain to have come from his hand, we have a picture of communities of faith struggling with a variety of issues and challenges. What is fascinating are the many personal details that reveal surprising aspects about Paul inside those letters—many of which have been seemingly unnoticed or ignored for the past 1900 years. John Knox was an exception. "Moreover, Paul's letters are unusually revealing, even for letters, and convey his personality in an extraordinary vivid and direct way."[10] Among the revelations we must include Paul's amazing openness to working alongside women in ministry and what had to be his story of shaping his life around the least respected and most subjugated people in his world. We will see communities of faith

---

[8] John Thorley, "Junia, A Woman Apostle," *Novum Testamentum* 38 (1996): 1, 18-29. For translations that use Junias (masculine) like the Revised Standard Version and the New International Version and those that retain Junia (feminine) such at the King James Version and the Latin Vulgate see Richard S. Cervin, "A Note Regarding the Name 'Junia(s)' in Romans 16.7" *New Testament Studies* 40 (1994): 464-70.

[9] The NRSV puts *her name* back in the text at Rom. 16:7 and then offers as an alternative the masculine name Junias. He's still hanging around even if he never existed!

[10] John Knox, *Chapters in a Life of Paul* (Macon: Mercer University Press, 1987) 75.

shaped from his preaching and missionary work who were not reinforcing standard social practices of the ancient world. There is evidence that some of these assemblies continuing into the 2nd and 3rd centuries still practiced an unusual egalitarian set of values which they traced back to the teaching of Paul. But egalitarian values were also being *contested* as we see in the Pastoral Epistles coming in the early part of the second century. The memory of Paul was being reconstructed, by some, at least in such a way that Paul would *not* have recognized himself. I can only wonder if Paul would recognize himself as I proceed to recover Paul from his own letters.

1.1 My readers

Before I get too far with Paul, I need to be clear about why I am writing this book. I'm writing for the many I've known in my ministry who simply can't *understand* Paul's letters or who often *don't like* what they hear. To be sure people generally like to hear the 13th chapter of 1 Corinthians: "And now faith, hope, and love abide, these three; and the greatest of these is love" (1 Cor 13:13). That plays well at many a wedding, but nearly everyone that I know, both lay and clergy, have at least one verse from one of his letters, if not many, that lead them to have questions about St. Paul—some of which are very critical and serious matters to be sure.

With my background as a pastor, I want to address the questions the average person sitting in church will be wondering about when hearing the letters of Paul in a reading or when discussed in a sermon. I would hope that pastors reading this book will discover aspects of Paul's story that have often been ignored—or, more egregiously, been shaped by documents that were re-writing Paul's story.

I hope that there are a few biblical scholars who will be reading this book, but I must be honest that I am not writing this *for* scholars, though I could not write this book without their help. What I want the scholars who pick up this book to know is how much respect and admiration I have for your dedication. I can't begin to compare myself to the skills you acquired with regard to ancient languages, and in so many cases the decades of service you have given to your work.

It has been a true privilege for me in my retirement years to go back to school, as it were, with the many scholars whose names appear in the bibliography. I've had discussions with just a few listed there, as well as many emails. I feel like I know many of you because I've been blessed to have the time, resources, and patience of my loved ones, to pursue this research. I feel called upon to carefully add footnotes making sure these scholars get the credit they deserve. To be clear, this book is not a dissertation! It is one pastor's journey, somewhat late in life, to encounter Paul and to be *happy* to have found him. I hope many of my readers will also *find* the Paul that seemingly got lost. Please read on!

1.2 Preliminary concerns about the historicity of Acts

The one document that is the most troubling for this particular enterprise, with regard to its historicity, is "The Acts of the Apostles." I will refer to it simply as Acts. For most of us, including this author, Acts was, at best, the most reliable account regarding Paul because it filled in the blank spaces with questions unanswered from his letters. Its eye-witness accounts, from the earliest days after the resurrection, presumably pre-dated Paul's letters.

For the last 1,900 years, when preachers and biblical scholars wanted to share something about Paul, in *biographical* terms, they nearly always began with Acts for most details regarding Paul's story. There we find the dramatic account of his call to follow Jesus when Paul was on the road to Damascus. He was going to Damascus to continue his persecution of followers of Jesus. The same story, with a few variations, is told *three times* in Acts. Ever since, this story is *the* story most Christians know about Paul. He, who had been the one persecuting followers of Jesus, suddenly and dramatically became a "Christian."[11]

Each account of Paul meeting Jesus, in Acts, involved the question of the Lord, "Saul, Saul, why do you persecute me?" (Acts 9:4). The repetition of someone called to serve God fits a pattern from the Scriptures.[12] Further on in this book we will examine Paul's

---

[11] The word "Christian" appears in quotes because it wasn't a term that Paul used for himself in any of his letters. Acts (11:26 and 26:28) makes the reference to this term. The only other time it appears is in 1 Peter 4:16.

[12] There are four times when God calls to someone using their name twice. Those addressed this fashion were Abraham (Gen 22:11-13), Jacob (Gen 46:1-4), Moses (Exod 3:10) and Samuel (1 Sam 3:1-10). Jesus used the same nomenclature on two occasions: when addressing Martha (Luke 10:38-42) and Simon (Luke 22:31-32). The story of Paul's call, as framed by Acts, certainly places Paul in the context of other significant figures in the history of Israel.

own account of his call as *the* account we should trust. Paul's emphasis on being "called" is what stands out in his letters. My approach is to take Paul at his word and to question the reliability of Acts.

My skepticism about Acts, however, isn't consistent—nor should it be. Even with all my questions about Acts I understand it to be an important account of the development of early Christianity. There are also a couple of places where Acts definitely helps us tell Paul's story with one little detail helping us find a particular date for Paul in history—as explained in Chapter 2, "Paul in Arabia." Chapter 3, "Paul. What Does your Name Mean," allows us to consider the possibility that Paul's name had been Saul —his Jewish name before he went by *Paulus* as a follower of Christ. Acts did not explain Paul's name change but simply reported that Saul was also called Paul. (Acts 13:9) That becomes the name used for the rest of Acts.[13]

Did Paul ever have such a distinguished name as Saul? Was Paul ever "Saul" but didn't want any of his letter recipients to know his old name? That's highly unlikely. In Galatians 2:13-14 Paul tells of his own past deeply rooted in protecting the Jewish faith and practice. He does not use his Hebraic name there as a frame of reference. The same argument applies to Philippians 3: 4-6 where he emphasized his Jewish credentials:

> "If anyone else has reason to be confident in the flesh, I have more: circumcised on the eighth day, a member of the people of Israel, of the tribe of Benjamin, a Hebrew born of Hebrews; as to the law, a Pharisee; as to zeal, a persecutor of the church; as to righteousness under the law, blameless" (Phil 3:4-6, NRSV).

You would think Paul would have added, to that account, his most Jewish name "Saul" if he had such. There is much more to be said about Paul's name which I believe *is the story* of his life in Christ. In a kind of ironic twist, the author of Acts may have known this to be the case even as he turned Paul into the last standing hero of his account.[14]

---

[13] The name "Saul" does reappear in later chapters when the Damascus-road story is repeated, albeit with variations. (Acts 22:6-16 and 26:12-19).

[14] In Smith and Tyson, the suggestion is made that giving Paul the Jewish name Saul was a kind of literary device. Dennis E. Smith and Joseph B Tyson, eds. *Acts*

Acts, written most likely in the early 2nd century, is a carefully framed narrative by an author able to construct a compelling story. The work itself has been important within the life of the Christian community ever since, but it is *not* a reliable historical source, particularly with regard to Paul.[15] For centuries, however, nearly all scholars thought, at least in terms of its source material, that Acts *predated* knowledge of Paul's letters. Acts is a carefully structured account of heroes of the faith in the early church with Paul getting top billing. Fascinating and exciting stories are there about Paul's travels, miracles, escapes, imprisonments, and speeches, but a not a single mention about Paul ever writing letters.[16] Perhaps those *collections* of Paul's letters came later.[17]

As noted earlier the scholarly consensus for most of Christian history was that Acts offered eyewitnesses to the early church in its birth. The author of Acts also seemed to write as a co-worker of Paul. In one account the author said that he met up with Paul in Troas: "On the first day of the week, when *we* met to break bread, Paul was holding a discussion with them…" (Acts 20:7). A number of other passages follow in the later chapters of Acts where there is a reference to "we," especially with regard to traveling to new places. (Acts 21:1-8, 15-17; 27:1-8; 28:1, 11-16). Those accounts were taken at face value. Acts became *the way* to tell Paul's story. It continues to be the main source for many with regard to the life of the early church.

As we proceed with the focus on what Paul actually said *about* himself, however, there will be occasions to consider some critical

---

and Christian Beginnings: The Acts Seminar Report (Salem: Polebridge Press, 2013), 148.

[15] See John Dominic Crossan, *Render unto Caesar: The Struggle Over Christ and Culture in the New Testament* (New York: Harper Collins Publishers, 2022) for a recent critique of Acts which offers a Paul seeking accommodation with Imperial Rome.

[16] In an essay by William O. Walker, Jr. there are reasons to suspect that the author of Luke knew at least one of Paul's letters but choose not to mention that Paul wrote any letters. William O. Walker, "The Letters of Paul as Sources for Acts," in Smith and Tyson eds. *Acts and Christian Beginnings: The Acts Seminar Report*, 116-17.

[17] Trobisch thinks Paul saw four of his letters as a collection. It is the four letters speaking directly about a collection for the poor in Jerusalem (Romans, 1 & 2 Corinthians, and Galatians.) Collections were formed early in the 2nd century about the time Acts was composed. David Trobisch, *Paul's Letter Collection Tracing the Origins* (Minneapolis: Augsburg Fortress, 1994), 70.

biblical research from the past fifty years raising some serious questions about the veracity of Acts. I believe it is equally important to frame those questions in way that still respects the way that Acts has been a deeply ingrained part of the overall story of Christianity.

For the most part this account of *"Paul Found: In His Letters"* concentrates on the *autobiographical* details in the seven letters Paul wrote, while keeping Acts out of the picture as much as possible — even though it is totally impossible to ignore its account. It is the proverbial *elephant in the room*. Actually, it isn't the only elephant, because the Pastoral Epistles (1 & 2 Timothy and Titus also paint a different picture. Questions can also be asked with regard to 2 Thessalonians, Colossians, and Ephesians as will be noted further on in the book.

With the Pastoral Epistles we find a heroic Paul who isn't connected with other apostles since he was essentially considered *the Apostle*. By writing in Paul's name, and even as some scholars suspect re-writing parts of Paul's letters, there is clear evidence that the identity of Paul was already in dispute among early Christians. The Paul speaking in the Pastoral Epistles in a number of important ways sounds different from the Paul in the seven generally accepted letters. Consider the observation of Dennis MacDonald:

> With all due respect to the author of the Pastoral Epistles, when we read the *Acts of Paul* we recognize that not all Christians in the Pauline circle would have silenced women from teaching, trimmed the order of widows, exhorted slaves to continued servitude, and commanded obedience to Roman authority. We can in short, no longer assume that the Pastoral Epistles were the rightful second century heirs of the Pauline legacy.[18]

In recent church history with regard to the issues of the ordination of women we have continued the historic debate regarding the question of who are the rightful "heirs of the Pauline legacy." The issue still isn't resolved since some more traditional "heirs" believe only men can be ordained. They read as gospel the statement, "I

---

[18] Dennis R. MacDonald, *The Legend and the Apostle: The Battle for Paul in Story and Canon* (Philadelphia: Fortress Press, 1983), 15. The full title referenced by MacDonald is *The Acts of Paul and Thecla*, a 2nd century document indicating women in early ministry influenced by Paul. Tertullian, an early church father from the 2nd century saw her as a "heretical woman;" see Lionie Hayne, "Thecla and the Church Fathers," *Vigilae Christianae* 48 (1994): 209-18.

permit no woman to teach or to have authority over a man; she is to keep silent" (1 Tim 2:12).[19] As the debate took place in the Episcopal Church in the 1970s, however, that passage of scripture was weighed against the clear evidence that Paul had women working alongside him including Phoebe (a deacon[20]) and Junia[21] (an apostle, an ambassador). The General Convention of the Episcopal Church in 1976, after much discussion and many tears on both sides of the question, approved a change in its Constitution and Canons to permit women to be ordained both as priests and as bishops. [22] We were debating the legacy of Paul.

Benjamin White in *Remembering Paul* extends the arguments regarding Paul's legacy with his comprehensive study of early church documents. The Pastoral Epistles and Acts were hardly unique as there were many writings from the 2nd and 3rd centuries giving contrary pictures of Paul—or at least, at times contrary to what Paul said about himself. To be sure we will never have all the facts to discern the truth regarding Paul's identity. We only have a portion of what he wrote. Moreover, we do not have accurate eyewitness accounts from his contemporaries. There is evidence, however, of strong oral traditions from early communities which kept their stories about Paul while facing their own challenges in living their faith—or rather, their loyalty to Jesus, but we can only guess with regard to what they were saying.[23] We need to consider the possibility that some of the oral traditions might have carried *more* truth about Paul than the written records from the same period, but that isn't verifiable. We're left with his seven letters.

There is evidence that some second-century writers knew Paul's letters, but as will be emphasized in Chapter 8, Paul Found in Letters Heard, it was a world where "words were written down in order to be read out-loud."[24] Some of writings from the early second-century emphasized the legendary Paul. Others never mentioned him. All of

---

[19] A similar contentious passage is found in 1 Cor 14:34–35. It is discussed in Chapter 9 "Paul an Unmanly Man."

[20] Romans 16:1.

[21] Romans 16:7.

[22] In 1973 approval had been given for women to only be ordained as Deacons.

[23] Benjamin White, *Remembering Paul: Ancient and Modern Contests over the Image of the Apostle*, (New York: Oxford University Press, 2014), 6, 13–14.

[24] Birger Gerhardsson, *The Reliability of the Gospel Tradition*, (Peabody, MA: Hendriksen Publishers, Inc, 2001), 113.

them, including the Pastoral Epistles would have been performed. But were people really hearing Paul? White frames the questions this way: "Which Paul? then, is the first question we must ask of each invocation of the Apostle. Is it the legendary Paul? If so, which legend? It is the epistolary Paul? If so, which epistle(s)?"[25]

In a sense Paul beyond his letters, encased in the contested memories and the struggles of various Christian communities, is multi-faced. Once more, White summarizes a number of different images of Paul:[26]

- the heresy fighter and caretaker of the household of God in the Pastorals
- the great Martyr in Ignatius
- the writer to the fractious Corinthians in 1 Clement
- the wise teacher for Polycarp
- the challenger of traditional society in the Acts of Paul and Thecla
- the public speaker and missionary for Luke (Acts)

Sitting in most churches the average person would guess Paul wrote most of the letters in the New Testament. When there is a reading from 1 or 2 Timothy the name of Paul is nearly always said to be its author. Few pastors would offer a preface to such a reading doubting that it came from Paul, even though that would represent the consensus of most biblical scholars. There is rarely, if ever, such a preface to explain that this letter (say, 1 Timothy) came from a community that treasured Paul, but which disagreed with some of the things that Paul had written. It probably won't help, in that worship, to say this reading reflected a community, maybe 50 or more years after he died, honoring the "legendary" Paul. In the context of this book, though, we will lend more credence to letters from Paul himself.

To take this account of the early contested images of the Ambassador Paul just a little further, it helps if we see that whoever was writing in Paul's name was, in a sense, doing the work of a historian. In a changed and changing world they were reaching back and bringing Paul forward. The historian Edward Carr emphasized that each historian "mirrors the society in which he (*sic*) works."[27]

---

[25] White, *Remembering Paul*, 55.
[26] White, *Remembering Paul*, 63.
[27] Edward Hallett Carr, *What is History* (New York: Vintage Books, 1961), 51.

Reading the Pastorals we find a far more organized church, but one facing a set of heretical challenges most likely in the early second century.[28] As noted earlier in this introduction there are three other letters that are seriously debated with regard to their authenticity: 2 Thessalonians, Ephesians, and Colossians. Each may reflect a different set of circumstances and issues than those common to the other seven. Those three epistles, as it were, may reflect or mirror a different time.

There is another much longer story to be told about Paul's identity as derived from his letters. So many scholars in Christian history seemingly have concentrated on his brain— on what Paul believed. Paul's letters, especially in the Reformation and the centuries since, have been mined for their wisdom regarding Christian theology and doctrine. A nineteenth-century biblical scholar, Ferdinand Christian Baur, is a particularly important figure in this story

Baur (1792-1860) came out of a tradition focused on Paul's theology. After giving credit to Paul for basically being the founder[29] of Christianity, Baur maintained that there were only four legitimate letters from Paul: Romans, Galatians, and 1 and 2 Corinthians. He dismissed all the others for their presumed tendencies to present a more "Catholic Paul."[30] Baur, essentially, set the pattern, still dominant at times in parts of the Protestant world, which in his case meant using the basic four letters as ". . . polemical weapons against both the Catholic Church and Judaism. . . ."[31] N. T. Wright laid the same charge against Baur, but in a slightly different way: "F. C. Baur forced upon the material his rigid and anachronistic analysis of the two 'isms', Judaism and Hellenism, the latter to be preferred over the former."[32]

Paul for Baur became, and for many since, the great architect of Christian dogmatics. For Baur and many other biblical scholars the pursuit of Paul has been to understand Paul's theology and not so much the man himself. An example of this approach is seen in the

---

[28] Richard Pervo, *The Making of Paul: Constructions of the Apostle in Early Christianity* (Minneapolis: Fortress Press, 2010), 83.
[29] An idea held by few today.
[30] White, *Remembering Paul*, 21-23.
[31] White, *Remembering Paul*, 24.
[32] N. T. Wright, *Paul and His Recent Interpreters: Some Contemporary Debates* (Minneapolis: Fortress Press, 2015), 1477.

Pauline scholar James D. G. Dunn. In his *The Theology of Paul the Apostle*, he singles out just one letter as the quintessential way to discover Paul's theology: "In short, Romans is still far removed from a dogmatic or systematic treatise on theology, but it nevertheless is the most sustained and reflective statement of Paul's own theology by Paul himself."[33]

It isn't as if my journey in this book into the story of Paul will ever ignore what Paul thought and believed, but this is *not* another book on Paul's theology, except as it relates to *his story*, and the faith communities he founded and visited.

There is one more reality regarding Paul's place in history, especially as it relates to Christianity, and what might have been, at the time, his *minor*, seemingly insignificant role as a leader. He wasn't, as he admitted, even a significant or key witness to the resurrection. Peter was the first witness and Paul was the last.[34] "Last of all, as to someone untimely born, he appeared also to me" (1 Cor 15:8).

When we encounter the reality of many legends about Paul, we can see how they were shaping the early Christian communities in the 2nd century, but also how those communities were divided by theological quarrels and debates. That is the period in history when we find Paul taking on a much more significant role than he had in his own time. Patrick Gray has observed, "It is uncertain whether Paul was as significant during his lifetime as he came to be in later centuries."[35] To be sure, with regard to the communities that received his letters he was important, but we have no way of ascertaining how far his actual reputation spread in those early days. By his own admission there were divided opinions about him in Jerusalem. In that setting some opposed him, others like Peter, but maybe only for a brief time, were favorable because Paul was sent to the Gentiles. Even though there were "false believers" in Jerusalem

---

[33] James D. G. Dunn, *The Theology of Paul the Apostle* (Grand Rapids: William B. Eerdmans Publishing Company, 1998), 25.

[34] Did Paul not know that the first witnesses were the women? See Matt 28:1–10. Consider, sadly, that the men who heard the witness of women in Luke 24:1–12 thought that the report of the women was "an idle tale" (Luke 24:11). In John's gospel Mary Magdalene is the first to see the Risen Lord (John 20:14–18). In Mark, once more, it is the women who discover the empty tomb, and then do not tell others "for terror and amazement had seized them" (Mark 16:8).

[35] Patrick Gray, *Paul as a Problem in History and Culture: The Apostle and His Critics Through the Centuries* (Grand Rapids: Baker Academic, 2016), 24.

(Paul's report in Gal 2:4) both he and Barnabas had the "right hand of fellowship" extended to them by James, Cephas and John, as they were sent on their way to "go to the Gentiles" (Gal 2:9).[36] Sadly, the Jesus people in Jerusalem, along with the first disciples, died out or were enslaved with the destruction of Jerusalem in 70 C.E.

In a very real sense, the controversial Paul will always be in view in this analysis of his letters, but he may not be the "larger than life Paul" of some accounts such as we find in Acts and the Pastorals, or even in some of the 2nd and 3rd century legends about him. More likely we will be discovering a complex man, with a deep faith, and an extraordinary constitution able to handle all kinds of adversity who was so very conscious of the historical significance of what "God has done in Christ."

In what follows neither Acts nor the Pastoral Epistles will be ignored. Nor should they be. A more detailed analysis of the complicated issues with regard to these particular documents, however, will be covered in in what is called an *excursus* at the end of this opening introduction. An excursus is a digression from the main topic, but which, nonetheless, offers relevant information.

1.3 The Focus on Paul's Seven Letters

What is important in discovering Paul's identity is that we *have* letters he clearly wrote. In those letters he was *present* to those who received them. This concept of presence may be hard to grasp, given our desire to hear and see someone as the way in which they are present to us. The actual process of sharing the stories of our lives no longer takes place in writing letters. We live in a world of emails, text messages, and twitter statements, all of which can be lost in an electronic blizzard. We are blessed with the letters of the past as we tell our own family stories. My worry is that with all our digital and screen technology we may not be passing on to the future the letters of our lives. Paul's letters, though, allow us to hear him, and to gather a better picture of the man himself.

There are 13 letters in the New Testament with Paul's name attached. Not all of those epistles, however, were written by Paul.

---

[36] Paul in his words had the commission to go to the Gentiles (Gal 1:16). What we cannot account for is how Acts disputes this claim with Peter's speech at the Council of Jerusalem where Paul was present. Peter's assertion is that he was the voice "through whom the Gentiles would hear the message" (Acts 15:8).

One or two may actually catch Paul's voice, perhaps by those who knew him and worked alongside. Other letters seem to paint a totally different picture of Paul. Consequently, there are three different categories differentiating the degrees of certainty with regard to authenticity.

The seven letters that nearly all scholars agree were written by Paul are: Romans, 1 Corinthians, 2 Corinthians, Galatians, Philippians, 1 Thessalonians, and Philemon.

There are three other letters that Paul might have written: 2 Thessalonians, Colossians, and Ephesians.

The Pastoral Epistles carry Paul's name, but this particular designation can be rightly questioned because they are so different in many respects from the other ten letters: 1 Timothy, 2 Timothy, and Titus

In the early days of television there was a game show called "What's My Line. There were three contestants all pretending to be someone with a particularly unique job or skill. They would all be introduced with the same name. Each might say "My name is Joe Adagio. I repair expensive violins." Questions of the contestants followed, but then the judges needed to vote. After the judges cast their ballots for the one they thought was the real person, the host would ask "Will the real Joe Adagio please stand."

The example of the game show is relevant to this work because we have three different kinds of letters in the New Testament, and the narrative of Acts makes a fourth candidate for whoever is to be called the *real Paul*. At one time I imagined Paul as a contestant on this game show and heard the Game show host ask, "Will the real Paul, Apostle to the Gentiles, please stand up?" Sadly, even as I try to let us hear Paul's voice, I'm not so sure there is a "Real Paul", but there are aspects to Paul's story sometimes ignored or forgotten which are discovered here.

Further on in eighth chapter "Paul Found in Letters Heard" we will look more closely at the six contested letters that bear Paul's name. The question there is "Can we still hear Paul?" For the purposes of discovering more of Paul's story, given the premises of this account, we have an abundance of material in the seven letters clearly bearing Paul's imprint. My strategy is simple: closely examine the seven letters and let Paul tell us who he really is, even though in his own time, others saw him in their own way. At times Paul tells us what others thought about him. In the years that followed, of course, other legends and stories of Paul continued in the oral world of the early Jesus communities. Some of these accounts and letters, like the *Acts of Paul and Thecla*, for example may carry truthful aspects of Paul's story, but their veracity becomes a matter for scholarly debate.

Beker reflecting on Paul in the Pastoral Epistles presents a different problem, because of the different voice of Paul emerging from what clearly are letters written decades after Paul. The situation of these early followers of Jesus had certainly changed as they faced issues of securing a stable position of acceptance for the practice of their faith in the Roman world. The Paul in the Pastoral Epistles stands alone, not in the context of the other early leaders who claimed apostolic status. Beker commenting on Paul in the Pastoral Epistles said, "…Paul is the *sole* apostle, the person who enjoys indisputable authority."[37] It may or may not trouble us, but it seems these *later* documents were written to make Christianity more respectable. "Now Paul was sufficiently domesticated to serve the needs of a church increasingly eager to gain social acceptability."[38]

In contrast to the Pastoral Epistles marginalizing the ministry of women, we find considerable evidence on the positive role that women played in the ministry of the communities founded by Paul *in* those seven letters. The evidence of Paul's positive views on shared leadership stands in stark contrast to some particularly difficult passages coming from 1 & 2 Timothy and Titus which present a Paul who cannot support women in leadership. It is important to consider a few examples.

Could Paul really have written the following? "Let a woman learn in silence with full submission. I permit no woman to teach or have authority over a man; she is to keep silent" (1 Tim 2:11–12). What a contrast this statement is to the reality that women were allowed to pray or prophecy just as men were doing in public worship in the Corinthian assemblies[39] (1 Cor 11:5).

---

[37] J. Christian Beker, *Heirs of Paul: Their Legacy in the New Testament and the Church Today* (Grand Rapids: William B. Eerdmans Publishing Company, 1991), 47.

[38] MacDonald, *The Legend*, 89.

[39] "Paul and his co-senders apparently see no problem with women praying and prophesying during a worship meeting in 1 Cor 11.5, thus participating in an active role in the assemblies," Kathy Ehrensperger, *Paul and the Dynamics of Power: Communication and Interaction in the Early Christ-Movement* (New York: T&T Clark, 2009), 172.

With regard to the prohibition of women having authority, there was his respect for Junia as an apostle (Rom 16:7) Consider also that he entrusted the delivery of the letter to the Romans in the hands of Phoebe. (Romans 16:1-2) To be sure there is another passage in 1 Corinthians 14:24-36 that declared that women should be silent in church. Some scholars are quite confident that Paul didn't write those words as his words.[40] A few scholars consider this passage as an "interpolation", meaning that some scribe, reflecting a later time in the church, gave these words to Paul in making a copy of this letter. This passage receives deeper scrutiny in Chapter 9 (*Paul an Unmanly Man*). It may be that Paul was quoting words from Corinth, and then as I will explain there, completely refuting them.

Paul *found in his own letters* is really quite different from most of other men in the first century when it comes to his view of women. In some surprising passages he uses metaphors that only a woman would be expected to use. So many of his co-workers were women as well. The patriarchal Paul is certainly present in the non-Pauline letters, while a *less manly man* emerges in the seven letters we are confident he wrote. There will be a dialogue in what follows with documents coming after Paul, but greater confidence will be placed in what Paul actually said, rather than the words put into his mouth by others who came after him.

In summary, *Paul tells much of his own story in his letters.* When there is information from other sources that can confirm or substantiate something about Paul, it clearly will be helpful to this enterprise. Acts, for example, is not always at odds with what Paul wrote. The other side of this process, of course, is the premise that any stories or facts that contravene something Paul said must be treated with great suspicion.[41]

---

[40] MacDonald, *The Legend*, 86–88.

[41] My intent is not to denigrate Acts or to have it removed from the New Testament canon. We can bring historical criticism to this account and still admire the creative narrative handed down to us by the author of Acts, while questioning its historicity. I would hope the readers of my book appreciate that I am taking Acts as an important account of the emergence of early Christian communities, and I am treating it in a serious manner. I would wish for the same assessment accorded to an earlier Biblical scholar, John Knox, who questioned the historicity of Acts. It was said of him that he did "...indeed take Acts with the utmost seriousness; instead of *assuming* its reliability he subjected it to the rigorous cross-examination that is required in good historiography." Douglas R. A. Hare, "*Introduction*" in John Knox,

1.4 Paul is not at his desk writing theology

The Paul met in these pages is not some kind of dour pipe-smoking theologian tucked away in a book-filled office writing systematic theology. To this day so many of the books about Paul focus on what was in his head, instead of the kind of man he was. Beker's observation is relevant to this focus on his seven letters. Beker wrote "we continue to treat Paul as an abstract-propositional, dogmatic thinker. . . . Most of us perpetuate the custom of reading Paul in a historical manner by universalizing some of his theological ideas while ignoring its socio-historical setting."[42] I would hope Professor Beker would be pleased to discover that there is no dour pipe-smoking theologian sitting in a comfortable study with the picture of Paul in what follows.

The genesis of this particular study looking at Paul's narrative in the context of the seven letters stems from my discovery of *"Pauline Autobiography: Toward a New Understanding"* which was the dissertation project of George Lyons.[43] Professor Lyons limited his project to Galatians and 1 Thessalonians, with regard to the autobiographical reflections from Paul found in each letter. Lyons' thesis was that whenever Paul made reference to himself, and it wasn't often, he, nonetheless, was following a practice and pattern frequent in the Greco-Roman world, or what is called Hellenism. In his conclusion Lyons stated that "Paul writes in the autobiographical mode only reluctantly and almost always apologetically."[44] Once I read the book by Lyons, I began to read these seven letters thinking that Paul's story, or shall we say Paul's *stories*, were there to be discovered.

In this account I can assure my readers that Paul emerges as a fascinating man in the midst of conflicts and also in the context of unique emerging communities of equals living together in a way that few could have thought possible.[45] He was a passionate man.

Chapters in a Life of Paul (Macon, GA; Mercer University Press, 1987), p. xl.

[42] J. C. Beker, *Heirs of Paul: Their Legacy in the New Testament and the Church Today* (Grand Rapids: Eerdmans Publishing Company, 1991), 28.

[43] George Lyons, *Pauline Autobiography: Toward a New Understanding* (Atlanta: Scholars Press, 1985).

[44] Lyons, *Pauline Autobiography*, 223.

[45] Zerbe notes that Paul perceived "a redistributive program that moves toward equality (*isotēs*) against the redistributive, tributary machine of the Roman imperium that moves toward ever greater inequality," Gordon Mark Zerbe, *Citizenship: Paul on Peace and Politics* (Winnipeg, Manitoba: CMU Press, 2012), 75.

He had strong feelings and opinions. He was also surprisingly gracious, forgiving (at times) and tender. The one thing lacking, at least from our limited point of view, may have been a sense of humor. [46] He certainly lived with a sense of purpose and direction and was not afraid of challenges. In the end he left a legacy that I doubt he never even worried about having.

Paul knew one thing would happen when he was writing those letters and sending them off with co-workers: they would represent him well. It was that *his presence* would be felt as those letters were shared. We have to stop thinking that the letters were read by individuals. They weren't read as we do with books like this. They were performed. They were embodied in a performance. They were voiced by those who carried them, not just in scrolls, but in their memory. Readings of Paul's letters were more like a theatrical event in the context of worship, and it is highly likely that letter performances would be repeated in the same way that some of us watch the same movie more than once. As the letters were read those who knew him were hearing his voice and sensing, once more, his presence.

This Paul is still with us. We may have to blow the dust off him when we find him in some long-forgotten theology books in a seminary library. We know we must be suspicious of reports about Paul that came later. But we can read his letters with fresh eyes. That's what this book is all about.

1.5 The Structure of the story — Chapters 2-14

A major concern in these chapters is to place Paul properly in the history of his times. The social, cultural, and history of the first century needs to be context in which we listen to the stories of Paul. This can't be a traditional biography as we simply don't have much documentary evidence.

Without knowing when or where Paul was born, given our premise to use just his seven letters, we can, nonetheless, make some reasonable guesses regarding *when* Paul began his ministry as Ambassador to the Gentiles. It is also possible to offer a rough course

---

[46] John Knox, *Chapters in a Life of Paul*, rev. ed. (Mercer Ga: Mercer University Press, 1987), 87. Elsa Tamez also notes the anomaly of an emphasis on "joy" in Paul's letter to the Philippians. This is a topic seemingly absent in the other six letters, but there was Paul writing from a prison cell emphasizing joy. Maybe he alone could smile in prison; Tamez, "Author's Introduction," 187.

of his ministry based on information found in his letters, without relying on Acts. Paul's revelation from God that Jesus was the Messiah may have happened within three years of the crucifixion of Jesus—maybe within a year! The two were most likely close in age, with Jesus being perhaps a few years older. God's revelation to Paul was connected to Paul's journey to Arabia (**Chapter 2**).

He went to Arabia following God's revelation to him of Jesus as Messiah. (Gal 1:17). It is a fascinating story to tell involving Galatians 1:17 and two stories of Paul escaping from Damascus in a basket (2 Cor. 11:11-33 and Acts 9:23-25). Some research into the international intrigue linking Galilee, the Nabatean Kingdom and Rome makes it possible to even determine an approximate date *when* Paul probably first went to Arabia. There is no other clue in any of the other letters ascribed to Paul's hand, where it possible to ascertain a particular date in the first century with regard to any of Paul's travels or letters. The one clue we have, though, is sufficient.

The story Paul offers is not that of the self-made man. But there is something of his story with regard to the possibility that he wanted a new name to coincide with God's apocalypse of Jesus Messiah. **Chapter 3** *"Paul: What Does Your Name Mean?"* asks more questions, than it provides answers, but it sheds light on what I think was Paul's *adopted* name. In this chapter I also offer some more traditional images of Paul that stand in stark contrast to the story he was living.

Since a major premise of this account is that we can learn a great deal about Paul from just seven letters, **Chapter 4** *"Paul Living the Story"* lays the groundwork for much that follows. Here we place Paul in the first century as a diaspora Jew living under Roman occupation. We pick up some small details and wonder what lies behind a claim he made such as having an "untimely birth" (1 Cor 15:8). There are few references to his being a child, but enough to offer some reasonable questions. It's also probably accurate to say that Paul's recognition of Jesus as God's Messiah, however, and when it happened, was the single most life-changing part of his story. Was it a conversion or a call? The never-ending question must be asked again and again.

Once more staying with the theme of finding Paul in the cities in various Western provinces, **Chapter 5** suggests we might have found Paul carrying his tools, but determines he was difficult to find as he must have looked like the majority who were poor. It is titled

"Paul Lost in the Crowd." Here I ask some sociological questions regarding Paul's social status. I presume he was lost in the crowd of the majority of those who poorly clothed and who, for the most part, lived a day-to-day existence. Where he lived and the trade at which he worked placed him alongside the most marginal members of his world. There is a continued scholarly debate regarding the social economic makeup of early communities of Jesus followers, with some emphasizing the role played by those with wealth. This debate is also considered.

Chapter 6 is titled *"Paul Sent to the Nations."* Paul's Jewish identity is critical to his account, because of the tendency to think he somehow became "a Christian." He wouldn't know what the word meant. Here, I wrestle with the problem of translating *"ethnē"* as "gentiles," since the latter as a category didn't exist. What is clearly emphasized is that Paul, who follows Jesus, is deeply Jewish, albeit in some way that are anomalous.

Chapter 7 *"Paul in Community* might also have been titled *the extroverted Paul.* He has friends all over. Daily he had to be thinking and praying about the various communities he founded. He has various teams engaged in ministry with him, and many were women. This gives me a chance to partly right the ship that for too long has labeled Paul a misogynist and his friends (and maybe his opponents) back in Jerusalem and the other faith communities he founded.

They were all participating in the drama of God's story, not just has it has been known, but as it was unfolding before their eyes. When Paul discovered, in Corinth, for example, that there were divisions (factions) replicating the hierarchical social distinctions in the world, he was deeply concerned. Unity was to be found only in Christ, and all the worldly differences having no importance. Here we will discover community where respect and dignity for "other" was a non-negotiable ethic.

Chapter 8, *"Paul Found in Letters Heard,"* offers some ideas about the presentation of Paul's letters that have been only rarely considered, even by seminary trained clergy. What is here was news to me in my research, but it was most welcome news. We need to leave behind the image of his letters as dry and hard to follow. Going back to their collaborative composition it's also important to see how as they were delivered. It was as if Paul himself had become present as trusted friends performed them.

The Paul so very present in his letters had to also be extremely bewildering to at least many of the men in the various communities who knew him. Thus, in **Chapter 9** we meet *"Paul the Unmanly Man."* He was hardly the model of success in his world, having left behind a secure honored way of living as a religious elder, to have a peripatetic life as a laborer. He had joined what Rebecca Solnit termed "the empires of the ill, the frail, and the failing."[47] As a man he crossed unexpected boundaries to become a Gentile *other*, and to give respect and dignity to women in a patriarchal culture keeping women in a second-class status no matter their nationality or tribe. His call to men to follow him with regard to these attitudes had to be most bewildering.

The sister chapter to "Paul the Unmanly Man" is **Chapter 10** *"Paul Slave of Christ."* We will be looking at the scars on his back and exploring the harsh reality of life for slaves in the Roman world. One thing that cannot be ignored are the troubling passages from other letters in the New Testament which Paul didn't write, where we find *a* Paul who was endorsing slavery. (i.e., Eph 6:5–8, Col 3:22–25, and 1 Tim 6:1–2) The evidence of a great many slaves attaching themselves to these new communities of followers of Jesus indicates something positive regarding what they heard from Paul about belonging to Christ. Onesimus is one slave who was Paul's most unusual friend. That story is evocative of Paul's radical understanding of the dignity of all people.

To understand Paul in reference to his letters means placing him in the context of the first century, particularly the reality all knew so well which involved the horrors of a slavocracy and an unimaginable cruel, vicious, and violent rule in which one-third all people were non-persons.

Paul most likely died at hands of Nero and was considered a traitor. **Chapter 11,** *"Paul in a Troubled World"* has two parts. With the question "Was Paul a failed pastor?" we look at the problems Paul addressed regarding accusations made against him in Corinth. Some intricate exegesis of 2 Corinthians unearths a story helping us to see Paul's leadership skills. In the second part of the chapter, we are looking for Paul in his letter to Romans. The social and political history of Rome is in view as we discuss Paul's understanding of *justice*.

---

[47] Rebecca Solnit, *The Faraway Nearby* (New York: Penguin Books, 2013), 128.

Paul was not just a theologian offering carefully composed doctrinal works. This highly passionate and emotional man had visions. **Chapter 12,** *"Paul the Mystic,"* offers a side of Paul often overlooked in the world of biblical scholarship. It considers Paul's emphasis on the place of the *spirit,* (the *pneuma),* in so much of his story and the life of the communities he addressed. Paul was not defined by a single vision but belonged to a spirit-inspired world centered in Christ. "And we speak of these things in words not taught by human wisdom but taught by the Spirit (*pneumatos*), interpreting spiritual things to those who are spiritual" (1 Cor 2:13). Important in this context will be 2 Corinthians 12:1-10 which bears the title "Paul's Visions and Revelations" in my NRSV. Paul wasn't always in his study writing letters, but often on his knees in prayer!

"Paul's Watch" (**Chapter 13**) comes at the end, because Paul thought he was living at the end of time. Christ would return and usher in a new creation. The days of the current rulers were numbered. Here we look at Paul's sense of time, but not as we usually measure time. The days of the world's evil rulers were numbered in Paul's mind, because of the judgment to come with the return of the Messiah. The passion of Paul was for a kind of justice grounded in the mercy of God, which would shape a new world—a new creation. That faith would guide him and his companions as they took a collection from Pauline communities to Jerusalem. From there Paul would pass through Rome and with their support he hoped for his mission to Spain. We do not know how it all ended for Paul but in this chapter, we wonder if Paul wanted to go to Spain to reach those most recently enslaved and subjected by Rome.

The concluding chapter, **Chapter 14,** *"Paul and the Kingdom to Come"* includes reflections on this journey back in time to meet Paul in the first century. I'm reluctant to leave him there. One of the most surprising things is how Paul was found—not rejected—by slaves in America as their voice for freedom. The real voice of Paul is one heard over and over. Thus, it is good to ask: What does it mean that 2,000 years later we still pray "Come Lord Jesus, come!"? My sense is that Paul has much to remind us about the importance of church unity grounded in a sense of justice for the least in our world.

Excursus 1.1 Terms I'm reluctant to use

In the chapters that follow you will seldom find terms like "gentile," "church" or "apostle", to list just three of many words that can confuse our understanding of Paul's message. To be sure, knowledge of Greek is not required to follow any parts of this argument. Greek words will be transliterated. One troublesome English word is Gentile (singular) or Gentiles (plural). *They* only existed from a Jewish perspective.

Finding Paul means seeing the ways in which he remained a Jew who developed a focus and passion inviting all *others* no matter what nationality or tribe to know the story of God culminating in the resurrection of Jesus. We have a problem, though, with terminology if we use either *"gentiles"* or the phrase *"non-Jews"* as if such existed in Paul's world. We have a long history in English bibles of translating the Greek word *ethnē* as *Gentiles*. But no one, so labeled in that world, would have ever described themselves as an *ethnē*. The Greek word *ethnē* is best translated as "nations" knowing that each entity had its own unique sense of identity, often grounded in a common language. In Paul's world you would receive a very strange look had you called a stranger a *Gentile*. "They would argue that they were Greeks, Corinthians, Macedonians, or some other ethnic/linguistic designation. Then and now, ethnicity and nationality are fundamental elements of identity."[48]

The Greek word for someone who gets called a "Jew" in English bibles is *ioudaioi*. It is derived from the name Judah, which was one of the 12 tribes of Israel. When the Babylonian Exile took place with the Jerusalem leadership displaced for three to four generations (ca. 586-537 BCE) they began to call themselves the Yehudim. They named themselves after the land where Jerusalem would be found. When we come to the 6th chapter, I will have more to say about *ioudaioi* as a word that can be translated either as Jews or Judeans. No matter what the translation we are not dealing with anything close to antisemitism as it emerged in history.

Questions of terminology will surface quite often. While Paul likely focused his preaching and ministry on people who were not Jews, it would be misleading for us to say that Paul was reaching *non-Jews* because that would create a designation that frames Paul's mission in a negative way.[49] To be sure major translations like the

---

[48] Paul Trebilco, *Outside Designations and Boundary Construction in the New Testament: Early Christian Communities and the Formation of Group Identity* (New York: Cambridge University Press, 2017), 156-57.

[49] My thanks to Bernard Brandon Scott for this observation in a conversation we had.

NIV and NRSV do not translate *"ethnē"* as non-Jews, but they consistently use the term "Gentiles." Because most English translations always capitalize "Gentiles" it seems on the surface as if there were such people in Paul's world. As noted above, however, the term "Gentiles" would not mean anything to anyone in Paul's world, except to Jews who referred to all the others in their world, but not necessarily in a derisive way.

In the scriptures we find a number of prophets seeing the *ethnē* as part of God's world. They have an eschatological vision of people from all the world (all *ethnē*, all nations) coming to worship God with their gifts in Jerusalem. Paul was taking up a collection from the *nations* as represented by the communities of faith he founded to take to Jerusalem. The collection will be a matter for our consideration further on in this book. For now, what is important is to see that *all these nations* and their representatives are envisioned doing something quite honorable and favorable to God. Elliott summarizes Paul's vision:

> "In his frenetic activity in Asia, Macedonia, Achaia, and Italy he intended to organize a caravan of the "first fruits" of the nations, holy gentile men and women marching into Jerusalem in fulfillment of the prophetic scenario of the last days (Isa 2:2-4, 12:3, 25:6-8, 60:3, 66:18; Jer 16:19; Mic 4:1-3; Zech 8:20-23). Paul understands this work as an act of worship." [50]

Paul's vision to reach the *ethnē*, the nations, was shaped in large part by these more positive ideas of a day when the whole world would come to worship the one God, whose story included creation and the calling of Abraham (i.e., Zech 8:20-23). These two aspects of God's story were central to the teaching of Paul. From this point on, except when quoting from other sources that use the term *gentiles*, I will either use the Greek word *ethnē*, or the word "nations."

Another term that is problematic is *"Apostle."* This is the traditional way of referring to Paul as *Apostle*. It is important, however, to discuss some legitimate concerns regarding this designation. To be sure in many of his seven letters Paul began by

---

[50] Neil Elliott, *Liberating Paul: The Justice of God and the Politics of the Apostle* (Minneapolis: Fortress Press, 2006), 175.

using the Greek word *apostolos*, to describe himself.[51] The word comes to us as a transliteration of the Greek word, which has the meaning "one who is sent from."

In parts of Christianity that reflect a more traditional kind of ecclesiastical and hierarchal structure both Paul and Peter are called the first in the historic line of apostles. I believe Paul would be as surprised as any to be included in such august company and, he would be most surprised to be placed at the head of the line. More than once in this account we will wrestle with Paul's personal identity as "Last of all, as one untimely born..." (1 Cor. 15:8)

The main problem with the term *"apostle"* is that it appears to be an official title, which at least in our world, is the result of an election or an appointment. You even can wear special clothes as a modern-day *Bishop*, perhaps in the historic line of succession tracing its way back to the first apostles. All the bishops I know are easily recognizable in their ecclesiastic garb. As I suggest in Chapter 5 "Paul Lost in the Crowd," we wouldn't have picked him out in a crowd, for he dressed as one who was poor.

As a substitute term for *apostle*, I was tempted to follow the lead of Bernard Brandon Scott who gave Paul the title of "envoy."[52] The term *envoy* captures the sense of the verb "sent" which lies at the root of *Apostolos*, but as Scott admitted to me in an email the better title to give Paul is that of "Ambassador." The more official title of *Ambassador* connects powerfully with our understanding of Paul as *called* or, as he says in the introduction to Romans, "set apart" (Rom 1:1). We will be exploring in some depth the scholarly debate asking whether Paul was called or converted, but suggesting that the former (i.e., called) fits with Paul's own statements about his story. Both "envoy" and "ambassador" can describe Paul.

Another detail that must be discussed before heading into the main chapters of this book regards my reluctance to use the words "Christian" and "church." The focus here is on Paul's ministry in the years 30 to 60 in the first century. We are not sure if the word "Christian" had even been coined in that time period. The word "Christian"[53] appears three times in the New Testament, but only

---

[51] Please note that at places in this account I will also use the Greek word *apostolos*, especially when it relates to Paul's own Greek in one of his letters.

[52] Bernard Brandon Scott, *The Real Paul: Recovering His Radical Challenge* (Salem: Polebridge Press, 2015), 42.

[53] Actually, the term is *Christianos*.

from documents composed near the end of the first century, perhaps even from the early 2nd century. The references to Christians are found twice in Acts (11:26; 28:28) and once in 1 Peter (4:16).

Scholars believe the term was used to *condemn* these strange people worshipping a crucified messiah.[54] The label "Christian" was first used *against* the followers of Jesus, and only adopted as a distinctive, more positive, label in the second century.[55] I will use the terms "followers of Jesus" or the "Jesus movement" as a way to describe members all these early assemblies.

What we call church isn't at all a good translation of the Greek word "*ekklēsia.*" Church in our world implies an institution, and it can mean some kind of distinctive building. It is also the term that separates Jews (with their institutions of synagogue and temple) from Christians who gather in churches. Paul's *ekklēsia* were united—Jew and Gentile together—to Christ. The term *ekklēsia* applied to all kinds of associations in the first century. It was also the word in Paul's Greek bible (the *Septuagint)* used for the assembly of all the people before God.[56] Horsley described the term this way: "*Ekklēsia* is thus a political term with certain religious overtones."[57] There's little doubt that Paul opposed the dominant ideology of the Roman Empire, but rarely in a blatant attacking mode. When writing to the Philippians, for example, Paul "…tells them his own story, the story of how he had abandoned his status and privileges in order to find the true status and privilege of one in Christ, and he encourages them to imitate him."[58] Obviously Paul has a vision of community quite different from the vertical and hierarchal world of the Roman Empire.

---

[54] Ernst Haenchen, *The Acts of the Apostles: A Commentary* (Philadelphia: The Westminster Press, 1971), 368. In a footnote he suggests that the term "*Christianos*" may have originally been used by Roman authorities to designate a sect of political conspirators. If Luke, however, had known of the origin of this term, if it was so, it would have undermined the main theme of Acts regarding the friendly treatment offered the followers of Jesus.

[55] Dennis E. Smith and Jospeh B. Tyson, eds. *Acts and Christian Beginnings: The Acts Seminar Report* (Salem: Polebridge Press, 2013), 136.

[56] Paul Trebilco, "Why Did Early Christians Call Themselves ἡ ἐκκλησία?" *New Testament Studies* 57 (2011): 444.

[57] Richard A. Horsley, "Building an Alternative Society: Introduction," in *Paul and Empire: Religion and Power in Roman Imperial Society,* ed. Richard A. Horsley (Harrisburg: Trinity Press International, 1997), 208.

[58] N. T. Wright, "Paul's Gospel and Caesar's Empire" in *Pauline Perspectives: Essays on Paul* (Minneapolis: Fortress Press, 2000), 182.

One problem that must be recognized when using the NRSV translation for most of the quotations from the New Testament is its choice of consistently translating the Greek word *ekklēsia* with the English word *"church."* For example, in the beginning of Galatians we find this address "To the churches of Galatia" (Gal 1:1 NRSV). I think it is wise to consider the counsel of Anders Runneson:

> In light of this ancient terminological and sociopolitical context it becomes quite clear that the English translation "church" is inappropriate and misleading, since it conjures up not only a (modern) religious non-civic, non-political setting, but more importantly, imposes on the ancients a separate non-Jewish institutional identity for those who claimed Jesus to be the Messiah.[59]

In what follows, when thinking about those assemblies of early Jesus followers, I will more often use Paul's term *ekklēsia*. At times I will also talk about "assemblies" because the practice of gathering for worship was a critical marker for membership in the *ekklēsia*. This book concludes, however, with the implications of Paul's story for those of us, including myself, who also treasure the word *church*. We need the story of Paul to reclaim an even more profound understanding of *ekklēsia*!

Excursus 1.2 Can the Historical Paul Ever Be Found?

An honest appraisal of doing history involves all that we don't know and what we may never discover. The historian Eric Hobsbawm wrote "Much about the behavior of people *of all classes* today, is in fact, as unknown and undocumented as was much in the lives of common people in the past."[60] What may set apart Paul's letters and all that was written in his name and about him in the centuries following his death, is that many honoring Paul were living *undocumented* lives. They even wrote letters in his name and didn't want to be remembered by their own names. They were pseudo-biographers, which sounds to our ears like they were criminals. It just wasn't a crime back then. We shouldn't see it that

---

[59] Anders Runesson, "The Question of Terminology: The Architecture of Contemporary Discussions of Paul," in *Paul Within Judaism*, ed. Mark Nanos (Minneapolis: Fortress Press, 2015), 72.

[60] Eric Hobsbawm, *On History* (New York: The New Press, 1997), 215; italics in original.

way, either. What mattered in the issues of their time, years after Paul, however, was to let him speak to their time and their issues, and what better way than to write in Paul's name.

There were different ways to hear Paul's voice and teaching in the years after he was martyred. Certainly, different communities had copies of some of his correspondence, and read them in worship. As those documents started to wear out, or when other communities wanted a copy, then copies were made. At that point discrepancies in the texts appeared — some unintentional, and others to amend something Paul might have said, but which no longer applied. At other times some took the liberty to write in Paul's name, and in a few cases, it might even have been someone close to Paul in his ministry. (Sometimes it is suggested that Paul was not the author of Colossians and Ephesians, but rather they were written by followers close to Paul.[61]) In other instances there were oral stories and legends about Paul which in a few instances were eventually written down and passed around from one community to another. The goal in all these different ways of continuing Paul's voice was to "... make the apostle useful and relevant for later times, as well as the theological perspectives that informed them."[62]

A question that we can never answer from our 2nd and 3rd century church documents is "Who got Paul right....?"[63] It would also be presumptuous to lead my readers astray to think that getting Paul "right" is the way this account ends. Whoever takes a stab at "finding Paul" will have to be honest about their own social location in history in the first place, and their place in the theological issues of their own time. The historical task with regard to the 2nd century, for example, is to understand Christ-followers struggling in a pagan world in which they were often seen as a threat to a more traditional way of life. Christ-followers, after all, weren't showing up for the gladiatorial games or participating in other public celebrations of civil life. Moreover, living in the context of Judean ethics they were

---

[61] Richard Pervo in *The Making of Paul* thinks Colossians fits with "the development of Pauline thought" (65) but describes the author of Ephesians as a "stranger" to Paul (72). At the opposite extreme is Douglas Campbell, *Framing Paul: An Epistolary Biography* (Grand Rapids: William B. Eerdmans Publishing Co., 2014). He maintains that Paul is the author of Colossians and Ephesians, the latter of which Campbell argues is the lost letter to the Laodiceans, 252-338.

[62] Pervo, *The Making of Paul*, 38.

[63] White, *Remembering Paul*, 174.

living in visibly different ways from their neighbors.

Another way to be realistic about the different "*Pauls*" in early church history comes from Wayne Meeks, who mentioned the great divergence in those who were identifying Paul as the "most holy apostle" while others called him the "apostle of the heretics."[64] Meeks goes on to note the many "inconsistencies" in Paul (i.e., in his letters) and says, "Paul is the Christian Proteus." In the Odyssey of Homer "Proteus was a *daimon* of the sea who could assume any form he chose."[65] It was Paul, of course, who boldly declared that "I have become all things to all people" (1 Cor 9:22).

Those early legends about Paul outside of his letters are examples of different communities of faith finding Paul's voice for their issues of living the Jesus story. Paul did not live to see the way his teachings and his story would continue, but that is true for each of us. We all step into a past that begins to shape us, but we also don't have the benefit of knowing what the future will do with our legacy when we are no longer alive.

Paul was aware of adversaries and controversies which arose in communities he founded, but little could he image how diverse this story of Christ crucified would become in the immediate centuries to follow, and how many opposed to each other would each claim him for their own arguments regarding Christianity. There would also be large segments of developing Christian communities *without* any stories or legends of Paul. The amazing travels of Paul extending from Arabia going West toward Rome (hoping for Spain), nonetheless, left large parts of the Mediterranean world untouched by his ministry or his letters. Patrick Gray noted "that there is ample evidence for the early spread of Christianity to Rome, North Africa, Syria, Cyprus, and other areas untouched by the Pauline Mission network."[66]

The "historical" Paul is a kind of fiction. Who he *is* depends on *who* is seeking him, and *what* is their historical context. My own story is that for a long time I usually avoided Paul. Rarely, in the first forty of my fifty plus years of preaching, did I base a sermon on passages from Paul's letters. When I first became more interested in Paul it was in pursuit of understanding a particular doctrine of his that

---

[64] Wayne A. Meeks, "The Christian Proteus," in *The Writings of St. Paul*, ed. Wayne A. Meeks (New York: W.W. Norton and Company, 1972), 435.

[65] Meeks, "The Christian Proteus," 435; italics in original.

[66] Gray, *Paul as a Problem*, 204.

fascinated me. I realized I had never studied in much depth the "doctrine of justification by faith" which was the central focus of the Protestant Reformation. Talk about a contested area among Pauline scholars! I found it. What I also learned is that there was much more to Paul than a particular theology or doctrine.

So, if we err in reading Paul through the different pictures from the early legends and the pseudepigrapha bearing Paul's name, do we not equally fail if we cannot see how others in our times influence our view of Paul? N. T. Wright has observed, "… There are plenty of serious-minded people in the world today who read Paul through a series of lenses bequeathed by Luther, Kant, Bultmann and others, and then interrogate Paul as to his perceived inconsistencies and aporiae as though these were there in his writings rather than in the cross-eyed effect produced by the lenses."[67] The danger in reading Paul is that we do so through the issues affecting us or those who study Paul with a particular worldview that seems amenable to us.

What if we take a step back, however, and let Paul speak for himself? That is the question I found framed by a number of scholars that have informed this effort. Going back to his letters we can find a consistency in Paul that seeks to model the story of Jesus which rather boldly (or so it can seem) involves Paul's claim that others should follow his example as he was following Jesus. In a more colloquial way Wright translates an assertion of Paul in 1 Cor 11:1 this way: "'Copy me, just as I'm copying the Messiah.'" The short sentence that follows suggests this is a statement that helps us *find Paul*. "With that we are touching bedrock."[68]

The *example* of Paul is what we will be looking for in this account. We will leave the issues of his contested identity for others to study, while we listen for Paul's frequent autobiographical statements. Thankfully his letters are not abstract philosophical or theological treatises. Paul was living and breathing all the while dictating his letters. Yes, dictating. Others were always in the room or in prison with him. We meet many of them as well. They were working alongside of him—alongside the Paul who can be found!

---

[67] N. T. Wright, *The Faithfulness of God* (Minneapolis: Fortress Press, 2013), 67.
[68] Wright, *The Faithfulness of God*, 1510.

Chapter 2
Paul in Arabia

Arabia is a vague word.[1]

From Paul's seven letters we are able to only discover *fragments* of a man's life. That is the best we can do. This can never be a biography in the traditional sense of that genre. Obviously, if we let Acts frame our account, we would have more material, but not enough to satisfy real biographical curiosity. Even though extended narrative accounts are infrequent in his letters[2] there is still much to be learned about Paul in the issues he faced and the company he treasured. The best place to begin to find Paul is with his own account of how God found him.

Finding Paul must begin with Paul's description of God's *call*[3] for him to be an *apostolos* and how the Messiah was *revealed* to him.

> But when God, who had set me apart before I was born and called me through his grace, was pleased to reveal his Son to me, so that I might proclaim him among the Gentiles, I did not confer with any human being, nor did I go up to Jerusalem to those who were already apostles before me, but I went away at once into Arabia, and afterwards I returned to Damascus (Gal 1:15-17).

Paul went to Arabia! He waited three years! He added this information to the story:

---

[1] G. W. Bowersock, *Roman Arabia* (Cambridge: Harvard University Press, 1983), 1.

[2] Stanley E. Porter, *Paul in Acts* (Peabody: Henricksen Publications, 2001), 194.

[3] In Chapter 4 "Paul Living the Story", and at other places in this book, the emphasis is on Paul's call and not his conversion. There are many scholars (i.e., Alan Segal) who believe it was a *conversion* in Alan Segal, *Paul the Convert* (New Haven: Yale University Press, 1990). It's a debatable topic, to be sure. The landmark book emphasizing Paul's *call* was written by Krister Stendahl in *Paul Among Jews and Gentiles and Other Essays* (Philadelphia: Fortress Press, 1976).

Then after three years I did go up to Jerusalem to visit Cephas and stayed with him for 15 days; but I did not see any other apostle except James the Lord's brother" (Gal 1:18–19).

There are no clues in this report about *when* Jesus was revealed to Paul, but there are some chronological clues to be followed in what Paul says. A critical comment is the disclaimer made by him after he was called to proclaim Jesus among the Gentiles (*ethnē*). He declared that he *did not* "go up to Jerusalem to those who were already apostles before me." Between his call and a visit with Peter in Jerusalem was a three-year period. After that comes an even more perplexing vacuum in Paul's life that lasted fourteen years. With another revelation (*apokalypsis*) he went up to Jerusalem for the second time. This is what he charted in this narrative.

Paul called. God reveals his son to him	Year 1 (Gal 1:15
Paul in Arabia. At some time returns to Damascus	Year 1–3 (Gal 1:17)
Paul's first visit to Jerusalem	After year 3 for a 15-day visit (Gal 1:18)
The missing years	14 years (Gal 2:1)
Makes second visit to Jerusalem	17 years after his call (Gal 2:1)

What was the date when he was visiting Peter for the first time? It was probably in late 36 CE or early 37 CE.[4] when Paul met Cephas (Peter). This means that somewhere around 33CE or 34 CE Paul was *called to be an apostolos to the ethnē*, and by his own account, traveled to Arabia. There is no real way to say how long he stayed in Arabia, but there is one clue from another letter that he was there long enough to get into some kind of trouble.[5] As you will discover Paul did not work with a travel agent to get to Jerusalem. The premise of this chapter is that it was a last-minute decision to save his life.

Paul's call to follow Jesus might actually have happened within a year or so of the crucifixion. Was Jesus crucified around 30 CE?

---

[4] The *Excursus* at the conclusion of this chapter explains in great detail the story behind our certainty for this approximate date for Paul's escape from Damascus.

[5] Douglas Campbell believes Paul was there for the entire three years; see Douglas Campbell, "An Anchor for Pauline Chronology: Paul's Flight from the Ethnarch of King Aretas: 2 Corinthians 11:32-33," *Journal of Biblical Literature* 121 no. 2 (2002): 279-301.

That is a possible date as is 33 CE. The actual dates are less important than knowing that Paul and Jesus were contemporaries. There's no reason to think Paul ever met or heard Jesus. Certainly, you would think there would be evidence in one or more of the letters if that had happened. He does report in a couple of places having received a word of the Lord, and those passages point to the mystical side of Paul. (See Chapter 12)

Based on Paul's recounting we have *intervals of time* between events. John Knox observed that the *intervals* are more crucial than the actual dates. "For the understanding of Paul it matters little, if at all, just when, in terms of calendar years, his work began or just when it ended. What matters is what happened in it — the order of events and the intervals between them."[6] I would simply add, following the basic strategy of this account, we want to-rely on Paul's own accounts.

Acts states that Paul encountered the Risen Jesus as he "approached Damascus" (Acts 9:3). In Galatians Paul declared that he "returned to Damascus" (Gal 1:17) after going to Arabia. It is logical to assume that Damascus was one of the places where Paul was, "violently[7] persecuting the church of God and was trying to destroy it" (Gal 1:13). But why?

2.1 Why did Paul persecute the early followers of Jesus?

Among the details imbedded in Paul's story in Galatians we discover Paul's acknowledgment of having persecuted early Jesus followers, or more accurately not individuals but the *"ekklēsian"* of God (1 Cor 15:9, Gal 1:13).[8] He found something wrong and even dangerous in those Judeans declaring that Jesus had risen from the dead and was the expected Messiah. I think we need to challenge the usual picture of "Paul the Persecutor," and look at the real possibility that he was acting as "Paul the Protector." Paul was, after all, a staunch defender of the Judean faith.

As mentioned earlier we can also presume that Damascus was the city where Paul was known to be a Pharisee. (Phil 3:5) With these

---

[6] Knox, *Chapters in a Life*, 67.

[7] Further on in the next section I will contest the translation describing Paul's persecutions being marked by violence.

[8] Arland Hultgren, "Paul's Pre-Christian Persecutions of the Church: Their Purpose, Locale and Nature," *Journal of Biblical Literature* 95 no. 1 (1976): 109. I have changed his "churches" to the Greek *"ekklēsia."*

details in mind Paula Fredriksen imagined what the Judeans in Damascus were thinking when early missionaries (other *apostoloi* perhaps) might have come from Galilee with the message about the messiah who had been crucified and then arose from the dead. Did these missionaries have occasions to preach during Sabbath synagogue services? If so, they may have been preaching to a mixed congregation of people from many parts of the world, because there were God-fearing *others* (even Romans) interested in the Hebraic story and way of life in Judean communities throughout the Roman Empire.

What Fredriksen emphasizes is that this particular message was dangerous, even seditious. The core of the message from these Jesus followers might have been the vision of the end of the world with the expected return of the Messiah. "…this was dangerous. If it got abroad, it could endanger the whole Judean community."[9]

More than the news itself, we must also consider Paul's passion for preserving ethnic identity where Judeans lived beyond the borders of Judea. Trained as a Pharisee he wrote in Galatians, "I advanced in Judaism beyond many among my people of the same age for I was for more zealous for the traditions of my ancestors" (Gal 1:14). Having been trained as rabbi meant Paul would have memorized the Bible. Teaching was by recitation. After hearing the same passage three or four times it was expected that the text would be memorized.[10] The Bible was not a book or set of scrolls that Paul carried around with him in a knapsack, but it was always there with him—in his head.

It wasn't just scripture that mattered. Paul had to know the political realities facing the Judean way of life. For example, in Jerusalem itself, in the beginning of the first century there was a tense relationship between the authorities in Jerusalem and the occupying Roman army. Clearly whatever Paul knew about those early Jesus followers troubled him, especially if it could provoke Roman retaliation. We can only presume to consider Paul's early concerns, because they were never spelled out in his letters. At the same time, he never denied his persecution of the community to which he would devote himself. He admitted it in three of his letters.

---

[9] Paula Fredriksen, *From Jesus to Christ: The Origins of New Testament Images of Jesus* (New Haven: Yale University Press, 1988), 154.

[10] Richard A. Horsley, *Text and Tradition in Performance and Writing* (Eugene: Cascade Books, 2013), 10.

(1 Cor 15:9; Gal 1:13, 23; and Phil 3:6). It could be that Paul was simply trying to preserve space for Judeans to practice their faith without troubling or alerting the Roman authorities.

In trying to understand Paul's early opposition to the news of the resurrection of Jesus, we know the problem was not resurrection *per se*. As a Pharisee Paul believed in the eventual resurrection of the dead, with the coming of the Messiah.[11] The problem was not belief in a Messiah because those ideas had been in the air for 400 years. But it had to be difficult to comprehend how one crucified as a criminal and rebel was the expected Messiah—whose death was understood as what Roman did to those considered traitors. Commenting on Paul's declaration in 1 Corinthians about the message of the cross as foolish, Richard Gordon wrote, "…it would indeed have been 'folly' (1 Cor 1:23) as well as an anti-Roman political statement to proclaim and organize communities around a crucified political criminal as a central symbol."[12]

Rome had already, through a decree of Augustus, recognized that Judeans could send a temple tax back to Jerusalem, and were permitted in some provinces to keep their Sabbath day practices. Fearing some kind of reaction from those loyal to Rome may have led Paul to what he termed his "earlier life in Judaism" when he was "persecuting[13] the *ekklēsia* of God" (Gal 1:13). We must also consider that in the eyes of the Romans, who alone had the legal right to inflict crucifixion on a criminal or for someone charged with treason, Jesus was "…perceived to be a political threat. He had aroused multitudes with his preaching of the kingdom of God; he criticized the Temple establishment in Jerusalem, which bore allegiance to Rome and through which Roman colonial power was maintained; and he seemed generally to have been a regular disturber of the peace."[14] Paul could have shared that sentiment prior to his unexpected "call."

With regard to the kind of persecution Paul might have administered as a synagogue official—if that is what he was—it would have been a discipline called *makkot*, which was a lashing. The

---

[11] Pamela Eisenbaum, *Paul was Not a Christian: The Original Message of a Misunderstood Apostle* (New York: Harper Collins, 2009), 53.

[12] Richard Gordon, "The Veil of Power," in *Paul and Empire: Religion and Power in Roman Imperial Society*, ed. Richard A. Horsley (Harrisburg: Trinity Press International, 1997), 141.

[13] Note that this is a word that will be considered shortly.

[14] Eisenbaum, *Paul Was Not*, 146.

law allowed a maximum of 39 lashes! Paul, himself, received that punishment, by his own recollection, five times. (2 Cor. 11:24). He never disclosed the reasons his back bore those scars, but they must certainly have been visual evidence of such punishment.[15]

Paul's earlier fear of a Roman response to a rebellion in Judea was not something he lived to see. The rebellion which began in 66 CE broke out first in Alexandria and then spread to other cities including Damascus. It finally culminated with the destruction of Jerusalem in 70 CE. At that point Judeans lost the privilege to send their temple tax to Jerusalem. Instead, they found themselves building a Roman temple with a new tax designed just for them. This new tax would be building a pagan temple. Clearly this tax meant all diaspora Judeans were violating the first commandment.

Jerusalem was still standing when Paul saw the early Jesus followers as a danger to Judaism. To be sure most translations of Paul's use of the Greek word *diōkō* use the English verb "*to persecute.*" But the first meaning of the word in my lexicon is to "hasten, run, press on," with "persecute" as the second meaning. Other possible meanings of the word are: drive away, drive out, run after, pursue, even to strive for or seek after."[16] Given the reality that as a Pharisee Paul had to be part of a community constantly discussing issues and challenging various interpretations, I have to believe Paul was more argumentative than persecutorial with this new sect of Jews proclaiming Jesus Messiah.

Paul's analytical mind must have given him some clear reasons to oppose this new and fervent sect. What is hard to accept is the account in Acts regarding Paul having been *sent by* Jerusalem authorities to Damascus where was supposedly "ravaging houses" and "breathing threats and murder" (Acts 8:1-3; 9:1-2). We are on safer ground, as I have suggested, to consider that Paul, already living in Damascus, may have been trying to preserve privileges that existed within a kind of tolerance from Roman authorities protecting Judeans who were practicing their faith. Bridgett Kahl suggests that they were accorded greater concessions than other defeated tribes and territories. "In Paul's time the Jews, like the Galatians, had by

---

[15] N. T. Wright emphasizes that the marks on his back proclaim that Paul's identity had always been connected to his belonging to the life of the synagogue. Wright, *Paul and the Faithfulness*, 1441.

[16] William Danker et al., *A Greek-English Lexicon of the New Testament and Other Early Christian Literature* (Chicago: The University of Chicago Press, 1978), 201.

and large rather successfully gained an "insider" status and, for some of them, even upper status in the eastern part of the Roman empire."[17]

Even if we consider Paul trying to protect Judaism from Roman reprisal for this new sect, we can discover in his letters how far he traveled away from that view. By the time Paul was writing to the Galatians it is clear he had concluded that Jewish accommodation to Roman protection was ultimately an inconsistent and even contrary stance for a true Jew to take. Paul, in other words, changed from preserving some space in which Jews were protected by Rome to challenging it as a faithless compromise of key elements of Jewish beliefs.

Kahl offers some clarity on the conflict inherent in Jews accepting accommodation with Rome and its many gods. It was so at odds with the insistent and uncompromising monotheism of the first commandment: "I am the Lord your God, who brought you out of the land of Egypt, out of the house of slavery; you shall have no other gods before me" (Exod 20:2). By minimally accepting some allegiance to Rome, Kahl maintains, Jews were accepting Rome's sovereignty over them. She went on to explain, "This was a politically viable solution, though full of inherent contradictions and significant theological problems. The Torah of the one God who would not tolerate other gods had in effect become a favor granted by the supreme representative of idolatry, the *one other god*, Caesar."[18]

To be sure, probably influenced by Acts, many translations have Paul violently persecuting the new sect. "In Luke's writings [i.e., Acts] the term "persecute" has a severe connotation, and in his descriptions of Paul as persecutor Luke portrays him as engaged in severe activities against his victims."[19] I agree with Hultgren's conclusion that we should see Paul with "an intensity of zeal (not an intensity of violence)"[20] The adjective "violent" is frequently a *mis*-interpretation of the Greek word *hyperbolē*. Part of the problem, as

---

[17] Bridgett Kahl, *Galatians Re-Imagined: Reading with the Eyes of the Vanquished* (Minneapolis: Fortress Press, 2008), 211.

[18] Kahl, *Galatians Re-Imagined,* 216; italics in original. Kahl concludes that Paul never opposed Torah in Galatians. His negative comments about the "Law" were connected to those who as Jews were making accommodations to Roman law.

[19] Hultgren, *Paul's Pre-Christian Persecutions,* 107.

[20] Hultgren, *Paul's Pre-Christian Persecutions,* 110.

explained by Steve Mason[21], is that this word functions as an intensifier, and the translator must take the context into account. He noted that in other ancient documents the word can have the sense of "surpassing aim, extravagant, or even extremity of need." The literal meaning might be "above measure." The King James translation is "beyond measure."

The phrase "intensity of zeal" can give us a picture of the argumentative Paul (as seen in his letters), along with his dogged determination (also always in evidence) living with the commitment he had to God's call. Once claimed by Jesus Messiah, Paul had the same intensity as an apostle. *Intensity* rather than *violence* is thus the better way to describe Paul's earliest response to those following Jesus Messiah. And once he was called to preach Jesus as Messiah his ministry was marked by the same *intensity*.

2.2 Paul's Call—Then Comes the Question: Did He Follow Abraham's Journey?

There is just one clearly identifiable story of Paul's call to be an *ambassador* to the *ethnē*. It is found in the story in Galatians. Unlike the three accounts in Acts, Paul offers few descriptive clues. The call is a statement of fact: "But when God, who had set me apart before I was born and called me through his grace, was pleased to reveal his Son to me (Gal 1:15). The purpose of the call was "so that I might proclaim him among the Gentiles" (*ethnē*).

What must be noted is the difficulty of translating into English Paul's statement about being called by God. The problem is with the infinitive "to reveal." "Reveal" is a word we might use to describe the opening of the curtains to begin a play. If that is the picture in our minds, the curtains draw back as we find Paul in the middle of his life. If we have curtains slowly opening, however, what is missing is the real drama of what happened. It was a revelation of dramatic consequences. What we cannot verify is if it was a dramatic encounter such as we find three times in Acts. To be sure that is the story most familiar to many.

Understanding one little Greek word in this verse is critical. Thus: "But when God, who had set me apart before I was born and called me through his grace, was pleased to reveal (*apokalypsai*) his Son to me" (Gal 1:15-16).

---

[21] Email correspondence with Steve Mason, Oct. 20, 2020.

The Greek in that passage comes from the word *apokaluptō*.[22] This is the Greek word for something dramatic and unexpected that can be both visual and audible, but for Paul it did not mean the world would be shattered to pieces. The connection to the life of Paul, sometimes overlooked with all the emphasis on Paul the thinker, is that Paul was more likely a Jewish mystic. There are serious reasons to question the idea that Paul's call was somehow his first and only mystical experience with the holiness of God. In a further chapter the focus will be on Paul's mysticism and his charismatic gifts. As Ashton points out there was enough in Paul's story — including his openness to mystical experiences — that led some people to think he was crazy[23] (see 2 Cor 11:16). And he may have been a little out of his mind to travel to Arabia.

In the extensive, even exhaustive, literature about Paul, there seem to be only a few scholars who have proposed some explanations for Paul's journey to Arabia, and fewer still who place it in a historical context. There was a direction in Paul's life, and, indeed, a dramatic turn in it with his travel to Arabia. The Excursus at the end of this chapter focuses on the historical events affecting Herod Antipas and other players on the stage of politics in the region stretching from Arabia to Damascus. That history provides the context in which we find Paul heading to Arabia and back to Damascus. The quote of the philosopher McIntyre, at the beginning of this chapter, speaks of lives with their unpredictable events, which, nonetheless, seem to have a teleological character.

There is also a place for wondering what Paul was doing in Arabia, and how his experiences there may have framed his ministry in the second half of his life. The bible in Paul's head with its stories of Abraham may have been pointing the way for Paul's journey. What I am offering here are some proposals and ideas about Paul in Arabia that are not based on a plethora of evidence, but there are so many interesting clues to investigate. Paul's journey to Arabia is one the least discussed pieces of his story in all the books on Paul I have read. Most scholars simply ignore this detail. Others are like Kirsopp Lake, writing in 1919, who mentioned it, almost in passing, said of

---

[22] The form of the verb used in Gal 1:15 is an aorist infinite, which simply means it was an action completed in the past. In English we have the noun "apocalypse" and the adjective "apocalyptic" but there isn't a similar verb.

[23] John Ashton, *The Religion of Paul the Apostle* (New Haven: Yale University Press, 2000), 138.

Paul's involvement in the Nabatean kingdom of Arabia, "the question is not of primary importance."[24]

Others suggest that what Paul needed after this call was some quiet time. "What is likely is that he earnestly desired a time of quiet recollection."[25] I once heard a seminary professor make an off-hand remark on Paul in Arabia. "It's like he was off to seminary. Better to keep him silent for three years, before he gets his first parish!"

Perhaps, more insightful, and helpful to our understanding of Paul's motivation to travel to Arabia is a comment by Barclay noting that what had to haunt Paul, in all the years that he was the traveling ambassador, was his earlier zeal in opposing the very faith that now claimed his life.[26] In some ways, being called to follow Jesus as Messiah placed the young man Paul in a difficult situation. Could he just go back to his Pharisaic friends and tell them of this revelation — this apocalypse? The answer is obvious; not now, probably never! Neither could he just appear at a gathering of early disciples celebrating the Lord's Supper, especially in Damascus, and say "Let me join you." He had no credibility in either camp!

Rather than see Paul's journey to Arabia as some kind of escape or even retreat (i.e., Deissmann), my thesis is that Paul connects his call with a key part of his Jewish faith. He was going to follow in the footsteps of Abraham. At least two of Paul's letters (Romans and Galatians) have arguments grounded in God's call to Abraham with this subsequent declaration; "All the Gentiles shall be blessed in you" (Gal 3:8).[27] The Abraham story clearly shaped Paul's outreach to all others to be included in the family that knows Jesus as Lord. Pamela Eisenbaum has noted the similarity between both Paul and Abraham in that both lived with "others" who were far from their families of origin. "Like Abraham, God's call to Paul resulted in his living an itinerant life among people who were not his kin."[28] The first part of Paul's journey took him to a land Abraham also knew.

---

[24] Kirsopp Lake, *The Earlier Epistles of St. Paul: Their Motive and Origin* (London: Rivingtons, 1919), 271.

[25] Adolf Deissmann, *Paul: A Study in Social and Religious History* (New York: Harper and Brothers Publications, 1927), 247.

[26] John. M. G. Barclay, ""Offensive and Uncanny": Jesus and Paul on the Caustic Grace of God," in *Jesus and Paul Reconnected: Fresh Pathways into an Old Debate*, ed. Todd D. Still (Grand Rapids: William B. Eerdmans Publishing Company, 2007), 13.

[27] See also Romans 4:1–12.

[28] Eisenbaum, *Paul Was Not*, 174.

In a most interesting journal article N.T. Wright wrestled with the connections of Paul's visit to Arabia and its most famous mountain *Horeb,* also more familiarly known as *Mount Sinai,* where Moses stood when encountering the "thunderous" voice of God (Exod 19:19) and where he received the 10 Commandments.[29] Mount Sinai also appears in a notable story from 1st Kings when the prophet Elijah fled to it for safety from Queen Jezebel's threat to kill him. There Elijah encountered an earthquake, a wind, and a fire, but God was not in any of those events. And then he heard "a sound of sheer silence" (1 Kgs 19:12). God's word to the prophet meant that he was to return to Damascus. Wright mused on that command and Paul's statement in Galatians "I went away at once into Arabia, and afterwards I returned to Damascus" (Gal 1:17b). Wright emphasizes a connection between the violence Elijah had demonstrated against the Baal prophets and Paul's admission of "violently[30] persecuting the church."

What is relevant is the second reference Paul makes in the letter to the Galatians to Mount Sinai. "Now Hagar is Mount Sinai in Arabia and corresponds to the present Jerusalem, for she is in slavery with her children" (Gal 4:25). Jewish scholars must shake their heads at this unique and unusual comparison of Mount Sinai with Hagar, because it appears nowhere else in Scripture.[31] For now it is simply important to note the possibility that Paul may have seen Mount Sinai while in Arabia. Certainly, while there he was thinking about his most unusual call — that Jesus was the Messiah.

In further chapters we will explore in more detail the implications of Paul's understanding of his role as ambassador to the ethnē. Paul's vision of community uniting Jew and ethnē depended, in large part, on his unique and creative interpretation of the covenant and promises that God made to Abraham in Genesis. Romans and Galatians are the two letters where Paul's concentrated theology swirls around his reading of that narrative.

---

[29] N. T. Wright, "Paul, Arabia and Elijah (Galatians 1:17)," in *Pauline Perspectives: Essays on Paul* (Minneapolis: Fortress Press, 2013), 152–9.

[30] Keep in mind my argument with this translation from the NRSV. Maybe the prophet was just "intense", but tell that to the prophets of Baal.

[31] J. Louis Martyn, *Galatians: A New Translation with Introduction and Commentary* (New Haven: Yale University Press, 1997), 436–37.

2.3 Was a sketch of Paul's face hung at the Petra Post Office?

What did Paul presumably do while in the Arabian kingdom to be declared, as maybe he was, an enemy of the state, or perhaps simply one who caused dissension and divisions? There are some scholars like Betz who believe Paul was acting as a missionary while in Arabia. [32] There may be some truth in this matter, but most scholars, giving some thought to the Arabia visit, seem to ignore the fact that, first of all, Paul needed to work at something in order to earn a living. Could it have been in Arabia that Paul learned the trade that would support him for most of his ministry?[33] It is not a question we can answer.

In Chapter 5, "Paul Lost in the Crowd," I explore questions regarding the kind of work he did, and why, at certain times, he also accepted help having someone as his patron. There are a few aspects of Paul learning to work with his hands and taking up a trade while in Arabia that make sense. First of all, it is clear he could not have continued a life as a Jewish rabbi, as a respected member of the Pharisees. As Horsley explains, "...Paul presumably would have received support in the tributary system of the Jerusalem Temple state...."[34] That could not be the case anymore.

We do not know why Paul chose to travel to Arabia upon receiving his call, but we can be certain that there were Jews there. Fredriksen wondered if he contacted other followers of Jesus while he was in Arabia but thinks he did not based on his comment that he did not "...confer with flesh and blood" (Gal 1:16) with regard to Jesus."[35]

In that period of time when Paul pursued followers of Jesus Messiah, while still an active Pharisee, I think it is fair to assume he heard stories about Jesus and especially the assertion from his followers that he was alive. Then came God's call to know Jesus as

---

[32] Hans Dieter Betz, *Galatians: A Commentary on Paul's Letter to the Churches of Galatiam* (Philadelphia: Fortress Press, 1979), 74.

[33] We must also consider the reference in Acts 18:2–3 about Paul meeting Aquila and Prisca in Corinth after they were expelled from Rome. Paul it was said was "of the same trade" as they were. It does not say they taught him this trade.

[34] Richard A. Horsley, "1 Corinthians: A Case Study of Paul's Assembly as an Alternative Society," in *Paul and Empire: Religion and Power in Roman Imperial Society*, ed. Richard A. Horsley (Harrisburg, PA: Trinity Press International, 1997), 249.

[35] Fredriksen, *From Jesus to Christ*, 157. I read that differently. Paul was asserting his independence from those in Jerusalem with the story of God's call making him an apostle.

God's son. Where could he go? Did Paul, in deciding to travel to Arabia, wonder if he might travel there without his reputation as one who opposed the early believers? Would there be Arabs there, Godfearers, just like those throughout the Empire interested in the Jewish faith?

Given the realities of the diaspora[36], it is highly likely that there were Jews in the major cities of the Nabataean Kingdom. Some of them may have heard about Jesus and been convinced he was the Messiah. What we know for certain is that Paul was heading to a land filled with foreigners from all over the world. The Roman historian Strabo was told by a friend and informant that Petra was a city "full of foreigners."[37]

Making it possible for Paul to have a living in the land of the Nabataeans was their Semitic language with similarities to Aramaic[38] and Hebrew—languages Paul knew in addition to Greek.[39] Equally important for understanding Paul in Arabia is that his first language was Greek. Paul must have traveled with traders fluent in Greek—a language they needed in order to trade in Damascus, but also when they traveled toward the East. Peter Frankopan, in *The Silk Roads: A New History of the World*, reminds us that following the military achievement of Alexander the Great 300 years before the time of Paul, the Greek language was spoken "...all over Central Asia and the Indus Valley."[40]

Like so many in his world Paul was multilingual. As Kathy Ehrensperger framed it such people have "...'a distinct compound

---

[36] I think it is fair to add that the term "diaspora" would not have been familiar to Paul. It is a term in our world applicable to people from any ethnicity or national identity living away from their homeland.

[37] Bowersock, *Roman Arabia*, 61.

[38] Martin Hengel, "Paul in Arabia," *Bulletin for Biblical Research* 12, no. 1 (2002): 47. A comment regarding the Nabataen traders: "by the end of the third century BC, they are reported to have corresponded in Aramaic, although they spoke an Arabic dialect."

[39] Kathy Ehresperger suggested "that Paul was brought up in a Jewish family who knew Hebrew/Aramaic as well as Greek. . . . His Greek is good but not 'stylistically grand'," *That We May Be Mutually Encouraged: Feminism and the New Perspective in Pauline Studies* (New York: T& T Clark International, 2004), 131. Please note: I have not found any scholars declaring that he spoke Latin.

[40] Peter Frankopan, *The Silk Roads: A New History of the World* (New York: Alfred A. Knopf, 2016), 8.

state of mind—*multicompetance'*."[41] Paul's being an ambassador to the *ethnē* certainly makes great sense given his language skills. A few other connections with those living in the Nabataean Kingdom may have worked for Paul. Nabataeans were the only other people in the 1st century world known to practice circumcision.[42] Most important of all they may have embraced Abraham and Sarah as their ancestors.

Perhaps it was in Arabia, and maybe in Petra, when Paul began to see the possibility of creating a unique community of equals (Jews and non-Jews) living in the context of the second coming of the Messiah.

The non-Jews in the Nabataean Kingdom could have been from as far way as China and India. Arab traders carried goods and human cargo to cities in the Roman empire. Describing the fall of Babylon (i.e., Rome) the Revelation of John lists the cargo of all the merchants of the world. The list concludes with "cattle and sheep, horses and chariots, and human lives" (Rev 18:13).

Paul would have found Jews living in Arabia with a lifestyle with which he was familiar. His work and relationships must have included many interactions with his Arab neighbors. Life for Jews in the diaspora created its own questions about how to live with non-Jewish neighbors. It meant constantly negotiating a life which kept Jewish traditions (maybe not all of them) while at the same time maintaining relationships with non-Jews through work and daily living. We know from Paul's letters that what to eat and with whom to share meals were challenges in Corinth and Rome, and, most likely, equally so in Petra. It is not possible to say when Paul came to the conclusion that "all foods were clean" (Rom 14:20), but his openness to non-kosher food might have started in Arabia.[43]

What was it, though, in Paul's convictions about Christ as the culmination of God's story that could have caused him trouble from the very beginning of his ministry? The answer must lie in our understanding of the demands and expectations Paul had for the way that this gospel was to be lived and shared.

---

[41] Kathy Ehrespereger, *Paul at the Crossroads of Cultures: Theologizing in the Space Between*, (New York: Bloomsbury T & T Clark, 2013), 56. Ehrespereger is quoting A. Pavlenko. *Emotions and Multiculturalism*. Cambridge: Cambridge University Press, 2005), 12. Italics in original.

[42] Ehrenspereger, *Paul at the Crossroads*, 50.

[43] See also 1 Cor 10:23-28.

The gospel creates and names a world, a "kingdom," a people, a social and political body in practice in which the reign of Christ dissolves the loyalty claims of all other kings, lords, powers, empires, social orders, economies, and nations." [44] Many of us instead live in a world where our religious commitments are negotiated alongside other responsibilities and interests. Paul's message was so different! Perhaps he was as outspoken about his assurance that Jesus was Messiah in a way that others could not accept. Somehow, he became a marked man, and in a few years he would escape from arrest by the Nabatean governor of Damascus and go to Jerusalem. (2 Cor 11:32-33)

No evidence in any documents from the first century can inform us with complete certainty why that governor in Damascus, connected to the Nabataean king, wanted to arrest Paul. In his preaching or teaching, however, Paul must have asked for a loyalty to Christ that preceded and likely precluded other loyalties valued in the Arab world where his ministry began. It certainly wouldn't be the last time some authority tried to lock Paul up.

There is one more piece of this puzzle to consider. We must entertain the possibility that Paul's call to preach Christ crucified began inside the Jewish communities he knew and must have loved. Was he stirring up trouble in Petra among that community of Jews which must have also extended a welcome to god-fearers? Given his penchant so clear in his later letters with a passion for reaching people of all nationalities and tribes, was he unusually focused on bringing people into the local synagogue. Given some reflections on a question Paul asked in Galatians we must also ask if this was a time when Paul was preaching circumcision (See Gal 5:11)

These are important questions to raise because one recently suggested theory is that Paul's early preaching may have included the demand that *ethnē* be circumcised. Paul said, for example, that his gospel began in Philippi. "…because of your sharing in the gospel from the first day until now" (Phil 1:5). Did it not begin when he went to Arabia? So, what was he preaching there? Garroway suggests, based on a question Paul asked in Galatians, that Paul, perhaps in the beginning, was preaching a "Gospel of circumcision" given Paul's argumentative question in Galatians: "But, my friends

---

[44] Douglas Harink, *Paul Among the Postliberals: Pauline Theology Beyond Christendom and Modernity* (Grand Rapids: Brazos Press, 2003), 89.

why am I still being persecuted if I am still peaching circumcision" (Gal 5:11). Could it mean that at one time Paul was preaching to Gentiles that they could be followers of Jesus Messiah, but circumcision was required? Was that his message in Arabia?[45]

Much of this account of Paul in Arabia has been about unanswerable questions. The reason given in Acts for Paul's escape blames the Jews who were trying to kill Paul. (Acts 9:23-25) According to Acts "Saul became increasingly more powerful and confounded the Jews who lived in Damascus by proving that Jesus was the Messiah" (Acts 9:22). Jews seeking to have Paul arrested would evolve into a continual theme in Acts, but it cannot be confirmed within Paul's letters. The very next verse (Acts 9:26) has Paul in Jerusalem.

With the little story in Acts 9:22-25 and with 2 Corinthians 11:32 we have the clue we need to place Paul in history. He *was* in Damascus. The Nabateans controlled the city, if only for a brief time, and it was during the time of King Aretas IV. Once we consider the background of 1st century politics involving the Arab Kingdom, Judea, and Damascus we can discover a *date,* or at least a period of time from which it is possible to say when Paul made his first and second visits to Jerusalem. Even more interesting is how this one date (in late 36 or early 37 CE) may place Paul's *call* within a year or two of the crucifixion of Jesus.

From Paul's account of his escape from Damascus he had to have some idea of what he did while in the Nabataean Kingdom that placed a warrant on him as a wanted man. He was about to be arrested by the governor of that city.

> In Damascus, the governor under King Aretas guarded the city of Damascus in order to seize me, but I was let down in a basket through a window in the wall, and escaped from his hands (2 Cor 11:32-33).

The way Paul framed the story about making his first visit to Jerusalem coming three years after his call leads to the logical assumption that Paul, upon reaching the ground outside the wall of Damascus, made his first visit to the holy city. First century politics involving Roman provinces and tensions with Parthia were in the background when Paul escaped from the clutches of the Nabataean

---

[45] Joshua D. Garroway, *The Beginning of the Gospel: Paul, Philippi and the Origins of Christianity* (Cham: Palgrave MacMillan, 2018), 27-68.

governor. Paul, who never played a role in the larger historical events, nonetheless, had his own story to tell.

Certainly, if Paul had just gone to Arabia on retreat, it would be hard to find a cause for arresting him. It seems plausible that he was in Arabia for a considerable time—two or maybe three years—long enough to establish some kind of reputation.[46] Paul may have been one of the most surprised citizens of Damascus after his sojourn in Arabia when the Nabataean king took control of the city in which he was living.[47] Unlike the account in Acts my suspicion is that Paul had a little time, maybe not much, to prepare his escape. We have to wonder if he did not make sure that the tools of his trade were also in that basket on his way out of Damascus?

Excursus 2.1 A Date for the Attempted Arrest of Paul

Paul knew about Arabia but he could not have placed it on a map like we use. He lived in a one-dimensional, or "odological," world. It is what prevailed in antiquity.[48] To the extent that they had maps they were the distances between places and towns, or the days to travel from one port to another. Distances were often measured with regard to what a Roman army could traverse in a day.[49] The Romans placed distance markers along significant routes. Those planning travel thought of it "...in terms of sequences or itineraries, like beads on a string."[50] The kind of mental map that Paul must have had also seemed to go in one direction on that day he left Arabia to go back to Damascus. From that point on Paul's "map" had an "...underlying itinerary or sequence that ran from east to west."[51]

Our map of the Middle East would seem strange to Paul for another reason: the boundaries marking off national states from one another would make little sense to him. The countries encompassing parts of the desert Paul knew as Arabia now include Saudi Arabia,

---

[46] Horsley and Silverman think it was a three-year sojourn; Richard A. Horsley and Neil Asher Silverman, *The Message and the Kingdom: How Jesus and Paul Ignited a Revolution and Transformed the Ancient World* (New York: Penguin Putnam, 1997), 124.

[47] There are some scholarly questions about *when* Aretas took control of Damascus which are addressed further on.

[48] Susan P. Mattern, *Rome and the Enemy: Imperial Strategy in the Principate* (Berkley: University of California Press, 1999), 39.

[49] Mattern, *Rome and the Enemy*, 29.

[50] Campbell, *Framing Paul*, 275.

[51] Campbell, *Framing Paul*, 275.

Yemen, Oman, United Arab Emirates, Jordan, Kuwait, Iraq, Iran, and Israel. Arabia, though, was not a nation state in any sense of the term in Paul's world. Upon reaching Arabia, Paul would have been told he was inside the Nabataean Kingdom whose boundaries were sand. More likely, the absence of any Roman military presence is what would have told him that he was in a different part of the world.[52]

Some background about the Nabataean's will be helpful for determining as precisely as we can the date of Paul's escape from Damascus. Our knowledge of the history of the Nabataeans does not go back very far because they left few written documents. Their legacy, however, continues with the survival of parts of their magnificent cities carved out of stone. They are a lasting testimony to Nabataean creativity and prosperity.

Their economy was based in trade, which led to their dominance and control over Western sections of the Silk Road—never a single road or route, by the way. At two points in our story their power over this key trade route extended up to its Western terminus which was Damascus. A portion of this road bearing the ancient name "The Kings Highway" connected Syria with the Gulf of Aqaba far to the south.

The capital of the Nabataean Kingdom was Petra, the most popular tourist attraction in Jordan today. Called a "rock-bound city" it was located in the cavernous mountains southeast of the Dead Sea. It was an almost impregnable fortress-like city fortunately supplied with a constant stream of water—engineered through a series of manmade aqueducts. There have been many archeological excavations of various Nabataean cities which have "…brought to light a prosperous civilization in that territory which was at its peak by the time of Paul's visit."[53]

What matters to this discussion is a brief interval when the Nabataeans controlled Damascus for the second time in their history. According to G. W. Bowersock, their control of this city, was quickly and shrewdly abandoned in the face of a Roman army returning from the East sometime in late 36 CE or early 37 CE.[54] The

---

[52] Robert Bryan Lewis, *Paul's Spirit of Adoption in its Roman Imperial Context* (New York: Bloomsbury T & T Clark, 2016), 6.

[53] Betz, *Galatians*, 73.

[54] G. W. Bowersock, *Roman Arabia* (Cambridge: Harvard University Press, 1987), 69.

story itself involves shifting alliances with regard to Rome's control of Judea and other provinces in East Asia, as well as the tabloid-pages character of Antipas, the third son of King Herod (the Judean king at the time of the birth of Jesus).

King Herod died in 4 CE. Herod's rule was remembered for its harsh brutality and onerous taxes. He may have called himself "King of the Jews," but he never held the affection of Jews, whether in Jerusalem or Judea.

King Herod's third son Antipas[55] was named tetrarch of Galilee.[56] It may not seem to have been a significant part of the world, but Galilee was along major trade routes extending up to Damascus (Southern Syria in our maps today). Roman armies were stationed in this territory as well as in the neighboring provinces of Syria, Judea, and just to the east in parts of modern-day Jordan.

Excursus 2.2 The Nabataean Kingdom and the Fall of Herod Antipas

The Nabataean King Aretas IV (8 BCE. to 40 CE)[57] had a long mostly peaceful and prosperous rule over his kingdom. At some point in the middle of Tiberias' rule as Emperor (14–37 CE) Antipas married Phasaelis, a daughter of King Aretas IV. Aretas obviously had his own motivations in approving this alliance, as it must have had something to do with the all-important trade routes so essential to the success of his kingdom.

Antipas, following somewhat in the footsteps of his father King Herod, made it a point to curry favor with whoever was emperor. It was on one of his visits to Rome that he fell in love with the wife of his half-brother. Her name was Herodias, the daughter of another half-brother Aristobolus. At this point Antipas, while still in Rome, determined to divorce Aretas' daughter, Phasaelis. Herodias, in turn, would be divorced from her half-brother, to marry Antipas.

Word of the intentions of Antipas to divorce Phasaelis came to her while Antipas was still in Rome. To stay in Galilee would give Antipas opportunity to have her murdered. Several generals, supposedly connected to Aretas, helped her escape back to the safe

---

[55] There is some confusion regarding which title and name should be used for Antipas. He is called King in one biblical account (Mark 6:14), and sometimes bears the name Herod Antipas (i.e., Josephus). For more on this matter see http://www.jewishencyclopedia.com/articles/1597-antipas-herod-antipas.

[56] In some historical accounts he is known as Herod the Tetrarch.

[57] Bowerstock, *Roman Arabia*, 55.

custody of her father. From any Middle Eastern point of view, even today, such a set of public events involving a daughter was considered outrageous and immoral—it was a matter of *honor* as well.[58] Bowersock says that Aretas was "enraged."[59] The King needed revenge, but with patience waited for the right opportunity to strike back.

Death and politics played the critical roles in this narrative. Two deaths occurred which gave Aretas his opportunity to strike against Antipas. The first death took place in 33 CE when the appointed governor of Syria (which included Damascus) died. Tiberias sent General A. Vittelius to be its governor. Vittelius chose to live in Antioch from which Parthia was east. Rome had reason to fear that the Parthians might mount military aggression against their Roman provinces. Through 35 and 36 CE Vittelius negotiated with Artabanus, the Parthian leader, a peace settlement that included an exchange of hostages. At the end of this agreement Tiberias asked Antipas to oversee the final arrangements.

Antipas was always one to curry favor with the emperor and did so on the occasion of this important settlement, thereby upstaging Vittelius. "Antipas, Josephus tells us, definitively upstaged Vittelius after the latter's diplomatic triumph by being the first to report to Tiberius, in detail, the news of this important agreement. (*Ant.* 18.104-5).[60] This was also the moment that King Aretas chose to take out his revenge against Antipas.

In late 36 CE the Nabataean army won a decisive victory over the forces of Antipas, who received no help from Rome. It seems that Vittelius, with his army still in the East, heard about the Nabataean attack and was pleased to see the defeat and humiliation of Antipas.[61] Tiberias died in early 37 CE.[62] The next emperor Caligula ended up banning Antipas and his family to Gaul.

---

[58] Paul and all, including Aretas, lived in a *group-oriented world*, where what others thought of you mattered a great deal and it was also "a culture where honor [was] regularly claimed or defended." See the excellent research of Bruce J. Malina and Jerome H. Heyrey, *Portraits of Paul: An Archaeology of Ancient Personality* (Louisville: Westminster John Knox Press, 1996), 95.

[59] Bowersock, *Roman Arabia*, 65.

[60] Campbell, *An Anchor*, 294.

[61] Campbell, *An Anchor*, 287. See below for a contrary view that it was earlier in 29 CE.

[62] A small detail noted by Michael Bird regarding the death of Tiberias was that he had made a promise to Antipas, namely, to enact revenge on Aretas IV. It was

King Aretas took control of Galilee and his army proceeded to march through part of the Decapolis all the way to Damascus. But when he heard that Vitellius was returning with his Roman army, which would obviously want control of the territory of Damascus, Aretas suddenly abandoned the city. It was, then, for about six months in late 36 or early 37 CE that the Nabataeans were in control of the city to which Paul had returned from his own visit to Arabia.[63] Most likely Paul's escape in that basket was planned and carried out by friends he had made there who also were Jesus followers. There may be questions around the escape itself, but it happened.

2 Corinthians 11:32-33 reports his nighttime escape from Damascus, but Paul did not say in that account where he went. We cannot say for sure that he chose to go to Jerusalem on this occasion, but it is possible. Two passages in the New Testament mention Paul's first visit to Jerusalem. The first account, chronologically in terms of authorship, belonged to Paul. It was his statement in Galatians, that after three years [we presume *after* his *revelation*] he went for 15 days to visit Peter in Jerusalem. The second passage is from Acts. The story of Paul's escape from Damascus is immediately followed by "When he had come to Jerusalem, he attempted to join the disciples…" (Acts 9:26)." Obviously Acts has a different view of Paul's reception by the first apostles, but then the Paul we find in the rest of Acts spends lots of time in Jerusalem, where he becomes in the assessment of Tom Phillips *the rehabilitated Paul*, which he concludes describes what the author of Acts was trying to achieve.[64]

Aretas that had the final word on the matter. See Michael F. Bird, *An Anomalous Jew: Paul Among Jews, Greeks, and Romans* (Grand Rapids: William B. Eerdmans Publishing Company, 2016), 215.

[63] There's also general agreement about the period of time in which these events occurred, though there are some questions about other dates, particularly when Aretas defeated Herod Antipas. Justin Taylor is a scholar who dates that victory happening in 29. If so this date precludes the presumption above that Aretas went to Damascus when the Roman general Vittellius had his back turned toward Parthia. Those defending this view suggest that Aretas was in Damascus with his representative at the behest of Rome which "pursued a policy of granting territory to favored client rulers," Justin Taylor, "The Ethnarch of King Arestas at Damascus: A Note of 2 Cor. 11.32-33," *Reveu Bibliqué* 99 (1992): 718-728; the reference to his *ethnarch* or governor in Damascus is also a topic of scholarly debate, but it does not need to concern us here. Whether Aretas defeated Herod Antipas in 29 CE or 36 CE we can still reasonably date Paul's escape to the later date.

[64] Thomas E. Philips, *Paul, His Letters*, 195.

We have a long way to go in this account of finding Paul, but the real truth is that as we take him at his word, we discover some things about Paul you will never find in Acts. For one thing he was not taking orders from Jerusalem. He had in his company his trusted associate Timothy and never mentioned that he was circumcised though that is to be found in Acts 16:1-3. Why did Paul not mention it in one of his letters? Maybe it never happened. Also, of note women in leadership are sorely absent in Acts, but not in Paul's ministry as reflected in his letters. The contrasts between Acts and the seven letters will be a theme throughout the following chapters.

Paul Found is about the missing Paul. Only he was always there in his letters.

Chapter 3
Paul: What Does Your Name Mean?

> "The art of perspective is to see yourself small on the stage of another person's story."
> *Rebecca Solnit*[1]

Rebecca Solnit's quote provides us with a perspective on Paul, who did indeed see himself small on the stage of others' stories. That has not, however, been the way his story was told in Acts. It is not the image of him emerging from the Pastoral Epistles. It is also not the picture from artists in the Middle Ages and the Renaissance which depict Paul as a tall, muscular, well-dressed leader. He was rarely seen as "small," though that is what his Latin name means.

How, then, did we come to see him as such an imposing figure? The Paul *remembered* in the Pastoral epistles, the Acts of the Apostles, and early 2nd century apostolic writers like Tertullian and Irenaeus not only stands as the singular apostolic voice from the first century, but as one who could be endorsed in the struggles of apologists for the Christian story. He was seen as an ally in the serious issues with those considered heretics — and, ironically even embraced by many heretics as their hero!

I am beginning this chapter with a focus on the Acts of the Apostles because it has played such a significant role in planting the image of Paul in our minds. More often than not all that is reported in it has been accepted as fact, not fiction. But it seems likely that it contains both fact-and fiction. The first evidence in early Christian documents referencing Acts came from the work of Justin Martyr[2], who was born around 100 CE, and active in what others called a heretical ministry as a Christian philosopher until he died the death of a martyr somewhere between 162-168 CE. According to

---
[1] Rebecca Solnit, *The Faraway Nearby*, 29.
[2] Calvin Roetzel wrote that Justin Martyr revered Paul to the extent that in his edited bible removing much of the Jewish story, Paul was the "measure of truth and the core of his Bible;" Calvin Roetzel, *Paul: The Man and the Myth* (Minneapolis: Fortress Press, 1999), 154.

Haenchen "Not until Justin Martyr can a knowledge and use of Luke's two works be established." Haenchen went on to note that Acts was not at that time "considered an authoritative book to which one might appeal."[3] Even Paul's letters had failed to achieve much authority in Christian circles by the middle of the second century.[4]

Consider also what Bridgett Kahl said about Acts. ". . . [W]e should understand him [i.e., the author of Acts] to be rewriting the history of the early Jesus movement and of Paul within the parameters of the post-70 Roman imperial context of special concern about security, particularly with regard to movements deeply rooted in Judaean history and heritage."[5] At the time Acts was written Jerusalem stood in ruins having been devasted by Roman armies totally crushing the Jewish revolt.[6] Thousands had lost their lives or been enslaved. Luke's silence about that part of the history can be attributed to accommodations he and others were making to Rome's authority. In other words, Kahl sees Acts as defending the movement from further attacks from Rome.

Acts falls into the category of early Christian apologetics. Thus, "By default, Paul is interpreted not within his own historical context but within the framework of gentile Christian apologetics and polemics from the early second century and later."[7] Most recently John Dominic Crossan notes how the basic theme of Luke-Act is that "…Rome must adapt to Christianity and Christianity must adapt to Rome in the acculturation envisioned as Roman Christianity."[8]

On its own Acts is a fascinating story of successive leaders in the early church. The apostle Peter is on the stage through its early chapters, with the story of Stephen, the first deacon, added into the narrative. The apostle Philip makes a cameo appearance in a story about an Ethiopian eunuch. Then Paul's story, his conversion on the road to Damascus, begins in chapter nine, interrupted briefly by Peter's encounter with the Roman centurion Cornelius. Peter makes

---

[3] Haenchen, *The Acts of the Apostles*, 8–9.

[4] White, *Remembering Paul*, 46.

[5] Bridgett Kahl has called it "the most influential 'life of Paul' ever written." *Galatians Re-Imagined*, 137.

[6] John G. Gager, *The Jewish Lives of the Apostle Paul* (New York: Columbia University Press, 2015), 89.

[7] Elliott, *Liberating Paul*, 71.

[8] John Dominic Crossan, *Render unto Caesar: The Struggle over Christ and Culture in The New Testament* (New York: Harper Collins Publishers, 2022), 201.

one more brief appearance with his arrest and a dramatic deliverance from prison.

The story of Paul in Acts begins with the stoning of Stephen, an event observed by a young man named Saul, who our author says, "approved of their killing him" (Acts 8:1). This negative portrait quickly gives us another unseemly view of Paul who "was ravaging the church by entering house after house dragging off both men and women, he committed them to prison" (Acts. 8:3). Whew. It didn't take long for Paul to get a reputation among early followers of Jesus as someone to fear. Even the chapter that describes his conversion on the road to Damascus adds to the charges against Paul:

> Meanwhile Saul, still breathing threats and murder against the disciples of the Lord, went to the high priest and asked him for letters to the synagogues in Damascus so that if he found any who belonged to the Way, men or women, he might bring them bound to Jerusalem (Acts. 9:1-2).

The author of Acts provides the picture of a vengeful Paul. Even though Paul himself admits to persecuting followers of Jesus Messiah he *did not* describe it in terms of the violence and devastation implied in Acts. There are scholars who believe the author knew about a number of Paul's letters,[9] even though that reference was left out of the Acts account. He could have been using his literary license to magnify the vicious side of the early Paul

For most of Christian history Acts has been the primary way to tell Paul's story, while his letters were mined for his theology. Pamela Eisenbaum characterizes the role of Acts in this way: "Because the book of Acts comprises a single, well-structured, chronological narrative, the events of Paul's life appear connected and sensibly ordered. By contrast, the bits of information in Paul's letters do not help us construct a tidy narrative of Paul's life. Furthermore, Acts is more entertaining reading than the letters."[10] I

---

[9] William O. Walker notes a number of parallels between Acts and Paul's letters indicating the author's familiarity with the letters. Leaving out any mention of Paul's letter was a strategy, Walker suggests, to present to the church of his time a more "orthodox" Paul. Indeed, that is what we find in Acts, rather than the more controversial Paul found in his letters, "*The Letters of Paul as Sources for Acts,*" in *Acts and Christian Beginnings: The Acts Seminar Report*, eds. D. Smith and J. B. Tyson (Salem: Polebridge Press, 2013), 116-17.

[10] Eisenbaum, *Paul Was Not,* 11.

agree with Eisenbaum about Acts as "entertaining reading," and I agree that I cannot present an organized biographical story regarding Paul. Those random "bits of information" in his letters which I follow in this book, do give us, however, some ideas about Paul that are worth considering.

One engaging concept from Acts is the material on Saul as Paul's former name. There is no confirmation outside of Acts that this apostle to the nations was ever known in the first century by any other name than Paul. What we have to ask, though, is this: Did this one we know as Paul, adopt that name after God's revelation of Jesus as Messiah? We must also wonder if there is the possibility that the author of Acts invented a former name for Paul because he knew of the stories from 1 Samuel of Saul trying to kill David (1 Sam 19-27). Paul, after all, by his own admission opposed the early followers of "the one who was descended from David" (Rom. 1:3).

When the author of Acts first replaces the name Saul with the name Paul it happens in the story of the conversion of the proconsul Sergius Paulus (Acts 13:4-12). He is Paul's first convert from among the nations—and he is a Roman official! Please note that this is a man with two names, or the technical terms are *praenomen* (a given name) and *nomen* (related to *gens*, one who founded the family). He may have had a third name, termed the *cognomen* or the family name. While three names were common in more elite Roman families, Sergius Paulus, expresses what was customary in Rome. You would really be known by your *cognomen*, and in many cases just a single name. In the first century there was an ancient superstition about having three names. "Thus the superstition that a Roman at any rate *ought* to have three names is of considerable antiquity."[11] Paul, like many a slave had just one name.

What about the possibility that Paul's original name was Saul[12], since the name is clearly a Judean name. Paulos is a Latin name. By his own account Paul's world, from his earliest days, was grounded

---

[11] A. E. Douglas, "Roman *Cognomina*," in *Greece and Rome* 5 no. 1 (Mar. 1958): 66.
[12] In a fascinating Journal article Michael Kochenash (2019) compares the violent part of Paul to King Saul's attempts of kill David. (1 Samuel 19-27) He also roots the opposition to Paul with a parallel from stories associated with cult of Dionysius. Considering Luke as the author of Acts, Kochenash notices "Luke's proclivity to use names in creative ways;" Michael Kochenash, "Better Call Paul 'Saul': Literary Models and a Lukan Innovation," *Journal of Biblical Literature* 138, no. 2 (2019): 437.

in Judaism (Phil 3:4-6). Paul walking to the synagogue on a Sabbath morning, in the company with others, he might have been called *Sha'ul* (a Hebrew name) or *Saoulos*.[13] Latinized the name becomes *Saulos*. The transliterated Greek of Acts 13.9" here reads: "*Saulos de ho kai Paulos*." In what follow we do not have Acts to help us but an Italian philosopher has some fascinating insights.

3.1 A Case of *Metanomasia*

It is conceivable that, born a Judean, Paul would have been given a famous biblical name like Saul. As a Pharisee, by his own account, he had admirable credentials. Then he came to Jesus or Jesus came to him. What is also possible is that having experienced such a profound change in his own identity Paul decided on his own to change his name. Such an act — called *metanomasia*[14] — can be understood as a profound erasure of a past identity no longer appropriate for a person determined to live a different life.

He would also be following the biblical pattern of Abraham and Sarah. In Genesis 17:5 God changed Abram into Abraham. That does not sound significant to our ears, but in Hebrew Abraham went from "exalted ancestor" to a name which meant "ancestor of a multitude." Obviously, that fits with the content of the Abrahamic covenant and the night-time vision of the star-filled sky when God asked Abram to count the stars if he was able to do so. Then God said, "So shall your descendants be" (Genesis 15:5).

Two chapters later God also told Abraham that his wife's name was to be changed from Sarai to Sarah (Gen 17:15). With the change of a single letter, she went from being a "princess" (i.e., Sarai) to being a ruler (i.e., Sarah). If this analysis is correct, the change of a single letter for Paul went in the opposite direction: from bearing the royal name of Saul (tall and handsome) to bearing a Latin name far away from any claims of importance. "The substitution of *sigma* by *pi* therefore signifies no less than the passage from the regal to the insignificant, from grandeur to smallness..."[15] Paul, bearing a

---

[13] From the Septuagint. Sometimes it is spelled: *Saulus*; Giorgio Agamben, *The Time That Remains: A Commentary on the Letter to the Romans* (Stanford: Stanford University Press, 2005), 6.

[14] Agamben, *The Time*, 10.

[15] Agamben, *The Time*, 9.

Latin name which could have easily been given to a slave, would tell and live a story alongside the least and the dispossessed.

This change is not leading him to be the hero in the story of his life. On the contrary we see in Paul, what Welborn called "...the reversal of the conventional polarities of knowledge and power: the low and despised experience divine favor, while the cultural elite are put to shame."[16] Paul's stature had been a proud one through the first half of his life. He declared in Philippians that he was "circumcised-on the eighth day, a member of the people of Israel, of the tribe of Benjamin, a Hebrew born of Hebrews" (Phil 3:5). Regarding those credentials he declared that nothing in his previous life mattered any more. Richard Hays gives us a translation far more accurate than the more sanitized version we usually hear when this passage appears in the Sunday lectionary. Hays explains that Paul's "encounter with Christ led him to empty himself of these claims and privileges. He has left his former status behind declaring 'I've suffered the loss of all things, and I consider them crap [sic], in order that I may gain Christ and be found in him.'"[17] What Paul once knew was still inside him. His Hebraic faith was central to his understanding of Christ, but he shared the remainder of his life among most vulnerable and expendable people in the first century. Paul remained eloquent in his writing, persuasive and determined with some of his opinions, argumentative in places, and surprisingly open to living alongside people from all parts of the world—especially the least in his world.

Paul's change of name in Christ set the direction he would follow for the rest of his life. It is highly likely that others who came to believe in Jesus Messiah based on Paul's preaching, teaching, and example may have found themselves being asked by Paul, "What shall we call you, now that Christ is your Savior?" The philosopher Agamben has pointed out how that seemingly throw-away line from Acts— "Saul who is also called Paul" (Acts 13:9—is actually declaring that Paul is his new *surname*, which will be his last name—

---

[16] L. L. Welborn, *Paul, the Fool of Christ: A Study of 1 Corinthians 1-4 in the Comic-Philosophic Tradition* (New York: T & T Clark Publishing, 2005), 161.

[17] Richard Hays, *The Moral Vision of the New Testament: Community, Cross, New Creation* (New York: Harper Collins, 1996) 30.

his only name— from this point on in the story. The Greek is *ho kai Paulus* (literally "who is Paul") and that is his name within the context of living in Christ.[18]

Such name changes happened quite frequently in the early church, often using the exact same formula as found in Acts. Agamben gave a few examples from his book *The Time That Remains*:[19]

> *Januarious qui et Asellus*
> *Lucius qui et Porcellus*
> *Idelbrandus qui et Pecora*
> *Manlius qui et Longus*
> *Amelia Maura qui et Minima*

Asellus in Latin in a small ass or donkey. *Porcellus* is a young wild boar. *Pecora* is the Latin word for livestock or animals. The other two were tall and quite small.

Translated we are talking about new followers of Jesus Messiah who cast off their former names, common and honorable, for the kind of name a master might give to a slave. Translated:

> *Januarious qui et Asellus* (also known as small donkey or small ass)
> *Lucius qui et Porcellus* (also known as small wild boar/pig)
> *Idelbrandus qui et Pecora* (also known as one of the livestock)
> *Manlius qui et Longus* (also known as long)
> *Amelia Maura qui et Minima* (also known as small)

It is hard to comprehend someone willing to take on a name that will only evoke scorn and disdain, but that seemed to be the case with at least some in the early years of the Jesus community, including Paul. His name, according to Agamben, carried with it an "onamistic prophecy" which meant that "...those things that are weak and insignificant will, in the days of the Messiah, prevail over those things the world considers to be strong and important."[20]

---

[18] Margaret Williams, "The Use of Alternative Names by Diaspora Jews In Graeco-Roman Antiquity," *Journal for the State of Judaism* 38 (2007): 307–26. She notes that *Saulos* (the Greek version of Saul) was an adjective describing "the *loose wanton* gait of courtesans." She infers a different reason for his name change. I do not find it convincing, as she simply alludes to this definition.

[19] Agamben, *The Time*, 8–12.

[20] Agamben, *The Time*, 10.

To be a slave in the first century, whether you were captured in a war or born into slavery, meant having your master assign you your name—often just a single name. Frequently the names described some obvious physical quality that was observable. Embracing the name of Paul shows that he willingly accepted being known as a slave of Christ (See Chapter 10, "Paul Slave of Christ"). As part of a rhetorical introduction in the letter to the Galatians he asked if his readers thought he was trying to seek human approval or to please people? He responded, "If I were pleasing people, I would not be a slave of Christ" (Gal. 1:10).[21]

A theme which will be emphasized throughout this study are all the different ways in which Paul called himself the least and last of the *apostoloi*, and how much he emphasized "weakness." Gorman suggests that Paul's decision to work with his hands in a slave-like trade was an example of "self-enslavement." He writes, "For Paul, who as an educated Roman citizen came from a higher social class, the decision to work as a tent maker was an act of self-enslavement — deliberate socio-economic self-abasement, self-humiliation, and status renunciation."[22]

Though this exploration of Paul has just begun, already it challenges many traditional images of Paul, particularly those in Western painting and sculpture. In the painting below the artist Raphael (1515) envisioned Paul wearing rich robes of bright red and green, standing tall on a platform, with other well-dressed gentlemen standing and sitting mesmerized by his sermon in the middle of Athens. I see him almost lost in a crowd of the very poorest carrying a bag of tools, wearing rags, in conversation with other people on their way to work. The legendary image of Paul in Western art in contrast to the image of the Paul I am finding in his letters is the topic in the Excursus that follows.

---

[21] Note many translations, including the NRSV, translate it as "I would not be a servant of Christ." A translation of the Greek word *doulos* as "servant" suggests someone was in a much softer and more acceptable role in contrast to being a "slave." "*Slave*" is the proper translation of *doulos*.

[22] Michael Gorman, *Cruciformity: Paul's Narrative Spirituality of the Cross* (Grand Rapids: William B. Eerdmans Publishing Co., 2001), 183. Note that I disagree with claiming Paul was a citizen, but that is debatable. This is discussed further on.

Raphael (1483-1520) depicted Paul preaching in Athens in a painting and in a tapestry. In each Paul is dressed as an important Renaissance man with arms raised speaking to at least three groups in the audience: two converts kneeling, men paying those attention, and others arguing among themselves.

Excursus 3.1: A Problem – Our Traditional Images for Paul

Raphael's Paul is clearly tall and able to command the attention of a crowd. The artist was hardly alone in seeing a tall Paul, though you would think in a church that still used Latin for its worship (up until Vatican II in the 1960s) that many of its artists through the centuries would have known his name meant "small." I conducted my own brief survey of images of Paul in both paintings and sculpture from the past 1900 years and only in one painting did I find a rather "small Paul." It is a painting titled "The Conversion of Paul," by Michelangelo (1542–45) in which a blinded stunned Paul with rather *short* arms lies on the ground bathed in light.

The Conversion of Saul was a fresco painted by Michelangelo (1542-1545) which is found in the Vatican. There are a great many figures in the fresco, angels in heaven and many others on the road. Reproduced here is the central point the story. Paul with seemingly strong but short arms is being assisted by a man reaching out to help him.

It makes sense to begin in Rome, where tradition has it that Paul was beheaded by Nero.

Next to St. Peter's Cathedral and inside the walls of the Vatican is an immense sculpture of St. Paul. It is not very old, though, having been carved only in 1848 on the orders of St. Pius IX, who wanted to replace the smaller sculpture of "St. Paul outside the Walls."[23]

---

[23] http://www.waymarking.com/waymarks/WM61H9_Saint_Paul_in_St_Peters_Square_Vatican_City_State.

The "new" Paul is about eighteen feet tall. And he is inside the walls![24]

Pope Pius IX (1848) ordered that a new statue of Paul be erected in Vatican Square with the height to equal to the temple dedicated to Peter. He holds a very tall sword in this right hand as tradition had it that the was beheaded and not crucified as was Peter.

This is a muscular noble-looking Paul glancing down at a book held in his left hand. The greatest irony is displayed with his right hand clutching a very sharp sword pointed to the sky. Why was it not a pen? Part of the historical reason given for featuring Paul with a sword is that was the instrument Nero commanded to be used to execute him. It is common in many depictions of Paul.

The early church story of the martyrdoms of Paul and Peter—supposedly they died at the same time at the command of Nero—is that one died by the sword and the other was crucified. Why was Paul beheaded? Supposedly, because he was a Roman citizen! Or was he? Once more, following our theme of taking Paul letters as our main authentic source for all things Paul, we are asking some serious questions regarding his status within his world. He may not have had the respect and authority of a Roman citizen as some have

---

[24] http://stpetersbasilica.info/Exterior/StPaulStatue/StPaulStatue.htm.

thought and as Acts declares where his being a citizen was a statement on the lips of Paul (Acts 22:25).

In the history of Western art there are images of a young man Paul, and many of an older, wiser, and more thoughtful Paul. Rembrandt was particularly taken with paintings of the latter. Rembrandt's painting of St. Paul in Prison (1627) is a particularly marvelous interpretation of a worried and pensive Paul. He is also a well-fed Paul who must have eaten more than vegetables. With pen in hand, sitting on the edge of a bed, surrounded by tattered codex compilations of various texts, like any good writer, he is waiting for inspiration or searching his brain for the right word. He is not a small man.

Painted in 1627 when Rembrandt was 21 there would be a number of other paintings of Paul to follow. This is a rather large Paul deep in thought holding his pen in his left hand. He even has his sword next to him.

El Greco, whose gigantic paintings must be seen to be believed, once painted a gaunt angular Paul with fingers you might find on a classical pianist— long and delicate and hardly at all affected by the manual labor that so defined his life as an missionary.[25] The

---

[25] This particular El Greco painting is really only about 36 inches tall.

traditional sword hangs down in an almost casual manner from his right hand, while a small hand-written note with a few words is held out in a delicate manner in his left. Through the centuries St. Paul is often found and presented in the image of the artist and of the times in which the saint is re-discovered as it were. El Greco's Paul bears much facial similarity to some of his paintings of Jesus, and that is a detail that I think Paul would find appealing.

This painting in Museo del Prado in Madrid is remarkable. Paul is standing alone but reaching out to someone with this note in his left hand distinguished by extremely long, even delicate, fingers.

While the artistic world must struggle from the silence of the ancient sources to capture Paul in their paintings or sculpture, there is another part of the religious world which to this day continues the practice of *metanomasia*. In a number of Roman Catholic religious communities, the initiate who is finally accepted as a brother or sister receives their new name in Christ as the final stage of making their life vows. It is a practice also maintained within some orthodox traditions for those ordained to the priesthood.

I have a friend with the name Father Krikor. I do not remember his old name, but I was privileged to be present when he received his new name. While still a deacon he had been serving a newly organized Armenian Orthodox community in California, but he had not been ordained as a priest[26] in a period of time when he was married and assigned to start this church. At the ordination the archbishop laid hands on his head to make him a priest. Then asking him to stand, the archbishop in a loud voice said his new name three times.

It was time to welcome, greet, and meet their new priest Krikor (Krikor is the Armenian name for the famous third century bishop Gregory who courageously confronted the king who was persecuting Christians at that time. The king was baptized by Gregory). As you might suspect Krikor never even thinks about using his old name. Paul, in his letters, seems to have forgotten his previous name, as well.

3.3 Conclusion

In this chapter I have presumed that Paul changed his name. Once more, a word of caution is in order, because he never mentioned his old name. We needed Acts to help make the case for what it might have been.

We will have many more unanswerable questions—also asked from the silence of our documents. Some of them may help us picture the real Paul. For example, did Paul just blend in with the majority of faceless, almost nameless, people that composed the population of every city in the Roman Empire, many of whom also bore names easily disparaged? I can imagine someone walking down a crowded alley framed by the workshops of various

---

[26] According to the traditions of his church he could be married as a deacon, and then ordained a priest. Had he been single when made a priest he would not be allowed to then be married.

craftsmen who might have bumped into Paul carrying a bag of his tools.

"Excuse me," the stranger said, "You OK?"

"Fine, no problem," Paul said, "Where you going so fast??

"I just wanted to get away from this horrible crowd."

"Here let me show you a short cut to the plaza down this alley. What's your name?

"Lucius. And yours?

"Paulus!"

"That means short or little. Does it bother you to have that name?"

"Not at all, especially now that I know a special story."

The two men continued down that alley, with the plaza ahead, as Paul began to tell him a few stories about Jesus.

Chapter 4
Paul Living God's Story

> "Our ordinary and extraordinary day depends on the stories we hear. One piece of news, a change of intention, even a revision of memory, a secret, a disclosure, a piece of gossip may change our lives."[1]

> It is not that stories are part of human life, but that human life is part of a story.[2]

> "From the beginning to the end of the *Dogmatics* (the end simply where [Karl] Barth was forced to stop), Barth was attempting to show that Christian speech about God requires a transformation not only of speech itself but of the speaker."[3]

We can discover a great deal about Paul with a careful reading of just his letters, and we know he had stories to tell, but in reality, there was only one story that mattered. Paul was living in the context of what Hans Frei described as a "providentially governed biblical history."[4] In short, he was living and breathing the story of God traced back to creation, in the footprints of Abraham, culminating in the crucifixion and resurrection of Jesus Messiah.

---

[1] Barbara Hardy, *Tellers and Listeners: The Narrative Imagination* (London: The Athlone Press, 1975), 16.

[2] Leslie Newbigin, *The Open Secret: An Introduction to the Theology of Mission* (Grand Rapids MI: William B. Eerdman's Publishing Company, 1995), 82.

[3] Stanley Hauerwas, *With the Grain of the Universe: The Church's Witness and Natural Theology* (Grand Rapids MI: Brazos Press, 2001), 176.

[4] Hans Frei, "Apologetics, Criticism, and the Loss of Narrative Interpretation," in Stanely Hauerwas and L. Gregory Jones, eds, *Why Narrative Readings in Narrative Theology* (Eugene, OR: Wipf and Stock Publishers, 1997), 63.

Like all of us Paul had "a particular social identity".[5] Born into a family tied to the land of Judah, his call led him to travel large parts of his world in what Crites called "a story that "creates a world of consciousness and the self that is oriented to it."[6] It was scripture that Paul carried with him in his head and in his heart.[7] He did not need to use a concordance to discover a passage in scripture. As he was writing Romans, according to Richard Hays his many references to the Psalms and Proverbs were the "images of God that were in his bones."[8] The Biblical story was not just what God had done in the past, but what all could know of the God of Israel through the story of Jesus, and all who embraced him as their Lord (*Kyrios*) and Messiah (*Christos*)[9]

With scripture so important to Paul, and really to the mindset of Jews throughout history, we should not be surprised to see just how often Paul's letters reflect the biblical world. Whether it was an allusion to Adam, Paul's exegesis of the Abraham and Sarah saga, or the prophets, Paul was seeing its relevance to the whole world. He belonged to a communal story that wasn't of his own making. This is true for each and every one of us. The difference is that in our world we tend to think of ourselves as unique discrete individuals. That wasn't the case in Paul's world.

He wasn't thinking of himself as having discovered the truth about God's story on his own. This is in such contrast to our

---

[5] Alasdair MacIntyre, *After Virtue: A Study in Moral Theology* (Notre Dame: University of Notre Dame Press, 2007), 220.

[6] Stephen Crites, "The Narrative Quality of Experience," in *Why Narrative? Readings in Narrative Theology,*" eds. Stanley Hauerwas and L. Gregory Jones (Eugene: Wipf and Stock Publishers, 1997), 71.

[7] Note that my reference is to "scripture," not to the Old Testament. It wasn't old at all for Paul. Paula Fredriksen wrote that Paul worked "beneath a canopy of biblical promises." Paula Fredriksen, "The Question of Worship: Gods, Pagans, and the Redemption of Israel," in *Paul within Judaism: Restoring the First-Century Context to the Apostle,* eds. Mark D. Nanos and Magnus Zetterholm (Minneapolis: Fortress Press, 2015), 201.

[8] Richard Hays, *Echoes of Scripture in the Letters of Paul* (New Haven: Yale University Press, 1989), 43.

[9] Note that Paul often uses these two words in reference to Jesus. For the people of Israel who were looking for a messiah, this is how Paul saw Jesus. *Christos* (from which we have the word "Christ") was the Greek word for messiah. It meant *anointed one.* The Greek word for anyone who was a *master* or *lord* over others was *kyrios.* Calling Jesus your *kyrios* was actually a kind of subversive expression since Caesar was considered the *kyrios* for all in the Roman empire.

perception of an Einstein who discovered the theory of relativity, or an Isaac Newton who invented calculus.[10] MacIntyre, the Aristotelian philosopher, notes, with some regret I might add, "...we live in a world that assumes the egoistic nature of human beings – that we are primarily individuals."[11]

Paul wouldn't understand our focus on being individuals doing their own thing. Never would he sing along with Simon and Garfunkel the lyrics, "I am a rock, I am an island."[12] As we will learn, many of his letters might have even been composed with the help of his co-workers. Paul would be one of those people we meet every now and then who use the plural pronoun "we" when talking about something personal. Paul had the mindset of Bishop Tutu, who brought us to understand the "deeply spiritual" sense of the Zulu word *Ubuntu*, Paul, following Bishop Tutu would say "A person is a person through other persons . . . We need other human beings in order to be human.".[13]

Essentially the Jesus story as Paul lived it is well expressed by the theologian Amos Wilder: "That which makes the peculiar mystery of the life of a Christian is that the world plot plays itself over in him, yet in such a way that it is always unprecedented..."[14]

It is clear that Paul was convinced there was a single history of the world that extended back to creation and to the story of Adam. Paul, with his rootedness in Torah and a special Hebraic way of life, had in his past a community of friends and family devoted Judeans who shared a common life of faith and practice. For the first part of his life that story gave him an ethnic identity. Then he changed. What changed was his understanding of *who belonged* to that story. The category of *ethnicity* (that which set him apart from all others at one point) no longer mattered. As we will see, the categories of slave/free and male/female also disappeared into some kind of cosmic dust.

---

[10] That was his claim, and history generally gives him the credit, but during Newton's life a claim was made by Leibnitz that he should be credited with having discovered calculus. Thus, the modern world of individualism was already in existence.

[11] MacIntyre, *After Virtue*, 229.

[12] From the song, "I am a Rock" written by Paul Simon.

[13] Desmond Tutu, *The Wisdom of Desmond Tutu*, comp. Michael Battle (Oxford: Lion Publishing, 1998), 36.

[14] Amos Wilder, *Early Christian Rhetoric* (Cambridge, MA: Harvard University Press, 1971), 58

His grounding in scripture gave him the insight that God's grace extended to *all*. It had been part of God's plan all along, especially as it was revealed to Abraham, father of all the nations. The basic dichotomy in Paul's world when he was growing up had been "Judean" or Non-Judean." Those divisions had lost all their power to divide the "worthy" and the "unworthy" when Paul became "the least of the apostles" (1 Cor. 15:9). In the world of Jew or Greek, slave or free, and male or female privilege always went with one side. Gaventa says, "the gospel brings these privileges to an end, but the pairs no longer exist."[15] Building on that idea it helps to hear Elizabeth Schüssler Fiorenza: "Women and men in the Christian community are not defined by their sexual procreative capacities or by their religious, cultural or social gender roles, but by their discipleship and empowering with the Spirit."[16]

As a young man Paul knew himself privileged to be a Judean — recipient of the promises of the covenant. After God's revelation to him of Jesus Messiah, however, he would claim those same promises only as they fully extended *to everyone* in the world. As he revisited the Abraham story and God's covenant it became the springboard into his ministry to the nations (*ethnē* — not *gentiles*), where his message would challenge Rome's ideology.

Paul's world, especially in political and military matters, was dominated by Rome. The Romans divided their world in terms of themselves and *all others* who were either just Greeks or Barbarians. Judeans, who were considered strange by the Romans, were also in the category of Barbarians.

The lens of ethnicity is still with us. For many it is still the world of "we" (our world as we like it) and "them" (all the others, no matter who they are). We are not like them. We don't think like them. Rather than reproach human beings holding views which allow them to claim a unique identity vis-à-vis others, however, we also need to understand the *positive side* of a social identity which shapes a view of the world and of others, where our differences are in view. And it always involves politics. Miroslav Volf was commenting on an idea of Charles Taylor regarding "the politics of difference." Volf described it as that recognition we give to others in

---

[15] Beverly Roberts Gaventa, *Our Mother St. Paul* (Louisville: Westminster John Knox Press, 2007), 72.

[16] Elizabeth Schüssler Fiorenza, *In Memory of Her: A Feminist Theological Reconstruction of Christian Origins* (New York: Crossroad, 1998), 212–13.

which we appreciate their "investment in a particular language, religion, customs, their construction of gender and racial difference, etc."[17] The assemblies Paul was writing to were composed of people wherein differences remained, but which were, in Paul's view, not to be regarded as divisive.

Paul's embrace of all humanity had to come as an unexpected turn in what had been a proud heritage. He declared in Philippians that he was "…circumcised on the eighth day, a member of the people of Israel, of the tribe of Benjamin, a Hebrew born of Hebrews…" (Phil 3.5). Yet just two verses later he declared that nothing in his previous story, the admirable credentials he once assumed, were important or mattered any more. "Yet whatever gains I had, these I have come to regard as loss because of Christ" (Phil 3:7). What Paul once knew was still there in memory, but of such insignificance. The past was still inside him, but it wasn't directing his new life. He began living a life in a community he would never have imagined.

In his past life, by virtue of the title Pharisee, Paul had lived a separated life. The Greek word for such is *aphorismenos* which meant *separated*. "Aphōrismenos [sic] is nothing more than the Greek translation of the Hebrew term [Pharisee]."[18] In actuality, Pharisees distanced themselves from common people, called the "people of the land" (In Hebrew the "*am-ha'aretz*, people of the earth, were the ignorant farmers who did not follow the law").[19] The rough callused hands those farmers developed were going to become Paul's hands. Paul would have friends and co-workers who had to struggle literally for "daily bread." In the second part of his life, he was not *separated* from them.

Our story of Paul examines the times he looked back on his previous life, but not with regret! In his book, *Ethics in the Conflicts of Modernity*, MacIntyre emphasizes that those who lead "excellent lives" (his term) are those who identify and learn from their mistakes. He maintains that the "capacity for rationality over any extended period of time" requires engagement "in mutual criticism

---

[17] Miroslav Volf, *Exclusion and Embrace: A Theological Exploration of Identity Otherness, and Reconciliaition* (Grand Rapids: Zondervan Publishing, 1996), 19.
[18] Agamben, *The Time that Remains*, 45
[19] Agamben, *The Time that Remains*, 45-6

with those who share their practical concerns."[20] This is exactly the perspective found in Paul who admits his mistakes (i.e., as one who began persecuting followers of Jesus and as one who made a painful visit to the Corinthians (2 Cor 2:1)).

Paul seems to have been capable of a healthy adaptation described by the philosopher Alasdair MacIntyre as a way to question "the social and cultural tradition" which we inherit, and in the process we may arrive at "…conclusions which initially they [we? Paul?] did not know how to formulate…" He proceeds to suggest that we can look back on our lives seeing both failures and success and can also discern a "directedness" in our lives that brings us to "conclusions" that we could never have formulated in the beginning.[21] It is that *directedness* which frames much of this account especially as we try to comprehend Paul's sense of time and in the end his desire to take the gospel to Spain. (Chapter 13)

4.1 Imprints from Paul's early years

The truth about telling Paul's story is that we actually do not know much. In McIntyre's formula, we do know something of the "stage" which Paul entered onto with its turbulent history and with the large literary output from the first century. In those resources are Paul's seven letters. A few of those letters he wrote were unusually long for letters in that world. Though Paul's shadow looms large in the story of early Christianity, it is likely he was mostly unknown in terms of the way Rome was writing its history. Many details will never be discovered. When and where was he born? Acts offers an answer about the where (Tarsus), but not about when. As noted in our chapter on Paul in Arabia we are on stronger footing taking a guess about when he was born, rather than where. We also know nothing about his family, except for a brief reference to a relative at the end of Romans (Rom 16:21). Acts also mentions the help given by the son of Paul's sister who gave a warning to Paul allowing him to escape a deadly trap. (Acts 23:16.) It is a small detail from Paul's life—maybe it *is* true.

Paul never made mention of his own family, but there was one woman whom he cherished as a mother. Years after meeting Jesus,

---

[20] Alasdair MacIntyre, *Ethics in the Conflicts of Modernity: An Essay on Desire, Practical Reasoning, and Narrative* (Cambridge: Cambridge University Press, 2017), 224.
[21] MacIntyre, *Ethics in the Conflicts*, 74.

while Paul was waiting to go to Rome, and by this time an older man, he declared that the mother of Rufus had been a mother to him. "Greet Rufus, chosen in the Lord; and greet his mother—a mother to me also" (Romans 16:13). Many of us can testify to having more than one mother in our life, in the sense of someone who cared for us as a mother would.

More questions come to mind. What about his early years as a child and a youth? There is nothing direct in any of his letters, but we ought to take notice of some references that suggest a more tender and understanding appreciation of the challenges facing children. Was he possibly an orphan? He shows empathy for a child alone in the world when writing his first letter to the Thessalonians. He wrote: "As for us brothers and sisters, when, for a short time, we were made orphans by being separated from you—in person, not in heart—we longed with great eagerness to see you face to face" (1 Thess. 2:17).

Perhaps Paul would have resonated with the title of the folksong "Sometimes I Feel like a Motherless Child." And there are echoes in Paul of what it is like for an orphan to be adopted into a family. Writing to the Romans Paul said, "For you did not receive a spirit of slavery to fall back into fear, but you have received a spirit of adoption. When we cry, "Abba!"[22] Father!" It is that very Spirit bearing witness with our spirit that we are the children of God" (Rom 8:15-16). The Romans also used adoption, but not in way Paul had in mind. For Roman aristocracy adoption was a way to preserve a family's reputation and place of honor in the world. For a man to die without a male heir meant the end of that family name. To be sure a typical Roman man would not use family images as Paul did.[23]

When Paul writes "we are all the children of God" (Rom 8:16) he was not reflecting the world of the Roman father.[24] Family images

---

[22] "*Abba*" is the Aramaic word for "father." Paul knew they had this Aramaic word in their vocabulary.

[23] See Robert Lewis, *Paul's Spirit of Adoption in its Roman Imperial Context* (New York: T & T Clark, 2016).

[24] The baby born to a Roman father would be placed on the floor before him. If the baby is picked up by the father he would be raised as his child. Otherwise, the baby was placed outside to die, or to be raised by someone as a slave. See Theodore Jennings, *Outlaw Justice: The Messianic Politics of Paul* (Stanford: Stanford University Press, 2013), 129.

and terms are discovered in nearly all of Paul's letters. In letters to Corinth and Philippi he addressed "his children" (1 Cor 4:14–21; Phil 2:22). We explore in Chapter 10, *Paul Slave of Christ*, his special relationship with Philemon who he called "His child" (Phlm 10). Paul may never have been married, but he had those he called his *children*.

Paul remembered being a child.[25] "When I was a child, I spoke like a child, I thought like a child, I reasoned like a child" (1 Cor 13:11). That phrase can evoke all kinds of memories for each of us, and it must have done the same for Paul. Was he remembering certain words he said when people corrected his pronunciation? Most likely! Did he remember having some argument with his father, but learned that the reasons he offered didn't persuade his father? Perhaps.

It is important to note that childhood was very different from what any of us experience. It basically was not a time to be nurtured! Mary Beard in her history of Rome notes that many children "worked as soon as they were physically capable, whether slave or free."[26] Beard discussed the archeologists who've studied the bones of the children in a cemetery outside of Rome. What those bones and joints reveal are signs of the hard physical labor those children endured. Paul saw those new followers of Christ needing the same kind of care that small children need. He called those in Corinth "infants in Christ."

The attention children did receive in Paul's world was for the purpose of control and guidance. Paul discussed the role that Torah played in the lives of those who were raised within the Jewish world. He said, "…the law was our disciplinarian until Christ came, so that we might be justified by faith" (Galatians 3:24). The NRSV used the word "disciplinarian" to translate Greek word "*paidagōgos*." Krister Stendahl suggested that "custodian" was a better translation. He favored the RSV translation "the law was our custodian until Christ came."[27] That was the role played by the law "until Christ came."

---

[25] The Greek word translated as child could also be properly translated as "infant;" Danker et al., *A Greek-English Lexicon,* 671. Using "infant" there lends a different meaning to the text.

[26] Mary Beard, *SPQR: A History of Rome* (New York: Liveright Publishing Corp, 2015), 448.

[27] Stendahl, *Paul Among Jews and Gentiles,* 18.

The word *paidagōgos* is a compound word connecting the word for child *"pais"* with the word for someone who is a leader—an *"agogos."* The genitive construction of *pais* is *paidos*. The child, as it were, was never without the one who leads. Indeed, in Paul's world a child from a household of wealth, when leaving home, was to be accompanied by their *paidagōgos*, or literally their tutor. Often the tutor, or custodian, was one of the slaves, albeit one with some education. That person was, therefore, responsible for protecting the child.

Notice that a word which could have simply been translated as "tutor" becomes in some translations "one who disciplines." To be sure some of the stories from that world were of stern, disapproving, even harsh servants bearing the title of *paidagōgos*. But Stendahl offers a more holistic understanding of a *paidagōgos* as "...a sort of ambulant babysitter, a slave who took children to school, taught them outward manners, saw to it that they did not fall into sin and difficulties..."[28]

Paul used the word *paidagōgos* in another passage with a tone of irony, if not disdain. We must remember that no one of any rank and status hoped to have their son grow up to be a *paidagōgos*, or what in English we term a *pedagogue*. The word might have some positive implications for us—but maybe not for Paul. Writing to the Corinthians Paul said they "might have ten thousand guardians (*paidagōgous*) in Christ, but not many fathers. Indeed, in Christ Jesus I became your father through the gospel." (I Cor. 4:15) The NRSV translation of the Greek word *paidagōgos* as *guardians* misses Paul's irony. Dale Martin noted that Paul referred to the other leaders in the Corinthian communities as "mere pedagogues."[29] Even though we encounter many times when Paul denigrates his own importance, there are times, and this is one example when he asserts himself. Dale Martin went on to note that "Consigning other teachers and leaders to lower positions, he implicitly claims a high-status position, also by calling on the Corinthians to imitate him."[30] Margaret Mitchell sees this same claim as conciliatory, rather than boastful. She argues that Paul was not adding to the factionalism that was rampant in Corinth, but instead contested "fractious

---

[28] Stendahl, *Paul Among Jews and Gentiles*, 21.
[29] Dale Martin, *The Corinthian Body* (New Haven: Yale University Press, 1995), 66.
[30] Martin, *The Corinthian Body*, 66.

boasting and self-interest seeking."[31] Her perspective helps us see that Paul's claim to be their father is subsumed in relation to Jesus Christ, i.e., "in Jesus Christ I became your father" (1 Cor 4:15).

When Paul was using metaphors like that of a pedagogue protecting a child or making the claim of being their father in knowing Jesus as Messiah he was connected to small communities of early Jesus people. What we see is the advice Paul gives about the way to live together as followers. The reality of shared convictions brings those communities together. Many of these convictions, as we can see in Paul's writings, also fell into the category of not being negotiable. Moreover, these convictions were shaping their lives and in particular determining how the community reflected the gifts, the grace, and the Spirit of God at work in their midst.

This wasn't just *information* that came to Paul and which he passed on to others. It was stunning news (indeed, Gospel) that required a whole new way to live the story of God with all in the world. The new friends to be made in this process were not coming from a vertical world of privilege and power, but often were among the most marginalized, now hearing, probably for the first time, that their lives mattered. That's why the family images in Paul's letters are so critical.

Context also mattered. There was a special sense of God's history which stirred in Paul for these early Jesus Messiah communities. They looked forward to the second-coming of Christ. Apocalyptic expectations had been swirling around Judeans in the 1st century for almost 400 years. That sense of God in history was characteristic of Hebraic concepts of God. The scriptural stories from God's walking in the Garden to the call of Moses, and the raising up the prophets, speak of those *unexpected* times when something from God's world was unveiled and disclosed on earth.[32] The real sense of revelations of God, though, was of something that was meant to happen. Especially with the prophets it was a window into the future—a future made present, as it were.

---

[31] Margaret Mitchell, *Paul and the Rhetoric of Reconciliation: An Exegetical Investigation of Language and Composition of 1 Corinthians*, (Louisville: Westminster/John Knox Press, 1991), 222.

[32] N. T. Wright, "Paul as Preacher: The Gospel Then and Now," in *Pauline Perspectives: Essays on Paul, 1978-2013*, ed. N. T. Wright (Minneapolis: Fortress Press,) 321.

There is something else in this view of revelation in the sense that God *is acting in history,* but the main actors are often the ones least expected to play a significant role in what ultimately matters in history. David Toole suggests that we find power in unexpected places: "To adopt an apocalyptic style is to follow the biblical lead and turn our attention away from the power of kings and toward the power of ravens and peasant prophets in the wilderness."[33]

Paul was *not* thinking that he or others could actually influence the course of history. He saw consequences coming, however. Some parts of the coming history would simply be unavoidable. In Philippians Paul proclaims the end coming to those who were the "enemies" of the gospel. "Their end is destruction, their god is their belly, and their glory is their shame; their minds are set on earthly things" (Phil 3:19). What followed were Paul's thoughts on already having a citizenship that is in heaven and a future glory. Paul's best advice isn't to change the world, but to live as God's people to be ready when the world ends, or more accurately, is marked by the new creation. (Rom 8:28-23)

Paul was asking followers of Jesus to live the Jesus story like he himself was doing and let that be their witness to God. In a very real sense, while seeing God changing the trajectory of the Roman Empire, Paul was called to proclaim this reality all the while living in an alternative society which "…is in its very existence a point of resistance because of the way in which it recodifies power relations."[34] Paul was sharing leadership with others. He worked alongside them and earned his daily bread. He even thought of himself as a "slave." That community, moreover, would hear over and over the reconciling forgiving love of God, and the call to consider the needs to the least in their world.

The way we view history in our "post-modern" world includes the great and not-so-great decision makers acting as reported in the daily news accounts. "We take for granted a deterministic, even mechanistic vision of human affairs," says Yoder.[35] All that is usually making the news is also devoid of imagination, and, more often than not, reflective of fear. We have come a long way from what once was. The philosopher Charles Taylor describes a long

---

[33] David Toole, *Waiting for God in Sarajevo: Theological Reflections on Nihilism, Tragedy and Apocalypse* (Boulder: Westview Press, 1998), 210.

[34] Toole, *Waiting for God,* 224.

[35] Yoder, *The Politics of Jesus,* 234.

process in which the world has been purged "of its connection to an enchanted cosmos."[36] Compare those views to Paul steeped as he was in the possibility of always seeing God's hand at work in this world: "Ever since the creation of the world [God's] eternal power and divine nature, invisible though they are, have been understood and seen through the things he has made" (Rom 1:20). It's fair to say Paul always kept his eyes open to the possibilities of God incarnate!

4.2 The Story of Paul's Calling to be an Apostolos

Paul's way of telling the story of being called to be an apostle is quite different from the account in Acts, which clearly is more dramatic and memorable. That version deserves our consideration, but when we let Paul have the last word on what happened, we will see a different Paul and his *calling*. We cannot say he was converted. Paul said he was "called to be an *apostolos*." To be called doesn't mean there is less drama in the story, but it may not give us the cinematic picture offered from the accounts in Acts.

Those amazing Renaissance artists with their paintings of the *conversion* of Paul sometimes depict a face of a man absolutely stunned and blinded. Did you ever hear a reference to Paul getting thrown off his horse when he met Jesus? That's a detail found neither in Paul nor Acts. Caravaggio, the Italian Renaissance painter created a masterpiece titled "The Conversion of St. Paul" (1601). The artist saw Paul, who has met the Lord, fallen off his magnificent horse looking up at the light shining from above. It's a gorgeous painting[37] — but not true!

With Galatians we have Paul's own account of what happened to him. God "*called me through his grace, [and] was pleased to reveal his Son to me*, so that I might proclaim him among the Gentiles... (Gal 1:15-16a).

---

[36] Taylor, *The Secular City*, 155.

[37] https://www.pathwaystogod.org/sites/default/files/styles/banner/public/Caravaggio-Conversion-of-Paul.jpg?itok=0TGKEoyd.

Completed in 1621 this painting clearly has Paul blinded by the shock of light from above. He's been thrown from his horse while two men seek to help him, and a Roman soldier backs away.

In Paul's understanding of his call, it had been pre-ordained when he was in his mother's womb.[38] Like the prophets of old, whose words were inside Paul, his belief was that God had set him apart before he was born. He wasn't born again, to leave behind his Judean identity as a Christian. He was part of a divine plan. He did not see it initially unfolding before him, but this event was what compelled him to the ministry he had for years preceding his letter to the Galatians.

One word that needs to be unpacked in Paul's account is the word "revealed." The NRSV uses the word "reveal" for the Greek word *apokalypsai*. This is the source for our word *apocalypse*, which can be used as an adjective. Paul had what I call an "apocalyptic experience." The basic story of God that shaped and formed him was always there! Stendahl's emphasis on "call" didn't take anything

---

[38] Lopez suggests that Paul is presenting himself as "fatherless" and that's exactly in the model of "the First Testament prophets." Davina C Lopez, *Apostle to the Conquered: Reimagining Paul's Mission* (Minneapolis: 2008), 134.

away from his past, but that apocalyptic experience allowed him to have "a new understanding of his mission, a new understanding of the law which is otherwise an obstacle to the Gentiles."[39]

The picture from Acts is so different. It's as if his whole life flashed before him and then was changed. The way it is often told is that Paul dramatically and suddenly realizes all that was wrong with his past life. He would now live in a different way. That is the conversion story of Paul, but it is not to be found in his letters.

Whatever happened, the meaning took time to be fully embraced. Segal in his book *Paul the Convert* explains it this way: "Although conversion is often thought of as a sudden change that alters one's life immediately, the study of modern conversions shows that Paul's own description is more characteristic....That Paul claims the conversion took place without the help of flesh and blood underlines the extraordinary circumstances of the religious decision, but it does not mean that he immediately realized all the implications of his conversion experience. Only time could've disclosed these to him."[40]

Another way to understand this *apocalyptic experience* recorded in Galatians, is that it most likely was something familiar to Paul. In Chapter 12 (Paul the Mystic) I explore the many deep mystical and spiritual experiences that Paul recorded in his letters.

Before we leave Paul's account of God's call behind it is helpful to remember Paul's clarity regarding his credentials as one called to proclaim the Lord Jesus Christ to all people. He never went to seminary or went through an examination process to be certified and ordained for this ministry. The letter to Galatians begins this way: "Paul an apostle — sent neither by human commission not from human authorities, but through Jesus Christ and God the Father" (Gal. 1:1). That was not how the author of Acts remembered Paul. There Paul takes his orders from Peter and James (see Acts 15:1–21). Paul, as captured in Acts and the Pastoral Epistles, is not the independent missionary we find his letters.

Benjamin White in *Remembering Paul* explains how the written sources from the 2nd and 3rd centuries dealt with issues which divided and challenged the early Christian communities. They nearly always appealed to Paul when seeking an authoritative voice

---

[39] Stendahl, *Paul Among Jews and Gentiles*, 9.
[40] Segal, *Paul the Convert*, 13.

to defend and support a particular belief or practice. And they did so ignoring his letters, or never knowing about them. A perfect case in point regards Marcion (140? C.E.) who knew of Paul's letters. Marcion, however, sought to uproot Christianity from its Judean roots. In the process Marcion, according to some of more orthodox church fathers, tried to edit out elements of Paul's letters to accord with his own non-Judean understanding of Jesus. (Editing Paul's letters seemed to also have been practiced by those who came from more orthodox circles.)

Followers of Marcion continued to remember his views for centuries afterwards in places as far apart as France and Syria. Congregations with Marcionite beliefs may have lasted into the 10th century in places far off to the east in Iran and Afghanistan.[41] To this day Pauline scholars like N.T. Wright invoke the term "Marcionism" to refer to any attempt to pull Christianity from its Jewish roots.[42]

If Marcion stands for placing the Judean story at a distance, the author in Acts endorses a connection with the prophetic tradition of Israel, but also paints a picture of Jewish priests harassing first Jesus (i.e., Luke 20:20-40) and then the apostolic movement in its earliest days in Jerusalem. It is a mixed message. There is a Judaism in Acts that could appeal to God-fearers who admired certain parts of the Jewish world, but which would not require adherence to Jewish cultural practices.[43] The story of Luke focused on the way the priests opposed Jesus. In a strange way the author of Acts also fails to fully embrace Paul as he is never known as one of the apostles in Acts.[44] At the same time Luke in both the gospel and Acts portrays the "Christian movement [as including] the true heirs to the best of the Jewish tradition (the prophetic tradition), while associated non-Christian Jews with the worst of the Judaism (the priestly tradition)."[45] In another paper Tyson concludes that Acts was telling

---

[41] Diarmaid MacCulloch, *Christianity: The First Three Thousand Years* (New York: Viking Press, 2010), 126.

[42] N.T. Wright, "Romans and the Theology of Paul," in *Pauline Perspectives: Essay on Paul, 1978-2013* (Minneapolis, MN: Fortress Press, Kindle Edition 1995), 107. "Yes, the Torah simply intensifies the sin of Adam in the people of Israel. No, this does not lead to Marcionism."

[43] Thomas E Phillips, "Prophets, Priests, and Godfearing Readers: The Priestly and Prophetic Traditions in Luke-Acts," in *Contemporary Studies in Acts,* ed. Thomas E. Phillips, (Macon: Mercer University Press, 2009), 238.

[44] Smith and Tyson, *Acts and Christian,* 36.

[45] Phillips, "Prophets, Priests," 239.

the success of the early Jesus movement against the background of the "final failure of the Jewish mission and the Jewish rejection of the Gospel."[46] Paul, in his time, prior to the fall of Jerusalem, knew of the Jewish resistance to Jesus Messiah, but he also proclaimed one day "all Israel will be saved" (Rom 11:26).

Paul's ministry meant bringing all kinds of people to see the world through the biblical story. He was in the words of Richard Hays inviting them "to understand themselves now as descendants of the characters who appear in the pages of Scripture."[47] They would be asked to see themselves as the sons and daughters of Abraham and Sarah. They would learn that they were all (male and female, slave and free, Greek and Jew) made in the image of God. (Genesis 1:26) And when it came to the story of Jesus on the cross Paul made sure they understood that in spite of all the defeats and inhumanities any might have experienced, which he knew as well, "we (*plural*) are more than conquerors through him who loved us" (Rom 8:37). In what some might have thought to be just casual encounters with this Judean philosopher or teacher, or however they saw him, what they were meeting was a *witness* for Christ.

Giorgio Agamben helps us understand how Paul could bring so many with him into the story of Christ crucified for he was both the witness and the one whose apocalyptic experience and visionary encounters made him credible. The Latin for "witness" is "*testis*" which is like the party sitting on the witness stand describing how they saw the accident take place. Such a witness (a *testis*) "…is in the position of a third party."[48]

The second Latin word is "*superstes*" which describes someone "who has lived through something, who has experienced an event from beginning to end and can therefore bear witness to it."[49] Cephas, as a *superstes*, had lived as a disciple of Jesus, and then seen the Risen Lord. Paul is a "*superstes*" with regard to his call as an *apostolos*. He saw the risen Lord! "Last of all, as to one untimely born, he appeared also to me" (1 Cor 15:8).

---

[46] Smith and Tyson, *Acts and Christian* 136–37.

[47] Richard Hays, *The Conversion of the Imagination: Paul as Interpreter of Israel's Scripture* (Grand Rapids: William B. Eerdmans Publishing Company, 2005), 9.

[48] Giorgio Agamben, "Remnant of Auschwitz," in *The Omnibus Sacer*, ed. Giorgio Agamben (Stanford: Stanford University Press, 2017), 772.

[49] Giorgio Agamben, "Remnant of Auschwitz," 772.

The word for a "witness" most often used within the Christian story is *martyr*. Its root is the Greek verb *martureō*. (The noun in Greek is *martus*.) In the many uses in the New Testament, it doesn't mean "dying for what you believe," but, more prosaically, means being a witness to some person, something, or some truth. To describe someone as a *martus* in the New Testament means they are standing for something or declaring some truth. Consider Paul's use of this word in the introduction to Romans, "For God, whom I serve with my spirit by announcing the gospel of his Son, is my witness (*martus*) that without ceasing I remember you always in my prayers" (Rom 1:9). It is God who is the witness (*martus*) for Paul!

At the end of Paul's life, according to the traditions of the church he was martyred. The Letter of 1 Clement (dated somewhere between 80–140 CE) gives to Peter and then to Paul the distinction of being *martyrs*, in what has become the more traditional interpretation of that work. Peter is placed first and simply says, "There was Peter who by reason of unrighteous jealousy endured not one not one but many labors, and thus having borne his testimony went to his appointed place of glory" (1 Clem. 5.4). A little more was said about what Paul endured but the account concludes with the same simple commendation. "He had borne his testimony before the rulers, so he departed from the world and went unto the holy place, having been found a notable pattern of patient endurance" (1 Clem 5.6).[50]

No matter how much we want to know more about the earliest witnesses to Jesus Messiah and how they shared that story, we are always left with more questions than answers. I doubt that many in their world even knew, or perhaps cared, who they were. If we had seen Paul walking into Corinth for the first time, perhaps with some tools in his knapsack, would we think he was somebody? Probably not. He would simply be one lost in the crowd. This takes us to the next chapter.

---

[50] J. B. Lightfoot translation of 1 Clement of Rome. http://www.earlychristianwritings.com/text/1clement-lightfoot.html.

Chapter 5
Paul Lost in the Crowd

> Exploring and narrating the Pauline story can be a means to articulate a counter narrative, a challenge to this (and other) dominant narratives, a means to envisage human communities in which a different story constructs a different sense of identity and undergirds different patterns of community practice.[1]

> Let him wander through the city, an exile from the bridge and the hill. Let him be the least among the raucous beggars. Let him pray for the crusts of rotten bread thrown to the dogs.
> - Epigram on the Death of a Poor Man[2]

By the time we find Paul in any of the seven letters under consideration we have found a poor man. We could not have picked him out from a crowd of people walking into a city in Asia Minor. Had we walked along one of the narrow alleys where traders and crafts people hawked their wares, we would have seen what he had for sale, but we would not have known him as a follower of Jesus. He was just another man struggling for his living.

His reference at one point to having "far greater labors" (2 Cor 11:23) than others had might easily include the work he did, but also all the other things he endured to proclaim the gospel. There is also Paul's comment in the 15th chapter of Corinthians in which he lists all those who has seen the risen Lord. He acknowledges that he was the *last*. Some had questioned whether he was fit to be an apostle, and Paul stated, "I worked harder than all of them—though it was not I, but the grace of God that is with me" (1 Cor 15:10).

---

[1] David G Horrell, "Paul's Narratives or Substructure: The Significance of Paul's Story," in *Narrative Dynamics in Paul: A Critical Reassessment,"* ed. Bruce W. Longenecker (Louisville: Westminster John Knox Press,2002), 170.

[2] Greg Woolf "Writing Poverty in Rome," in *Poverty in the Roman World,"* eds. Margaret Atkins and Robin Osborner (New York: Cambridge University Press, 2006), 95.

If you passed by his confined workshop, I believe you would have seen a man enjoying his work. But he *never* mentions in any of the seven letters what he made with his hands. Acts tells us it was tents. Obviously, there was more to his work, because that workshop had to be his pulpit as well. It had to be one of the places where others learned about Jesus Messiah. No one could have guessed that the one so passionate about God's story was once a member of a distinguished religious party in the Jewish world. Yet there was something strange about this man who worked from dawn to dusk alongside the nameless others in the world of the poor. He was not poor in his previous life.

Not all Biblical scholars, though, have seen Paul as "highly vulnerable and needy." A number have suggested that Paul had wealthy friends and may have even benefited from those relationships. Gerd Theissen is known as a sociologist and a New Testament scholar. He has argued that Paul's wealthy friends in Corinth played a significant role in terms of Paul's ministry. Thus, he writes "the majority of Corinthian Christians come from the lower strata," and then suggests that what is noteworthy is that "all of those baptized by him belonged to the upper strata: Crispus, Gaius, and Stephanus."[3] That emphasis on those with elite status continues with Theissen's assessment of Paul. He focuses on Paul's Roman Citizenship—not as probable but as fact—and his work as a craftsman making him independent. Paul, moreover, could offer a message about Christ that allowed him to "win for Christianity those who belonged to the upper strata."[4] Such an understanding about Paul has been around for a long time.

An older source on Paul is Adolf Deissmann. His book, *Paul: A Study in Social and Religious History*, first published in 1912, emphasizes Paul's deep concern for those living in poverty. But Deissmann still talked about Paul's world as having a class system such as he knew in 1912: "The people whose souls were moved by the mission of Paul and his faithful companions were—the overwhelming majority at least—men and women from the middle and lower classes."[5] The presence of a "middle class" at that time *is*

---

[3] Gerd Theissen, *The Social Setting of Pauline Christianity: Essays on Corinth* (Philadelphia: Fortress Press, 1982), 102.
[4] Gerd Theissen, *The Social Setting*, 102.
[5] Adolf Deissmann, *Paul: A Study in Social and Religious History* (New York: Harper and Brothers Publishers, 1912), 241.

now a questionable assessment of the economic reality facing what Meggitt called "the lived reality of the other 99% of the population."[6]

A problem with the concept of social class is that "class" is primarily defined in *economic terms* in our world. But *class* in Paul's world was a *legal* term[7] and was restricted to an extremely small segment of society. There were really only two classes in Rome: the *senators* and the "'*equestrians,*' or 'knights' (equites)."[8] According to Beard the "equites" were substantial property owners, often involved in financial and commercial businesses. Below these two categories were *all the rest*, lumped indiscriminately, into the category of the common poor that included some who were free, but a vast number who were slaves. The economy of the empire depended upon them, and it was especially so in Italy with slaves concentrated in agrarian and mining enterprises. It has been estimated that there were between 2 to 3 million slaves in Italy in the first century alone, out of a total population of 7.5 million.[9]

My argument in this chapter is that Paul's ministry was one meant to include everyone—but with a special focus on those excluded. There were so many ways in which people were marginalized and disregarded. Further on there will be a section describing the life of the urban poor. That is where Paul lived. But he also knew of those with some privilege and wealth, as Theissen noted who were part of the community in Corinth. Throughout this book we will be discussing those who had a sense of privilege and who were either confused by Paul or simply dismissive of him. The one thing for which we can be grateful is that because they were on Paul's radar, we learn so much about Paul. As an example, consider a series of questions addressed in his first letter to the Corinthians:

> Where is the one who is wise?
> Where is the scribe?
> Where is the debater of this age? (1 Cor 1:20)

What if we place Paul's name into these questions? I think there is a good chance Paul could at one time have told us he was all those

---

[6] Justin J Meggitt, *Paul, Poverty, and Survival* (Edinburgh: T & T Clark, 1998), 13.
[7] John G. Gager, "Shall We Marry our Enemies: Sociology and the New Testament," *Interpretation* 36 no. 3 (July 1982): 262.
[8] Mary Beard, *SPQR*, 262.
[9] Robert Jewett, *Romans: A Commentary*, Hermeneia (Minneapolis: Fortress Press, 2007), 51.

people. Remember he had great confidence in his story, "circumcised on the 8th day, a member of the people of Israel, of the tribe of Benjamin, a Hebrew born of Hebrews; as to the law a Pharisee; as to zeal, a persecutor of the church; as to righteousness under the law, blameless" (Phil 3:4-6). At the very least in the context of his Jewish world he had been among the educated, the orators, and the philosophical elite of his community. Thus, these could be the questions he asked in light of the way his life changed after his revelation of Jesus Messiah.

> Where is Paul who was wise?
> Where is Paul who was trained in skills like unto a scribe?
> Where is Paul who took pride the in the debates of his age?

Wherever Paul was raised, it had to be in the context of a somewhat elite Jewish community with leaders having deep theological questions regarding holy scripture and the meaning of their faith in such trying times. Paul also knew the scribes, which was a slightly different guild than the Pharisees. But he could read and write, albeit with large letters. (Gal 6:11)[10] At the same time, given the reality of living in a Greek world, Paul and others knew the legacy of philosophical inquiry that required immersion into the *ideas* of Aristotle and Plato. As Robbins points out the first century world nurtured a literary culture that existed without the printing press.[11]

Paul's last question might even reflect the reality that he was formed in the oral Hebraic traditions which shaped discourse in a more concentric narrative style than was characteristic of Greek philosophy.[12] For both Greeks and Jews it was a rhetorical culture

---

[10] A quality of a scribe was the ability to write very small letters and use every inch of a piece of papyrus. See chapter 8 "Paul Found in Letters Heard." See also Steve Reece, *Paul's Autographic Subscriptions in the Light of Ancient Epistolary Conventions* (New York: Bloomsbury T. & T. Clark, 2017). Reece (p. 68) notes that adding a subscription by the author was normal in the ancient world. It was the trained scribe with the gift of writing small.

[11] Vernon Robbins, "Oral, Rhetorical and Literary Cultures," *Semeia* 65 (1994): 78.

[12] See Kenneth Bailey, *Paul Through Mediterranean Eyes: Cultural Studies in 1 Corinthians* (Downers Grove, IL: IVP Academic, 2011). The entire commentary on Corinthians by Kenneth Bailey (2001) reveals the chiastic character of every argument in that letter. This means that the most central part of every argument is found in the middle of a passage.

that combined written and oral materials. Paul was clearly part of that world. "Decidedly Yes!" write Robbins.[13]

Was he, though, ever one of the great debaters of this age? The author of Acts answered that last question in the affirmative with his story of the speech Paul gave in Athens in front of the Areopagus and the council of its leaders. (Acts 17:16-34) One scholar who examined that speech concluded that it shows the extent of Paul's training in the world of the classical Greek orators. "Supporting his argument by quotations from Epimenides and Aratus of Soli, Paul employs a line of reasoning not unlike that of classical Greek orators."[14] That is an old argument. As will be emphasized in the next chapter Paul, the Pharisee, was grounded in the Judean world of scripture.

We also do not need Acts to tell us that Paul visited there, because we have his own words. (1 Thess 3:1) The difference from Acts is that Paul said he was alone when he was in Athens. We can't verify from the story in Acts 17:16-34 that he actually debated with the philosophers there. There is real evidence, however, in 1 Corinthians that Paul took issue with Greek philosophical tradition. Consider this challenge from Paul:

> [22] For Jews demand signs and Greeks desire wisdom, [23] but we proclaim Christ crucified, a stumbling block to Jews and foolishness to Gentiles, [24] but to those who are the called, both Jews and Greeks, Christ is the power of God and the wisdom of God. [25] For God's foolishness is wiser than human wisdom, and God's weakness is stronger than human strength (1 Cor 1:22-25).

We are dealing with a distinct contradiction We are in the *either/or* world of Paul's thinking. In Chapter 11 we will see the consequences for Paul in opposing those claiming wisdom and privilege in the Jesus community. Welborn explains it this way: "To such elite Christians, Paul would have been an embarrassment, owing to the weakness of his person, the defects of his oratory, his banausic occupation, and the content of his gospel."[15]

---

[13] Vernon Robbins, "Oral Rhetorical," 78.

[14] J. Daryl Charles, "Engaging the (Neo)Pagan Mind: Paul's Encounter with Athenian Culture as a Model for Cultural Apologetics (Act. 17:16-34), *Trinity Journal* 16 (Spring, 1995): 52.

[15] L.L. Welborn, *Paul, The Fool of Christ*, 129.

But how did this Pharisee with privileges and status become a common tradesman? And why? One thesis proposed by Willis is that his choice was "intentional, in order to relate best to his converts."[16] He goes on to affirm that Paul intentionally chose manual labor[17] and he also states at another point that Paul did not really experience true poverty.[18] Lastly the term he uses for Paul's story as the title of his journal article indicates "downward mobility." That is not a term or concept I am using here.[19]

We need to remember what was said earlier about Paul's apocalyptic experience of Messiah Jesus. It was a *calling*. It was probably the last thing he ever expected, but once he had time to consider it in light of God's story his path was set for him. To follow Messiah Jesus meant finding his place alongside the most expendable in his world. In that solidarity Paul also found his voice that spoke against the "wisdom of the world" while proclaiming that the weakness of God (dying on a cross) is *stronger* than human strength.

Paul would declare that God's weakness was more powerful that human strength. And he would align himself with all who were weak. Paul emphasizes in more than one place in 1 Corinthians is that he, himself, was familiar with weakness. "And I came to you in weakness and in fear and in much trembling" (1 Cor 2:2). A few chapters later Paul said "To the weak I became weak so that I might win the weak. I have become all things to all people" (1 Cor 9:22). We should not think this means that weakness was a strategy for Paul. The scholar Willis points out the deeper meaning of the Greek word for weakness (*asthenēs*) He said, "it is probable that here too ἀσθενής [*asthenēs*] refers to Paul's being considered contemptible (by some)."[20]

There is just one more word Paul uses of himself that allows us to see him in the midst of the very poor. It is the Greek word *tapeinos*

---

[16] Wendell Willis, "Paul's Downward Mobility," *Journal for the Study of Paul and His Letters, Summer* 5.1 (2015): 110.

[17] Wendell Willis, "Paul's Downward Mobility," 123.

[18] Wendell Willis, "Paul's Downward Mobility," 124.

[19] This is a sociological term with the negative connotation of someone who has made mistakes, or who missed opportunities to move up in terms of social status. None of that applies to Paul's story. It would not apply, for example, to the story of St. Francis or Buddha.

[20] Willis, "Paul's Downward Mobility," 121.

often translated as "humble" in the NRSV. We think of humility as a virtue, but it was not so in Greek or Roman eyes. We need to consider the radical nature of Paul's comment when he told the Corinthians he was "humble when face to face with you, but bold toward you when I am away" (2 Cor 10:1). That was never an admirable trait in Corinth. In another letter, Paul used a version of the word humble but coined a new word in Phil 2:3 in reference to a community practice *(tapeninophrosune)* namely *practiced humbling themselves* and in 2:8 described Jesus who "humbled [*etapeinosen*] himself." In reference to community Paul took the word *tapeinos* [what is low, poor, undistinguished],[21] consequently "lowly," or "despised" and combined it with the Greek word *phronesis* (in Phil 2:3) which meant a practice or a virtue. Eve Marie Becker who has written a marvelous book on this one word translates it, somewhat awkwardly perhaps, as "the practice of low-disposition."[22] This is what Paul endorsed for himself and his community living the story of Christ crucified.

5.1. The visible poor

Wherever Paul traveled in the Roman Empire—and travel it he did—he saw the dominance of Rome and the subjection of all who had been conquered by Rome—including Jerusalem, Judea, and Galilee. Their status wasn't that of being citizens. Maybe a few could call themselves citizens but be assured it wasn't a category embraced by most. A few rights and privileges were also carved out for Jews under Roman law to continue their religious and community life, but they were tenuous agreements at best. The experiences Judeans like Paul lived through and remembered, moreover, were of distrusted tyrants, such as Pharaoh. In Paul's world there was another tyrant in the form of Caesar who didn't just tower over Egypt, but over the entire Mediterranean world.

Paul was born sometime during the end of the reign of Octavian, also known as Caesar Augustus. (27 BCE–14 CE). A year before he died, he wanted all in the empire to know and remember not only his accomplishments but the indomitable power of Rome over all others. He ordered inscriptions on various arches and temples

---

[21] Danker et al., *A Greek-English Lexicon*, 989.
[22] Eve-Marie Becker, *Paul on Humility* (Waco: Baylor University Press, 2020), 77–78, 83. This is further explained in Chapter 7 (Section 7.3).

throughout the empire which would display for all to see his many accomplishments—meaning his victories over his enemies. It was called the *Res Gestae* ("What I have done!"). It is long document—over 2700 words in Latin—all of which were inscribed in stone and marble throughout the empire.

The manifold ways in which people were reminded of the power of Caesar and his divinity (being called the "son of God") also included the coins that bore his image. Even Jesus gazed at one of those coins. (Mark 12:13-17) Asked by the Pharisees if it was lawful for Jews to pay taxes to the emperor, Jesus asked to see the coin in question. He most likely would have looked at a relief of Caesar. One coin is called the Lugdunum 2BCE - 11CE.[23] The legend circling his profile reads "CAESAR AVGVSTVS DIVI F PATER PATRIAE": "Caesar Augustus Divine F (for *Filius*, i.e., "Son of God") Father of the Country" (Meaning all in the Empire!).

The image of Caesar Augustus was pervasive because of the coins bearing his image and so-called peace insured by his military victories. The shields used in war on the opposite side have been laid to the ground. Coin from the collections of Nickle Galleries, University of Calgary. Photo: Brittany DeMone. Used with permission.

The reply Jesus made after looking at whatever coin he was shown had to be understood by all in the audience as a subversive message in the context of the commandments proscribing the use of graven images and the ridiculous assertion of Caesar claiming divinity. Basic to Judeans was having only one God, and it certainly could not have been Caesar, though he claimed to be the son of God.

---

[23] http://academic.brooklyn.cuny.edu/classic/wilson/coin/ric206.htm.

Those who asked the question of Jesus "would have known full well that according to the covenantal tradition of Israel/Judea, now subjected to direct Roman imperial rule, it was not 'lawful to pay taxes to the emperor.'"[24]

What is especially important to this chapter with its suggestion that Paul would have been amongst the nobodies of his world, is how often all of those who had been conquered by Rome and considered its enemies were constantly reminded of their status as "*others.*" Born in the later years of the reign of Caesar Augustus, Paul had to know that wherever Jews lived they were considered in the eyes of Rome as just one of the "...many defeated and incorporated peoples"[25] living inside the Roman empire. Even though Paul did not live to see Jerusalem destroyed by the army of Vespasian in 70 CE, he would not have been surprised to see the coin following his "so-called" victory which is known as the *Judaea Capta*.[26]

The defeat of Judea (70 CE) by Vespasian, now the emperor, was celebrated with this coin which depicted on the reverse side an image of a tall victorious Roman soldier, and disconsolate defeated women symbolizing all Judeans (female and male). Coin from the collections of Nickle Galleries, University of Calgary. Photo: Brittany DeMone. Used with permission.

As expected of an imperial coin, the image of the emperor is found on one side of the coin—this is an image of Vespasian. What

---

[24] Richard Horsley, *Hearing the Whole Story: The Politics of Plot in Mark's Gospel* (Louisville: Westminster John Knox Press, 2001), 36.

[25] Davina Lopez, *Apostle to the Conquered: Reimaging Paul's Mission* (Minneapolis MN: Fortress Press, 2008), 25.

[26] https://www.biblicalarchaeology.org/daily/ancient-cultures/ancientisrael/judaea-capta-coin-uncovered-in-bethsaida-excavations/

interests us in terms of the iconic propaganda is the story on the other side of the coin of the suppression of conquered peoples. A palm tree growing tall indicates the agricultural prosperity of Judea. There are two figures on either side of the tree. One is a tall, proud, muscular Roman soldier and the other is a defeated woman with her head held in a despairing pose. As Davina Lopez noted with regard to this image "…it is not unusual for individual representation of the Roman imperial period to use women's bodies as personifications of territories and defeated peoples."[27] Even Jewish men, following the destruction of Jerusalem, regardless of where they lived inside the extensive boundaries of the Roman Empire, had to see that *they (as men!)* were considered in the category of a defeated woman — like that woman holding her head in shame.

What the Roman semiotics of public spaces, inscriptions and coins created was the constant reminder of conquest over all considered in the category of *others*. Paul's call was to be one of the others — already so as a Judean! Paul is to be found, as it were, among the *plebs urbana, misera ac ieiunia*.[28] A friend of mine offered translations of this phrase that help us see the people (plebs) Cicero had in mind. A simple basic translation is "urban, squalid, and starving." There is irony, however, in the Latin word *ieiunia* as it can mean "fasting." We might see "fasting" as a chosen spiritual discipline, but in the lives of the poor it is not "chosen" but a daily reality. Thus, we might translate that phrase as "Urban common people: hopeless and forced into fasting." [29]

This was the life Paul shared. He described his life as marked by "…great endurance, in afflictions, hardships, calamities, beatings, imprisonments, riots, labors, sleepless nights, hunger" (2 Cor. 6:4-5). The same theme was repeated a few chapters later where he described a life "often near death" (2 Cor. 11:23). Paul knew from firsthand experience the world of the urban poor, who lived "in toil and hardship, through many a sleepless night, hungry and thirsty, often without food, cold and naked" (2 Cor. 11:27).

---

[27] Davina Lopez, *Apostle to the Conquered*, 37; with thanks to Brother Glen Lewandowski of Holy Cross Priory, Onamia, Minnesota.

[28] A quote of Cicero, *Epistulae ad Atticum* 1.16 as cited in Justin Meggitt, *Paul, Poverty and Survival*, 97.)

[29] With thanks to my friend Brother Glen Lewandoski, The Crozier Community of Onamia, MN.

The sleepless nights were not in the comfortable bed of someone's Roman villa. Those who lived in such villas would never be found doing anything that resembled toil. What are to make of Paul's reference to being naked? Not in any of the Renaissance art that I know do we see much of Paul's skin. Few in Paul's world had anything like a closet full of clothes. He most likely wore the same patched clothing day after day!

When he arrived in Galatia wearing such rags, he remembered how he arrived in their midst with "a physical infirmity." We don't know what it was, but it may have meant he was hard to look at because Paul admitted that they were "put to the test." The entire passage reads:

> You know that it was because of a physical infirmity that I first announced the gospel to you; though my condition put you to the test, you did not scorn me or despise me, but welcomed me as an angel of God, as Christ Jesus (Gal. 4:13-14).

Bridgett Kahl came to a stunning conclusion about the way the Galatians welcomed Paul and nursed him back to health. "He came to them as Jewish *other*, highly vulnerable, and needy, and they could've treated him as an enemy or just let him die, but they took him in as neighbor and brother. In his *weakness* and *repulsiveness*, he embodied the dying and crucified Christ for them (4:14), and in their solidarity with him they brought him back to life."[30] It is the vulnerable Paul we must consider as we look at the reality nearly all faced on a daily basis.

5.2 The life of the urban poor

It may be almost impossible for any of us to imagine what life was like for those living in any of the major cities in the Roman empire, and that's because life was so precarious and fragile for the majority of people. Most of the population of Rome, for example, lived in the upper levels of four and five story tenements or in the rear spaces of a shop. It was estimated that up to 90% of Rome's population was housed in tenement buildings. There wasn't such a thing as "privacy," and "sanitation" didn't exist either. It was what Jewett describes as a form of "vertical zoning" in which the overall

---

[30] Bridgett Kahl, *Galatians Re-Imagined*, 283. (My italics)

density was estimated to have been 300 per acre, a number "almost two-and-a-half times higher than modern Calcutta and three times higher than Manhattan Island."[31] That's where most of the desperately poor lived in Rome.[32]

Jewett's observation that Paul was writing to "tenement churches" helps us to understand just how desperate their lives were and even where they slept. What they called "home," as if the word even applied, were the poorly built tenements. They contained many small cubicles in which people were densely packed at night. The sanitary conditions are almost unimaginable in contrast to our world.

> Tenement cubicles were smoky, dark, often damp, and always dirty. The smell of sweat, urine, feces, and decay permeated everything; "dust, rubbish, and filth accumulated; and finally bugs ran riot" ... Outside, on the street, it was little better. Mud, open sewers, manure, and crowds. In fact, human corpses – adult as well as infant — were sometimes just pushed into the street and abandoned."[33]

Imagine the challenges the early followers of Jesus faced to find a place where they could gather together. It's clear from the fragile archeological evidence of the tenements in Greek and Roman cities, reviewed above, that there wasn't space for more than 8 or 10 people in most of the apartments of the poor. But were there wealthy members with houses, or in that world "villas," of a size that could hold 30 to 50 people at a time? One such gathering seems to be referenced in Paul's letter to Philemon with the opening greeting "...to Archippus our fellow soldier, and to the church [the *ekklēsia*] in your house" (Phlm 2). There is another reference to a "house church" in the home of Prisca and Aquila. (Rom 16:3-5) Gerd Theissen looking at the social context for early Christianity suggests

---

[31] Jewett, *Romans*, 54.
[32] Jewett, *Romans*, 65.
[33] Rodney Stark, *The Rise of Christianity: How the Obscure, Marginal Jesus Movement Became the Dominant Religious Force in the Western World in a Few Centuries* (New York: Harper Collins Publishers, 1996), 154. Stark relies on two historians for this description: Jerome Carcopino, *Daily Life in Ancient Rome* (New Haven: Yale University Press, 1940), 44; and John E. Stambaugh, *The Ancient Roman City* (Baltimore: John Hopkins University Press, 1988).

that there were also gatherings at the homes of Phoebe and Gaius.[34] Though a few homes may have been welcoming to early followers, finding places to meet still had to be a challenge.

In his extensive study of Christian meeting places Adams suggests a myriad of possibilities open to early assemblies. They could easily rent barns in a nearby countryside, or simply find a free open public space next to a lake, a river, or the ocean. Perhaps they rented dining rooms (called *popinae*) for their weekly Eucharist. There is also evidence of gatherings at burial sites, and those included funeral meals as well. The usual assumption is that early Jesus communities always met in houses, but Adams challenges that idea, because his research demonstrates that "… Christian groups could possibly have met in a variety of other places too."[35] Most recent scholarship suggests that the term "house-churches" is entirely inappropriate to use in describing the urban fellowships known to Paul.[36] Given the social status of most of the early followers there are two or three other reasonable places that they met for worship and teaching, including a rear space perhaps even in the shop where Paul worked, ate, and slept.

Most likely we would find Paul in his shop making things. He worked in what was called a *taberna,* which combined a counter displaying goods open to a narrow alley in which people came to shop. There would have been room in the back of the *taberna* for some stools or maybe a chair or two. Whoever rented that space for work probably cooked in the back and maybe slept on the roof. Perhaps there was space for small groups to gather in the evening.[37]

The reality of poverty in Paul's world is identified in Meggitt's book by the final word in the title: *Paul, Poverty, and Survival*. Most of those whom Paul knew and with whom he shared his life were struggling at or near the economic level of basic subsistence. That was the life Paul knew for his life in Christ.

---

[34] Gerd Theissen, *The Social Setting,* 89. Romans is written from the home of Gaius (Rom. 16:23).

[35] Edward Adams, *The Earliest Christian Meeting Places: Almost Exclusively House* (London: Bloomsbury T. & T. Clark, 2013), 200.

[36] Edward Adams, *The Earliest Christian Meeting Places,* 201–2.

[37] Meggitt, *Paul, Poverty and Survival,* 62–67.

Excursus 5.1: The Extent of Poverty in the First Century — A Scholarly Debate

In this chapter I maintain that we find Paul sharing the life of the poorest members of his world. The questions that remain regards the extent of that poverty. Should we also not consider the rich friends, like his patron Phoebe in Romans who obviously had befriended him? (Rom 16:1-2) Turning to the sociologist Rodney Stark is one place to begin. In his book *The Rise of Christianity* he offers the thesis that the early Jesus movement "was not a proletarian movement but was based on the more privileged classes."[38]

We need to take Stark's analysis seriously, even though Paul's comments as I understand them place him among the most oppressed. In stark contrast — pun intended — Stark's view along with some contemporary New Testament historians is that Paul had his "greatest success among the middle and upper-middle classes."[39] One problem with this assumption is that we have such little data from the first and most of the second century. What evidence is there, moreover, of the growth and impact of those early Jesus communities except for the survival and growth that followed in the second century and beyond? To be sure we have the letters and the gospel accounts, but there is no archeological evidence until about 180 CE to find traces of their existence.[40]

Where Stark is of most help in situating Paul in the middle of the first century is his estimates of the total number of what he calls "Christians" in the Roman Empire between the years 40CE and 350 CE. He estimates that the number of Christians grew by 3.42 percent per year, or 40 percent per decade. This table[41] is helpful, for our purposes, because it shows just how *few* knew the Jesus story in the time of Paul.

Christian Growth Projected at 40 percent per decade

Year	Number of Christians	Percent of Population
40	1,000	0.0017
50	1,400	0.0023
100	7,530	0.0126

---

[38] Stark, *The Rise of Christianity*, 7.
[39] Meggitt, *Paul, Poverty and Survival*, 45.
[40] Meggitt, *Paul, Poverty and Survival*, 9.
[41] Stark, *The Rise of Christianity*, 7.

150	40,496	0.07
200	217,795	0.36
250	1,171.356	1.9
300	6,299,832	10.5
350	33,882,008	56.5

Stark's analysis leads us to see how fragile and marginal were the earliest followers of Jesus Messiah in the first century. He suggests that the problem was that Christianity was a new religion. Paul's message to Romans, according to Stark, was for them "to embrace a new worldview, a new conception of reality, indeed, to accept a *new* God."[42] The gospel Paul preached was not, in fact, some new religion; deep down it was the Jewish story, now understood to be for the whole world. To follow this Jesus, as will be emphasized in this book, is to call others (the *ethnē*) to live Jewishly.

Paul was inviting people from all nations, not just Rome, to know the Judean story of God, a historical account of God through Israel, particularly in light of the Abrahamic covenant reaching the whole world. To be sure those coming into this community, along with others in their social network (something Stark, the sociologist, rightly emphasizes) would be practicing their faith in a way counter to what many of them had known in the past.

Instead of its roots among the powerful, and by implication according to Stark, those protected from reprisal from Imperial Rome,[43] I am asserting that the communities Paul founded were comprised of people who were not only living *counter to what many of them had known in the past,* but also counter to the conformity that Roman authorities demanded of the lower classes. I am taking seriously Paul's troubles that landed him in prison. I don't know that Stark considered this fact. And Paul *knew* poverty! His was a life marked by "toil and hardship, through many a sleepless night, hungry and thirsty, often without food, cold, and naked" (2 Cor 11:27).

The historical problem is that the poor are those who in numbers far more than we can't count, who "failed to leave any significant

---

[42] Stark, *The Rise of Christianity*, 38.

[43] Stark, *The Rise of Christianity*, 46, "If as is now believed, the Christians were not a mass of degraded outsiders but from early days had members, friends, and relatives in high places—often within the imperial family—this would've greatly mitigated repression and persecution."

mark in the historical record."[44] There were some poor within Rome, however, who left a mark on a few tombstones detailing the endeavors of their occupations that society demeaned. In other words, as Morley notes,[45] they were proud of their work, and there's evidence of that attitude from Paul as well. At the same time, poverty for the working masses was a reality.

It is one thing to see Paul hard at work in his shop working with his hands, but it is much harder for biblical scholars to connect the extreme poverty he knew to his work as an ambassador and as a creative Jewish theologian. Thus, Friesen says, "For the most part, however, specialists have not assimilated Paul's economic life into their portraits of 'Paul the apostle' or 'Paul the theologian.'"[46] There is no doubt that Paul had at times stayed in someone's house — houses he could never have called his own. He also received some gifts. The danger is that we might think of Paul as a poorly paid pastor, who nonetheless, gets free housing in the church's parsonage and who receives a few chickens from time to time. The real truth is that he didn't even want to be a poorly paid pastor. He was a self-supported one, albeit not exactly prosperous.

The best picture of Imperial Rome's social strata I was able to discover in my research comes from Steven Friesen who offered a seven-point poverty scale for the first century of the Roman Empire. In the following table I have listed each group, a brief description, and the percentage of those in each category.

---

[44] Neville Morley, "The Poor in the City of Rome," in *Poverty in the Roman World*, eds. Margaret Atkins and Robin Osborne (New York: Cambridge University Press, 2006), 31.
[45] Neville Morley, 35.
[46] Stephen J. Friesen, "Poverty in Pauline Studies: Beyond the So-Called New Consensus," *Journal for the Study of the New Testament* 263 (2004): 350.

Friesen's Poverty Scale (modified by author)[47]

Category Title	People in this category	% of the total
PS 1: Imperial Elites	Imperial family, senators	0.04%
PS 2: Regional or Provincial Elites	Equestrian families, provincial officials, retired military	1.00%
PS 3: Municipal Elites	Decurial families, few wealthy non-office holders, some veterans, merchants	1.76%
PS 4: Moderate Surplus	Some merchants, traders. Artisans who employ others. Military veterans	7%
PS 5: Stable, Near Subsistence Level	Merchants. Artisans, shop owners, some farm families	22%
PS 6: At Subsistence	Small farm families, laborers (skilled & unskilled) most merchants, traders, shop owners	40%
PS 7: Below Subsistence Level	Some farm families, unattached widows, orphans, beggars, disabled, day laborers	28%

What are we to make of this picture of the economic reality that faced the vast majority in Paul's world? Friesen states it bluntly: "For nearly everyone in Paul's assemblies, as for nearly everyone in the Roman empire, poverty was a way of life."[48]

---

[47] I have shortened some of the descriptions Friesen used in his chart of poverty.
[48] Stephen J Friesen, "Poverty in Pauline Studies." 358.

Even if we place Paul in the category "PS 5: Stable Near Subsistence Level," we are talking about 22% of the population that is an illness or a broken bone away from near disaster. It is a world where over 90% of the people are near, at, or below subsistence level.

With Paul we certainly have a "religious genius," but we should bear in mind that that didn't give him a social status which offered him much security. Meggitt expresses it clearly:

> Undoubtedly Paul was not a 'typical' artisan of the Greco-Roman world — he would not have left such a mark on history if he had been — but his uniqueness, particularly the uniqueness of his religious genius, should not blind us to the fact that his experience of material existence is far from unusual: it was nothing less than the arduous and bitter experience of the urban poor.[49]

5.2 Excursus: Like the Gentile "others"

Susan Eastman makes a claim for Paul that is key to our understanding of "Paul lost in the crowds." She asserts that "...only by crossing the boundaries *to become like the Gentile "others,"* without first requiring that they become like him, can Paul firmly communicate the grace of God who took the initiative to liberate enslaved humanity."[50] The Jewish Paul is still Jewish, but in terms of how he lived his life and how he looked, he was one of the *others*. Paul, in terms of his dress, his occupation, and his chosen companions (other Diaspora Judean, non-Jews, and the poor) would be seen as people of no significance or importance.

Had Paul remained *a Pharisee — and he continued to oppose the new Jesus Messiah movement —* there is no doubt, considering at least one factor of life in the Middle Eastern world: he would easily have been identified in any particular crowd walking through any city in the Roman Empire. The New Testament scholar Kenneth Bailey, with over forty years of living and teaching in the Middle East as part of his background, said that in the time of Jesus [and Paul] there were two ways to identify a "stranger." It was either by talking to him and hearing his dialect, or by looking at his dress. There was a clear

---

[49] Justin J. Meggitt, *Paul, Poverty and Survival*, 96–7.
[50] Susan Eastman, *Recovering Paul's Mother Tongue: Language and Theology in Galatians* (Grand Rapids: William B. Eerdmans Publishing Company, 2007), 186. (Italics mine.)

difference between Hellenistic and Judean garb. Bailey noted, "...even separate villages of Palestine and Lebanon had their distinctive dress."[51]

Stowers makes the important point regarding the urban world of the first century that everyone made judgments about others with regard to dress, speech, posture, and even the way you walked.

> This was a culture where people believed that you could determine another's character, class and ethnic origins not only from dress and speech but also from such things as posture, the way one walked, how one sneezed and whether one scratched one's head or not. Paul was a Jew and a leather-worker. It is doubtful that he could have overcome the stigma of these roles even if he had sought to do so.[52]

Paul, though, no longer claimed membership in the community of Pharisees by the time he was writing any of the seven letters we are considering, but he was "working with his hands" at some kind of "labor." Based on Paul's claims to be working with his hands, and experiencing hunger and thirst, we can envision him wearing the tattered and patched clothes of the majority of those surviving from day to day.

There are small terracotta sculptures from the 1st century showing mime actors, those clearly at the bottom of society, who are wearing a *chiton*, which was a short frock, patches of small fabric sewn together.[53] Contrary to our Renaissance paintings of a well-clothed Paul wearing wool garments for a cold day, we need to consider a barely clothed Paul carrying some equally shabby bags with his tools as he walks into the next city to bring the gospel of Christ.

When we look to the gospels for indications regarding clothing, the references are not numerous, but we do know that the clothing Jesus wore at the time of his arrest was a prize, as it were, for the soldiers who even gambled for his tunic. There is one telling

---

[51] Kenneth Baily, *Poet and Peasant and Through Peasant Eyes: A Literary-Cultural Approach to Parables in Luke*, vol. 2 (Grand Rapids: William B. Eerdmans Publishing, 1976), 42.

[52] Stanley Stowers, "Social Status, Public Speaking and Private Teaching: The Circumstances of Paul's Preaching Activity," *Novum Testamentum* 36 no. 1 (1994): 74.

[53] L.L Welborn, *Paul Fool of Christ*, 39.

condemnation on the lips of Jesus, however, regarding the dress of "the scribes who love to walk around in long robes" (Luke 20:46). We have a phrase the "clothes make the man" and the meaning of that proverb carries across the world and back into the time of Jesus and Paul.

Excursus 5:3 Paul as seen by others

Earlier in this chapter I discussed Paul's references to weakness and how the so-called humility he claimed for himself, was the disdain in which he was held by some. But was he really small? In Latin the word *Paulus* meant small. To be a small man in the world of the Roman Empire was not a deficit, however. One specific physical description of Paul comes an early 2nd century document called *The Acts of Paul*.[54] In it a man with the name of Onesiphorus welcomed Paul to his house:

> And he saw Paul coming, a man small of stature, with a bald head and crooked legs, and a good state of body, with eyebrows meeting and nose somewhat hooked, full of friendliness; for now he appeared like a man, and now he had the face of an angel.[55]

What Onesiphorus initially saw in Paul was a man with "a good state of body." As noted earlier in this chapter this was certainly not what the Galatians first saw when Paul came to them: "You know that it was because of a physical infirmity that I first announced the gospel to you" (Gal 5:13). With a miserable looking Paul, by his own account, we, nonetheless, see the Galatians having treated him as an "angel." That little detail coincides with what Onesiphorus saw.

Perhaps, what is striking about Onesiphorus' eye-witness description of Paul—the only one we have—is that he saw in Paul one who made the same kind of impression on the viewer as did Caesar Augustus. According to another 2nd century writer Suetonius, author of *The Lives of the Caesars*: "He (Augustus) was unusually handsome and exceedingly graceful at all periods of his

---

[54] Benjamin White, *Remembering* Paul, 67-8, suggests this literature is a form of hagiography. Paul is a hero to the author. In hagiography it is rare to find a balanced picture.

[55] Acts of Paul, 3.2 as quoted in Bruce J. Malina and Jerome H. Neyrey, *Portraits of Paul: An Archaeology of Ancient Personalitiy* (Louisville: Westminster John Knox Press, 1996). 128.

life... He had clear, bright eyes... His teeth were wide apart, small, and ill-kept; his hair was slightly curly and inclining to golden; his eyebrows met. His ears were of moderate size, and his nose projected a little of the top and then bent slightly inward. His complexion was between dark and fair. He was short in stature...but this was concealed by the fine proportion and symmetry of his figure."[56]

Not all the details in this picture of Augustus match Onesiphorus' description of Paul, but if there is a comparison to Augustus Paul is not just an ordinary person. The similarities are in terms of stature, nose, and physical quality. Malina and Neyrey offer an analysis of Paul based on what the ancients called *physiognomics*, which essentially means discernment of the *character of a person* by how *they looked*.[57] What these authors found in that description of Paul were all admirable traits, many of which described successful Roman generals. It's fair to say that when we admire someone, we nearly always have a positive picture of them no matter what others might see.

5.4 Finding Paul in the crowd

Something else important comes from Malina and Neyrey. In their unique study of personality, as it was defined in this ancient world, they help us understand Paul in the context of a world that primarily defined people in terms of *generation, geography, and gender*. "To know someone [in that world] means to know their roots, ancestry, and genealogy."[58] What was most respected was being a group-oriented person, because in that world anyone claiming *individuality* was really defining themselves as a *deviant*. What we will find is that these new communities founded by Paul have the same kind of group-oriented values stemming from Paul's Jewish background, albeit bringing together in a unique way those mostly discarded as non-citizens, nobodies, and even those whose identity as slaves placed them as living in a category of "suspended death."

When we return to the rhetoric of Paul that began this chapter,

---

[56] Suetonius, The Lives of the Caesars 2.79.1–2 as quoted in Bruce J. Malina and Jerome H. Neyrey, *Portraits of Paul: An Archeology of Ancient* Personality (Louisville: Westminster John Knox Press, 1996), 130.

[57] Bruce J. Malina and Jerome H. Neyrey, *Portraits of Paul*, 5.

[58] Bruce J. Malina and Jerome H. Neyrey, *Portraits of Paul*, 24.

we ought to hear those questions from the perspective of those in Corinth who were not respected or fully welcomed with dignity and respect by those with privilege. They knew how those questions were addressed in the story of Jesus Messiah. The questions were:

> Where is Paul who was wise?
> Where is Paul who was trained in skills like unto a scribe?
> Where is Paul who took pride the in debates of this age?

Paul's challenge to the Corinthians, as is clear in this letter, was to focus on "Christ crucified" as the key to understanding the mysteries of God. For God would choose the things that "low and despised in the world, things that are not, to reduce to nothing things that are" (1 Cor 1:28). It's an upside-down world for Paul, and we have to believe his was also a story of being turned upside-down. As one who was "down" he literally could be "one" with that vast majority, and that became the source of nearly all his friends in Christ. And yet he will always stand out in this account for his unflinching determination to be nothing more than "one of the crowd." That is where he made friends for Christ.

Chapter 6
Paul Sent to the Nations

Unless we learn to think within first-century categories rather than medieval ones, we will never understand either the ancient Jewish world or Paul.[1]

I am quite confident that Christianity will survive a completely Jewish Paul, just as it evidently survived a completely Jewish Jesus.[2]

Barth was fond of quoting the response to the query of Frederick the Great for a proof of God's existence—Sire, the Jews.[3]

6.1 Paul was always a Jew: seeing Muggles in God's story

The story of Harry Potter began on the eve of his 10th birthday when a letter of acceptance came from Hogwarts School of Witchcraft and Wizardry. The only problem is that his Uncle Vernon and Aunt Petunia destroyed that first acceptance letter and all the others that followed on subsequent days. Finally, Uncle Vernon, in a desperate attempt to find a place where no letters could possibly be sent, escaped with the whole family to a cold miserable cabin on an isolated island. Then when they arrived in the middle of their first night in a dark freezing cabin came the thundering presence of Hagrid, Keeper of Keys and Grounds at Hogwarts. Hagrid knocked down the door to that ramshackle cabin in order to personally deliver the invitation to Harry. On this evening Hagrid told Harry that he was a wizard, and not a *muggle*. Harry had never even heard

---

[1] Wright, *Faithfulness*, 115.
[2] Zetterholm, "Paul Within Judaism," 34.
[3] Hauerwas, *With the Grain of the Universe*, 170. Note: Barth was one of the co-authors of the Barmen Declaration approved by a small number of Confessing Churches in Germany in 1934 after the Nazi government took over the largest Christian denomination. No government, it said, could rule the church. Soon after, Barth lost his teaching position. After his expulsion from Germany in 1935 he taught in Switzerland.

the word *"muggle."* Hagrid looked at Uncle Vernon and Aunt Petunia and burst out, "A Muggle...it's what we call non-magic folk like them. An' it's your bad luck you grew up in a family o' the biggest Muggles I ever laid eyes on."[4]

In the Harry Potter world, it didn't matter where a Muggle lived, what language they spoke, or what their race. From the wizard perspective, *all who weren't wizards were Muggles*: those who could not do magic. The term was invented by the author J.K. Rowling, based on the English word "mug" which meant "someone who is easily fooled."[5]

Paul didn't know anything about Muggles, but it is a good way for us to understand the *binary nature of Paul's world*. Paul was molded into the mindset of a Hebraic heritage knowing and believing that Jews were distinct from all *others* in the world--the *ethnē*, or what is commonly translated in most of our Bibles, as "Gentiles

Steve Mason makes the point that Paul's ethnic identity was *Ioudaios* (i.e., Judean) because he was from *Ioudaia* (i.e., Judaea). He points out that it is "a simple transliteration."[6] What happens in our world was true 2,000 years ago. We ask someone where they are from, and with their answer we presume to think we know something about them. Paul knew himself as a Judean. As Pamela Eisenbaum also noted anyone in the first century hearing one of Paul's letters, even if they never met him, would know they were Jewish letters "because they were authored by a Jew, and they contain Jewish language, imagery, and concerns."[7]

Some Judeans were the first to cherish the teachings and the example of Jesus with the affirmation that he was risen from the dead and was the "Mashiach — the Hebrew word for one whom God "anointed" as king." We know the word as *Messiah*. Paul's story as he told it in Galatians was an apocalyptic experience that Jesus was Messiah — which in Greek was *Christos*. And then Paul lived out

---

[4] J. K. Rowling, *Harry Potter and the Sorcerer's Stone* (New York: Scholastic Press, 1998), 53.

[5] http://www.huffingtonpost.com/entry/american-wordformuggle _us _ 563a 6b29e4b0b24aee489e20.

[6] Steve Mason, "Paul without Judaism: Historical Method over Perspective," in *Paul and Matthew among Jews and Gentiles*, ed. Ronald Charles (London: T & T Clark, 2021), 9–40.

[7] Eisenbaum, *Paul Was Not a Christian*, 7.

a vision of Isaiah of a day to come when the God of Israel would "gather all nations and tongues, and they shall come [to Zion] and shall see my glory" (Isa 66:18). The messengers would be sent to the farthest places including Tarshish (Isa 66:19.) This was the story Paul lived as one of the messengers. The word apostle meant someone who was sent. As will be discussed in the last chapter Tarshish was in Spain and that was where Paul wanted to be sent.

Bringing the story of Jesus Messiah to non-Jews would be part of Paul's missional strategy framed by what Pamela Eisenbaum noted as "his profound concern to rescue gentiles from their idolatry."[8] Paul who spoke of Christ living within him (Gal 2:20) invited the world to live inside the world of Judaism without actually becoming Jews. It's a complicated idea as expressed by Nanos. Those who follow the teaching of Paul would be demonstrating to "many of their family members and neighbors that they were acting Jewishly, practicing Judaism, the way of life developed by Jews — and that is indeed what Paul promoted that these non - Jews should do, although insisting they do so while remaining non - Jews."[9] We will explore what this looks like in the sections that follow.

6.2 What did Paul's claim to be a Pharisee mean?

Toward the end of Acts the narrator described a scene in which Paul stood before a council of the chief priests of Jerusalem. There Paul said, "Brothers, I am a Pharisee, a son of Pharisees" (Acts 23:6). As a member of that community came his affirmation of belief in "the resurrection of the dead" (Acts 23:6). Acts makes it clear this was not a doctrine that the Sadducees endorsed (Acts. 23:7-8). The author's next verse gives the picture of "certain scribes of the Pharisees group [who] stood up and contended, 'We find nothing wrong with this man'" (Acts 23:9). It seems like Paul is safe, but in the next verse violence breaks out and it seemed to the tribune they would "tear Paul to pieces" (Acts 23:10). The threat lasted over the night. "In the morning the Jews joined in a conspiracy and bound themselves to an oath to neither eat nor drink until they had killed Paul" (Acts 23:12). The final confrontation that faced Paul in Acts

---

[8] Eisenbaum, *Paul Was Not a Christian*, 74.
[9] Mark D. Nanos, "Reading Paul in a Jewish Way "O be joyful all you peoples, with God's People" (Rom 15:10): Who Are the People?," in *Reading Paul Within Judaism: Collecteed Essays of Mark D. Nanos Vol 1*, Mark D. Nanos, ed. (Eugene, OR: Cascade Books, 2017, Kindle Books), Loc. 4163 of 5769.

was preceded by accounts earlier in the narrative in which Paul visited a synagogue when he first arrived in a city. In nearly every instance the Jews turn against him. At the same time there are many favorable impressions of Jews in Luke and Acts.

At times, especially in the early parts of Luke and Act we find admirable accounts of Jewish piety, but it is not a consistent theme. The *conspiracy to kill Paul* though is characteristic of the threat that hung over Paul's head throughout Acts. What is offered is basically a dismal picture of the Jewish people. They are "fanatic, hostile and vindictive" and they are "obstinately imperceptive and unheeding."[10] Those are the conclusions of the New Testament scholar Joseph Tyson who did an amazing careful and balanced study of the way Judaism was portrayed in both Luke and Acts. Both accounts were written some decades after Paul's letters—later in the first century following the destruction of Jerusalem. We can surmise from Acts as well that it was a time in which the followers of Jesus were becoming somewhat detached from their Jewish identity.

To be sure, Acts states that belief in "the resurrection from the dead" was something Pharisees affirmed and which the Sadducees denied. The major difference was that the Sadducees (tied to the temple) were stricter in their interpretation of scripture than the Pharisees who were considered lax and casual when it came to matters of the way to follow daily practices of living as a Jew. The historical reality is that there was no one way to be Jewish. As Sanders has observed we have to be careful about any generalizations we make about first-century Judaism. Most Jews, he explains were monotheists, for example, but some were not. Most observed the Sabbath or didn't eat pork, while some ate the pork and didn't observe the Sabbath.[11] For a man who spent his life helping scholars understand Judaism in the ancient world he offered this unexpected statement, "I do not think that I know what the essence of Judaism was."[12]

Just as Judeans were enmeshed in Hellenism, we also find pagans visiting synagogues and debating Jewish scriptures. Some

---

[10] Joseph Tyson, *Images of Judaism in Luke-Acts* (Columbia: University of South Carolina, Press, 1992), 188. None of these characterizations accord with what Paul wrote in Romans 11.

[11] E.P. Sanders, *Comparing Judaism and Christianity: Common Judaism, Paul and the Inner and Outer in Ancient Religion,* (Minneapolis: Fortress Press, 2016, 42.

[12] Sanders, *Comparing Judaism,* 49.

avoided pork while others observed the Sabbath. A few even underwent proselyte circumcision. These are the examples that Paula Fredriksen gives when explaining what she calls the "inner-ethnic socializing" so characteristic of life in the first century.[13]

One of the most interesting things about the history of Judaism is that it has fostered what Shaye J. D. Cohen termed "the creation of a society which tolerates disputes without producing sects."[14]

There are two overlapping ways in which Jewish intellectuals converse. In their study and reflections on scripture what they are doing is called *Aggadah*. With commentaries and explanations of texts from a variety of rabbis through the ages we have a continual discussion of biblical texts and stories. Other commentary over the centuries is found in what is called *Halakhah*. It is best described as rules and guidance for living the Jewish story. Dorff describes "*halakhah* as a discourse, an ongoing conversation through which we arrive at understanding, however tentative, of what God and Torah require of us."[15] *Halakhah* is where we find Jewish ethical thinking, and that is also where we find Paul in nearly all his letters.

Paul does, of course, often use the Greek word *nomos* which is translated as law. We should not think of it though as what we might find in the law books gracing a lawyer's office.

Paul was a participant in this discourse that has always involved conversations and interpretations of God's story. Living the story, in accordance with these interpretations was the moral side of the Jewish faith called *halakhah*. Jews not only converse about the meaning of story, but also about the way to live the story. We see this matter reflected in Paul's letters with regard to his expectations for those he welcomes into a faith that calls Jesus the Messiah.

Paul was not thinking about an institutional set of laws which had structured enforcement by a government. His mind was on Torah and the better way for understanding it is the word "Teachings." That is how his rabbinic mind would have understood Torah not only as the first five books in scripture, but the whole of scripture. As Michael Bird perceptively points out, "The law – or perhaps we should call it "Torah," to get away from purely legal

---

[13] Paula Fredriksen, "To See Paul Within Judaism," *Journal of Biblical Literature* 141, no. 2 (2022): 367-69.

[14] As quoted in Elliot N. Dorff, "Borowitz on Halakhah, Aggadah, and Ethics," *Journal of Jewish Ethics* 1 no. 1 (2015): 61.

[15] Dorff, "Borowitz on Halakhah," 68.

connotations — is a mixture of story, promise, and command."[16] Bird goes on to emphasize that "promise" is all connected as well to Paul's understanding of the call of Abraham. And this in turn is an example of the interplay of *Aggadah* and *Halakhah*.

6.3 Paul would not be separated from others or from his Jewish story

Paul never said that his Jewish identity had come to an end, as so many have often assumed. Biblical scholar, Karen Armstrong, for example stated that his call to follow Jesus "...snatched Paul away from everything that had hitherto given meaning to his life. . . ."[17] It's not true. How do we account for what Paul said in Romans: that God has never rejected "his people" (Rom 11:2; meaning Paul's brothers and sisters, the people of Israel)? Paul meant that "all Israel will be saved" (Rom 11:26).

What changed for Paul was an understanding of *who belonged* to God's covenant story. To speak Southern for a second and say *Y'all* means to speak Paul's theology: namely *everyone* in the world, *all* who were disobedient, including Israel, would be saved.[18] In his role (with his *call*) he would be God's emissary reconciling and breaking bread with those from whom he once was separated. Having been devoted to maintaining purity and holiness apart from all who were "*ta ethnē*," he now was called to bring the gospel to all *the nations*. As discussed in the second chapter he first went to Arabia.

Reflecting back to the second chapter and Paul's mission to Arabia, it was simply the first of many destinations throughout the Roman Empire that Paul would visit and where he would put down roots. Based on the way Paul made friends it's unlikely he went to Arabia on a private spiritual retreat. He must have been telling others what God had revealed to him about Jesus. He also became a marked man in the eyes of the Nabatean authorities. We can also wonder if while in Arabia he learned to take meals with others besides Judeans. Somewhere along the way he did.

---

[16] Michael F. Bird, *An Anomalous Jew: Paul Among Jews, Greeks and Roman* (Grand Rapids: Eerdmans, 2016), 149

[17] Karen Armstrong, *St. Paul: The Apostle We Love to Hate* (Boston: New Harvest, 2016), 26.

[18] See Theodore Jennings, *Outlaw Justice* (Stanford: Stanford University Press, 2013), 174.

What we see in two of Paul's most important letters, Galatians and Romans, is a focus on the story of Abraham as singularly significant for Jews and for *all* followers of Jesus—i.e., the *ethnē* from all nations. In *Paul Was Not a Christian*, Eisenbaum makes a striking comparison between Paul and Abraham. "Like Abraham, God's call to Paul resulted in his living a life among people who were not his kin."[19] The key word to be considered is *"kin"* or *"genos* in Greek"— that factor of identity with shared story and history, that gives any community is unique identity.

The Greek word *"genos"* means a social group sharing a common history and a common name that see themselves unique and different in significant ways from all others. Kinship, in Paul's world, was *genos*. Our term "ethnic" as in "ethnic food" or "ethnic dress" has connotations of belonging to a specific group of people, but in Paul's mindset *ethnē* meant *all* other peoples or *nations*. Two thousand years ago *genos* referred to what we would call a specific ethnicity, while *ethnē* referred to "all others," particularly those not like us, even barbarians and pagans.[20] This contrast between ancient and contemporary definitions of *ethnē* and *genos* is important because Paul made a rather stunning redefinition regarding Jewish identity.

Paul was essentially challenging the narrow definition of "genos" in his world. It is likely he first explored this idea in Arabia where there were, at least, in contrast to other places where he would go, most likely people who knew Abraham's story. By emphasizing Abraham as the singular father for everyone in the world, Paul was crossing all the boundaries of "us" and "them" that defined all loyalties and oppositions in Paul's world.[21] The same language system plagues us in this world with regard to the status of refuges and those fleeing persecution and often not being welcomed. Here is what Paul said in Romans about why God called Abraham:

> The purpose was to make him the ancestor of all who believe without being circumcised and who thus have righteousness reckoned to them, and likewise the ancestor

---

[19] Eisenbaum, *Paul Was Not a Christian*, 174.

[20] Love L. Secrest, *A Former Jew Paul and the Politics of Race* (New York: T & T Clark, 2009), 107-108.

[21] A case can be made that Abraham remains the one figure still connecting Jews, Christians, and Muslims together. It's often forgotten.

of the circumcised who are not only circumcised but who also follow the example of the faith that our ancestor Abraham had before he was circumcised (Rom 4:11-12).

In the letter to the Galatians, Paul said: "the scripture, foreseeing that God would justify the gentiles (*nations*) by faith, declared the gospel beforehand to Abraham, saying, 'All the gentiles shall be blessed in you'" (Gal 3:8). Paul carried this whole idea to a level of identity astounding to many of his contemporaries: he was a Jew living like a gentile (*ethnē*)! "Friends, I beg you, become as I am, for I also have become as you are" (Gal 4.12). What we must not forget is that he still lived, breathed, and taught the Jewish story now framed in the shadow of the crucifixion and resurrection. But he saw Abraham as the spiritual father of *all* the peoples of the world. He saw himself with the rather unexpected task of taking this Jewish story—now that of Jesus messiah—to the nations. The only catch to this is that wherever he went, he could find *ethnē* inside of Jewish worship.

Though we have no way to estimate the numbers, there were numerous people throughout the Roman Empire interested in the way Judean people lived according to what was obviously an ancient faith. There is much evidence pointing to the so-called "God-fearers" who attended Jewish synagogues in the first century. Nanos makes the point that when Paul was writing to the Romans, he knew that his listeners in that Jewish community would include what he called "righteous gentiles."[22] It is likely that few communities of some size in the Roman world were without some Jewish population or more likely *communities* (plural). Neither were there Jewish communities without outsiders supportive of their rights to worship, or more importantly, curious enough to want to learn more.[23]

The ease with which Paul could call up various names like Moses, David, or Abraham, when writing to communities of believers from the nations suggests that he knew his readers were aware of the basic stories, either because the core of his ministry

---

[22] Mark D. Nanos, "The Jewish Context of the Gentile Audience Addressed in Paul's Letter to the Romans", *Reading Romans within Judaism: Collected Essays of Mark D. Nanos, Vol. 2* (Eugene, OR; Cascade Books, 1918), 99.

[23] Gager suggests that there were outsiders to Judaism who weren't converts, but occupied an "intermediate status" within the synagogue communities in the Roman Empire; John G. Gager, *Reinventing Paul* (New York: Oxford University Press, 2000), 67.

involved teaching those stories, or because they had already experienced and learned them through a nearby welcoming synagogue community. Most importantly, though, Paul was teaching *ethnē* to think of themselves as *belonging* to the story of Israel, not defined by land per se, but by the kind of family God intended all along. Richard Hays explained it this way:

> the "Israel" into which Paul's Corinthian converts were embraced was an Israel whose story had been hermeneutically reconfigured by the cross and resurrection. The result was that Jew and gentile alike found themselves summoned by the gospel story to a sweeping reevaluation of their identities, an imaginative paradigm shift so comprehensive that can only be described as a "conversion of the imagination."[24]

While I like the title of the book by Hays, we need to see its broader corporate dimensions. A kind of extreme individualism marks our contemporary world. "Finding yourself" is supposedly that adventure of personal discovery. Such an idea would have been extremely perplexing to Paul, raised up as a Judean with a tradition extending back to the creation of the world. It was also never a story closed to others per se, though its obligations extended to practices (circumcision, food restrictions, and Sabbath practices) often at odds with pagan cultural practices. Those obligations, more importantly, were more about faith in God's protection and forgiveness through all the centuries. As we find him in his letters, he never left Judaism behind. Daniel Boyarin has written, "I treat Paul's discourse as indigenously Jewish. . . . This is an inner-Jewish discourse and inner-Jewish controversy."[25]

Also relevant to our discussion of Paul the ambassador to the nations is the meaning of what happens when one is a convert to Judaism. There is a name change! You are either "ben Avraham" or "bas Avraham", which is to say you *become* either a "son or daughter of Abraham. The convert is adopted into the family and assigned a

---

[24] Hays, *The Conversion of the Imagination*, 5–6.
[25] Daniel Boyarin, *A Radical Jew: Paul and the Politics of Identity* (Berkley, CA: University of California Press, 1994), 205.

new "genealogical" identity."[26] Boyarin added that in the Genesis story, Abraham represents the first convert to the Jewish tradition.[27]

6.4 A more holistic understanding of Torah and Judaism in the 1st Century

If we are going to understand the historic reality of Christianity breaking away from Judaism, the most important part of this story is that it happened *after* Paul, and not during his lifetime. It was a process, as Boyarin points out in *Border Lines,* that took over four centuries.[28] For our purposes, we need a more nuanced understanding of what it meant for any Jew in the first century to maintain a Judean identity.

At this point we need to enter into conversation with scholars (Jewish and Christian alike) who *counter* the dominant image of Paul being a convert *from* Judaism. To be sure the picture from 1 Timothy is the converted Paul (see 1 Tim 1:12–16). As Pamela Eisenbaum notes, if we only had the seven letters of Paul, we would have never discovered a "converted Paul." "He never even uses the language of repentance in reference to himself."[29] The only thing he regrets is his early persecution, noted before, with regard to the early followers of Jesus Messiah. Segal also noted that Paul never used the terms found in born-again Christianity.[30]

If Paul didn't convert from Judaism, how do we explain what happened to him? I think Segal gets is right. It was a transformation. That indeed is the very language Paul used in many of his letters. Along with his love of the Jewish narrative of God's story, Paul was grounded in experiences of the spirit: "And we speak of these things in words not taught by human wisdom but taught by the Spirit, interpreting spiritual things to those who are spiritual" (1 Cor 2:13).

To be sure Paul was something of a puzzle to other Jews. As Bird in his book *Paul an Anomalous Jew,* explains, "It wasn't that Paul converted from one religion to another, but he ventured beyond the

---

[26] Boyarin, *A Radical Jew,* 241.

[27] Fredriksen might beg to differ with Boyarin's use of the word "convert." She notes that pagans interested in Judaism were "adherents" but not "converts;" Paula Fredriksen, "What Does it Mean to See Paul," 369.

[28] Daniel Boyarin, *Border Lines: The Partition of Judaeo-Christianity* (Philadelphia: University of Pennsylvania Press, 2004).

[29] Eisenbaum, *Paul Was not a Christian,* 42.

[30] Segal, *Paul the Convert,* 21.

margins of conventional Judaism."[31] The places where he "ventured" were for the most part his adoption of living with others, which meant not keeping up traditional markers of Jewish identity or what Boyarin called "...those observances of Torah which were thought by Jew and gentile alike to mark off the special status of Jews: circumcision, kashruth, and the observances of Sabbath and the holidays."[32]

While reference was made to eating Kosher food (i.e., *kashruth* above) Paul could accept even food offered to idols, as perhaps innocuous. Paul said of that food and therefore, by implication, food sold in a temple meat market, that it may not have mattered since "no idol in the world really exists" (1 Cor 8:4). The real problem for Paul wasn't the food per se, but who was welcome at the table. Nanos looked at Paul's condemnation of Peter in Galatians. That Peter withdrew from table fellowship with ethnē meant he was using the criteria of who was and who was not worthy to be at the same table together. That was replicating the class structure of table fellowship known both in Judea and Rome, in direct contrast to the table fellowship of those following Jesus Messiah.[33]

Jews, we should note, were marked by a set of values, not evident in much of the Roman world, regarding family and an ethical focus on the poor, the orphans, and widows. Those sharing in synagogue life were called to live in a new way different from their neighbors. Those decisions most likely had consequences, such as the persecutions Paul mentioned in 1 Thessalonians. They had "turned to God from idols, to serve a living and true God" (1 Thess 1:9). But they had also suffered. In fact, Paul began by stating they had been persecuted (1 Thess 1:6) and later said opposition had come from "your own compatriots" (1 Thess 2:14). They were living with a difficult and challenging new faith.

Boyarin quotes a definition from Mary Louise Pratt of the in-between space where two or more cultures meet as a place "...where disparate cultures meet, clash, grapple with each other, often in

---

[31] Bird, *Paul an Anomalous Jew*, 46.

[32] Boyarin, *A Radical Jew*, 53. Note that the word *kashruth* refers to the foods that are prohibited, and to all matters relating to keeping Kosher.

[33] See Mark D. Nanos, "How Could Paul Accuse Peter of 'Living *Ethnē*-ishly' in Antioch (Gal 2:11–21) if Peter Was Eating According to Jewish Dietary Norms?" *Journal for the Study of Paul and His Letters* 6, no. 2 (Fall 2016): 213-4.

highly asymmetrical relations of domination and subordination."[34] The presumption of a superior status is also at work in a nation seeking to colonize a less advanced civilization—i.e., Roman attitudes toward unconquered nations and tribes. One consequence of hybrid interactions on the cultural or religious level is that one side disowns the other. If there was one common denominator uniting Judeans and all the others conquered by Rome, it was that whatever their culture contained—with regard to story, music, art, cuisine, etc.- it was not equal to the myth of Roman superiority. Both Jewish followers of Jesus along with non-Jews in their worship assemblies needed additional skills. These Paul had.

6.5 Paul's bi-cultural and bi-lingual skills

Paul's status in his early ministry was most likely akin to those of immigrants and refugees in our world—needing new skills and language to make a new life for themselves and their loved ones. What made Paul different from our more contemporary refugees is that he wasn't escaping from terror and violence. He wasn't seeking new opportunities for freedom. Paul moved into new circumstances, not to get sustenance from them, but to give something to them— the story that he was called to tell.

And, clearly, he had or developed the skills he needed to tell that story. With his roots in what is modern day Syria he already spoke more than one language. We don't know exactly what the level of competence was, but he had facility with the Greek language, which was almost a requisite in the world of commerce, trade, and politics of Rome. While Romans tended to see Greek as a lesser language than their own Latin, it was nonetheless common for those seeking any "linguistic prestige and socio-economic advantage"[35] to have facility in both Greek and Latin.

Paul also knew well what it meant to live as one conquered and ruled by Rome. He would travel among a great many of them. By some estimates traveling over 10,000 miles in his ministry, again and again, he would walk into trouble and persecution, even spending considerable time in various prisons.

---

[34] Daniel Boyarin, *Border Lines*, 18, quoting Mary Louise Pratt, *Imperial Eyes: Travel Writing and Transculturation* (London: Routledge, 1992), 4.

[35] Stanley E Porter, *Paul's World*, (Boston: Leiden, 2008), 135–36. As noted earlier, however, I have found no evidence that Paul spoke Latin.

Like all his Jewish brothers and sisters, even those who never ventured outside the walls of Jerusalem, Paul was navigating a Greek culture under the military rule of Rome, with a Judean upbringing and way of life. A key question regards how Paul adapted himself and his way of life to that world. To what extent did he become at home in the Greek world? Do we end up with a Hellenistic Paul more than a Jewish Paul?

In asking these questions we find ourselves inside what N. T. Wright describes as "the old divide between those who suppose Paul to be basically a Jewish thinker and those who see him as having borrowed his fundamental ideas from Hellenism."[36] It should be obvious that I am making the case that Paul was a Jewish thinker. At the same time, we must recognize that he had the skills to communicate and probably be fairly convincing when addressing people who didn't know the Judean story.

Wright suggests that the historical tendency in Biblical scholarship has been to read Paul in a context of Hellenistic philosophy. The quest for the Paul who presumably rejected Judaism meant looking for the supposed Hellenistic, non-Jewish, sources of Paul's religion."[37] More traditional scholars, in a similar vein, explain Paul's idea of justification by faith to be in opposition to the Jewish law.[38] My argument in this chapter is that Paul is grounded in the Hebraic story. Inside its life of synagogue worship, he addresses non-Jews and Jews alike. That is clearly at the heart of the letter to Rome. We see Paul continuing to apply Judean ethics to all the problems he addresses. In the chapters yet to come we will also look at Paul as he brings scripture and the story of Jesus to bear on common issues affecting marriage and family, and how to live in a time when the end of time seems so close at hand.

In finding Paul we must look to those who experienced oppression and subjugation within Rome, to be sure, but also in the context of Hellenistic culture that was male dominated and ruled by violence over women, conquered people, and slaves. Ehrensperger emphasized that Paul was part of a discourse from below. "It was a

---

[36] N. T. Wright, "Gospel and Theology in Galatians," in *Pauline Perspectives: Essays on Paul, 1978–2013* (Minneapolis: Fortress Press, 1994), 80.

[37] N. T. Wright, *Paul and His Recent Interpreters: Some Contemporary Debates* (Minneapolis: Fortress Press, 2015), 17.

[38] See the excellent chapter "The Traditional View of Paul," in John G. Gager, *Reinventing Paul*, 21-42.

discourse about subjugated people accommodating and distancing themselves from dominant power claims; inside their own communities and stories."[39]

To be sure, Paul's ability to write in Greek included his foundation in the Greek version of the Bible called the Septuagint. Agamben tells an interesting little story about Paul's writing. A famous scholar years ago was walking with the Philosopher Taubes. He said he had been reading Paul's letters. He said "But [it] isn't Greek, its Yiddish!" Taubes agreed and said that's why he understood it.[40] Agamben added to that with the observation that Paul also inhabited the language of exile.[41] The four hundred years preceding Paul in Jewish history had been reflections on the exile that somehow continued even though the Jerusalem temple had been rebuilt. Paul, the Jewish ambassador to the nations, would take the longing for what once was into those segments of society where there was the least promise of life and only a dismal future. Paul, the man of hope, would inspire them with words like these: "And now faith, hope, and love abide, these three; and the greatest of these is love" (1 Cor 13:1).

---

[39] Ehrensperger, *Paul at the Crossroads*, 217.
[40] Agamben, *The Time that Remains*, 4.
[41] Agamben, *The Time that Remains*, 4–5.

Chapter 7
Paul in Community

"And there is something on the stage of history that was not there before: a community that calls itself by the name of the crucified Messiah."[1]

"God settles into the recesses formed in the world by the little ones, the nothings and nobodies of the world, what Paul in First Corinthians calls *ta me onta*."[2]

It is not that stories are part of human life, but that human life is part of a story.[3]

7.1 To see a most unusual leader

A major part of the story behind this book is that I had gone through many years of ministry as a pastor and preacher thinking that I knew what was in the Bible, and that included knowing what I thought was essential to the Pauline letters themselves. New Testament scholar Paul Meyer says this about that problem: "No curse lies more heavily upon our study of the Bible, especially in a theological seminary, than the confidence that we already know what is written on its pages."[4] What I'm offering here *isn't* what I thought I knew.

We need to consider that the mysterious workings of the Holy Spirit which originally inspired Holy Scripture are still there waiting to erupt into life, or better yet erupt into the lives of those of who are ready to open its pages. Is it possible that ordinary pastors and people can have something akin to the experience Karl Barth

---

[1] Paul Meyer, *The Word in this World: Essays in New Testament Exegesis and Theology* (Louisville: John Knox Press, 2004), 14.

[2] John D. Caputo, *The Weakness of God: A Theology of the Event* (Bloomington: Indiana University Press, 2006), 45; *ta me onta* can be translated either as "nobodies," or literally "those without a being."

[3] Leslie Newbigin, *The Open Secret: An Introduction to the Theology of Mission* (Grand Rapids: Eerdmans, 1995), 82.

[4] Meyer, *The World in this World*, 15.

reported having while working on his earth-shattering commentary on Paul's letter to the Romans? "During the work it was often as though I caught her breath from afar, from Asia Minor or Corinth, something primeval, from the ancient East, indefinably sunny, wild, original that somehow is hidden behind the sentences."[5]

I'm not sure that I've caught Paul's breath but finding the implicit and explicit stories of Paul in his letters lets me see him in a different light. It isn't a Paul striding assuredly through the history of his time, but a Paul whose own life, and the certainty he once had, was guided by God's spirit to a life he never would have imagined. What appears in nearly all his letters—perhaps with Romans as the outlier—is an emotional honesty that may be the most neglected reality in the way many of us were taught to read Paul.

The worries of Paul are visible in nearly all his letters. What emerges from Paul's 2nd letter to the Corinthians, for example, is a picture of Paul's "grieving soul." An anguished Paul is how I describe Welborn's portrait of Paul in the book *The End of Enmity: Paul and the Wrongdoer of Second Corinthians*. The paintings of Paul discussed in a previous chapter were inspired by the imaginations of artists in the Renaissance and beyond, depicting a tall, well-fed, and muscular figure. In contrast Welborn finds a Paul expressing "psychological distress"[6] over the rupture of a relationship with a dear friend—never identified by name in any letter.[7]

The *usual assumptions* are that Paul must have been a strong leader, with the usual set of skills possessed by those with power and authority. This is not the reality we see in his letters. He followed a strange path and used unusual metaphors for a man who could be considered an admirable leader. This Paul would be equally weird in our world. A leader writing a letter of tears isn't exactly standing tall (2 Cor 2:4). A leader talking about his escape from arrest by being let down in a basket over the walls of Damascus isn't an example of strength (2 Cor 11:32–33). Rarely will a leader remind people of a terrible disability that launched their relationship. Paul did. He arrived in Galatia in some physical state

---

[5] James B. Smart, trans. *Revolutionary Theology in the Making: Barth – Thurneysen Correspondence, 1914–1925* (Richmond: John Knox Press, 1964), 43.

[6] L. L.,Welborn, *An End to Enmity: Paul and the "Wrongdoer" of Second Corinthians* (Göttingen: Walter de Gruyter, 2011), 436.

[7] The first part of Chapter 11 "Paul in Trouble" is based on this matter.

that would ordinarily elicit *scorn* (Gal 4:14). Unlike a proud leader, he lists the terrible things he had endured as *badges of honor*. (2 Cor 11:23-33) He even told the Corinthians he was "content with weaknesses, insults, hardships, persecutions, and calamities for the sake of Christ" (2 Cor 12:10). Jerry Sumney calls him the apostle of weakness."[8] I can think of only a few leaders of our times such as Gandhi, Martin Luther King, and Nelson Mandela who proclaimed a similar story.

7.2 A Network of Jesus Messiah Communities

We have many forms and shapes of communal life in our world, but it also a world which proclaims the message "Do your own thing!" Advertising immerses us in the idea that we *deserve* the very best. Religion in places has been transformed into what one sociologist has called "Moralistic Therapeutic Deism."[9] The underlying philosophy is that we can choose our own religion; no one should try to persuade anyone else about what to believe. Brad Gregory explains that this modernistic and individualistic approach to faith is meant to make one "feel good and happy about oneself and one's life." Gregory adds that God becomes something like "a combination Divine Butler and Cosmic Therapist."[10] Paul would be appalled.

For Paul, the way to have God in one's life is radically different from what is currently offered up. The extreme example of this comes from J. R. Kirk's book "Jesus I Have Loved, but Paul?" Kirk is not an advocate for self-serving theology, as his exaggerated emphasis on the word "My" shows in this quote:

---

[8] Jerry L Sumney, "Paul's 'Weakness' An Integral Part of His Conception of Apostleship," *Journal for the Study of the New Testament* 52 (1993): 90.

[9] Christian Smith as quoted by Brad S. Gregory, *The Unintended Revolution: How a Religious Revolutions Secularized Society* (Cambridge: The Belknap Press of Harvard University, 2012), 170.

[10] Gregory, *The Unintended Revolution*, 170-1.

"My heart. My life. My relationship with God. My alienation from God. My repentance. My faith. My allegiance. My Lord. My justification. My sanctification. My membership added to the church. My quiet time. My closed-eye self-examination at communion. My route to heaven. My escape from the coming conflagration. My soul with Jesus forever."[11]

These claims to selfhood are what Colin D. Miller sees as peculiar to the age we live in: "We are, in other words, a historical oddity: we are "selves." "A 'self' is the 'core' of an 'individual' who has no telos, no virtues, no vices, no authority, and no story. We live in a way that our classical forefathers, if MacIntyre is right, could hardly recognize as human."[12] The same sentiments are echoed by the anthropologist Talal Asad who notes that in the world emphasizing personal freedom the question becomes, "…what should human beings do to realize their freedom, empower themselves and choose pleasure?" He calls it the "the increasing triumph of individual autonomy."[13] It is a question that would leave Paul looking bewildered.

As we examine Paul in community, we find ourselves in a network of communities sharing historical continuity. Bound inside the story of Israel meant they were telling time within a Jewish perspective. We happen to be living in *nuclear-time* and thus we fear the possibility of a dismal future. Paul was grounded in a more confident concept of apocalyptic time which, in the words of Moltmann, "awaits the end of time with passionate hope: 'Come, Lord, Jesus, come soon (Rev. 22:20).[14]

Relevant to time as Paul knew it is the meaning of the Greek word *eggus*, known to us in the phrase "the kingdom of God is present (*eggus*)," which is to say "it is near." The Greek phrase is not about watching a clock or looking at a calendar, but it is more of a

---

[11] J. R. Kirk, *Jesus I Have Loved, But Paul? A Narrative Approach to the Problem of Pauline Christianity* (Grand Rapids: Baker Academic, 2011), 53.

[12] Colin D. Miller, *The Practice of the Body of Christ: Human Agency in Pauline Theology after MacIntyre*, (Cambridge: James Clarke and Co., 2014), 39.

[13] Talal Asad, *Formations of the Secular: Christianity, Islam and Modernity* (Stanford: Stanford University Press, 2003), 71.

[14] Jürgen Moltmann, *The Way of Jesus Christ* (Minneapolis: Fortress Press,1999), 159.

spatial term, in the sense of being "close by," or "just around the corner."[15] It is also, as Moltmann emphasizes, a matter involving followers of Jesus certain that "the signs of the messianic era are already visible."[16]

7.3 Not a Community of Conversions

Christian Revivalism may have been somewhat unique to America, but a more direct connection to its roots according to Diarmaid MacCulloch goes back to the 18th century Moravians and John Wesley. What emerged was Methodism and an evangelical emphasis among many denominations all rooted in the story of the Great Awakenings in America. It created what MacCulloch called "a lasting pattern: an appeal to the need for personal conversion and 'revival" in the Church."[17] *All of this occurred* under the larger umbrella of the Protestant Reformation with its focus on the conversion of individuals. As an example, consider a passage from 2 Corinthians 5:17, which has often been quoted in reference to a conversion experience. Two translations follow:

King James Version (KJV)	New Revised Standard Version (NRSV)
"If any man be in Christ there is a new creature..."	"So if anyone is in Christ, there is a new creation..."

These two versions are basically the same, except that the NRSV substitutes the more inclusive pronoun "anyone." The first problem with both translations is that there is *no* Greek pronoun in this verse. The second issue is with the translation of Greek word *ktisis*. Is it "creature" or "creation"? The Greek word can be translated either way.

What matters is that Paul wasn't preaching in a tent and calling for individual conversions. But he was creating unique communities, the make-up of which was different from what anyone in that historical era had seen or experienced. Paul had a new *creation* in mind, not a new individual, or a new *creature*.

---

[15] Danker et al., *A Greek-English Lexicon*, 271.
[16] Moltmann, *The Way of Jesus*, 97.
[17] MacCulloch, *An Unintended Revolution*, 757.

This phrase *new creation* was at the heart of Paul's argument in Galatians. "For neither circumcision nor uncircumcision is anything; but new creation (*ktisis*) is everything" (Gal 6:15). The powerful inclusive vision of what is to come is clearer in this translation of 2 Cor 5:17 offered by N.T. Wright: *"If anyone in Messiah, new creation!"*[18] There isn't a verb in that translation just as it was not be found in the sentence in Greek in Paul's letters. We might call it a *statement*, but more precisely it was an *announcement*.[19] No matter where you come from, you belong to something new on the face of the earth, and we all belong together.

What will distinguish Paul's concept of *belonging* from what is emphasized in many of our churches is the importance placed on *belonging* to the story of Christ, and far less on *knowing* the story. There was no such thing in Paul's world as a "confession of faith," unless it was understood to be the Shema: "Hear, O Israel . . ." (Deut 6:4), which continues with "You shall love the Lord your God with all your heart, and with all your soul, and with all your might" (Deut 6:5). What is dramatically different is not the proclamation of the oneness of God, but that *all* are brought into that story through Christ.

What we find in Paul's understanding of community is a standard of ethical practice that was antithetical to values maintained by those in power in first century Rome. At that time, Rome was an empire more than a city, and an empire founded on principles of violence and domination.

While those in power lived in palaces and seaside estates, Paul lived among those whom Caputo identifies as "marginal, the outsider, the left-out, the least among us, the poor existing individuals, the destitute, the *anawim*, those who are plundered and ground under."[20] Describing those known to Jesus, John Caputo

---

[18] Wright, *Paul and the Faithfulness of God*, 1072.

[19] Note how Steve Mason translates *"the euangelion"* (usually translated as The Gospel): "The unmissable theme of 1 Thess, the earliest known text by a follower of Christ, is what Paul calls The Announcement (τὸ εὐαγγέλιον)" in "Paul Without Judaism: Historical Method over Perspective," in *Paul and Matthew Among Jews and Gentiles*, ed. Ronald Charles (London: Bloomsbury T & T Clark, 2021) 26.

[20] Jack Caputo, "In Search of a Sacred Anarchy: An Experiment in Danish Deconstruction," in *Caputo: Essential Selected Writings*, ed. K. Keith Putt (Bloomington: Indiana University Press, 2018), 309. In this essay Caputo claims it is

made the point that the very same people are clearly depicted in our times with the movie *Slumdog Millionaire,* where we see massive numbers of people wearing rags digging through garbage to find anything of value. Our modern day "slumdogs" have their counterparts throughout history.

Thankfully the few letters from Paul's hand offer us a picture of one man who was willing to contend for the dignity of the "least" in his world. Paul's first letter to the Corinthians begins with his observations regarding the *divisions* that had taken place which did not affirm the dignity of all its members. Indeed, the Corinthian *ekklēsia* had become a competitive environment undermining the essential aspects of community, or *koinonia.* Paul expected followers of Jesus to live as he did, making no distinctions about who was more worthy than another, but they were divided in Corinth. Paul addressed that issue directly in 1 Corinthians 1:10-11 with two Greek words: *schismata* and *erides.* The word *schismata* in verse 10 is translated in the NRSV as "divisions." The Greek refers to factions or serious conflicts in the community. The second word, *erides,* from verse 11 is related to the name of the Greek god of discord, name Eris. In the words of Margaret Mitchell, Paul "was addressing "a serious social threat to the life of the church community."[21]

What Paul wanted was for all to be united in their loyalty to Christ. What he saw were factions at work claiming different allegiances: to Paul, to Apollos, to Cephas, or to Christ. Paul asks the rhetorical questions: "Has Christ been divided?" (1 Cor 1:12-13) Then, after noting that someone had said "I belong to Paul," and another "I belong to Apollos" (1 Cor 3:4), Paul clearly assumed priority over Apollos by making the contrast between them as one who planted a garden and one who watered (1 Cor 3:5). The early community of Jesus Messiah followers was the garden *planted* by Paul. Apollos got out the hose to water what Paul started. Paul's message: both were God's servants.

We cannot avoid the clear assumption that Paul is claiming an *originating* authority. By this term—not borrowed from anyone

---

among such in this world where God is to be found. His use of the word "*anawim*" is found in Amos 8:4 where that is the Hebrew word for the "poor."

[21] Margaret M. Mitchell, *Paul and the Rhetoric of Reconciliation: An Exegetical Investigation of the Language and Composition of 1 Corinthians* (Louisville: Westminster/John Knox Press, 1991), 72; see the entire exegesis 65-83.

else—I am recognizing that Paul sees himself as a *father* (and as we shall also see as a *mother*) to those in assemblies he founded. Lest we jump to the conclusion that this represents *patriarchal* power we need to remember that in so many ways Paul was not a typical man in his world.

The crucial question is this: are Paul's patriarchal assumptions any different from those in the prevailing culture? To be sure Paul never shirked from claiming credit for the assemblies he founded. At the same time my contention is that he was *unlike* any *father* or *master* the members of these Jesus Messiah communities had ever known. He was claiming authority and the responsibility for teaching and preaching the meaning of the gospel, and he expected a degree of obedience to the norms he understood to be essential to their common life. Moreover, Paul offered practical advice, meant to bring members of the community together, all the while sharing in the peace of Christ. Paul, however, had little respect for the patriarchal premises that diminish the worth of others.[22]

Cynthia Kittridge sees in Paul what she calls "a vision of equality struggling for expression within the dominant patriarchal culture."[23] That struggle is apparent in what Paul advised to those who first responded to his gospel after he had come to Corinth: "Consider your own call, brothers and sisters: not many of you were wise by human standards, not many were powerful, not many were of noble birth" (1 Cor 1:26).

Paul's declaration regarding God choosing "things that are not" flew directly in the face of Greek philosophy which primarily gave license to the very *few* who claimed their place in the world based on the concept that they had a "being" (*ousia*) that preceded and precluded all the others in their world.[24] Notably, Paul is recognizing that the "things that are not"—have a much greater theological significance in contrast to the "things that are." Consider how Caputo understands the importance of this verse:

---

[22] In Chapter 9, "Paul the Unmanly Man" Paul's amazing affirmation of marriage is equality between a husband and wife.

[23] Cynthia Briggs Kittredge, *Community Authority: The Rhetoric of Obedience in the Pauline Tradition* (Harrisburg: Trinity Press International, 1998), 36.

[24] Caputo, *The Weakness of God*, 147.

God withdraws from the world's order of presence, prestige, and sovereignty in order to settle into those pockets of protest in contradiction to the world. God belongs to the air, to the call, the spirit that inspires and aspires, that breeds justice. God settles into the recesses formed in the world by the little ones, the nothings and nobodies of the world, what Paul in First Corinthians calls *ta me onta*.[25]

No wonder Paul includes a hymn exalting Christ who emptied himself and took the form of slave (Phil 2:5-11). Elizabeth Tamez points out that this hymn appeared in "a context where ambition abounds and people kill for the kind of power, wealth, and status that demands a servile prostration of its subjects." She concludes, "Reading the poem as a provocative political statement takes away the absolute dominion of the emperor and also highlights the emperor's unhealthy attitudes toward power, luxury, and grandeur."[26] Nearly every issue addressed in Philippians concerns a unity that seems to be in jeopardy because of the assertions of rights to status and influence by the very few. Paul addressed himself to those causing divisions because they had what Tamez has rightly called "unhealthy attitudes."

7.4 Reflecting on *ekklēsia*

Ekklēsia was a common word in the first century embraced by trade associations and almost any shared interest bringing people together. Its visibility is the reason Ascough is reluctant to attach politically revolutionary implications to this word.[27] The work of Richard Last also points out how many associations in the Roman world—religious, economic, trade-oriented, and social—used the same term to describe themselves. The basic understanding of

---

[25] Caputo, *The Weakness of God*, 45.
[26] Tamez, "Author's Introduction", 75.
[27] Richard Ascough, *Paul's Macedonian Associations: The Social Context of Philippians and 1 Thessalonians* (Tübingen: L. J. C. Mohr, 2003), 137.

ekklēsia is a call for togetherness. That is the idea stressed by almost every other known ancient association's title."[28]

Something more was at work, though in Paul's consistent use of this term: there were consequences of belonging to *ekklēsia* shaped by faith in Christ crucified. Rowan Williams explains that: "…the Christian *ekklēsia* is both an assembly for those who are not at home in the present order and a revelation of true order—as a sign of both disruption and of harmony."[29] The theologian Myron Penner emphasizes the meaning of the word *ekklēsia* as both "called out" and "called in," meaning that its participants find themselves in "conflict with all other commitments to the powers and institutions of one society" (i.e., Rome).[30]

Looking at Paul's use of the term as more politically subversive is Richard Horsley. He points out that we can see in Paul's letters, especially in light of his comments about the collection he will take to Rome (discussed more fully in Chapter 14) that there was a "network of assemblies [that] had an "international" political-economic dimension diametrically opposed to the tributary political economy of the empire."[31] While the actual numbers of followers of Jesus Messiah in the time of Paul was quite small as we saw in the last chapter with the work of Rodney Stark, they were found dispersed through many parts of the empire—even those not visited by Paul. Some of these were surely more subversive.

7.5 Paul and biographical memory

If you came across an unknown man while traveling in the world of the first century, you would identify him either by his dress

---

[28] Richard Last, "Ekklēsia Outside the Septuagint and the Demos: The Title of Graeco-Roman Associations and Christ-Follower Groups," *Journal of Biblical Literature* 137, no. 4 (2018): 959.

[29] Rowan Williams, *Why Study the Past? The Quest for the Historical Church* (Grand Rapids: William B. Eerdmans Publishing Co., 2005), 46.

[30] Myron Penner, *The End of Apologetics: Christian Witness in a Post-modern Context* (Grand Rapids: Baker Academic, 2013), 66.

[31] Richard A. Horsley, "1 Corinthians: A Case Study of Paul's Assembly as an Alternative Society," in *Paul and Empire: Religion and Power in Roman Imperial Society*, ed. Richard A. Horsley (Harrisburg: Trinity Press International, 1997), 251.

or speech.[32] If you shared the same trade you might want to ask him about how he learned to work with leather. Perhaps his accent would intrigue you, and you'd ask where he was born. The conversation would be about his story and yours.

We know already that Paul did not hide his identity as he wrote his letters. He didn't tell long complicated stories, but his autobiographical memory was wrapped up in his faith and his vision for living *in Christ*. His memory bank was full of many God-graced times, and, as we will see further on, it also included mystical experiences that were hard to put into words. Consider all the dangers Paul faced and how this extensive list reveals his dedication to follow Christ:

> Three times I was beaten with rods. Once I received a stoning. Three times I was shipwrecked; for a night and a day I was adrift at sea; on frequent journeys, in danger from rivers, danger from bandits, danger from my own people, danger from Gentiles, danger in the city, danger in the wilderness, danger at sea, danger from false brothers and sisters; in toil and hardship, through many a sleepless night, hungry and thirsty, often without food, cold and naked. And, besides other things, I am under daily pressure because of my anxiety for all the churches (2 Cor 11:25-28).

All the years seemingly lost to us were, nonetheless, filled with conversations with friends and strangers. And in all the months Paul spent in prison, according to his own accounts, he shared those times with fellow workers. The letter to the Philippians, for example, was written by Paul and Timothy (1:1), and we learn a few verses later that it was written while they were in prison. They had long days, and maybe even longer-seeming nights in which to talk and share stories.

Paul's memories of these events in the context of his ministry were never just his alone. They encapsulated the life he was living as one whose goal was to live "in Christ." Paul was sharing with the earliest followers of Jesus, known to him through his evangelistic work, two kinds of memory. They are "foundational or cultural

---

[32] Kenneth Bailey, *Poet and Peasant*, vol. 2, 42. Professor Bailey made these comments in reference to the problem any Jew would face with the naked man lying as if dead in the ditch, as in the story of the Good Samaritan.

memory" and "biographical memory." Credit for this distinction belongs to the historian Jan Assmann, who points out that the key question is always "What must we not forget?"[33] Memories aren't just stories but are the framework for judgments about life in the present, offering at the same time a way to see into the future.

"Biographical memory" is more immediate and social. In the words of Assmann, it "always depends on social interaction, even in literate societies."[34] This kind of memory isn't part of the institution or part of the mechanisms at work in the formation of group identity. It concerns the recent past, and only becomes relevant in a relational context, that is, when a personal experience can be related to someone else's experience or when one wants to form a relationship by connecting to someone with similar life experiences. When Paul spoke of the mother of Rufus at the end of Romans, for example, he said, "Greet Rufus, chosen in the Lord! and also greet his mother—a mother to me also" (Rom 16:13). I can imagine that others, not having ever met Paul in person, might have turned to the mother of Rufus when the letter was read and asked her, "How it is that you were like a mother to Paul?"

7.6 Cultural memory and rituals of belonging

Cultural memory is both nurtured and sustained in ritual and in various repeatable events. Such events, like a Seder meal, for example involve re-telling the major faith stories that give people their own identity and understanding of their shared history. The liturgical cycle of the Christian year is another example of cultural memory. Rituals of belonging, such as baptism or a bar mitzvah serve not just to welcome someone into the community, but to reaffirm its meaning for all members.

"Cultural memory" was always implicit in Paul's unequivocal ethical expectations for belonging to Christ and to one another. Paul's letter to the Philippians begins with a reference to the very first day they met (Phil 1:5) in what Paul called "the early days of the gospel" (Phil 4:15). As with so many of our own personal stories we begin by saying "Remember when?" The past is invoked so that

---

[33] Jan Assmann, *Cultural Memory and Early Civilization: Writing, Remembrances, and Political Imagination* (New York: Cambridge University Press, 2011), 16.
[34] Assman, *Cultural Memory and Early Civilization*, 37.

those coming into that culture will learn those stories, but, as Assmann points out, there is a counterfactual dimension to this process.[35] In recovering what has been forgotten or the times when the way was lost, the record a community keeps by remaining true to its foundation also re-creates itself for different times and challenges.

We can see repeatedly in Paul's letters a teaching based on what he considered to be the fundamental parts of the community along with the ground-rules for belonging. The basic, not-to-be-questioned ethic was *belonging with one another*. The one remarkable attribute in the kind of communities Paul created, as well as those in Rome (i.e., those he did not start), is that *those from many different ethnicities were drawn into the world of* the Judean story and a shared life shaped by knowing of Christ crucified. These communities sought to give dignity to all members, even the most vulnerable. Moreover, they had become *friends,* or more importantly siblings.

7.7 Paul's friends

At the end of Romans, we have a picture of a most diverse set of friends and co-workers connected to Paul—especially the women. Those mentioned are Phoebe, Prisca (of Prisca and Aquila), Mary, Junia (connected to Andronicus), Tryphaena and Tryphosa, Persis, the mother of Rufus, Julia, the sister of Nereus, and Olympus.

From the larger list of names Paul identifies those who worked alongside of him in ministry: Prisca and Aquila, Andronicus and Junia, Urbanus, Tryphaena and Tryphosa, and Persis. A number of those mentioned were probably Jewish members of the Jesus assemblies forced to leave Rome when Emperor Claudius expelled all Jews from Rome in 49 CE. That is probably how Paul first met Prisca and Aquila in Ephesus (Acts:18.1–3). This couple is mentioned first in the list of those greetings, perhaps because of their importance in Paul's life. Only in Acts do we learn that Paul worked alongside them as a tentmaker. This is not a detail we can confirm since Paul never mentions his trade. He comments in Romans 16:4 that they were his "co-workers alongside of him" and that they had "risked their necks for my life." We don't know what Prisca and Aquila did to save Paul's life, but the point that they

---

[35] Assman, *Cultural Memory and Early Civilization*, 51.

"risked their necks for him" in the Roman world meant risking execution, or "death by decapitation." *Citizens* could not be executed by crucifixion. This is a clue that at least Prisca and Aquila were citizens.

Paul wasn't a lone eagle when it came to ministry. Among those Paul called "co-workers" (*synergos* in Greek) were Andronicus and Junia (Rom 16:7). They were fellow prisoners with him at one point, but two other facts are most important in Paul's eyes. They were "prominent among the apostles" and "they were in Christ before I was." Were there women among the early apostles? According to Acts there weren't. Paul, however, said that his friends Andronicus and Junia were *both* apostles. What Paul also said about them, according to Jewett, is that they were *"outstanding* among the apostles."[36] Paul places this husband and wife team essentially alongside the others who were witnesses to the resurrection. It means they were active in ministry soon after the crucifixion.

With the mention of Rufus and his mother (Romans 16:13) we may be going back to the day of the crucifixion itself. In Mark's gospel a passerby, just coming in from the country, was compelled to carry the cross of Jesus.[37] He is identified as Simon of Cyrene, the father of Alexander and Rufus. Mark's gospel has also traditionally been connected to the community of early followers in Rome. Could a foundational memory of the Roman Jesus community have included the wife of Simon of Cyrene and their two sons Alexander and Rufus? Paul mentioned that Rufus was "chosen in the Lord." It was "an honorific title of one who has a long and tested record of discipleship."[38] Rufus and his mother may have been exiled by the edict of Claudius, and like Prisca and Aquila returned to Rome around 55 CE.

The importance of the reference to Rufus, if we have correctly identified him, means that in addition to meeting Peter and James and the early disciples in Jerusalem, Paul may have met another witness to the crucifixion of Jesus.

---

[36] Jewett, *Romans*, 963.
[37] Jewett, *Romans*, 969.
[38] Arland J. Hultgren, *Paul's Letter to the Romans: A Commentary* (Grand Rapids: William B. Eerdmans Publishing Company, 2011), 587.

What I see in just a few of these snapshots of various friends of Paul is the way his life and ministry was wrapped up in the lives of so many others committed to follow Jesus. To be sure, we'd love to know more. But the other part of this story is how much we actually can know by paying closer attention to what Paul was telling others in his letters.

Chapter 8
Paul Found in Letters Heard

"Lore, being lighter, travels faster than letter."[1]

"Greet all the brothers and sisters with a holy kiss. I solemnly command you by the Lord that this letter be read to all of them" (1 Thessalonians 5:26–27).

"Blessed is the one who reads aloud the words of the prophecy and blessed are those who hear and who keep what is written in it; for the time is near" (Revelation 1:3).

Scripta littera manet[2]

8.1 Letters meant to be performed

It is inaccurate to say people were "reading" Paul's letters, especially if we think they were sitting down in some kind of private setting to open them for their own pleasure. Brittany Wilson, in her book *Unmanly Men*, discusses only *hearers* and not *readers*, "because the majority of early Christians would have most likely heard the text read aloud."[3]

Among a number of significant questions Paul asked in the tenth chapter of Romans was, "How are they to hear without someone to proclaim him?" (Rom 10:14). A few verses earlier he made reference to the practice of confessing "with your lips that Jesus is Lord (Gr. *Kyrios*)" (Rom 10:9). The whole chapter is about sound! It's also a dialogue that brings in the prophetic voice of Isaiah, while addressing questions to a community ready to hear Paul's voice through that of Phoebe. Phoebe did more than simply carry a letter of Paul's to Rome. A number of scholars are sure it was *performed* by

---

[1] Dennis R. MacDonald, *There is No Male and Female: The Fate of a Dominical Saying in Paul and Gnosticism* (Philadelphia: Fortress Press, 1987), 21.

[2] Howard Thurman, *With Heart and Hand: The Autobiography of Howard Thurman* (New York: Houghton Mifflin Harcourt Publishing Company, 1979), 228; it means "The written word endures."

[3] Brittany Wilson, *Refigurations of Masculinity in Luke-Acts* (Oxford: Oxford University Press, 2015), 33.

her or by Tertius, the scribe.[4] No matter who read it, Paul's words commending Phoebe to the people in Rome indicate that she was the one charged to embody Paul's voice (Rom 16:1).

In nearly every worship service when we have a reading from one of Paul's letters, that is all it is—*just a reading*. People have asked me why we even *read* these letters, since they are so difficult to understand. Some churches print the texts of the readings so that people can follow along with the oral reading. The presumption is that people who see *and* hear the text can understand the content better. I'm not sure that is what happens. My usual experience is that the spoken readings, if they're not delivered by gifted readers, are dry and lifeless. Bozarth-Campbell explains the reason for that kind of experience in this statement:

> Words have no meaning in themselves, but meaning is in us, the human users of words. Words spring from human sources, and human beings are defined by the language that emanates from them through the intentional-acting of being. The notion of speech includes a *someone* standing behind the words, intending meaning through them, and the possibility of self-disclosure to the hearer. Utterances are self-involving in belief, performance, and commitment.[5]

What public worship needs are more dramatic readings of scripture. Arthur J. Dewey suggests that "Romans 10 needs to be performed to be truly understood."[6] That might be said of all Paul's letters. In our world the skills of reading and writing are thought to provide us all the insight we need. Thus, we have transported Paul's letters into our faith communities as documents to be studied and analyzed. But reading scripture in liturgy involves more than cognition.[7] It is probable from the way the letters were collected together and saved

---

[4] Jewett notes that Tertius, a slave and a scribe, wrote the letter and that *either* he or Phoebe did the public reading of it, *Romans*, 23.

[5] Alla Bozarth-Campbell, *The Word's Body: An Incarnational Aesthetic of Interpretation* (Tuscaloosa: University of Alabama Press, 1979), 55–56.

[6] Arthur J, Dewey, "A Re-Hearing of Romans 10:1-15," *Semeia* 65 (1994): 121.

[7] Horsley emphasizes that the entire gospel was performed before it was written. He comments on what it means when we treat the gospel as a *mere text*. "Reading Mark as a mere text reduces what was a living tradition of live performance to a fossilized skeleton of what it could be." Richard A. Horsely, *Hearing the Whole Story: The Politics of Plot in Mark's Gospel* (Lousiville: Westminster John Knox Press, 2001), 62.

in various communities that the letters themselves were not so much read but considered as holy icons. The way an epistle or gospel is read in the more liturgically oriented churches sets readings apart in an iconic way.[8]

Many of those on the receiving end of Paul's letters knew what he looked like and the timber of his voice. They had seen him when he was happy and when he was irritated. They had seen his gestures when he felt empowered, or perhaps his slumped shoulders when he was feeling discouraged. Only with the letter to the Romans did Paul write to communities who didn't know him from a previous visit, but even there, as we know from the 16th chapter, many knew him from other places where they had encountered him.

The thesis I am exploring in this book is that Paul wasn't hiding behind his desk writing esoteric theology. He was telling the story of God in the context of his own life. Walter Ong notes that the author of Mark's gospel is really hidden from view within the text of that gospel, while Paul is right before our eyes. "…Paul himself very much emerges in the text of his letters, which are thus more closely linked with orality than the written narrative is."[9]

If we are to appreciate how Paul's presence was felt and heard in those assemblies receiving Paul's letters it is important to imagine that one delivering the missive was performing it in a way that essentially embodied and reflected Paul's voice. The very experience of first hearing one of those letters, or more likely being present at repeated performances of those letters, had to mean being drawn into the very presence not just of the one sent by Paul, but actually feeling the presence of Paul himself. We're talking about the power of theater and performance that can draw us out of ourselves, almost as if we were on stage ourselves. Constantin Stanislavski, famous for his Actors' Studio in the 20th century said, of a particularly powerful performance, "You have come in and taken your seat as an onlooker, but the director of the play changes you into a participant in the life unfolding on the stage."[10]

---

[8] Horsley also discusses how Judean worship involved not just reading from the scrolls, but a "ceremonial exaltation, display, and "reading" served to enhance the sacred aura of the scrolls—a sacredness and mystery that continues in the Sabbath reading in synagogues today." Horsley, *Hearing the Whole Story*, 57.

[9] Walter Ong, "Text as Interpretation: Mark and After," *Semeia* 39 (1987): 15.

[10] Bozarth-Campbell, *The Word's Body*, 114.

Every missive that Paul sent required someone to bring that letter to life, or better yet, to reflect, as accurately as possible, the very voice of Paul. As Bozarth-Campbell puts there is "a *someone* standing behind the words."[11] There also ought to be a spiritual, or even mystical aspect to such reading in a worship context.

In many churches the Bible is held up, maybe by the preacher in the pulpit, or the deacon who reads the gospel. It should not be seen as just a prop. It is a sacred moment as the reading takes place.

Imagine a sacred performance of Romans 10:3-13, in Paul's time. Whoever carried and delivered the letter (whether Phoebe or Tertius) would have also been charged with interpreting it and answering questions that might be raised. The reader most probably gave an introduction to the reading, something like this:

> In this letter, Paul makes us feel that it's very important to remember Moses and his connection to the law. I know you are familiar with the story about the Ten Commandments. In my mind I see Moses, huge and strong, standing with the two stone tablets braced on his hip and urging the people of Israel to heed his words. First, we hear the words of Moses and *then* Paul's rhetorical questions.

The reader pulls her shoulders back and lowers her voice. "Moses writes concerning the righteousness that comes from the law, that 'the person who does these things will live by them.'" Then she looks at the listeners, and continues in a normal voice:

> But the righteousness that comes from faith says, '*Do not say* in your heart, "Who will ascend into heaven"[12] –'That is, who will bring Christ down?' 'Who will descend into the abyss?'" —that is, to bring Christ up from the dead.' But **what does it say?** 'The word is *near* you, on your lips and in your heart.'[13]

The speaker pauses and then repeats the last phrase touching her lips, then bringing her hands close to her heart. Letting the words

---

[11] Bozarth-Campbell, *The Word's Body*, 114.

[12] Note Paul is quoting Deuteronomy 30:12 here. Fisch calls this Paul's intertexual strategy to create a "torah of trust." Yael Fisch, "The Origins of Oral Torah: A New Pauline Perspective," *Journal for the Study of Judaism* 51 (2020): 54, 57.

[13] Note that I could use italics and bold print in this statement and assume the reader will see the significance of these marks.

sink in may be one of those theatrical moments of silence known to draw people's attention. Certain words are emphasized.

Then she says, "Hear Paul once more: 'But what does it say?' "The word is near you, on your lips and in your heart" (that is, the word of faith that we proclaim) because if you *confess* with your lips that Jesus is Lord and *believe* in your heart that God raised him from the dead, *you will be saved.'"*

She pauses often in that last section even allowing for a longer silent periods—bated breath, it is sometimes called. She looks intently at various people as she continues emphasizing certain key words. Her slow measured pace continues.

"For one *believes* with the heart and so is justified, and one *confesses* with the mouth and so is saved. The scripture says, "No one who believes in him will be put to shame." For **there is no distinction** between Jew and Greek; the same Lord is Lord of all and *is generous* to all who call on him. For, "Everyone who calls on the name of the Lord shall be saved."

She takes a deep breath and repeats that last verse: "***Everyone*** who calls on the name of the Lord shall be saved."

Maybe she puts the letter down on a stool. She really doesn't need it since the letter was memorized. Most likely, she keeps the audience in mind and in subtle ways notices how they respond to her words. The reading is interactive. It's gospel for Paul but also theater. She goes on, still pausing at various places. "Now listen to Paul's questions!"

"But how are they to *call* on one in whom they have not believed? And how are they to *believe* in one of whom they have never heard? And how are they to *hear* without someone to proclaim him? And how are they to *proclaim* him unless they are *sent*? As it is written, 'How beautiful *are the feet* of those who bring good news!'"

The reading is coming to a conclusion. But it ends with cautionary words from Isaiah. Perhaps her voice changes slightly. "But not all have obeyed the good news; for Isaiah says, 'Lord, who has believed our message?'"

She has one more verse to offer. And it is good news. She can smile and offer it in a strong voice: "So faith comes from what is **heard**, and what is **heard** comes through the word of Christ."

We do not know how these letters were performed, but they had to be delivered orally without the audience reading along.

Interpretation was also expected. Thus, I imagine Phoebe or Tertius simply saying, "*We are the people* who God always has had in mind."

I can also imagine heads nodding and some smiles. Perhaps all the different kinds of people Paul had in mind were looking at each other, men, and women together, different ethnicities, and a variety of ages and maybe smiling as one. I know from my experiences with great theater such as my wife and I experience at the Guthrie Theater in Minneapolis, we lose all track of time and place, when it is a moving performance. That very well could have been the case with Paul's letters in the first century.

8.2 Both an oral world and a literate world

Paul was a composer. Rather than being immersed in a world of musical notes, however, he dwelt in a world of stories and sayings along with the bible that was in his head as well as his heart. He wasn't a scribe as we know, but we do know that at least two of the letters were dictated to a scribe: Romans and Galatians. We know in fact that a scribe wrote most of the letter to the Galatians, with Paul only adding his signature at the end in the large letters a scribe would never use. (Gal 6:11)

Most important of all is that these were public letters— public for those in Jesus Messiah communities. Two of the quotes from the New Testament at the start of this chapter capture this reality. Paul demanded that the letter to the Thessalonians be publicly read. The author of Revelation expected the same. This was "…a world in which speaking had primacy, and both the production and consumption of manuscripts grew out of the living tissue of speech."[14]

Consider the image of reading Paul's letter to the Romans. If it was Phoebe she stood before a crowd holding the letter like an icon. The marks on that piece of papyri were letters, but they weren't letters that could be read without training. The Latin name for this kind of writing that was meant to pack as many words on a page as possible was "scriptio continua."[15] It looked something like this:

---

[14] Werner H. Kebler, "Jesus and Tradition: Words in Time, Words in Space," *Semeia* 64 (1994): 153.

[15] Alan Chapple, "Getting Romans to the Right Romans: Phoebe and the Delivery of Paul's Letter," *Tyndale Bulletin* 62, no. 2 (2011): 213.

recallmydescriptionofthereaderofpaulslettertotheromansp
hoebewhostoodholdingtheletterinonehandthatletterwaslik
eqaniconithadmarksonthepapyrithatwerlettersitwasntataal
ikethelettersonthispagethelatinnameforthiskindofwritingt
hatwasmeanttopackasmanywordsonapageaspossiblewassc
riptiocontinuaitlookedsomethinglikethis

If any contemporary book were written in text, as above, few books would be read. There are no marks of punctuation and no capitalization. (Capital Greek letters were the norm.) Where does one sentence end and the other begin? In the suggested performance above I'm giving clues used in the literate world. For example, the word "icon" was italicized. This typographical change signals that this word is especially important. If I were reading this paragraph out loud, I would emphasize the word icon with an inflection in my voice. In the spoken word, "italics" or "bold" are heard, not read. The reader of a Greek text, namely the performer, needed to know what the author, in our case Paul, wanted emphasized. But it is the reader as performer not the author who does the interpretation. What if the interpretation has what Allan Bozarth-Campbell called a "spirit-charged power of performance"? Then, as she notes, "it can have the effect of breathing new life into those who participate in its moment of revelation."[16] Very few of the public readings or sermons we have in contemporary worship reach this depth and power, but it's likely they had to when Paul's letters were first performed.

Maybe in our time we can find Paul in these letters even in worship. Perhaps if we had more dramatic readings of his letters, we would see a Paul with feelings and not just ideas. We would hear a Paul not only breathing threats as he does a few times, but also commending and praising those who have sacrificed so much for the sake of their common faith.

Writing to a friend, Roman philosopher Seneca commented that a letter truly brings a friend to life, for it "brings us real traces, real evidence of an absent friend!" He valued seeing "the impress of a friend's hand upon his letter..."[17] We may remember Paul's message at the end of Galatians, "See what large letters I make when I am

---

[16] Bozarth-Campbell, *The Word's Body*, 143.

[17] Stanley K. Stowers, *Letter Writing in Greco-Roman Antiquity* (Philadelphia: The Westminster Press, 1986), 29; quoting from Seneca, *Moral Letters* 40.1.

writing in my own hand" (Gal 6:11).[18] What would it mean then, to read Paul's letters and feel his presence? To hear him, as it were, 2000 years later, in a world yearning to feel Paul's messianic promise? It is my contention that we can hear Paul, if we give his words the kind of reading that his original followers heard.

All of us, whether now or thousands of years ago, also speak with our hands and facial expressions, along with inflections of our voice, as well as changes in the rhythm of our speaking. It wasn't as if there weren't literate people in Paul's world, but they were a clear minority. In the ancient Mediterranean world, it is estimated that maybe just 2% to 4% were literate.[19] Yet in a real sense, most were literate in that world, in ways that may exceed our skills in reading text from a book or scroll. It was a *rhetorical culture* in which written texts were available to a few who could read, but to a great many the same texts were stored and kept through memorization and familiarity with the stories of their past.

What makes the performance of Paul's letters not just another theatrical performance is that the recipients were *already* bonded in spirit as an audience sharing the narrative story of following Jesus Messiah. In the terms of Bozarth-Campbell, whose work focuses on the ways a poem or story can be *incarnated* in a communal setting, Paul's listeners were experiencing "acoustic space" — "the sound of life as it is happening."[20]

The point of trying to hear Paul's story in his own voice is that he really was *speaking* through his letters. Whoever was reading the letter to the *Galatians* had to pause and wonder *how* to deliver the opening line in the 5th chapter where we are supposed to hear Paul's voice: "Listen! I, Paul, am telling you that if you let yourselves be circumcised, Christ will be of no benefit to you." In my mind, whoever delivered that caustic sentence must have been coached by Paul about *how* he wanted that line to be delivered. I fear there are many similar passages in Galatians that pass by in most churches without any awareness of the *voice* that was behind that letter.

---

[18] The same "autographic subscription"—as it is called— comes at the end of 1 Corinthians, 2 Thessalonians, and Philemon. It indicates he *did not* write any of the preceding material in those letters. Thus, he had one or more scribes do it.

[19] Joanna Dewey, "Textuality in an Oral Culture," *Semeia* 65 (1994): 39.

[20] Bozarth-Campbell, *The Word's Body*, 52, quoting Leland H. Roloff, *The Perception and Evocation of Literature* (Glenview: Scott, Foresman and Co., 1973), 73, who was defining the technical term "acoustic space."

Galatians isn't the only letter in which Paul uses the first-person singular pronoun, but in this letter perhaps more than others, we sense how present Paul is inside the letter itself. Lest we also miss the significance of what Paul was saying, we need to understand that the Greek verb for "I testify" (*martyromai*) is the root word for *martyr*. Paul may not have claimed to be a martyr who dies for the sake of Christ since that connection came after him, but he meant his affirmations to be taken seriously. In the same letter he concludes with a passage in which his listeners are not only to hear him, but to see, or envision in their memory, his body. "From now on, let no one make trouble for me, for I carry the marks of Jesus branded on my body" (Gal 6:17). Paul's back was branded, as it were, just like that of any slave. There are so many ways to understand how Paul was present in his letters.

8.3 The Paul found in his letters vs the Paul "found" in Acts

One of the images of the Paul I thought I knew which I liked best for years preceding this book was from the Acts of the Apostles. It was the story of Paul in Athens, where he is "in the marketplace every day with those who happened to be there" (Acts 17:16-34).[21] That was a favorite passage of mine when I was planting a new Episcopal church. As part of my ministry, I felt it important to be visible and publicly involved in community life. In the account in Acts Paul comes off as one who is able to debate in the public square with some credibility, even though there were those who "scoffed" at what they heard. What is erroneous with that picture of Paul engaged with other philosophers of his day is that by his own words he wasn't all that great at public speaking and rhetoric. The author of Acts, however, depicted a Paul who could debate with the best, while those in Corinth concluded something quite the opposite: "For they say, 'His letters are weighty and strong, but is bodily presence is weak and his speech contemptible'" (2 Cor 10:9-10).

Who are we to believe? Acts or Paul? The premise in this book is that Paul is to be trusted especially with statements regarding his own story. When he says, "he didn't come to the Corinthians with lofty words or wisdom" (1 Cor 2:1), many might have remembered that they first met him in his workshop in a crowded noisy world of

---

[21] Raphael's painting is reproduced on page 61.

people at work. Maybe he needed to shout to be heard. Amongst his fellow workers his language was that of common people.[22]

When he asked these questions—"Where is the one who is wise? Where is the scribe? Where is the debater of this age? Has not God made foolish the wisdom of the world?" (1 Cor 1:20)—The answers to these questions must be: "Not here. Not here. Not here. Yes!"

In this passage Paul proclaimed himself as a fool for Christ. His message is that Christ crucified sounds like foolishness in direct contrast to the so-called "wisdom of this world." This proclamation leading toward salvation is, by the world's standards, foolishness. Thus, Paul admitted that his speech was lacking by the world's standards. "And I came to you in weakness and in fear and in much trembling. My speech and my proclamation were not with plausible words of wisdom, but with a demonstration of the Spirit and of power, so that your faith might not rest on human wisdom but on the power of God" (1 Cor 2:3-4).

My own assessment is that few if any call committees in most churches would accept Paul with the honesty about himself, we see in the previous passage. I remember the story my friend Walt Pulliam shared with me when he came for an interview at an American Baptist Church in the 1970s near to the congregation I served. He didn't come "in fear and trembling," but just before the interview began, he took out his pipe (unlit at the time) and said, "I guess I better tell you, I sometimes smoke this." His gesture did not end the interview. The members of the Call Committee laughed, and their lay leader said, "We already knew and figured we'd like you with your pipe." We can only wonder what the Corinthians first loved about Paul, especially since he was better at writing letters than giving speeches.

---

[22] "Linguistic studies have demonstrated that Paul's Greek is "not stylistically grand" ... that his vocabulary is not that of an average rhetorician or philosopher ... and that he does not show any knowledge of Greek literature or philosophical discourse, although there are sections in his letters where a quotation from such literature could be envisaged." Kathy Ehrensperger, "Speaking Greek under Rome: The Power of Language and the Language of Power," *Neotestamentica* 46, no. 1 (2012): 19; in other words, Paul was able to speak with ordinary people.

In his book *Paul, the Fool of Christ*, L.L. Welborn looks at the public theater of the ancient world and what he calls a common figure on stage, that of "the befuddled orator." Such an actor with hyperbole and sometimes revolting vulgarities caused raucous laughter at what was simply bad oratory.[23] Paul was not "a befuddled orator." His letters reveal an educated man with abilities "providing evidence of social origins far from the bottom of Greco-Roman society."[24] Paul, however, had little regard for those who puffed up themselves, and he met their attitudes of superiority with irony and paradox. Paul may have learned those rhetorical devices from the banter of his co-workers, those discounted in that world

8.4 Paul and the interlocutor

Did you ever notice how many questions Paul was asking, especially in the first few chapters in Romans? Asking questions is Paul's way to interact with those receiving this letter, and he even constructed a few imaginary dialogues around these questions. It allowed him to give voice to other ideas even if they were never ever his. We simply should not say or think that everything in Romans, or in the other letters as well, is what Paul wanted us to believe or understand. In the letters we hear other voices than that of Paul.

Stanley Stowers makes this important observation: "Paul wrote in dialogical exchanges, ring compositions, transitional false conclusions and rejections, various rhetorical figures, speech-in-character, and so on."[25] Among the many devices he used, it is clear that Paul loved rhetorical questions to which the *implied* or *expected* answer was either "Absolutely!" or "Never!"

For example, in Romans Paul asked, "Should we continue in sin in order that grace may abound?" (Rom 6:2) Paul answers his own question all in the same verse with an imperative followed by another sharp question: "By no means! How can we who died to sin go on living in it?" Chances are that disturbing statement was one Paul had heard in his missionary endeavors. Within a few sentences it is obvious where Paul stands.

---

[23] Welborn, *Paul: the Fool for Christ*, 92, 94.
[24] Welborn, *Paul: the Fool for Christ*, 253.
[25] Stanley Stowers, *A Re-Reading of Romans: Justice, Jews and Gentiles* (New Haven: Yale University Press, 1994), 11.

Examples of Paul asking questions that have ready answers abound in his letters. It is sort of like a father examining the dented fender of the family car after his teenager returns home and asks rhetorically: "You think I'm blind? You ran into something. What happened?" The same kind of rhetoric is found early in Galatians. Paul, having stated that no human commission or authority made him an apostle, asked a few verses later, "Am I now seeking human approval, or God's approval. Or am I trying to please other people?" (Gal 1:10) The obvious answer from the frame of the question is clearly "No." Paul simply adds to this, "If I were still pleasing people, I would not be a servant of Christ." His ethical admonitions at the end of the letter bear a different sentiment. They come as imperatives: "Bear one another's burdens and in this way you will fulfill the law of Christ" (Gal 6:2).

What becomes more difficult to discern, but which is important to our *ability* to read his letters arises in those places where we find what is called "speech-in-character." In simpler terms that means that in order for us to hear Paul's letters, we need to understand that Paul was often *quoting others* or expressing thoughts and ideas that belonged to others. Sometimes the words came to him as a matter of inquiry as they did in 1 Corinthians 7 which begins with the concerns around marriage which had been addressed to him: "Now concerning the matters about which you wrote" (1 Cor 7:1). But there were other ways in which Paul was in dialogue in his letters.

Paul could portray a known person in his writing as he did with Peter in Galatians, even though Peter was given no lines. Paul was addressing him with a sarcastic question (see Gal 2:14). Or, in a more creative way, Paul could invent an imaginary character and a dialogue in which he himself participated which is found in Romans. The scholar Stanley Stowers maintains that Romans is best understood by assuming that Paul has "an encoded audience,"[26] which meant those receiving the argument could perceive two or more voices.

There are a number of places in Romans where Paul was clearly in dialogue with some other person or character. Not surprisingly it seems likely that Paul knew of someone or some people in the community who would maintain a theological idea opposite to his own. Equally possible was the literary license Paul assumed as he

---

[26] Stanley Stowers, *A Re-Reading of Romans*, 22.

made up an imaginary foil for his argumentative purposes in various places.

A good place to wrestle with this idea is Romans 3:1-20. I can imagine the perplexity of any ordinary lector faced with this reading. However, a congregation following the Revised Common Lectionary—as many mainline churches do—will never face this task, for, much to my dismay, there are no readings from Romans chapters 2 and 3 in any of three years covering all possible Sundays in the liturgical cycle. Many a pastor, I assume, is relieved. Here, at least, I can tackle one such passage.

The term often used by biblical scholars for the imagined (or some cases also a real) person "engaged in" dialogue with Paul is called the "interlocutor." That is not a derisive term. It simply means someone who takes part in a conversation or dialogue. What follows is the version of Romans 3:1-9 rearranged, so that it looks like a movie script, without any advice regarding lighting, sound, or staging. There are just two characters: Paul and one labeled the "Interlocutor." Stowers describes him as *a fellow Jew* and calls him a teacher who objects "to Paul's insistence on God's impartial judgment."[27] We can see the interlocutor's concerns in his questions. We can imagine that a single reader may have been coached how to voice the two parts.

Romans 3:1-9

Interlocutor: [v.1] Then what (*ti oun*) advantage has the Jew? Or what is the value of circumcision?

Paul: [v.2] Much, in every way. For in the first place the Jews[a] were entrusted with the oracles of God. [v.3] What if some were unfaithful? Will their faithlessness nullify the faithfulness of God? 4

I: [v.4] By no means! (*mē genoito*) Although everyone is a liar, let God be proved true, as it is written,

"So that you may be justified in your words, and prevail in your judging."

P: [v.5] But if our injustice serves to confirm the justice of God, what should we say? That God is unjust to inflict wrath on us? (I speak in a human way.)

---

[27] Stowers, *A Re-Reading of Romans*, 159.

I: [v.6a] By no means! (*mē genoito*) For then how could God judge the world?

P: [v.6b-8] But if through my falsehood God's truthfulness abounds to his glory, why am I still being condemned as a sinner? And why not say (as some people slander us by saying that we say), "Let us do evil so that good may come"? Their condemnation is deserved!

I: [v.9a] What then? (*ti oun*) Are we any better off?

P: [v.9b] No, not at all (*ou pantōs*); for we have already charged that all, both Jews and Greeks, are under the power of sin.

This passage is full of passionate objections and questions. It contains what Stowers called "false conclusions" as we twice see the expression "By no means! (*mē genoito*)" (3:4,6) and Paul declaring "No, not at all (*ou pantōs*" (3:9). Then there are the leading questions of "Then what? (*ti oun*)" (3:1) and "What then? (*ti oun*)" (3:9) What is happening here is a continuation of an argument Paul began in Romans 1:19, when he declared "For what can be known about God is plain to them, because God has shown it to them."

At the heart of the early chapters of this letter Paul is making the argument that there is a place for Gentiles as full members of the Jewish story of God. What Paul opposes is any concept of "a one-sided, partial mercy toward Jews alone."[28] Thus Paul asked at the end of this passage "Are we Jews at a disadvantage?"[29] Note also how prominent the pronoun "we" is in this dialogue.

This was not like a reading as we know that word. Paul lived a world of sound. It wasn't a book culture as we know it, but it was a reading culture in that readings were public events for its members. Judaism was a scripture-based community. To be sure all the recitations of scripture were connected to traditions that existed in writing, but what mattered was hearing![30]

---

[28] Stowers, *A Re-Reading of Romans*, 174.

[29] Stowers notes that a translation like that found in the NRSV misses the mark. The question there is "Are we any better off?" The passage begins with the question "Then what advantage has the Jew?" The last part gives his answer. Jews are in. So too with the *ethnē*! *A Re-Reading of Romans*.

[30] Bernard Brandon Scott, "Blowing in the Wind: A Response," *Semia*, 65 (1994), 184.

The period of manuscript Christianity had not arrived, however, in the time of Paul.[31]

What we do know from the epistolary evidence of letters bearing Paul's name is that Paul made himself present in the lives of communities which he had known personally (except for Romans). Those letters in turn, allowed him to remind others not only of the story of God in Christ, but of their stories and memories of Paul, including the many conversations and teachings which he mentioned in his letters. Those letters made its recipients vicarious participants. May it be that it is still the case with us!

8.5 Paul and Romans 7: the world's story or his?

The main theme of this book is that we can learn so much about Paul from his seven letters. If St. Augustine, who was called "the first modern man" by Stendhal, could be reading this book, he would be ready for me to say that Romans 7:7-25 is certainly autobiographical. Stendahl declared, "His *Confessiones* are the first great document in the history of the introspective conscience."[32] There are also four Latin words echoing from the theological tradition connecting Augustine to Luther. They are: *simul Justus et peccato*. It means: made just or righteous *and* a sinner. That is the introspective conscience identified by Stendahl who made this judgment about Paul: "Here is a man with a quite robust conscience. Here is a man not plagued by introspection."[33] But what about the agony and despair of this unnamed person in chapter 7 who cannot do good he wants to do, and does the evil he does not want to do (Rom. 7:19)?

I think there are two ways—and maybe many more—to read what sounds like a personal confession by Paul in Romans 7:7-25. One is by Paul Meyer who states that this is Paul's way of understanding the demonic power of sin. The second way to read this is with the insights of Robert Jewett who sees Paul wrestling with his past life as a vigilant, maybe arrogant Pharisee. Following Paul wherever he went was this former identity as one who opposed the early followers of Jesus.

---

[31] Joanna Dewey, "Textuality in an Oral Culture," *Semeia* 65 (1994): 55.

[32] Krister Stendahl, "The Apostle Paul and the Introspective Conscience of the West," *Harvard Theological Review* 56, no 3 (1963): 205.

[33] Stendahl, *Paul Among Jews and Gentiles*, 14.

The biblical scholar Paul Meyer declared that Romans 7:7-25 is not Paul's personal story. The passage, instead, nonetheless evokes in many readers their own experiences of struggling to do good and avoid evil.[34] Meyer notes that Paul is describing the "demonic nature of sin in its power to pervert the highest and best in all human piety, typified by the best in Paul's world, his own commitment to God's holy commandment, in such a way as to produce death in place of the promised life."[35] Perhaps, most profoundly, Meyer discusses the Latin maxim "*corruption optimi pessimal*," the worst evil consists in the corruption of the highest good.'" He concludes this is not Paul's private experience, but Paul's "diagnosis of the condition under which all human religion suffers…"[36] We are thus not dealing with the sin as personal willfulness or intentional violation of the law. And it is not Paul's story.

What if Jewett, on the other hand, is correct in asserting that Paul reflects in this passage on his former life of arrogance with regard to living better than others as a Pharisee. I noted in Chapter 2, when discussing Paul's call (not conversion) to preach Jesus Messiah, that at one point in his life he admitted to persecuting the ekklēsia of God. (Gal. 1:13). I pointed out that the phrase violently persecuting as found in the NRSV is a mistranslation of the Greek word *hyperbolē* that implies intensity, not violence. Section 2.1 thus concluded, "*Intensity* rather than *violence* is thus the better way to describe Paul's earliest response to those following Jesus Messiah."

Jewett describes Paul's earlier life as belonging to the world where "competition in zeal promised honor and divine approbation."[37] Paul no longer lives in that world and condemns all those within the Jesus Messiah communities who assert privilege and power over others. The Paul who did that was what he called in the NRSV is termed a "wretched man", but the better translation for Jewett is "miserable man."[38] That is what died with his life in Christ. While he wonders at the end of Romans 7 who will rescue him, the truth for Paul is that he has been rescued. Thus, "Thanks be to God through Jesus Christ our Lord" (Rom 7:25).

---

[34] Paul W. Meyer, *The Word in This World* (Lousiville: Westiminster John Knox Press, 2004), 59.
[35] Meyer, *The Word in This World*, 71.
[36] Meyer, *The Word in This World*, 7.
[37] Jewett, *Romans*, 468.
[38] Jewett, *Romans*, 471.

In the end we are left with a dense inscrutable passage that seems autobiographical on Paul's part, but we can't be sure about this.

Excursus 8.2 Paul's Letters Collected and Other Stories Told

I haven't said much about the Pastoral Epistles (1 & 2 Timothy and Titus) here, but that's because it's easier to refer my readers back to comments on the disputed letters in the introduction. The voice of Paul coming on so strong as an authority and restricting the leadership of women in the disputed letters stands in such contrast to what we find in the undisputed letters. The picture to be found in the next chapter "Paul the Unmanly Man," is really about the recognition and dignity Paul ascribes to women in his communities, as is his call to men to not act in accordance with standard social expectations regarding masculinity. When we examine the words about what Paul expects of men and women in the Pastoral epistles and those in the seven uncontested letters, there are glaring contrasts.

It is a miracle that we have any of Paul's letters and all the other pages in the New Testament The first letter we have of his was written to the Thessalonians. Other letters followed, some of which were certainly lost, and others or fragments of which might have been pasted and copied into letters we still have. That first letter, though, is what mattered. It was saved. It was shared. Thus, began a process of reading (performing!) those letters, copying them, and passing them on to other communities of faith. More than the letters would appear. Obviously, the four gospels occupy a pre-eminent place in the life of the New Testament. All these treasures go back to Paul who felt he was called to be an apostle even before he was born. As Raymond Collins, so astutely noted, "In a very real sense the New Testament was born when that first letter of Paul was written."[39] We must be grateful for this miracle.

---

[39] Collins, Raymond Collins, *The Birth of the New Testament: The Origin and Development of the First Christian Generation* (New York: Crossroad, 1993), 213. (With thanks to Beverly Gaventa, *Our Mother St. Paul*, 173, who shared this comment in a footnote).

Chapter 9
Paul an Unmanly Man

> Then the apostle is seen as a "feminized," vulnerable, beaten, suffering apostle, a member of a conquered nation who in no way coheres with the image of the elitist ideal of masculinity in Greek and Roman perception.[1]

> He was not a believer in the inferiority of women. He did not advocate a secondary role for women in the Church. He did not teach some notion of a divine hierarchy, with husbands ruling over their wives.[2]

> We tend to read Paul as a triumphant power broker who dominated his recipients in a structured and authoritarian way, from a position of undisputed power.[3]

> O St. Paul, where is he that was called the nurse of the faithful, caressing his sons? Who is that affectionate mother who declares everywhere that she is in labor for her sons?
> (*Anselm of Canterbury*)[4]

9.1 A one-gendered world

The basic premise of this chapter is that Paul did not live up to standard expectations for a man in the first century of the Greco-Roman world. It was not simply that he was open and accepting of women as full participants in the *ekklēsia* centered on faith in Jesus as their Lord (*Kyrios*) and Messiah (*Christos*), but that his stories

---

[1] Kathy Ehrensperger, "The Question(s) of Gender: Relocating Paul in Relation to Judaism," in *Paul within Judaism: Restoring the First-Century Context to the Apostle*, eds. Mark D. Nanos and Magnus Zetterholm (Minneapolis: Fortress Press, 2015), 246.

[2] Bristow, *What Paul Really Said*, 2.

[3] Cynthia Westfall, *Paul and Gender: Reclaiming the Apostle's Vision for Men and Women in Christ* (Grand Rapids, MI: Baker Academic 2016), 252.

[4] Beverly Roberts Gaventa, *Our Mother St. Paul* (Louisville: Westminster John Knox Press, 2007): 15.

about himself, and even his language betrayed what others expected from men. Since this book is all about discovering Paul in his own words, what will surprise some about this Paul is that he cannot be categorized as a misogynistic patriarchal male who distrusted women. This Paul was a surprise to me, the author!

The concept of *gender* in Greco-Roman eyes is hard for us to comprehend, given our basic premise of living in a two-gendered world. The ancient world had a different model. It was a "one-sex" model of sexuality, in which men were the ultimate ideal, while women were "inverted" males. Many biblical scholars turn to Thomas Laqueur[5] to understand this strange way of affirming the superiority of the male sex—claims which continue to haunt our so-called modern world. Laqueur, in his book *Making Sex: Body and Gender from the Greeks to Freud*, explained it this way: "An anatomy and physiology of incommensurability replaced the metaphysics of hierarchy in the real representation of women in relation to man."[6] The key premise in Laqueur's one-sex model of sexuality is that it was based on assumptions of hierarchy, with the biological differences explained in a primitive description of anatomy in which the internal organs of women were the opposite of men. For Galen, the 2nd century C.E. physician, "Women… are inverted, and hence less perfect men."[7] Eventually the "one-sex" model fell apart due to science.

This *one-gendered world* evident in ancient texts is construed in hierarchical terms, with "man" at the top and "woman" at the bottom."[8] The Paul we meet in Corinthians isn't like this. Giving a married woman authority over her husband's body (1 Cor 7:4) and allowing a woman to lead in worship (1 Cor 11:5) did not cohere with the usual norms of that ancient world.

What was implied in a world defined solely by men was a polarity of power and privilege. It was what Wilson called a "vertical axis of power." She explained: "With these polarities of dominant/subordinate, active/passive, and self-controlled/excessive, the underlying assumption is that "man" is both a social superior and the unspoken norm. In other words, "man" is the type and "woman"

---

[5] Thomas Laqueur, *Making Sex: Body and Gender from the Greeks to Freud* (Cambridge MA: Harvard University Press, 1990.
[6] Laqueur, *Making Sex*, 6.
[7] Laqueur, *Making Sex*, 26.
[8] Wilson, *Refigurations of Masculinity*, 40.

is the antitype: "man" is the standard by which "woman" — or the "other" — is measured."[9] It was also the world that formed and shaped Paul — or rather, the Paul before he found himself inside the story of Christ, when he became Paul the *unmanly* man. His story of being found in Christ led him to undermine assumptions of privilege and superiority that demeaned or excluded others. Dale Martin notes that Paul "called into question any use of normal, upper-class status designations of honor within the church"[10]

Out in the patio in our backyard we used to have some large concrete flowerpots. Relief etching on the outside of those pots imitated Greek art in the time of Paul. You might even call them Hellenistic pots. To be sure, those concrete flowerpots honored the artistic balancing of form and shape so characteristic of that ancient world but knowing the realities of life in that world for the majority of those like Paul and his co-workers, the pots carry echoes of imperial violence and oppression. "Hellenism," as Horsley points out, was "a "system" of master-slave relations, slavery being one of the principal institutions of the ancient Hellenistic-Roman social-order."[11]

Our account of Paul's story regards his strange concept of using power to enhance the life of the *least* in the world, those most likely to suffer, be excluded, enslaved, or crucified. Ehrensperger notes, "Paul's Jewish tradition presents alternative perceptions to Greek and Roman notions of the use of power. Those notions in the latter part of the first century reflected an institution marked by patriarchal leadership and the silencing of women."[12]

Those patriarchal notions are read by some scholars as true to Paul. It is an argument that I contest. To be sure the accusation fits when we come to Acts and the Pastoral Epistles. With regard to Acts it is a form of *apologetic historiography* according to Judith Lieu who notes the degree to which its author places the narrative "within the

---

[9] Wilson, *Refigurations of Masculinity*, 40.

[10] Martin, *The Corinthian Body*, 63

[11] Richard A. Horsley, "Paul and Slavery: A Critical Alternative to Recent Readings," Semeia 83-84 (1998): 159.

[12] Kathy Ehrensberger,. "The Question(s) of Gender: Relocating Paul in Relation to Judaism", in *Paul within Judaism: Restoring the First-Century Context to the Apostle*, eds. Mark D. Nanos and Magnus Zetterholm (Minneapolis: Fortress Press, 2015), 246.

world of the Graeco-Roman Empire."[13] Paul in Acts walks with authority and influence and is still speaking at its end. That is what is at question in this chapter.

Paul lived in that world which gave power to men where even inside his own family the head of the household, the father, could dictate whether a newborn baby would be allowed to live. It was common for a Roman family to raise just one daughter, often placing another new-born female infant outside, where it would die, or be taken by someone who wished to raise the child as a slave. In this one-sex world defining every deviation from a masculine ideal, there was a de facto reality affecting all women, slaves, nations conquered, and any men who showed the slightest defects in character or manly behavior. They were demeaned and excluded.

In such a world, Paul's masculinity was something of a mixed bag. There are times when we can see him claiming authority that was typical in his Greco-Roman world, but then Paul used metaphors that had to be very strange coming from a man in his world — and in ours as well. The inconsistencies in Paul definitely rise to the surface with a Paul sharing his work alongside women, and then seemingly expecting them to be silent. (See Section 9.1.3 where we find a Paul welcoming the voices of women.)

What we find over and over in Paul is an honesty about his failings and weakness. We see this in what most scholars consider Paul's first letter 1 Thessalonians.[14] What preceded this letter was the experience of Paul, Silvanus, and Timothy in Philippi where they had "suffered and been shamefully mistreated" (1 Thess 2:2). We ought to be surprised that they admitted to being shamed, but honesty about things rarely considered admirable abound in 1 Thessalonians. In Paul's world the kind of work he did — that which required "labor and toil" and working "night and day" (1 Thess 2:9) — was not admirable in Jewish or Roman eyes.

Miroslav Volf wrote, ". . . as a rule, the kingdom of God enters the world through the back door of servants' shacks, not through the

---

[13] Judith Lieu, *Christian Identity in the Jewish and Graeco-Roman World* (New York: Oxford University Press, 2004), 90–91.

[14] There are two basic dates for this first letter: 40-41 or 50-51. That's a ten-year difference. Douglas Campbell makes a strong argument for the earlier date, but admits it is "a date that is embarrassingly early," *Framing Paul*, 252. That's scholarly talk about how others might receive his idea for this date. It does not affect how we find Paul here.

main gate of the Masters' mansions."[15] Paul knew that. There, in the world of the nobodies, Paul embraced what N.T. Wright called "the strange power of suffering."[16] He did so within the context of his Jewish identity and the apocalyptic lens that framed his world. "Suffering was itself a sign for Paul that one was living between the times, caught between promise and fulfillment, between the passing of sentence on the old world, and the final disappearance of evil. Hence the Jewish theme of 'tribulation,' which Paul recapitulates in a Christian key precisely as part of his 'not yet.'"[17]

E. A. Judge said Paul was "tortured by the problem of how to combine his sense of calling and authority over obstreperous converts with the self-renunciation to which he saw himself also called."[18] Paul's view was that those called to the story of Christ were the weak. (1 Cor 1:27) They would find their source of life in Christ and not in the world of competition and privilege. Strangely his resume had become that of a failed man, marked by the long list of sufferings and embarrassments he recorded in 2 Cor 11:23-30.

Jerry Sumney suggests that even before he ever came to Thessalonica Paul saw himself as *the apostle of weakness*.[19] To what seemed like the conclusion to a long list of unmanly experiences of endangerment, hardship and anxiety, Paul reported that he had to allow his friends to rescue him from prison by entrusting himself to a basket let down by a rope. (2 Cor 11:32-33) That escape at night from the hands of the Nabataean governor in Damascus is pictured by Antoinette Clark Wire as a humiliated Paul, something like a caught fish, dangling in thin air.[20]

We might smile at that image, but at the same time we need to consider the implications of one who could have chosen differently if manly pride mattered. How many with a life of privilege would choose such suffering. It was not the mandated suffering, known by many in Paul's world—and ours today, with the harsh

---

[15] Volf, *Exclusion and Embrace*, 114.

[16] Wright, *Faithfulness*, 1116.

[17] Wright, *Faithfulness*, 1117.

[18] E. A. Judge, *Social Distinctives of the Christians in the First Century: Pivotal Essays by E. A. Judge*, ed. David M. Scholer (Peabody: Hendrickson Publishers Inc. 2008), 35.

[19] Jerry L Sumney, "Paul's 'Weakness': An Integral Part of His Conception of Apostleship." *Journal for the Study of the New Testament* 52 (1993): 90.

[20] Antoinette Clark Wire, *2 Corinthians* (Collegeville, MN: Liturgical Press, 2019), 239.

institutionally supported realities of poverty, racism, ageism, and sexism. Wire's commentary includes an observation on a kind of suffering that is embraced in the context of tenderness and openness to others.[21] There we find a reflection on the connection Paul made between his own weakness and the power of Christ: "I am all the more glad to boast in my weakness, so that Christ's power may rest on me." [Her translation of 2 Cor 12:9][22]

The NRSV translation of the same passage has Paul saying that the "power of Christ may *dwell* in me." The Greek verb has the sense of taking up one's residence.[23] Another form of this word appears in the prologue to John's gospel: "And the Word became flesh and lived among us." This NRSV translation Greek of the verb *episkēnoō*, is improved by one scholarly friend of mine who says it means *to pitch one's tent*. Wire takes the translation a step further as the word *episkēnoō* can mean "may rest on me." She speculated that this may be Paul's subtle reference to the concept of the cloud of glory that hovered over the tabernacle in Ezekiel 40:34-35. The Hebrew word for this phenomenon is God's *shekinah*, which is the feminine form for the presence of God. She pointed out that the deeper meaning in all this is that "Christ is not alien from but intimate with, even at home in, the harsh realities of this human life."[24]

9.2 Paul as a *malakos*, mother and nurse

The Paul we meet on the pages of Acts is every bit the man you'd expect to find in the first century. In his letters it's a different Paul. In what follows I am dealing with passages from his letters suggesting a subordinate role for women. They have taken on canonical authority for centuries regarding the so-called "place of women in the church." We will discuss in this chapter two of the most prominent texts in 1 Corinthians that continue to haunt any positive re-envisioning of Paul.[25] The problem we are addressing is

---

[21] Credit for this observation belongs to Cynthia R. Wallace in a sidebar titled "Risky Generalizations" in Wire, *2 Corinthians*, 252.

[22] Wire, *2 Corinthians*, 249.

[23] Danker et al., *A Greek-English Lexicon*, 298.

[24] Wire, *2 Corinthians*, 259.

[25] A more comprehensive review of all the challenging texts, including those from the pastoral epistles is found in Frances Taylor Gench, *Encountering God in Tyrannical Texts: Reflections on Paul, Women, and the Authority of Scripture* (Louisville: Westminster John Knox Press, 2015).

well summarized by Elizabeth Schüssler Fiorenza, who has observed that "throughout the centuries, patriarchal theology and the church have silenced women, and excluded us from religious institutions of authority."[26] This was not Paul's mission.

To this point we've seen how Paul embraced his enfeebled masculinity as part of his identification with Christ crucified. For any man in the first century, we are dealing with unusual metaphors. Paul as "male wet nurse"? Paul who escapes in a basket over a wall in Damascus? He is not the brave Paul standing up to the governing authorities. We learn from Gaventa that Roman men who were less manly were called *malakos* — men "identified by his soft hair, sedentary habits, weak eyes, and small legs."[27]

In my years of study regarding St. Paul one of the things I never expected would be finding metaphors in Paul's letters which were grounded in the world of child-bearing women. My own story includes being brought up inside an androcentric world which also ruled the seminary I attended in the 1960s. It was a world that "failed to notice these astonishing references to the maternity of a male apostle."[28] There isn't a tsunami of scholarly work on this topic, but a number of more careful feminist biblical scholars are unearthing this amazing side of Paul by a reading of Paul's letters. Among these are Beverly Gaventa, Diana Swancutt, Sandra Polaski, Elizabeth Tamez, Lisa Rehman, Carolyn Osiek, Brittany Wilson, Frances Taylor Gench, Cynthia Westfall, and, most notably, Elizabeth Schüssler Fiorenza.[29] Among others, these have been particularly helpful to my understanding of *Paul the Unmanly Man*. They have enabled me to see a side to Paul overlooked for far too long. One of the more comprehensive scholarly studies in my mind is Gaventa's *Our Mother Saint Paul*.

It is also helpful to simply point out the number of texts in Paul's letters that use his most surprising metaphors. Consider the following passages from his letters in which Paul speaks both as a *mother* and as a *father*:

> Thessalonians 2:5-7: "As you know and as God is our witness, we never came with words of flattery or with a

---

[26] Fiorenza, *In Memory of Her*, 8.
[27] Gaventa, *Our Mother St. Paul* 48
[28] Gaventa, *Our Mother St. Paul*, 6.
[29] See the Bibliography for their books and articles that have informed this book.

pretext of greed; nor did we seek praise from mortals, whether from you or from others, though we might have made demands as apostles of Christ. But we were gentle among you, like a nurse tenderly caring for her own children."[30]

Galatians 4:19: "My little children, for whom I am again in the pain of childbirth until Christ is formed in you."

1 Corinthians 4:14–15: "I am not writing this to make you ashamed, but to admonish you as my beloved children. For though you might have ten thousand guardians, you did not have many fathers. Indeed, in Christ Jesus I became your father through the gospel."

1 Thessalonians 2:11 "As you know, we dealt with each one of you like a father with his children, urging and encouraging you and pleading that you lead a life worthy of God, who calls you into his own kingdom and glory."

1 Thessalonians 5:3 "When they say, "There is peace and security," then sudden destruction will come upon them, as labor pains come upon a pregnant woman, and there will be no escape."

1 Corinthians 3:1-3 "And so, brothers and sisters, I could not speak to you as spiritual people, but rather as people of the flesh, as infants in Christ. I fed you with milk, not solid food, for you were not ready for solid food. Even now you are not ready, for you are still of the flesh."

Romans 8:22-23 "We know that the whole creation has been groaning in labor pains until now, and not only the creation, but we ourselves, who have the first fruits of the Spirit, groan inwardly while we wait for adoption, the redemption of our bodies."

Galatians: 3:27-28 "As many of you as were baptized into Christ have clothed yourselves with Christ. There is no longer Jew or Greek, there is no longer slave or free, there is no longer male and female, for all you are one in Christ."

There was much going on in Paul's discourse that has often been missed, and probably none as critical as his unusual and, shall we

---

[30] Note the alternative reading discussed below of 1 Thess. 2:7 "We were infants among you, like a nurse taking care of her children."

say, unexpected metaphors. In most of the above passages we encounter what Susan Eastman termed "Paul's mother tongue."[31] What contrasts to the idea of a "mother tongue" is the predominant voice that Ursula Le Guin termed the "father tongue." "The essential gesture of the father tongue is not reasoning but distancing—making a gap, a space between subject and the object or other."[32] In other words the "father tongue" is the language of power.

Le Guin defined the *"mother tongue"* as conversation, grounded in relationships, exchanges, and networks. It isn't an instrument that divides, but one that binds and unites. It has to do with relationships, networks, and community. In light of Paul's message in so many of his letters he was clearly seeking unity and reconciliation and not an ordered hierarchy or a respectable societal institution. He was inviting others to a social vulnerability and shared economic footing with the "least of these" that Paul embodied in his own experience of being found in Christ. Equally significant is how much Paul sought for harmony, peace, and love to mark the common life of those belonging to Messiah Jesus. Paul we might say had a *mother tongue*.

There is a profound quote from Jurgen Moltmann which helps explain Paul's mother tongue, as he allied himself with those most vulnerable in the world of Pontius Pilate: "Anyone who is possessed by the sufferings of Christ becomes a stranger in the world of Pontius Pilate."[33] Even though the name of Pontius Pilate was never mentioned in any of Paul's letters, he had to be included in Paul's observation about the strange foolish wisdom that marked those in the world of Christ: "But we speak of God's wisdom, secret and hidden, which God decreed before the ages for our glory. None of the rulers of this age understood this; for if they had, they would not have crucified the Lord of Glory" (1 Cor 2:7-8).[34] Paul, as we saw earlier, admitted to having been part of the world of violence, but as his metaphors of mothers, birthing, and nursing show, it was a world left behind.

Those receiving Paul's letters and hearing his voice, clearly included women, some of whom might have been nursing a

---

[31] Eastman, *Recovering Paul's Mother Tongue*, 6-7.
[32] Ursula Le Guin, "The Bryn Mawr Commencement Address," in *Dancing at the Edge of the World: Thoughts on Words, Women, Places* (New York: Grove Press, 1988).
[33] Moltmann, *The Way of Jesus*, 210.
[34] Note that 1 Thess 5:3 also alludes to the Roman rulers who will be destroyed.

newborn child, others who were midwives and nurses. "The groaning of labor was probably a sound very familiar to Paul from the houses where he stayed and the churches he founded, as indeed it would have been a common experience of household life in the Roman world."[35] Imagine what these women thought when this man used metaphors from their world.

As we consider what Paul was learning from his awakened awareness of human needs and suffering, we need to confront Paul's mixed metaphors that may have brought a smile to some faces, and quizzical expressions on others. A good place to start is his first letter to the Thessalonians. (1 Thess 2: 6-7) In the important preface to this verse, Paul describes the role of apostles (*plural*) who neither used flattery nor sought praise. They could have made demands but did not do so. Paul is reminding his hearers that he is "*gentle among you.* That's what we read in the NRSV translation.

There's an alternate translation for the text, however. Paul might have said "we were *infants* among you" and not "gentle among you." If the intent was "infants," then we have a really confusing mixed metaphor: "But we were *infants* among you, like a *nurse* tenderly caring for her own children" (1 Thess 2:7). The word that describes this rhetorical device is an *anacoluthon*, in that the two parts are not at all consistent. Were they like *infants* and at the same time like a *nurse*? The translators who chose "*gentle among you*" were offering a sentence in which there is a logical connection between being *gentle* and serving as *nurses*.

But, based on ancient manuscripts it could be either the adjective *gentle* or the noun *infants.* Though we've wrestled with the possibility that some troubling passages have been interpolated into Paul's letters, that is not the case here, since the original manuscript has not been deviated from except for a change of one small letter, which could be a simple scribal error. The Greek word for being *gentle* is *ēpios*, while the word for *infant* is *nēpios*. Historical evidence is that many of the earliest manuscripts had the noun for *infants*. Those ancient manuscripts tell us that we might need to recognize that this is truly a mixed metaphor: that is, that the apostles were both *infants* and *nurses*. Gaventa points out that it is easy to

---

[35] Carolyn Osiek and Margaret MacDonald with Janet H. Tulloch, *A Woman's Place: House Churches in Earliest Christianity* (Minneapolis: Fortress Press, 2006), 62-63.

understand how a scribe might change "infants" to "gentle" — simply as an easier way to understand the passage.[36] Chances are Paul wasn't as straightforward as others might have wanted. Thus, the scribal alteration, choosing the word *nurses* could be a judicious attempt to make Paul more logical.

Gaventa also notes that such a mixed metaphor was "by no means uncommon in the letters of Paul."[37] Thus we should consider how the mixed metaphor might actually make perfect sense. Based on Paul's statements, he and other apostles came to Thessalonica "like a child," even like an infant;[38] 1 Corinthians 13:11 is translated "When I was a child, I spoke like a child" (NRSV). The word for child there is *nepios*, meaning either "child" or "infant." Members of the assembly in Corinth are also called "infants in Christ" (1 Cor 3:1), that is, full of innocence. Paul adds that they never used "words of flattery or with a pretext for greed, nor did we seek praise from mortals" (1 Thess 2:3-4). The context in which Paul makes this claim is significant. Paul was reminding the Thessalonians that the three of them (Paul, Sylvanus, and Timothy) had come after being mistreated in Philippi. (1 Thess 2:2) Their shameful treatment led them to be courageous in preaching the gospel. And yet, there they are, "gentle" among them, or as "infants" among them. We cannot resolve the difference between these two concepts, except that Paul described a ministry like unto that of nurses. A Paul who cares for his communities of faith does so not just with rhetoric, but with birthing images (discussed next) and nursing metaphors (discussed below).

In his letter to the Galatians Paul used not a mixed metaphor, but a confusing one addressing the Galatians about his vision for a new kind of community: "My little children,[39] for whom I am again in the pain of childbirth until Christ is formed in you" (Gal 4:19). The question is not just how a man can be in the pain of childbirth, but how this birth (if it is such) results in something being born inside the lives of those in these communities?

---

[36] Gaventa, *Our Mother St. Paul*, 18–25.

[37] Gaventa, *Our Mother St. Paul*, 19.

[38] 1 Corinthians 13:11 is translated "When I was a child, I spoke like a child" (NRSV). The word for child there is *nehrios*, meaning either "child" or "infant." Members of the assembly in Corinth are also called "infants in Christ" (1 Cor 3:1).

[39] The Greek there is "*tekna*" which is appropriate for a small child.

Once more Gaventa has some amazing insights on Paul's labor pains.[40] The word for such labor is *ōdinein,* which is not the same as another word in Greek which simply meant to give birth. The word *ōdinein* included the anguish and agony of the process. In the world of Jewish apocalyptic literature, it was often used to symbolize the coming of God's judgment, and the return of the Messiah.

We need to remember what happened to change Paul from persecutor to persecuted for the faith he once condemned. Paul could no longer be the man he once was. It didn't mean disassociating from that world, but it meant making new choices. What was changing was actually captured in the phrase "until Christ is formed in you." Paul used the root of the same word Kafka used in his novella "Metamorphosis" in Galatians 4:19. There the word is *morphōthē.* In that passage it is a passive verb. That means that the *shaping,* the *changing,* and the *forming* has an agent (a cause) from outside. For Paul that was the work of the Holy Spirit. That gift is promise. It is something to *await,* rather than *create,* like a birth. Like a woman.

Among the maternal images in Paul, there is also the picture of Paul as the mother who nurses her children. "And so, brothers and sisters, I could not speak to you as spiritual people, but rather as people of the flesh, as infants (*nepios*) in Christ. I fed you with milk, not solid food, for you were not ready for solid food. Even now you are not ready, for you are still of the flesh" (1 Cor 3:1-3). To be sure, Paul is not complimenting their mature faith in Christ at this point.

Paul's use of the nursing metaphor in 1 Corinthians, with its emphasis on their infantile status, is meant to show the sharp contrast to assumptions of spiritual accomplishments and status that some in their midst seem to have been proclaiming. (1 Cor 14:37). Paul instead declared they were not ready for solid food. McNeel notes that Paul used a breastfeeding metaphor: they weren't ready for the solid teaching Paul had in mind. What Paul would give them was "not the worldly philosophical wisdom that they long for, but the ethical and social implications of the gospel..."[41]

---

[40] Gaventa, *Our Mother St. Paul,* 29–39.

[41] Jennifer Houston McNeel, "Feeding with Milk: Paul's Nursing Metaphors in Context," *Review and Expositor* 111 (Fall 2013): 569.

9.3 Heads up: Paul fully affirms women in ministry and worship — 1 Cor 11:2-16

What we have with 1 Cor 11:2-16 is really difficult to decipher. MacDonald said it is "a linguistic labyrinth rivaling Daedalus's and befuddling a host of would-be-Thesaurus-users. Every turn in this maze forces the intruder to choose from among several paths."[42] MacDonald adds that we ought to read this as a passage that *Paul wrote*. A few verses in this passage are so at odds with what Paul affirms about women participating in worship that we must, however, consider that some of these verses came to Paul as *opinions of some men* in the Corinthian assembly.

One of the most-debated parts of Paul's letter to the Corinthians concerns the implication that the heads of some matter more than others. Should heads be covered or uncovered? Does the hairdo matter? With these questions we have issues of social class, protection of some women, and the questions of men and women participating in worship. All these matters arise in chapter 11 of 1 Corinthians — just the first 16 verses! Determining whether Paul actually wrote this entire section or may have repeated words that came to him from Corinth will inform our understanding of these various questions. There are five parts to be examined:

> Part A 11:2-3 — The ordering of heads
> Part B 11:4-7 — Men's heads uncovered and women (some?) were unveiled
> Part C 11:8-13 — Paul affirms men and women in worship and leadership
> Part D 11:14-15 — Who has long hair
> Part E 11:16 — Unity in worship

I maintain that Part B of this passage (verses 11:4-7) came to Paul as matters he chose to address. They were statements of belief or practice, most likely from male leaders in Corinth, asking for Paul to confirm what they were proclaiming. These verses reveal a *chauvinistic assumption of male superiority* clearly contrary to the unmanly Paul. It is so at odds with the other ideas which follow it cannot have represented Paul's understanding of the role of women in the life of these early communities of Jesus Messiah followers. In offering this analysis I am following the suggestions of Alan

---

[42] MacDonald, *There is No Male and Female*, 72.

Padgett[43] and David Odell-Scott, who wrote, "I take it that the position of 11.4-7 is not Paul's but is held by a faction in the Corinthian church."[44]

In this analysis of this highly contested set of verses it seems best for us to hear the words that came to Paul, not so much as a question, but as a statement of fact by some men in Corinth. As I let the men speak be assured, with one exception, that Paul presents a starkly contrasting view on the place of women in worship and leadership.

> Part A: 1 Corinthians 11:2-3
> I commend you because you remember me in everything and maintain the traditions just as I handed them on to you. But I want you to understand that Christ is the head of every man, and the man is the head of the woman, and God is the head of Christ.[45]
>
> Part B: 1 Corinthians 11:4-7
> Any man who prays or prophecies with something on his head disgraces his head, but nay woman who prays or prophesies with her head unveiled disgraces her head—it is one and the same thing as having her head shaved. For if a woman will not veil herself, then she should cut off her hair; but if it is disgraced for a woman to have her hair cut off or to be shaved, she should wear a veil. For a man ought not to have his head veiled, since he is the image and reflection of God; but woman is the reflection of man.
>
> Part C: 1 Corinthians 11:8-13
> Indeed, man was not made from woman, but woman from man. Neither was man created for the sake of woman, but woman for the sake of man. For this reason a woman ought to have a symbol of authority on her head, because of the angels. Nevertheless, in the Lord woman is not independent of man or man independent of woman. For just as woman came from man, so man comes through

---

[43] Alan Padgett, "Paul on Women in the Church: The Contradiction of Coiffeur in 1 Corinthians 11:2-16," *Journal for the Study of the New Testament* 6, no. 20, (Jan. 1984): 69. He included the last verse in this section (11:16) as part of "B," but I think it's a separate idea, akin to another passage a few chapters later.

[44] David Odell-Scott, *Paul's Critique of Theocracy: A/Theocracy in Corinthians and Galatians* (New York: T & T Clark, 2003), 168

[45] I argue below that verse 3 may have been what the men in Corinth believed. But Paul the Pharisee offers a clever exegesis.

woman; but all things come from God. Judge for yourselves: is it proper for a woman to pray to God with her head unveiled?

Part D: 1 Corinthians 14-15
Does not nature itself teach you that if a man wears long hair, it is degrading to him, but if a woman has long hair, it is her glory? For her hair is given to her for a covering.

Part E: 1 Corinthians 11:16
But if anyone is disposed to be contentious—we have no such custom, nor do the churches of God

My memory of going to church as a small boy in the late 1940s was that my mom usually had a hat on *in* church, and my dad always had a hat on his head as we drove to church, but never *in* church. The times have changed in many churches where today one would find almost no one wearing a hat. And I've seen some guys with baseball hats on in church!

Paul would have agreed that men should not have their heads covered in worship. It also was not seen in synagogue worship then.[46] It had everything to do with what it meant to worship Jesus as your Lord, your *Kyrios*. If your head was covered in worship then you were like all the other men in Rome, who followed the example of Caesar: "Pulling his toga up over his head . . . was the iconographic mark of a sacrificant presiding over a specifically Roman ritual, whether the emperor, a Roman priest, or a layman."[47] Brian Robinson points out that, therefore, the image of a man wearing a veil " can act as a public and political symbol of authority for the one wearing the veil." [48] Simply put, followers of Jesus Messiah should not act like Roman men in a temple.

---

[46] The tradition common in many parts of the Jewish world is for a man to wear a hat called a *yarmulka*. Some wear it whenever in public, others only in worship. It was not part of the Jewish world in the first century. See Samuel Krauss, "The Jewish Rite of Covering the Head," *Hebrew Union College Annual* 19 (1945-1946): 121-146.

[47] Neil Elliott, *Liberating Paul,* 210; quote of Richard Gordon, "The Veil of Power Emperors, Sacrificers and Benefactors," in *Pagan Priests: Religion and Power in the Ancient World,* eds. Mary Beard and John North (Ithaca: Cornell University Press, 1990), 202.

[48] Brian Robinson, *Being Subordinate Men: Paul's Rhetoric of Gender and Power in 1 Corinthians* (London: Lexington Books, 2019), 218.

The issue of head coverings or veils was much more guarded and restricted when it came to women. "Marriage and widowhood were the chief things a veil signaled...The veil was the flag of female virtue, status and security."[49] Quoting historian Roman de Vaux, the biblical scholar Dennis MacDonald wrote, "the veil in the ancient near East, including ancient Israel, made clear to others that a woman was the property of her father or husband, thus protecting male rights."[50] A woman with a veil belonged to the patriarchal order of the world which was the same throughout Paul's world.[51]

Nevertheless, there is a question regarding what women were expected to wear in worship, and what they wore while *leading* in worship alongside men. Critical to the way Paul framed this discussion is that he accepted women as leaders in worship. (Section 9.1.2 below deals with a difficult text that contests Paul's affirmation of women having active roles to play in worship.)

Custom dictated that women's heads be covered with a veil, or they were to have their hair bound up in a knot when they were in public.[52] That is essentially what 1 Cor 11:10 states when Paul wrote for a woman to have a "symbol of authority on her head." The issue of wearing or not wearing a veil is what follows here. We need to return to the passage a little further after this because the word "authority" is critical to understanding what Paul saw for women in the assembly as they wore their veils.

Not all scholars, however, agree that Paul meant that women should wear veils in assemblies. Richard Hays in his commentary on 1 Corinthians argued that Paul was talking about hair, rather than veils, because "It was not normal custom for women in Greek and Roman cultures to be veiled..."[53] In his commentary on 1

---

[49] Sarah Ruden, *Paul Among the People: The Apostle Reinterpreted and Reimagined in His Own Time* (New York: Image Books, 2010), 85.

[50] MacDonald, *There is No Male and Female*, 89.

[51] Daniel Marguerat, *Paul in Acts and Paul in His Letters* (Tübingen: Mohr Siebeck, 2013), 250.

[52] Uncovered hair on women which was ornately composed was more likely to be found in Rome; see Elizabeth Bateman, "Hair and the Artifice of Roman Female Adornment," American Journal of Archeology 105, no. 1 (Jan. 2001): 1-25.

[53] Richard Hays, *First Corinthians*, (Louisville: Westminster John Knox Press, 1977), 185-87.

Corinthians Gordon Fee asserts that there was "no first-century evidence" for veiling of women.[54]

Other scholars disagree. Bailey points out that wearing a covering over their hair was an ancient female practice in Paul's time. Clearly it is a tradition continuing in the conservative Islamic countries of today.[55] There were Greek and Jewish cultural expectations for women to have their hair carefully tied up *and* also covered when in public. In that first century setting a woman letting down her hair was something to be seen only inside her own home.

The veil, however, was *not a privilege* extended to *all* women. Appearing unveiled in public pointed out the status of women who were "degraded, vulnerable beings,"[56] not permitted to wear a veil. On the streets of Corinth if a woman had her head uncovered, she was either not a citizen or protected by her husband. The uncovered head, whether intended or not, was advertising "the availability of her sexual services."[57]

What Paul saw all around him in the cities where he spent most of his working life were some unveiled women (maybe the majority) and all the opportunities for men to have their way with those same women. As Dale Martin explained in *The Corinthian Body* the two things that troubled Paul the most from that pagan world were *porneia* (the Greek word for illicit sex) and *idolatry*.[58] Paul did not hesitate to condemn that behavior among those who followed Christ, though it does seem *porneia* was worse in Corinth, about which Paul said: "sexual immorality among you [is] of a kind that is not found even among pagans" (1 Cor 5:1). "In the time of Paul, the city of Corinth had become an infamous center of religious prostitution."[59] Four hundred years before the time of Paul, according to O'Connor, "Athenian writers vented their spleen by inventing words based on 'Corinth' to convey aspects critical of

---

[54] Gordon D Fee, *The First Epistle to the Corinthians: Revised Edition* (Grand Rapids: William B. Eerdmans, 2014), 576.

[55] Kenneth Bailey, *Paul Through Mediterranean Eyes: Cultural Studies in 1 Corinthians* (Downers Grove: IVP Academic, 2011), 300

[56] Ruden, *Paul Among the People*, 87.

[57] Sandra Hock Polaski, *A Feminist Introduction to Paul* (St. Louis: Chalice Press, 2005), 54.

[58] Martin, *The Corinthian Body*, 215–16.

[59] John Bristow, *What Paul Really Said about Women: An Apostle's Liberating Views on Equality in Marriage, Leadership, and Love* (San Francisco: Harper & Row, 1991), 51.

commercialized love: for example, *korinthiazesthai*, 'to fornicate'; *korinthiastês*, 'a pimp'; *korinthia korê*, 'a prostitute'."[60]

The women in that world who were not allowed to wear a veil would find an unusual friend in Paul. Laws in his world were made only by men. Westfall states that "laws were made and enforced that prevented women who were deemed without honor from veiling, which included prostitutes, slaves, freedwomen, and women in the lowest classes."[61]

Westfall's scholarship leads to the conclusion that the dignity and protection implied in wearing a veil was *not to be* a status distinction within the context of the early followers of Jesus when they came together for worship, but a symbol that there was *no* status to be gained by wearing a veil which would be a sign of status. Even the poorest women, or those who were slaves, were to be covered and look equal to those with the higher status who possessed the right to greater protection and equal dignity within the assembly as sisters in Christ. As Westfall insightfully notes, Paul was subverting cultural assumptions of his world "including the status and entitlement of men, as well as women of high status, who were the beneficiaries of the cultural regulations and restrictions on veiling."[62] This practice characterizes the theology that our differences may remain, but they no longer should determine our *place* inside the story of Christ crucified.

As I noted at the beginning of this when placing the text of 1 Cor 11:4-7 (Part B) and 11:14-15 (Part D) for consideration I suggested these were statements from the men in Corinth, who could not be expecting Paul's response. Paul concluded about women's heads in worship that no other man of his day might have imagined. Some had been removing their veils. And some had no veils to wear. Paul's response? *All* women—including slaves—would be wearing a veil while in worship![63] Thus in a context of early worship among followers of Jesus, if Paul required no man to have a head covering, the opposite was true for women. All women were to have the privilege of a veil. As Robinson states: "…Paul's commands would prevent the manipulation of veils as a source of distinction from and

---

[60] Jerome Murphy-O'Connor, *Paul His Story* (New York: Oxford University Press, 2004), 77–78.
[61] Murphy-O'Connor, *Paul His Story*, 33.
[62] Westfall, *Paul and Gender*, 69.
[63] Westfall, *Paul and Gender*, 37.

domination over lower-status members of the community."[64] Paul's sartorial instructions were not coming from a man asserting privilege, but from this unmanly man denying for himself and all other men the patriarchal assumptions of superior status with regard to women. Along with that radical concept Paul affirmed that women had authority that needed to be respected.

Part A: 1 Cor 11:2-3 and Part C: 1 Cor 11:8-13

It may seem strange to combine these two texts, but they really do belong together, and not to the previous argument about head coverings. We can assume that questions about what to wear on your head, and the asserted privileges of men came to Paul from the men in Corinth. What Paul does with this exegesis places Paul in the role of a rabbi handing on traditions as stated in 1 Cor 11:2 where he uses the plural of the Greek word for traditions which is *paradoseis*. A more literal translation of that passage is "I handed over (*paredōka*) the traditions (*paradoseis*) to you." Implicit is that these were traditions *handed* over to Paul That word is emphasized as the verb that begins the passage, i.e., I handed them, is *paredōka*.

Some scholars assume that "Paul's sense of gender differentiation is quite hierarchical."[65] It certainly seems to point in that direction with our discussion of the phrase "Christ is the head of every man, and the husband is the head of his wife" (1 Cor 11:3). This translation of the passage is what leads some to assume Paul believes wives are to be submissive to their husbands.[66]

The problem is with the NRSV translation of the first part of this passage. Note that the NRSV translates the word "man" as "husband." In English we can talk about "a man" without regard to his marital status. The same is true for the word "woman." It is not that clear in Greek. The Greek word *anēr* can be translated either *man* or *husband*, and the Greek word *gynē* can be translated either as

---

[64] Robinson, *Being Sub-ordinant Men*, 224.

[65] Faith Kirkham Hawkins, "Does Paul Make a Difference," in *A Feminist Companion to Paul*, eds. Amy Jill Levine with Marianne Blickenstaff (New York: T & T Clark International, 2004), 151.

[66] To be sure there are passages in Colossians (3:18) and Ephesians (5:22-33) expressing exactly that idea. This book discusses only the seven undisputed letters, and not those like Colossians and Ephesians. Some scholars think Paul authored them, but others disagree. I am in the company of those who don't believe that Paul wrote those two letters.

woman or *wife*. The context must determine the translation. The entire passage we are looking at discusses the relationship of men and women, particularly in the context of *worship*. This was not a question about marriage, but about women's heads when they were leading and participating in worship.

A better translation of 1 Cor 11:3 is found in the New International Version (NIV) which does not restrict the matter to marriage by using the word "husband": "Now I want you to realize that the head of every man is Christ, and the head of the woman is man, and the head of Christ is God." The question remains, however, where does this passage in Part A come from? It also had to come from the men in Corinth who were seeking Paul's agreement with *their position* regarding women in worship.

There are responsible scholars like Christopher Mount[67] and Richard Horsley[68] who offer compelling cases that both of our troublesome passages are not from Paul's hand. Is this an interpolation added later by some unknown scribe seeking to correct Paul? The harder road to take is to see these verses as words coming from Paul, but not as words bearing Paul's mark and stamp; that is, he wrote those words, but they do not reflect what he believed. This came from the men in Corinth. That is the path I am taking, following the lead of Alan Padgett and David Odell-Scott already referenced.

It is in Part C (1 Cor 11:8–13) that we *hear* Paul. It begins with a kind of midrash—which is to say a Jewish commentary on a passage of scripture—of the Genesis 2 creation story. The first verse reflects the story of Adam's rib used to make Eve. "Indeed, a man was not made from man, but woman from the man" (1 Cor 11:8).

What comes next contains words often mistranslated. Kenneth Bailey challenges the way we usually read 11:9-10 when he suggests that a small Greek word *"dia"* was used in two ways.[69] Bailey notes that many translations frame verses 11:9-10 in this way.

---

[67] Christopher Mount, "1 Corinthians 11:3-16: Spirit Possession and Authority in a Non-Pauline Interpolation," *Journal of Biblical Literature* 124, no. 2 (2005): 313–40.
[68] Richard A. Horsley, *1 Corinthians* (Nashville: Abingdon Press, 1998) 152.
[69] Bailey, *Paul Through Mediterranean Eyes*, 309–10.

9. For man was not created *for* [*dia*] woman
   But woman *for* [*dia*] man
10. *because of* [*dia*] this
    the woman should have authority on the head
    because of [*dia*] the angels.

The traditional understanding of this passage, in the patriarchal world, is to regard it as saying that women were created *for* the sake of men. Bailey claims this is not what the Greek text says. There is quite a difference if the correct translation of the passage doesn't use the word *for*, but choses the translation *because of* in the entire passage.

9. For man was not created *because of* the woman
   But woman *because of* the man
10. *because of* [*dia*] this
    the woman should have authority on the head
    because of [*dia*] the angels.

Bailey concludes, "It was not *Eve* who was lonely, unable to manage and needed help. Instead, it was *Adam* who could not manage alone."[70] The second part of the passage in Genesis has God declaring "I will make a helper for him" (Gen 1:18b). Using the word *helper, according to Bailey is the problem. It misses* the essence of the Hebrew word '*ezra*, which really means one who comes to save, which is the root of the name of Lazarus, namely "the one whom God helps/saves."[71] Westfall came to the same conclusion: "Therefore, we may infer that 1 Corinthians 11:9 means that man needed woman and knew it, which is a simple straightforward summary of Genesis 2:18-23."[72] Paul was affirming the strength and role of women and that led him into a passage emphasizing the *interdependence* of men and women.

I found the 1961 translation by the English scholar J. B. Phillips[73] in agreement with Bailey's work. "For man does not exist because woman exists, but vice-versa. Man was not created originally for the sake of women, but woman was created for the sake of man." In other words, the man needed the woman. Still does!

---

[70] Bailey, *Paul Through Mediterranean Eyes*, 310.
[71] Bailey, *Paul Through Mediterranean Eyes*, 310.
[72] Westfall, *Paul and Gender*, 103.
[73] J. B. Phillips, *Letters to Young Churches: A Translation of the New Testament Epistles,* (New York: The Macmillan Company, 1954), 56.

Earlier I quoted 1 Cor 11:10 with regard to what a woman wore that symbolized authority. At the time the focus was on a veil. It is important to consider what Paul meant by the word for authority. I will continue to emphasize the caution we must exercise with certain translations of the Greek bible. As an example, the NRSV translates 1 Cor. 11:10 this way: "For this reason a woman ought to have *a symbol of authority* on her head, because of the angels" (My italics).

The Revised Standard Version (RSV) took out the word authority (*exousia*) and substituted the word *veil* in the text. "That is why a woman ought to have a veil on her head, because of the angels." The word "veil" is not there.

If you want to see the translation that really messed up the passage, we have the Living Bible translation to consider: "So a woman should wear a covering on her head as a sign that she is under man's authority, a fact for all the angels to notice and rejoice in." This version adds the word *veil* and then assigns the word *authority* to men. It refers to the "head covering" as a *sign*, while the NRSV calls the *authority* a *sign*.

Walter Kaiser has called these various and numerous additions to 1 Cor 11:10 a "debacle" and "one of the weirdest twists in translation history."[74] The way out of this thicket is to consult the Greek, refrain from substituting words that are not there, and realize, once more, just how much respect Paul had for a woman to be equal to her spouse in marriage (1 Cor 7:2-4) and to have voice in the assemblies worshipping Jesus Messiah.

A "woman ought to have a symbol of authority on her head," is exactly the opposite of the message which expected women to be subordinate. As noted above 1 Cor 11:2-7 represented traditional Greco-Roman assumptions of male superiority. We don't see that in Paul, as we discover in re-reading these texts with the actual Greek in mind.

One further point about women having authority over their own heads: the primary meaning of the Greek word for authority (*exousia*) does not mean "power over." It primarily meant "freedom of choice, right to act, decide, or dispose of one's property as one wishes." The secondary meaning was the "ability to do something, capability, might, power." To be sure, the same word applied to

---

[74] Walter Kaiser as quoted in J. David Miller, "Translating Paul's Words About Women," *Stone-Campbell Journal* 12 (2009): 65.

rulers and officials.[75] We ought to keep the primary definition in mind as we consider how Paul expressed confidence in women making the right choices.

We can't pin-point why Paul introduced angels into his teaching, but Padgett wonders if they weren't like the women who worked alongside of Paul and who were sent in his stead as was Phoebe with the letter to the Romans. They were female messengers.[76] While women are definitely at a disadvantage as 1 Cor 11 begins, by this point as Odell-Scott noted, "male and female are co-originating and co-dependent."[77]

This interesting passage deserves more attention, but I don't want us to lose sight of our main theme. We must see Paul standing for the *unity* of men and women even if they are sharing it in a way that was quite out of the context of their world. Being "in the Lord" is the hermeneutical key to Paul's story. The ending of this dense part of 1 Corinthians 11:2-16 captures Paul's teaching about being in Christ.

> Part E— 1 Cor 11:16
> But if anyone is disposed to be contentious—we have no such custom, nor do the churches of God (NRSV).

With one simple verse, Paul sums up the basic issue confronting the Corinthian assemblies. They were divided and contentious. They had formed into parties and were bringing socially acceptable distinctions of worth, with their assumptions of privilege into the assembly. For Paul it was not be found among "all those who in every place call on the name of our Lord Jesus Christ" (1 Cor 1:2).

9.4 Women be silent in church?

This chapter has required us to be biblical detectives. We still need such skills particularly with the passage declaring women should be silent in the worship assembly. (1 Cor 14:34-35) To be sure many scholars think Paul wrote those words. Many Christian assemblies to this day follow this as their rule. Antoinette Clark Wire is not a biblical scholar who would ever embrace the exclusion of women from leadership or their subordination to men, yet she reads

---

[75] Danker et al., *A Greek-English Lexicon,* 352–53.
[76] Padgett, "Paul on Women", 81–82.
[77] David Odell-Scott, *Paul's Critique of Theocracy: A/Theocracy in Corinthians and Galatians* (New York: T & T Clark, 2003), 172.

the three chapters (11-14) in 1 Corinthians as Paul's attempts to silence women.[78] I have learned to read these chapters in a different light. What follows in the next section is a re-reading of these passages returning us to the Paul who said in Galatians 3:28 that all were equal.

Elizabeth Schüssler Fiorenza coined the term *ekklēsia gynaikon*, which is to say *women church*. She maintains that the essence of *women church* is a discipleship of equals.[79] This term relates to feminist and liberation theology, but it is useful in this analysis to see how Paul would understand *woman church*. I believe we should be ready to be surprised.

From my experience as a pastor my strategy in this chapter is to consider the texts which have most troubled women in the parishes I served. These two texts (1 Cor 11:2-16 and 14:34-35) are roadblocks, and not the kind you can just drive around. These two passages must be seen in the context of the entire letter reflecting ongoing conversations and concerns, some of which came to Paul in various reports. Those reports are stated explicitly at times, and it is important to consider that if a passage doesn't sound like Paul, it may not have come from him.

A point made by Kittridge regarding the authorship of the letters of Paul is relevant. She notes that Paul must be understood as a participant who is not at the *center* of a particular set of conversations, but *as* a participant. In her words he belonged to "dialogical interpretative communities."[80] We must also remember that these were occasional letters, very particular for each community. Most likely, Paul never thought he was creating doctrine for all time. He was sharing with others what it meant that their life together in Christ reflected the very story of Christ in terms of their questions and challenges.

Is it really probable that Paul would conclude his first letter to the Corinthians with the admonition that women should not ever be

---

[78] Antoinette Wire, *The Corinthian Women Prophets: A Reconstruction through Paul's Rhetoric* (Minneapolis: Fortress Press, 1990), 156.

[79] Elizabeth Schüssler Fiorenza, *But She Said: Feminist Practices of Biblical Interpretation* (Boston: Beason Press, 2002), 127–8.

[80] Cynthia Briggs Kittridge, "Rethinking Authorship in the Letters of Paul: Elizabeth Schüssler Fiorenza's Model of Pauline Theology," in *Walk in the Ways of Wisdom: Essays in Honor of Elizabeth Schüssler Fiorenza,"* ed. Shelly Matthews et al. (Harrisburg: Trinity Press International, 2003), 331.

heard inside their worship gatherings? Consider the background we've discovered regarding Paul in relationship to women who he saw as co-workers, and even Junia, who was an apostle in Christ *before* he was. Remember that the epistle to the Romans was entrusted to Phoebe who may have likely delivered it orally after being coached by Paul. She was at least in a role where others would ask questions of her regarding the letter and other matters as well.

Near the end of the 1st Corinthian section focused on worship we encounter the command for silencing women. The real conclusion to chapters 11-14 was Paul's hope that "all things should be done decently and in order" (1 Cor 14:40). How does that vision fit with the statement a few verses earlier: "As in all the churches of the saints, women should be silent in the churches. For they are not permitted to speak, but should be subordinate, as the law also says. If there is anything they desire to know, let them ask their husbands at home. For it is shameful for a woman to speak in church" (1 Cor 14:34-35).

This passage has been used for most of Christian history to great effect in keeping women from participating in leadership and also speaking in worship. The hard-fought battle has been won in some parts of the Christian world recognizing women as deacons, priests, and bishops, but women still haven't been recognized in significant parts of Christianity. Since the Roman Catholic Church, the Orthodox traditions, and major segments of the evangelical world resist the full involvement of women in all ordained ministry, this most arguable text continues to be used alongside texts from the Pastoral Epistles to restrict the opportunities for women to fully serve in holy orders, and in many cases any kind of leadership in these traditions.

Because all texts in the canon, even those we personally disagree with, need to be treated with respect, my task has been a careful examination of the broad spectrum of scholarship dealing with this command of *so-called* unequivocal clarity, when it is evident how much it flies in the face of other things Paul said. It must be noted, nevertheless, that it has been customary through history to defend this text as authentic because it is consistent with what is found in 1 Timothy and Titus regarding women in the life of the early followers of Jesus.

Please remember an observation made in the first chapter of this book regarding the difference between the Paul *of his letters* and the

Paul of *tradition* as heard through the Pastoral Epistles, Acts, and other 2nd and 3rd century documents. These later documents were written by historians, reflecting in their own times and with their own issues, positioning themselves and this new faith story in a more favorable light in the eyes of Roman authorities. I appreciate what Antoinette Wire has said regarding the delicate aspects of writing history: "historians know history is a piecing together of fragile textual and material remains."[81] For this analysis of Paul the focus must be on the early part of the first century when Paul's letters were actually written.

What we clearly have with the text silencing women is an "androcentric text." To this same text we must ascribe what Schüssler Fiorenza calls "the politics of otherness."[82] Defending this text as coming from the dictated words of Paul has been done throughout 2,000 years of Christian history and by many biblical scholars to this day. Wire, despite her insight about the fragmentary dependability of historical documents, does not support the interpolation theory regarding 1 Cor 14:34-35, but she also does not support the exclusion or submission of women. She believes, however, that this passage shows that Paul advocated "that others be silent, including women, who by tradition and propriety should not be speaking."[83]

Wire argues that the patriarchal Paul is the problem. With regard to silencing women (1 Cor 14: 34-35), this text must be understood as a form of "ecclesiastical patriarchy," a term, once more from Schüssler Fiorenza. "Reproducing societal patriarchy, Christian religious patriarchy has defined not only women but all subjected peoples and races as "the Other," as "nature" to be exploited and dominated by powerful men. Obedience, economic dependence, and sexual control are still the sustaining forces of societal and ecclesiastical patriarchy."[84] It is there in the text. But did Paul write these as his words?

What we have with Paul's text, whether or not he wrote it, is what Frances Taylor Gench calls a "tyrannical text." She argues that there are passages in scripture "that have legitimated the right of

---

[81] Wire, *The Corinthian Women Prophets*, 4.
[82] Fiorenza, *But She Said*, 200.
[83] Wire, *The Corinthian Women Prophets*, 153.
[84] Fiorenza, *But She Said*, 203.

some to exercise unjust power or control over others. They are "tyrannical" in the sense that they have circumscribed human lives and possibilities, functioning (and in many cases, continuing to function) as instruments of oppression."[85] Women through the 2,000 years of Christian history know all about being silenced by those who restrict the leadership in worship to men—men only!

Like many others I have found it very hard to believe that Paul actually wrote this most troublesome passage, though it is worth considering the proposal of Kenneth Bailey, who suggested that Paul was dealing with a problem of women talking (chattering?) during a worship assembly. Bailey's deep roots in the Mideastern world, where much has hardly changed in many aspects of their culture for thousands of years, led him to wonder if the women, sitting in a separate section (as it happens even in this day in places expressing more traditional Jewish and Muslim worship) were not paying attention when men were leading in worship. Was Paul telling the women "Stop your chatter and listen"?[86] John Bristow seems to think that this was Paul's intent. He noted that of the many Greek words for *speech*, Paul chose as his word for this admonition the Greek word *laleō*, (la-LAY-o)[87] which is the common word we would use if we saw two people talking over lunch. In this instance *laleō*[88] may have meant many different conversations.

That there may have been women talking and not paying attention in worship is an interesting proposal, but it does not address what we have already recognized as coming from Paul earlier in 11:2-16 where it was clear that women were welcomed to fully participate in the worship assembly. We also must consider how chapters 12-14 in 1 Corinthians are centered around issues of dignity and order in worship. All of Paul's concerns seem aimed at *whoever* might have been speaking in tongues or offering prophecies. He was reminding all of them that there were a great many spiritual

---

[85] Frances Taylor Gench, *Encountering God in Tyrannical Texts: Reflections on Paul, Women, and the Authority of Scripture* (Louisville: Westminster John Knox Press 2015), xi.

[86] Bailey, *Paul Through Mediterranean Eyes*, 416.

[87] Bristow, *What Paul Really Said about Women*, 62.

[88] Note that *laleō* is at the root of the word *glōssalalia*, the phenomena in worship which concerned Paul in 1 Cor. 14:1-19. Translated as "speaking in tongues" or simply "tongues" Paul had the gift of 'tongues,' but didn't think he should be praised for it. (1 Cor 14:18-19). He wanted strangers in worship to know what was being said, and thus preferred the gift of *prophecy*. (1 Cor 14:22-25).

gifts present in their assemblies and that none of those gifts mattered as much as a spirit of love that would inform all their cherished abilities. (1 Cor 13.)

When we come toward the end of Paul's discussion about matters affecting worship and find this command for women not to speak, it not only seems out of place and contrary to what we thought we heard earlier, but it clearly echoes the patriarchal sentiments of 1 Timothy. The similarities with the later epistle are notable and are spelled out below.

When the matter of an interpolation is considered, scholars attempt to see how many ancient manuscripts have what appears to be a scribal insertion, and which lack the same. That can be one clue for dating the possibility of such an addition. In the case of 1 Corinthians, though, *all* the ancient manuscripts have the words calling for the silencing of women. However, our earliest discovered written texts date no earlier than the 4th century. By that point in time there was consensus, or so it seems, that Paul had commanded women to be silent, or at least to avoid idle talk. In explaining the possibility that this troublesome text was an interpolation (i.e., bringing 1 Tim 2:11-13 into 1 Cor 14:33b-35) I am considering, but not endorsing, the suggestions of Dennis MacDonald and Gordon D. Fee, among many other scholars, that some scribe who knew the Pastoral epistles added these verses. The parallels seem telling.[89]

1 Corinthians 14:33b-36	1 Timothy 2:11-13
As in all the churches of the saints, Let women keep silence (*laleō*) in the churches	Let a woman learn in silence (*hēsychia*) in all subordination (*hypotagē*)
For they are not permitted (*epitrepetai*) to speak	And I do not permit (*epitrepō*) a woman to teach or have authority over a man, but to be in silence. (*hēsychia*)
But let them be subordinate (*hypotassesthōsan*) as even the law says.	For Adam was formed first, then Eve.

The difference to note here is that the Corinthian command to not talk, refers to a word about simple talk between people, while the Greek used in 1 Timothy (*hēsychia*) really does mean silence. It

---

[89] MacDonald, *The Legend and the Apostle*, 87. See also Fee, *The First Epistle to the Corinthians*, 781.

can also mean *quietness* or *rest*, but in this context that clearly isn't correct.[90]

In his analysis of this text MacDonald asked why the scribe adding these words, if indeed they were added, chose not to place them inside chapter 11? His answer is that since the 14th chapter was focused on those offering prophecies that could be heard and understood by all in the assembly (as opposed to the glossolalia that would be confusing to an outsider) it was this scribe's intention to counter women serving as prophets in worship.[91] Can we possibly ascribe to this long-forgotten scribe, if he ever existed, some saving motive for such an addition? Did he know and love both 1 Timothy 2:11-13 and 1 Corinthians? Could he have taken the passage in 1 Timothy, and paraphrased it into the end of Chapter 14? Or was it the other way around. Did that author copy from 1 Corinthians?

One answer possible, in the time of *Paul remembered*, is that there were those in some communities in the early church who were disturbed to think Paul fully accepted women in his shared ministry.[92] What they knew by then (40 to 70 years after Paul) was a more hierarchically ordered church struggling to be at peace in the Roman world. The androcentric leadership of the church, however, asserted itself. Decades after Paul, as MacDonald reminds us, there were "pious, dedicated, and skilled men—males of a particular social position and world view, who, in spite of their respect for the Pauline text, put their own signatures to his letters, thereby to some extent helped him write them. The Pauline corpus is mostly his, but also unmistakably theirs."[93]

Fee agrees with the interpolation hypothesis. In his massive commentary on 1 Corinthians, he found this passage on silencing women as "clearly intruding, and thoroughly unPauline, …vv. 34-35 are not authentic."[94] But we should remember there has been a

---

[90] Danker et al., *A Greek-English Lexicon*, 352–53.

[91] Note that this is also the theme of Antoinette Wire's book, *The Corinthian Women Prophets: A Reconstruction through Paul's Rhetoric*.

[92] For evidence that equality for women was in evidence in some parts of second-century Christianity see these sources: Jeremy W. Barrier, *The Acts of Paul and Thecla: A Critical Introduction and Commentary* (Tübingen: Mohr Siebeck, 2009) and Pauline Nigh Hogan, "Paul and Women in Second-Century Christianity," *Paul and the Second Century*, eds. Michael J. Bird and Joseph R. Dodson (New York: T&T Clark, 2009), 226-43

[93] MacDonald, *The Legend and the Apostle*, 89.

[94] Fee, *The First Epistle to the Corinthians*, 772.

tendency to take Paul's other words about things being done decently and in order (1 Cor 14:40), just as literally as the silencing of women. Not only are women not allowed to participate in leadership and worship, but the worship itself errs on the side of offering what Fee called "somber ritual, as though God were really something of a "stuffed shirt."[95]

The command regarding the silence of women in worship may *not*, at the end of the day, however, be an interpolation. That is the thesis of David Odell-Scott, who suggested that Paul was quoting words from the Corinthians themselves.[96] The logic of this suggestion is that the whole letter is framed as a response by Paul to questions brought to him on a number of issues facing this newly formed group of Jesus followers. Remember, the letter begins with Paul's reference to the quarreling and the schisms causing divisions in their midst. "For it has been reported to me by Chloe's people" (1 Cor 1:11). Further on Paul commented on a report of sexual immorality in the community. (1 Cor 5:1) Most telling of all was the way Paul began chapter 7: "Now concerning the matters about which you wrote: "'It is well for a man not to touch a woman.'"" (1 Cor 7:1) *Those were not the words of Paul!* It was a statement coming from Corinth which led to all of Paul's reflections on marriage, women, and celibacy.

If we take Odell-Scott's thesis seriously we don't need to speculate about a mysterious scribe reading and loving 1 Timothy, and then adding his own version to a copy of 1 Corinthians, thus becoming the *ipsissima vox* of Paul for all the centuries to come. Calling this passage an interpolation may be the easy way out, but it may also mean not hearing Paul's full affirmation of women to his first-century friends.

I suggest understanding how Paul was adding to his comments about order and decency in worship with one final point. *There were some who wanted to impose silence on the part of women in worship!* In their inquiry they wanted Paul to comment on what we read in 14.34-35. These are *their* words which they wanted Paul to affirm — namely that women should be seen, but not heard. I grew up hearing

---

[95] Fee, *The First Epistle to the Corinthians*, 774.

[96] David Odell-Scott, "In Defense of an Egalitarian Interpretation of First Corinthians 14:34-36: A reply to Murphy O'Connor's Critique." *Biblical Theology Bulletin* 17, no 3 (1987): 90-3; see also Yunk Suk Kim, *Christ's Body in Corinth: The Politics of a Metaphor* (Minneapolis: Fortress Press, 2008), 91.

those words from a grandfather when I was a small boy. In my grandfather's condemnation it was meant to include the whole world of children. It stung then as a child. This passage, when it seems to be coming from Paul, has hurt a great many women, in the same or worse way for far too long.

The NRSV placed the command about not touching a woman (1 Cor. 7:1) in quotes. The editors of the NRSV should have done the same with the silencing text. It would have been helpful if Paul had responded, "Now concerning your idea that women should be silent in worship...". If this letter was performed, and not just read, as suggested in the previous chapter, those listening to it would *hear* Paul. In this instance they might have heard Paul's anger.

Not too surprisingly, we also have an issue with recognizing *sarcasm* in Paul, but from what we know of him, we shouldn't be too surprised. Based on what we know about Paul and his women co-workers, as well as his affirmation of women participating in worship leadership (1 Cor. 11:2–16 above), we must expect that Paul would be offended by the command silencing women.

We should as well take the closing verse and mark it as Paul's sarcastic question. In Paul's true voice, 1 Cor 14:36 should read "**What!** Did the word of God originate with you? **What!** Are you the only ones it has reached?"

To be sure the translation in the NRSV doesn't contain the tone of his question. There we read, "Or did the word of God originate with you? Or are you the only ones it reached?" Seeing these as two questions helps. The "*What!*" is the suggested translation of a little word that is a single letter in Greek, namely *eta* which in Greek looks like this: η. As Odell-Scott noted this was "a two-fold negative rhetorical query."[97] If we read this as what Paul really wanted to say about the matter, he didn't feel a need to elaborate. Those who wanted to silence women were simply and flat out wrong. Odell-Scott, rightly concludes, "In fact, the text is one of the most emphatic statements *for* female participation in the worship of the church to be found in the New Testament."[98] As far as Paul was concerned Roman and Greek-speaking men were to show due respect to women as *equals* in worship.

---

[97] Odell-Scott, "In Defense of an Egalitarian," 100.
[98] Odell-Scott, "Let Women Speak," 90.

One final note: even the scholars behind the NRSV translation had their reservations about this command for women to be silent. They placed the entire passage in parenthesis. I doubt that the average reader even notices. It is not explained in a footnote in the NRSV. When it comes to Paul's views of women, we must resist the traditional interpretations which have often failed to see the context in which the Christian faith was initially formed. We need to look, not at the success of the patriarchal world that created an ecclesial Paul, but at the revolutionary aspects of Paul's message and his example that have been both forgotten and neglected. When it comes to issues of marriage, divorce, and celibacy the unmanly Paul was also out of sync with the norms of the Roman society.

9.5 Marriage, divorce, and celibacy in an eschatological frame

Earlier I made some comments about members of churches I've served who have never liked or understood Paul. More than once in my ministry I heard someone complaining about Paul the celebrate writing about marriage. What did he know about marriage? A few times in my research I have found a couple of scholars wondering if he ever was married and had become a widower. If so, he never mentioned it. In what follows you will find a Paul who could affirm celibacy, but who also had a view of marriage few Roman men could have endorsed.

Marriages in the ancient world were not based on love. They were arranged to maintain one's social class and to produce babies, primarily boys to carry on the family lineage. Girls were first married at about the age of fourteen and had no choice in the matter. Marriage for both was usually according to Sarah Ruden a "reality [that looked] rather joyless, with both husbands and wives—especially wives—locked into biological production."[99] What a different idea Paul had when it came to marriage. He also understood the real tragedy in divorce, and amazing for his time, affirmed celibacy. These topics are all found in 1 Corinthians 7.

By any measure coming from a man in the first century Paul had a most unusual and unexpected response to the issues facing this early Jesus community with regard to marriage, divorce, and celibacy. In particular, Paul addressed *both* men and women in this passage and did so in an argument that seems to contain "almost

---

[99] Ruden, *Paul Among the People*, 109.

monotonously parallel statements about the mutual obligations of men and women."[100] But did Paul see men and women as equal partners, not only in the context of belonging to the community of believers, but also in the context of their lives with regard to issues of marriage and celibacy? That level of egalitarianism will prove to be consistent with the other surprising aspects of Paul discussed above. Pauline scholar John Bristow has stated in regard to Paul's views on marriage and celibacy that "He was not a believer in the inferiority of women. He did not advocate a secondary role for women in the Church. He did not teach some notion of a divine hierarchy, with husbands ruling over their wives."[101]

The entirety of Chapter 7 encourages seeing a different Paul. Polaski has rightfully noted the "evenhanded tone as regards gender"[102] in this chapter: "Through most of the chapter, Paul instructs his readers as if women had the *same freedom* to choose their sexual and marital status as men."[103] To be sure Paul's eschatology was at work, counseling that it was best to stay as you are for this time. Polaski sums it up: "Those who are single or widowed should remain single; those who are married should not seek divorce. Even those who are engaged are commended for not going through with the marriage—unless, of course, the more serious problem of uncontrollable desire recommends marriage as the better option."[104]

Paul, while condemning any man visiting a prostitute (1 Cor 5:1-13), could affirm for marriage a kind of sexual equality to be at work based on the mutual needs of each partner. What stands out in his comments on marriage involving two believers, or even a marriage involving an unbeliever, is the complete mutuality Paul expected to see in such relationships. This is not what was affirmed in the Roman world or expressed even within Judaism. Paul wrote something completely unexpected with these words: "The husband should give to his wife her conjugal rights, and likewise the wife to her husband" (1 Cor 7:3). Authority in their relationship is to be shared. It is not for

---

[100] Margaret M. Mitchell, "Virgins, Widows, and Wives: The Women of 1 Corinthians 7," in *A Feminist Companion to Paul*, ed. Amy-Jill Levine with Marianne Blickenstaff (New York: T & T Clark International, 2004), 148.

[101] Bristow, *What Paul Said about Women*, 2.

[102] Sandra Hock Polaski, *A Feminist Introduction to Paul*. (St. Louis, MO: Chalice Press, 2005), 49.

[103] Polaski, *A Feminist Introduction to Paul*, 49.

[104] Polaski, *A Feminist Introduction to Paul*, 49.

one to have power over the other. Ruden states, "Paul comes up with something altogether new: husbands and wives must have sex with each other on demand, because they both need it—it's the reason they got married."[105]

More surprising was Paul's affirmation of celibacy, which he knew was not for all. It could easily be interpreted as subversive advice. Paul makes mention of apostles like James and Cephas who each traveled with a believing wife. He said he had the same right, but obviously, did not exercise it. (1 Cor 9:5) A theme in many of Paul's letters is his call to imitate him as he described his embrace of Christ of crucified.[106] The theme began with 1 Thessalonians where Paul applauded this community which had become "imitators of us and of the Lord" (1 Thess 1:6). While we might view a request to be "like me" as vain or pompous, Castelli viewed Paul's statement here as a matter of *historical fact*[107] regarding what she identified as a rather consistent theme in Greco-Roman antiquity. A great many rhetoricians and philosophers expected and called for their students to imitate them, or what in the Greek world was termed *memesis*.[108]

Paul's willingness not only to affirm his celibacy but to see this as a justifiable decision for other followers of Jesus was actually, in the words of Sandra Hack Polaski, the kind of commendation certain to "have risked Paul running afoul of the Roman authorities."[109] She points out that Roman law in the first century sought to make it a requirement that all between the ages of twenty and fifty must be married. What mattered were children, But Paul's advice about marriage focused on husband and wife, not children.

Another important context for understanding the dynamic situation in which many of these early followers lived was that some of them had a non-believing partner and, very likely, someone who was a pagan participating in the idolatrous practices Paul found repugnant. Paul had said that the unbelieving partner in such a marriage was made holy by the one who followed Christ. (1 Cor.

---

[105] Ruden, *Paul Among the People*, 101

[106] Paul's calling for others to imitate him will be discussed in more detail in Chapter 10 "Paul in Trouble."

[107] Elizabeth Castelli, "Paul on Women and Gender," in *Women and Christian Origins*, ed. Ross Sheppard Kraemer and Mary Rose D'Angelo (New York: Oxford University Press, 1999), 92.

[108] Castelli, "Paul on Women and Gender," 62.

[109] Polaski, *A Feminist Introduction to Paul*, 50.

7:14) Moreover, Paul deemed that their children, were made holy as well.

Dale Martin points out that Paul's views on the matter of impurity, such as "fears about pollution resulting from dangerous eating, sexual intercourse, desire, or unveiled women must seem very strange and archaic to modern ears."[110] However, with regard to the question of a follower of the Messiah living with a pagan spouse Paul did not seem to be worried about pollution. The direction in which purity flows is back *toward* the unbelieving spouse. Martin says that Paul "…insists that the purity of Christ holds such power that it may, in certain situations, purify even nonbelievers. The Christian is purified by his or her location "in" Christ; by extension, the unbelieving spouse is purified by his or her location 'in' the living spouse."[111] I find Paul's reference to the *holiness* of their children equally surprising because Paul never suggested that the purpose of marriage was procreation. This is the only reference in any of the undisputed letters where Paul made mention of children as part of the early messiah communities.

The matter of divorce had to come from questions the Corinthians addressed to Paul. What we find in Paul is his awareness of the command of Jesus forbidding divorce. (1 Cor. 7:10) The word for divorce, according to Ruden, was to "throw out," and was the same word for "disowning a child." A divorced woman was one put out on the street.[112] What had to be an amazing concession, in regard to divorce, Paul was giving permission to a woman to separate herself from her non-believing husband. Her choices, in that context would be to stay unmarried or be reconciled to her husband. Amazingly, Paul did *not* grant the same right to the man. He simply said, "the husband should not divorce his wife" (1 Cor 7:11). It has been noted that granting a woman the right to stay unmarried was counter to the command of Caesar Augustus. "Everyone between 25 and 60, single, widowed, or divorced, were required to marry or remarry and were expected to have at least three children."[113]

---

[110] Martin, *The Corinthian Body*, 136.
[111] Martin, *The Corinthian Body*, 218.
[112] Ruden, *Paul Among the People*, 113.
[113] Lewis, *Paul's Spirit of Adoption*, 129.

There is also what Polaski has called a *tenderness* in Paul, and a willingness to let his pastoral concern, not his theology, lead him into offering advice.[114] We see the same with regard to a believer living with a non-believer. The entire chapter (1 Cor 7) gives us a pragmatic Paul addressing questions from those who may shy away from maintaining existing marriages or entering into marriage. However, time was actually measured, the early Pauline communities were living with an apocalyptic mindset in which time was short.

In the spirit of this book, we have not found Paul to be a prude — his recognition of mutuality in marriage was remarkable in his world. How did others in his communities see him? I believe they saw him as an unmanly man. He did not define marriage from a man's point of view. Instead, Paul was embracing of all those who weren't accepted or honored in the patriarchal world of privilege.

Our wrestling with Paul at this point means we must acknowledge the reality of scripture as a gendered text. It was written by men, and most of its heroes are men. Everywhere Paul walked, whether in Thessalonica, Corinth, or the many other Romanized cities in which he walked, all of the public buildings and arches proclaimed an ideology of "gendered text."[115] Brittany Wilson captures the same picture with her comment that "gendered images depicting Rome's political dominance littered the imperial landscape."[116] While Wilson's scholarship uniquely focused on Paul as found in Acts, we have been looking for him in his letters. It is a most surprising Paul to be found there.

---

[114] Polaski, *A Feminist Introduction to Paul*, 52-3

[115] Davina C. Lopez, *Apostle to the Conquered*, 123. The exact quote is: "Ignorance of the gendered texture of Roman imperial ideology prevents New Testament scholars and other interpreters from fully grasping the alternativeness of Paul's call and subsequent work among the Gentiles."

[116] Wilson, *Unmanley Men*, 28.

Chapter 10
Paul Slave of Christ

> Much about the behavior of people of *all* classes today, is in fact, as unknown and undocumented as was much of the lives of common people in the past.[1]

> And there is something on the stage of history that was not there before: a community that calls itself by the name of the crucified Messiah.[2]

> But this freedom, freedom from the dreaded disease of bigotry and prejudice, according to Paul, is available to any and all who need it today. It has only to be claimed![3]

Eric Hobsbawm, the historian of history, discussed the emergence in the last century of "social history." It stood in contrast to "the old kind of intellectual history which isolated written ideas from their human context..." Hobsbawm asserted that wasn't his cup of tea. What he wished historians to attend to is this: "The social or societal aspects of man's being cannot be separated from other aspects of his being, except at the cost of tautology or extreme trivialization."[4] The danger implied here is relevant to our search for Paul as we pull him from the dusty bookshelves of dogmatic theologians. Paul needs to be discovered in the first century. If we could time-travel back to his world we would see him in the busy, noisy, smelly alleys lined with the workshops of hard-working, barely surviving artisans. We could find him, perhaps next door to Prisca and Aquila, asking for help with repairing someone's leather knapsack. Looking at how he was dressed we would probably conclude that he was a common

---

[1] Eric Hobsbawm, *On History* (New York, The New Press, 1997), 215.
[2] Meyer, *The Word in This World*, 14.
[3] Amos Jones, *Paul's Message of Freedom: What Does it Mean to the Black Church?* (Valley Forge: Judson Press, 1984), 67.
[4] Hobsbawm, *On History*, 75.

slave, but the clothes of those struggling for their daily bread didn't allow you to tell who was a slave and who was free.

The strategy here remains to find Paul in his letters. He was in prison in two of the seven letters he wrote. In his shortest letter, Philemon, he was not a prisoner of Rome, but titled himself "Paul, prisoner of Jesus Christ." Those are the first words in the Letter to Philemon. This letter is a major key for letting us see Paul's radical response to slavery in the Roman world.

Paul *remembered*, especially in Acts, was someone who never stayed long in any prison. At the end of the Acts account, nevertheless, he was still under house arrest in Rome. Though he could be arrested, as we learn at the end of Acts, his trump card in that account was his status of being a free man, indeed even a Roman citizen. What citizen of Rome, though, would ever begin a letter, to Rome of all places, declaring that his primary identity was as "slave of Christ"? (Rom 1.1) The second Greek word in that letter was *doulos* — "slave." Jennings makes the claim that this was a "gesture of solidarity with the dregs of the social order."[5] This understanding about the reality of slavery in the first century has taken a long time to be understood.

Biblical scholars for centuries relied on the field of classics to understand the history of Greece and Rome. Scholars in that world found "ancient Greek and Roman slavery...an embarrassment to be downplayed, hedged about with sophisticated apologies, or, if possible, explained away."[6] New Testament scholars were subsequently led astray, thinking, for example, that most slaves had a path to freedom with the process of manumission. Another assumption was that being a slave to someone of importance, say an emperor, or even Christ, meant having a special status. Only a few could tell that story.

Paul called himself a *slave of Christ*, but it is not what people hear from English translations frequently used in contemporary churches. In many translations Paul calls himself "a servant of Jesus Christ."[7] *A servant* and not a *slave*. In Paul's world a *doulos* was never understood as a *servant*. There was a perfectly good word in

---

[5] Theodore W. Jennings, Jr., *Outlaw Justice: The Messianic Politics of Paul* (Stanford: Stanford University Press. 2013), 17.

[6] Richard A. Horsley, "The Slave Systems of Classical Antiquity and Their Reluctant Recognition by Modern Scholars." *Semeia*, 83–84 (1998): 19.

[7] The NRSV translation. It's the same in the King James and the NIV.

Greek for a servant: *diakonos*. From it we derive our word deacon, and in many churches that designates an honorable and important ordained office.

The purpose of this chapter involves acknowledging the realities of slavery in the first century, and the absolutely incongruous message followers of Jesus had to confront with a Paul who expected them "through love to become slaves of one another" (Gal 5:13). Only as we explore the ramifications of that status in the context of Roman slave society will we begin to capture the provocative declaration of Paul declaring himself a "*slave of Christ*" (Rom 1:1).

This chapter is offering a Paul who sees slaves as *equal* members of *all* who belong to Christ, but this is a dramatic contrast with a later view of church leaders as *slave masters*. Once more the *remembered* Paul from writings decades after Paul offers a troubling picture. Dale Martin notes how Titus 1:7 "speaks of the overseers as *oikonomoi*[8] of God, as portraying local church leaders to be slave *masters* within the church."[9] Martin refers to the many places in the ancient world where Christian leaders used the term "slave of Christ" to identify those who "are active in the world as Christ's agents and wield his authority." He adds that such leaders expected to be "rewarded with higher status, more authority, and more power."[10] Martin makes a compelling case that from the *later* letters attributed to Paul that the title "slave of Christ" was a reference to the authority of the founding leader.[11]

The "remembered Paul"—and *not* the Paul calling himself "slave of Christ—is the Paul who offered advice to other slave masters in Titus. "Tell slaves to be submissive to their masters and to give satisfaction in every respect; they are not to talk back, not to pilfer, but to show complete fidelity, so that in everything they may be an ornament to the doctrine of God our savior." (Titus 2:9-10) As we've seen most of the most troubling statements attributed to Paul derive from the Pastoral Epistles. For example: "Let a woman learn in silence with full submission" (1 Tim 2:11). From that same letter came words that were gladly cherished by slave

---

[8] The Greek word for a household overseer.
[9] Martin, *Slavery as Salvation*, 55.
[10] Martin, *Slavery as Salvation*, 55.
[11] Martin, *Slavery as Salvation*, 56.

owners in the dark chapters of American history when slave ships brought a stream of captured Africans to the American ports. In church services on Southern plantations led by white ministers, many an American slave heard these words from 1Timothy: "Let all who are under the yoke of slavery regard their masters as worthy of honor, so that the name of God and the teaching may not be blasphemed" (2 Tim 6:1).

Some might wish that these sentiments be expunged from the Bible, but there they are. I am mindful of a collect from the Book of Common Prayer with this plea, "Grant us so to hear them, read, mark, learn, and inwardly digest them..."[12] It is a wonderful prayer. But there are some passages in the Bible that are hard to swallow or, as the prayer asks us to "digest." A significant example of hard-to-digest scripture is the story of Howard Thurman's grandmother. Thurman was a pastor, philosopher and theologian who became a mentor to Martin Luther King. I first encountered this story from the book by J. R. Kirk with the great title, *Jesus I have Loved, But Paul?* The book is more of a dialogue between the gospels and what Paul was saying. This is Kirk's account of the story:

> Howard Thurman, born in 1900...home for summer vacation from college, asked his grandmother why she would not allow him to read any of the Pauline letters. "During the days of slavery," she said, "the master's minister would occasionally hold services for the slaves. Old man McGhee was so mean that he would not let a Negro minister preach to his slaves. Always the white minister used as his text something from Paul. At least three or four times a year he used as a text:
>
> 'Slaves, be obedient to them that are your masters . . . , as unto Christ.'
>
> Then he would go on to show how it was God's will that we were slaves and how, if we were good and happy slaves, God would bless us. I promised my Maker that if I ever learned to read and if freedom ever came, I would not read that part of the Bible."[13]

---

[12] 1979 Book of Common Prayer, 236.

[13] J. R. Kirk, *Jesus I have Loved, but Paul? A Narrative Approach to the Problem of Pauline Christianity* (Grand Rapids: Baker Academic, 2012), 236.

My hope is that someone pointed out to Howard Thurman's grandmother that Paul did not write those words. There is no way, however, given where things stood in the world of biblical studies in the 19th century, that his grandmother would have known the research reflected here that dismantles the assumptions of racism, prejudice, patriarchy, and misogyny traditionally ascribed to Paul.

Fortunately, Howard Thurman didn't follow his grandmother's advice, though he knew the pain and sorrow from which she spoke. In his book *Jesus and the Disinherited* Thurman tells the same story and adds a haunted truth: "It cannot be denied that too often the weight of the Christian movement has been on the side of the strong and the powerful and against the weak and oppressed — this, despite the gospel."[14]

We're left with the question of whether Paul deliberately choose a slave name for himself as a follower of Jesus Messiah to mark his "rebirth" into a new identity? If so, he was doing what slave-owners commonly did as their first act of ownership: replace the slave's name with a new name having no connections with his or her past. The slave's former name died with his former self"[15] As was considered in Chapter 2, did a man with the proud name of Saul become a Paulus, meaning small?

10.1 A slave society

While the act of obliterating a slave's former identity may not seem violent, I have been stunned to discover how truly violent and oppressive the treatment of slaves was in first century Rome. There is no doubt that everyone living under Roman rule knew that slaves were always dangerously close to being beaten or killed — and that often meant crucified! No free person would ever want to trade places with someone in slavery!

The world that Jesus knew was marked by the same misery. Jennifer Glancy has paid particular attention to Jesus' teachings involving slaves. "In the parables of Jesus," she points out, "the bodies of slaves are vulnerable to abuse. Beaten, stoned, and executed, the figure of the parabolic slave is repeatedly the locus of

---

[14] Thurman Howard, *Jesus and the Disinherited* (Boston: Beacon Press.2012), 31.
[15] Orlando Patterson, *Slavery and Social Death: A Comparative Study*. (Cambridge: Harvard University Press, 1982), 55.

corporal discipline and other bodily violations."[16] She also notes how Jesus taught the disciples to be of service, that is, to be slaves of each other: "Whoever wishes to be first among you must be slave (*doulos*) of all. (Mark 10:44) His example at the last supper, in washing the feet of the disciples was done in light of that commandment. While we can picture Jesus doing a job reserved for slaves, we must recognize that slaves were also part of some of the parables he told. In those parables with slaves (i.e., Matt 22:1–14 and 24:45–51) they are simply characters in the stories. Wherever Jesus looked, he saw slaves. Did it bother him? We don't know except he died the death Rome reserved for traitors or slaves.

Rome was a slave society. A segment of America was also a slave society. Was there a difference between the two? In terms of the level of violence and degradation of other humans there was little difference. As James Cone states with a clarity few have been willing to express regarding the death of Jesus on the cross "…he died like a [lynched black victim] or a common [black] criminal in torment on a tree of shame."[17] Whether it was the rope that killed Sam Hose, one of the more than 5,000 African Americans lynched in the post-civil war era, or the cross, Cone writes "In each case, it was a cruel, agonizing, and contemptible death."[18]

The American system, however, was clearly based on race and skin color, while Rome made slaves out of the range of peoples under their domination. The economic demand in both societies continually required more slaves. One estimate is that from about 50 BCE to 150 CE Rome captured or gained through birth 500,000 new slaves each year. They were spread out, of course, throughout the Roman empire. The average number of new African slaves brought yearly to America in the first half of the 19th century was 28,000 with the greatest number to arrive in any one year being 65,000.[19] From the 17th century and well into the 19th century over

---

[16] Jennifer Glancy, *Slavery in Early Christianity* (Minneapolis: Fortress Press, 2006), Loc. 2026 of 3838.

[17] James H. Cone, *The Cross and the Lynching Tree* (Maryknoll, NY: Orbis Books 2011), 161.

[18] Cone, *The Cross and the Lynching Tree*, 161.

[19] Keith R. Bradley, *Slavery and Society at Rome* (New York: Cambridge University Press), 32.

11.5 million Africans rode on slave ships to the Americas.[20] As was true on the large estates of the Roman empire, slaves in the American South were needed in the agricultural sector. Slaves in Rome and in America produced a lifestyle of wealth and comforts for their masters with lives shortened for their unrewarded labor.

Not unlike the system that prevailed in the American South, the Roman slave owner had great power over any slave, as they were considered *property*. Slaves had no recourse to the law for anything that happened to them. This was *chattel slavery* which simply means they belonged to the household, alongside of the animals. Thus, Bryant noted, "Without question, the social reality of the Roman world meant that slaves endured uninterrupted violence."[21]

Keith Bradley, a classics scholar, offered research at the end of the last century that upended a long-held assumption that slavery in Rome was somehow more benign than other forms. As J. Albert Harrill noted in a paper commending Bradley, slavery in Rome was about as awful as anyone could imagine. Harrill notes how Bradley's work "suggests Roman slavery to have been more brutal than other forms in world history, precisely because the Romans lacked a biological or racial ideology for their institution."[22] In contrast to Aristotle's philosophy of slavery as natural, the Roman idea was a form of social control in which slaves were animalized.[23] They were like any other animal, that required beatings, and which could be sold and resold.

Another noted classicist engaged in revisionist studies of slavery in the Greco-Romans world is Orlando Patterson. He quotes the Latin term *"instrumentum vocal"* to point out that one's slave was regarded as a *speaking tool*.[24] In addition to implying the slave's being was simply functional, Patterson explained: "The typical slave in the Roman view was a "vocal instrument," a nonperson to be used

---

[20] Clarice J. Martin, "'Somebody Done Hoodoo'd the Hoodoo Man': Language, Power, Resistance, and the Effective History of Pauline Texts in American Slavery," *Semeia* 83–84 (1998): 208.

[21] K. Edwin Bryant, *Paul and the Rise of the Slave: Death and Resurrection of the Oppressed in the Epistle to the Romans* (Boston: Brill, 2016), 30.

[22] J. Albert Harrill, "Slavery and Inhumanity: Keith Bradley's Legacy on Slavery in New Testament Studies,". *Biblical Interpretation* 21, no 4–5 (2013): 511.

[23] Harrill, "Slavery and Inhumanity," 511.

[24] Patterson, *Slavery and Social Death*, 337.

sexually, disciplined with the whip, and questioned in court only under torture since his word was utterly without honor."[25]

If there were truly happy slaves, they surely were few in number. Bradley allows for that possibility. "At the individual level, certainly, slaves were at times positively embraced by their masters and treated with personal regard."[26] It was also true that if your master was a distinguished person in the world, his or her slaves might assume some of that status for themselves. Thus, Dale Martin writes, "...Naming oneself the slave of an important person was a way of claiming status for oneself."[27] He extends that argument to assert that Paul's claim to be a slave of Christ was of that nature. I explore this concept further on in the chapter.

To be sure the dreams slaves had for freedom led some to take desperate measures. The historian Bradley has examined slave-owners' documents that discuss slave resistance. Slave-owners had to be constantly on the alert lest a slave escape, commit theft, or simply exercise deceitful and mischievous behavior. In Roman and Greek comedies, slaves were often characterized as cunning. Bradley explained this common perception: "Slave behavior could only be construed as misbehavior by those it inconvenienced. Slaves themselves, Roman as much as any other, had to find every means possible to cope with adversity and they constructed in the process a morality that could be diametrically opposed to that of their owners."[28] There were only a few violent slave resistance movements in all the centuries of Roman rule. But far more frequently slaves ran away in a desperate attempt to gain freedom. Bradley recognized the "enormous courage and resourcefulness"[29] required by a slave runaway against the overwhelming odds of recapture and violent reprisal.

Almost any way out of slavery was impossible to achieve, but there was a legal way out called *manumission*. This was a one-way transaction, solely at the behest of the master. The word *manumission* can mean "given your freedom." It comes from two Latin words *manus* (hand) and *mittere* (to let go). In reality, a manumitted slave was still connected to his or her master with definite expectations of

---

[25] Patterson, *Slavery and Social Death*, 92.
[26] Patterson, *Slavery and Social Death*, 77.
[27] Martin, *Corinthian Body* 48.
[28] Bradley, *Slavery and Society at Rome*, 101.
[29] Bradley, *Slavery and Society at Rome*, 128.

loyalty and servitude as long as their master was alive. Manumitted slaves could earn money called a *peculium,* and if it grew in size, it might even purchase their freedom—*theoretically.* The indignity of being a slave would follow the manumitted slave into a freedom that was never, or rarely, truly free. As Bryant noted "manumission did not make one entirely exempt from the negative connotations associated with slave status."[30] And, should the freed slave die first, it was the master's right to inherit what the slave would leave behind. Freedom, though, was a word on Paul's lips.

Excursus 10.1 Paul's Message of Freedom
   The title of this section, borrowed from the book by Amos Jones, Jr., acknowledges that he is making an argument that challenges the views of many black preachers and theologians. Jones salutes Paul as "a dynamic revolutionary for freedom," not the Paul that "Black theologians...malign Paul and treat him roughly for what seems to be his endorsement of the institution of slavery."[31] What was fascinating for me to discover from the book by Jones and the book by Lisa Bowens is how many African American freed slaves and also those in bondage in the years preceding the civil war read Paul as a friend of their desire to end slavery.[32]
   What shaped Paul's ministry, or the direction in which it took him, was what Martin Luther King, Jr. called the gospel of freedom. As King ended his letter from the Birmingham jail he compared himself to Paul who had "...left his little village in Tarsus and carried the gospel of Jesus Christ to practically every hamlet and city of the Graeco-Roman world..."[33] Despite the hyperbole in that statement—there were many places where Paul did not go—the important message is that Paul's gospel was grounded in the concept of *freedom* which was at the heart of King's ministry.
   A powerful concept of social and historical change was central for Paul. The Jewish story of the Exodus was a major structural

---

[30] K. E. Edwin Bryant, *Paul and the Rise of the Slave: Death and Resurrection of the Oppressed in the Epistle to the Romans* (Boston: Brill, 2016), 109.

[31] Jones, *Paul's Message of Freedom,* 17.

[32] Lisa, M. Bowens, *African American Readings of Paul: Reception, Resistance, and Transformation.* (Grand Rapids: William B. Eerdmans Publishing Company, 2020). Some examples from her book are used in the concluding chapter of this book.

[33] Allen Dwight, Callahan, "Brother Saul: An Ambivalent Witness to Freedom," *Semeia,* 83-84 (1998): 247.

change that was and still is part of the annual remembrance of that event, namely *Passover*. It is in light of that formative event as it continues to shape Jewish consciousness to this very day, where we will find Paul living a story of freedom in the first century of the common era.

Another component of Paul's Judean faith involved a communal ethical commandment from God: "You shall not wrong or oppress a resident alien, for you were aliens in the land of Egypt" (Exod 22:21). It was this passage that led Rachel Adelman to conclude: "What raises us to 'chosenness' and confers a claim to that gift is the mandate of compassion for the stranger in our midst, and remembering that we were once (and on an existential level, may always be), strangers in a strange land. We are called upon to link living in the land with compassion for and just behavior towards those 'strangers' who dwell among us."[34] That compassion began with the call of Abraham, who clearly was a model for Paul, as he wandered farther and farther away from the land where he was born.

The warning of the theologian Amos Wilder rings in my ears regarding more academic appraisals of Christianity. He wrote, "We tend to think that Christianity began as a matter of ideas and ideals rather than as a bloody drama involving men's primordial relationships and loyalties and as a succession of trials, imprisonments, excommunications and family cleavages."[35] All of those human realities Wilder lists are reflected in the Biblical story and provide the background for each of Paul's letters.

The two equally dramatic events in the Jewish story that are key to understanding Paul are *exodus* and *exile*. To be sure the Exodus narrative is linked to the Patriarchs and Matriarchs (Abraham and Sarah, Isaac and Rebekah, Jacob, and Rachel). Jacob's son Joseph, sold into slavery, rose to wealth and prominence before he welcomed his own family and by extension the Hebrew people to Egypt to save them from famine. There they became forced laborers

---

[34] Rachel Adelman, ""My Father Was a Wandering Aramean . . . ": The Ethical Legacy of Our Origins in Exile (Parashat Ki Tavo, Deuteronomy 26:1–29:8)," Huffington Post, Dec. 7, 2016. Found at: https://www.huffpost.com/entry/my-father-was-a-wandering-aramean-the-ethical_b_57e1e98de4b05d3737be5099.

[35] Amos Wilder, *Otherworldliness and the New Testament* (Chicago: S.C.M. Book Club, 1955), 22.

for Pharaoh until that fateful Passover night that led them from slavery to the promised land.

The bookend story, and the memory haunting the Jewish community for 400 years preceding Paul, was the Babylonian exile. It was in this period of time that messianic expectations permeated Jewish thought since it seemed as if God had abandoned both Jerusalem and the temple. One day, though, God would return. "He would return in person. He would return in glory. He would return to judge and save. He would return to bring about the new exodus, overthrowing the enemies that had enslaved his people. He would return to establish his glorious, tabernacling presence in their midst. He would return to rule over the whole world. He would come back to be king."[36]

The story for Paul wasn't that Jews were not free from slavery in their deliverance from Egypt — in that sense they were free — but that the whole world was somehow enslaved in *sin*. No one was free! Thus, the story that had great significance to Paul was of Moses receiving the Torah, the law, or *the teachings*, on Mount Sinai. Paul was clear that this gift came four hundred thirty years after Abraham. (Gal 3:17) "But the scripture has imprisoned all things under the power of sin so that what was promised through faith in Jesus Christ might be given to those who believe" (Gal 3:22).

With the coming of Christ, the very idea of some claiming privilege over others was not to be found. In the words of Bridgett Kahl Paul was calling for a "new body of one-an-otherness..."[37] The Greek word *allēlōn* appears seven times in the last two chapters of Galatians. It means "one another." Where the vertical world sees the other as "less than," in the horizontal vision we do not compete against one another (Gal 5:26). The call is to "bear one another's burdens" (Gal 6:2). Only through *allēlōn* could true freedom be experienced. This was Paul's gift to those in slavery. Despite a system that words alone could not change, Paul called slaves to have an identity *in Christ* that gave them dignity and hope. They could have a place in the *ekklēsia* where there was to be mutual respect.

---

[36] Wright, *The Faithfulness of God*, 653–54.
[37] Kahl, *Galatians Re-Imagined*, 279.

10.2 Did Onesimus become free?

N. T. Wright begins his massive work entitled *Paul and the Faithfulness of God*[38] by focusing on Paul's shortest letter—the one addressed to Philemon. It was a plea from Paul to accept Onesimus back into his household as a *brother* and no longer as *slave*. How was it that Onesimus came to Paul in the first place? Paul does not say, but in the history of commentary on this letter most scholars have assumed Onesimus was a runaway slave, and now was being sent back to his master.[39] Wright supports this thesis (calling it "the majority opinion,"), though he acknowledges that there is a difference of opinion on this matter.[40] This "majority opinion" also supports the all-too-common attitude grounded in slave societies that slaves are untrustworthy.[41] Tertullian, writing in the second century wrote that "slaves were all spies who would betray their owners as a matter of course; they were not to be trusted at all."[42] Nonetheless, it is obvious from this very short letter that Paul trusted Onesimus and wanted him to be in ministry with him. We will need to consider that Onesimus had been *sent* to Paul and that will mean he was *not* a runaway slave.[43]

Noting Paul's willingness to cover any costs incurred by Philemon some scholars suggest that Onesimus also stole money from his master, or had incurred debts. Even Marcus Borg and John Dominic Crossan, who emphatically emphasize Paul's counter-cultural and anti-imperial rhetoric, subscribe to the view that

---

[38] Wright, *The Faithfulness of God*. The adjective *massive* is appropriate for a book with 1,658 pages.

[39] This theme can be traced back 1500 years to St. Crysostom. (349–407 CE). Christians still owned slaves in his world, centuries after Paul. The advice of Chrysostom, the Archbishop of Constantinople, was for the wealthy Christians to have just a few slaves. No matter how we might want to deny Christian support for slavery, it is part of our legacy of racism that haunts Christianity to this day.

[40] Wright, *Faithfulness*, 7.

[41] Jennifer Glancy notes that in Torah we find instructions for "ancient Israelites [to] shelter runaway slaves rather than return them to their owners." *Slavery in Early Christianity*, loc. 1768 of 3838.

[42] Bradley, *Slavery and Society at Rome*, 149.

[43] Allan D. Callahan, *Embassy of Onesimus: The Letter of Paul to Philemon* (Valley Forge, PA: Trinity Press International, 1997), 34–35. Callahan offers a unique theory that Onesimus, while not a run-away slave, was actually Philemon's real brother. The two had become alienated from one another. I could not find other scholars endorsing this theory.

Onesimus was in serious trouble with his master, seeking in Paul a friend of his master who would protect him.[44]

It is frequently noted that the name "Onesimus" is also a word that meant "useful." Followers of Christ might take on new name as discussed in Chapter 3, but slaves had to accept whatever their master called them, which was often, according to Horsley "a demeaning name."[45] Patterson defines the slave system as *"as the permanent, violent domination of majorly alienated and generally dishonored persons."*[46] In the letter to Philemon Paul speaks about Onesimus. "Formerly he was useless to you, but now he is useful both to you and me" (Phlm 11). Was this simply Paul making a pun on his name, or did it reflect the world in which the sexual use of slaves was normative.[47] Slaves did not have any rights to their own bodies! Marchal considers this a possible reality. "Onesimus's name reflects his own placement within this imperially gendered slave system, since it contains a constellation of characteristics sought by owners in their slaves. The slave exists not for his or her own benefit, profit, or pleasure but for the enjoyable use of the master, and Paul's description of Onesimus in terms of his utility . . . reinforces the status quo of this erotically kyriarchal system."[48]

I suggest we consider the possibility that Onesimus was *sent* to Paul who was in prison. Anyone in prison would depend on friends for their basic needs. To be in prison meant you were awaiting trial. To be sure, some prisoners were forgotten or died before they ever came to trial. The conditions could be horrible and the guards often had the despicable duty of being chained to the prisoners they guarded. If a prisoner was to receive food, or clothing, or anything for their basic needs it required help from friends outside of the prison. Wansink notes that visitors probably brought bribes for the guards and that "often made incarceration more tolerable, if not more humane. Sometimes they brought food and clothing. Sometimes they enabled the incarcerated to move to a better part of

---

[44] Marcus Borg and John Dominic Crossan, *The First Paul: Reclaiming the Radical Visionary Behind the Church's Conservative Icon* (New York: Harper Collins Publishers, 2009), 39; italics in original.

[45] Horsley, "The Slave Systems," 29.

[46] Patterson, *Slavery and Social Death*, 13. Italics in original

[47] See Excursus 10.2 below for more discussion on this topic.

[48] Joseph A. Marchal, "The Usefulness of Onesimus: The Sexual Use of Slaves and Paul's Letter to Philemon," *Journal of Biblical Literature* 130, no. 4 (2011): 760.

the prison. Sometimes they brought only moral support."⁴⁹ In his only other non-disputed prison letter, Philippians, Paul mentioned Epaphroditus who had been sent with gifts. (Phil. 4:18) It wasn't the first time that they had helped Paul. (Phil 4:16). The ministry of Onesimus, if he was sent to Paul in prison, most likely included gifts from the household of Philemon.

The sent-slave theory assumes that Onesimus did not come to Paul in desperation. Philemon, in other words wanted to help Paul who was in prison. Whatever help he offered had to be reflected in an earlier part of the letter where Paul said, "I have indeed received much joy and encouragement from your love" (Phlm 7a). When Paul said in verse 5 "I hear of your love for all the saints and your faith toward the Lord Jesus," it might have been a report from Onesimus who told Paul about the household in which he served.

The letter opens with greetings to three people: Philemon, Apphia, and Archippus. It is not a private letter. It is a community matter written to the *ekklēsia* in Philemon's house. Once more it is meant to be a letter *heard*. Moreover, each of the three individuals has a particular identity: friend, sister, fellow soldier. Though many interpreters suggest that Apphia might have been Philemon's wife, that is not the title Paul gave to her. I agree with Sara Winter's deduction: "Yet, if one analyzes the greeting in terms of social function, one notes that Apphia is addressed as "the sister" in her own right and not as the wife of one of the two men."⁵⁰

What was the status of Onesimus in Paul's eyes? He was sharing in the ministry alongside of Paul, and the Greek word *diakonē* is in Philemon 13. Paul also makes an appeal "on behalf of my child, Onesimus, whose father I have become during my imprisonment" (Phil 10). Paul's terminology reminds us of adoption as an important practice in Roman antiquity (see Chapter 4). It must have occurred with the baptism of Onesimus. Ironically Paul in his first letter to the Corinthians did not want people claiming their loyalty based on who performed their baptism. Here it mattered.

---

[49] Craig S. Wansink, *Chained in Christ: The Experience and Rhetoric of Paul's Imprisonments* (Sheffield: Sheffield Academic Press, 1996), 126.

[50] Sara C. Winter, "Methodological Observations on a New Interpretation of Paul's Letter to Philemon," *Union Seminary Quarterly Review* 39, no. 3 (1984): 206.

Another significant point is that Onesimus had no voice in this letter. Not surprisingly, there are no slave-authored stories from Roman times. As Harrill has noted, "The slave is a "living tool" caught between two 'masters' deciding on the use of his services."[51] Will he be returned to help Paul as requested, or will Philemon keep him as a slave, and most likely never hear from Paul again? While the question hangs in the air the entire community is *hearing* the letter with their eyes on Onesimus (the letter carrier) *and* Philemon.

What also should be emphasized is verse 13: "I wanted to keep him with me, so he might be of service [*diakonē*][52] to me in your place during my imprisonment." This isn't the word for a slave, *doulos*. Remember that Phoebe was called a *diakonos* in Romans 16:1, leading the NRSV to call her a *deacon*.[53] In giving this title to a woman (Phoebe) and to a slave (Onesimus) Paul indicates how he looked past their social status and measured their worth in terms of the shared life of the ekklēsia. Onesimus could be useful in ministry, perhaps working right alongside of Paul.

One little pronoun is significant. In so many of Paul's letters the second person plural pronoun is best understood with the Southern expression *Y'all*. From verse 4 in Philemon, however, it is the singular "you," meaning *you Philemon*. Paul expected this letter to be read in the context of worship, but knew that once the singular *you* was heard, all eyes would be on Philemon. What could they read on his face as Paul continued with what he called his "appeal?" ("…yet I would rather appeal to you on the basis of love" (Phil 9)). Philemon was being addressed with a theological question which might lead him to betray his place in society. Would Onesimus be sent back a free man? How would the other slaves react? What would others think? Did not his faith in Jesus

---

[51] As J. Albert Harrill has noted, "The slave is . . . services," in *Slaves in the New Testament*, Loc. 264 of 4260.

[52] The NRSV weakly translates this as "he might be of service to me," In the NIV Onesimus is there "helping" Paul. I think Paul was seeing Onesimus in a ministerial role.

[53] She is actually demoted in a number of translations to being *a servant* (e.g. King James Bible). Worse yet in the independent translation of Romans by Edgar J. Goodspeed she is called *a helper*. Also of note is that she is called a patron (*prostates*) in 16:2; see Jewett, *Romans*, 947.

Messiah and his relationship with Paul, mean that his slaves were his equals in Christ?

Paul's request to treat Onesimus as a brother is at the heart of the sent-slave interpretation of this letter. Winter points out how verses 8-14 "constitute a single, unusually constructed sentence."[54] She observes that the structure resembles what you would find in a petition before a court of law where you are might be asking for something or on behalf of someone. Indeed, those are Paul's words in verse 11, "I am appealing to you for my child Onesimus, whose father I have become during my imprisonment."

So many of the commentaries have their focus on the relationship between Onesimus and his master Philemon. What matters here, in direct contrast, is what Paul wanted with regard to Onesimus. He wanted to keep him as a coworker in Christ in his new status as a baptized follower of Jesus. Paul claims to be his father, which implied his baptism of Onesimus. Philemon is also beholden to Paul as we hear in verse 19, "I say nothing about your owing me even your own self." That may imply Paul having baptized Philemon as well. More than once, Paul called him his brother, as those in Christ were in a fictive family of brothers and sisters.

Paul also framed his relationship with the slave owner in economic terms. If the first part of the request involved a kind of legal petition, the second part of the letter involves more of a contractual relationship for which Paul took responsibility. Any debt that Onesimus might have had was assumed by Paul. Given the fact that freeing a slave also involved a tax paid Paul was willing to assume that part of the transaction.

In the context of where we might find Paul, however, with regard to slavery, I suggest that those favoring the "sent-slave" theory have a way of reading Philemon that leads toward a most radical conclusion. As I said above, I believe all eyes in that assembly hearing this letter were staring at the master of Onesimus. Those watching Philemon by name were Apphia, Archippus, and the "fellow workers" Mark, Aristarchus, Demas, and Luke (Phil 23-24).

---

[54] Winter, "Methodological Observations," 303.

This is not a private affair. It is something Paul wants all in the community connected to the ministry of Philemon to consider. The letter had to be read out loud first, and then this slave master would have to respond. Paul wrote that he expected as a result of the baptism, Onesimus' legal status would change. Paul stated he would like to have Onesimus back with him to work with him, but that could only happen if Philemon, as a result of the letter, recognized him not as his slave, but as his brother in Christ.

The key passage in this very short letter is this: "Perhaps this is the reason he was separated from you for a while, so that you might have him back forever, no longer as a slave (*doulos*) but more than a slave (*doulos*), a beloved brother—especially to me but how much more to you, both in the flesh and in the Lord" (Phlm 15-16).

The meaning of this for Winter is "slave and brother (Christian) are incompatible."[55] To be sure nowhere in the letter do we find the word "freedom." But in Paul's mind, because Onesimus was baptized in Christ, he no longer has a human master. The gospel of Christ is his freedom story.

We don't know how this all turned out, but there was a bishop of Ephesus at the end of the first century whose name was Onesimus. Could he be the one mentioned in Paul's letter? What we do know from the letter is that Onesimus *had* been a slave, but *no longer* could be such in Paul's eyes, or in the eyes of *any* claiming their identity in Christ, including Philemon.

10.3 Did Paul say, "Stay in slavery?" (1 Cor 7:21-24)

If the answer is in the affirmative, then we have significantly called into question what I suggested about the relationship between Paul and Onesimus, and in particular the response Paul hoped to receive from Philemon. The problem is posed by 1 Corinthians 7:21 which began with a question. "Were you a slave when called? Do not be concerned about it. Even if you can gain your freedom, make use of your present condition now more than ever."

This particular passage has had a most troubled history, particularly for those who were slaves in America and their descendants. Amos Jones has pointed out that 1 Cor 7:21 invites

---

[55] Winter, "Methodological Observations," 307.

"an erroneous and racist interpretation," coming from "conventional white theology and the majority of New Testament translations that convey the notion that Paul is exhorting slaves to remain in their state of servitude even after they receive the call."[56] There are other equally troubling passages. Does it mean the Bible should just be thrown away? That was a question asked by Frederick Douglass in regard to the experience of his people under the Fugitive Slave Bill (1850). He said,

"What do you do when you are told by the slaveholders of America that the Bible sanctions slavery? Do you go and throw your Bible into the fire? Do you sing out, "no union with the Bible!" Clear that thing is bad because I've been miss used, abused, and made bad use of? Do you throw it away on that account? No! You press it to your bosom all the more closely; you read it all the more diligently; improved from its pages that it is on the side of liberty — and not on the side of slavery."[57]

In her book *African American Readings of Paul* Lisa Bowens is aware of all the ways, mostly positive and affirming, that African Americans have found hope, dignity, freedom and promise not only in the Bible but in the words of Paul. She called it a "hermeneutic of trust."[58] That is the approach I am taking as we consider both 1 Cor. 7:21 above and 1 Cor. 7.24, "In whatever condition you were called, brothers and sisters, there remain with God."

The key to understanding where Paul stood involves not only his sense of being called to follow Jesus Messiah, but how his concept of *call* is central to understanding *who* belongs to Christ. It helps us to see that our troubled comments about slaves (1 Cor 7:21) come in an eight-verse part of the 7th chapter in which the word "call" or its cognate was used eight times. This passage in its own way is an echo of the way the letter starts with its emphasis on "calling" as the shared experience of all *in Christ*.

In the previous chapter, there was a serious exegesis of Corinthians 7:1-16. The second section (1 Cor 7:17-24) of that discussion begins with this statement, "…let each of you lead the life that the Lord has assigned, to which God called you" (1 Cor

---

[56] Jones, *Paul's Message of Freedom*, 48.
[57] Bowens, *African American Readings*, 297.
[58] Bowens, *African American Readings*, 298.

7:17). The next two verses are about circumcision. Paul did not recommend it as something necessary for those who had not been already circumcised. Then he wrote, "Let each of you remain in the condition in which you were called" (1 Cor 7:20). The same imperative sentence appears in 1 Cor 7:24 which thus becomes the frame for Paul's argument at this point. There is an amazing exception, however, to this rule presented in this concise set of verses.

We already know that Paul didn't stay as he once had been. He had been a Pharisee but was no longer. Even so, Fee thinks this passage has a kind of *double nuance*"[59] to it, in that it meant having both "faith in Christ" as their call *and* their station in life. There were a few times in the ancient world when calling meant "station in life, position, [or] vocation."[60] We need to consider that Paul was telling slaves that their *condition* was one of slavery. It was not their *calling*."[61]

What we have is a verse in the Bible, and not the only one by a long measure, that has been mistreated, or shall we say, mistranslated. As Bartchy noted the Greek word for calling (*klēsis*) was correctly translated into Latin as *vocatione*.[62] It did not at the time have the meaning of one's vocation, work, or profession, but by the time of Luther's Bible that was what happened with Luther's unfortunate choice of the German word *Beruf*."[63] which literally meant occupation or status. Had he stayed true to Paul's word *klēsis*, Luther would have chosen the German word *Ruf* which means call or summons.

The irony of this mistranslation by Luther is found in Paul's question relating *call* to *circumcision*. He asked, "Was anyone at the time of his call already circumcised?" (1 Cor 7:18). No one was called to be circumcised. It just happened if they were male Jewish babies. Slavery also happened, but it wasn't a calling. When we go back to Paul's world, only someone who owned slaves could begin

---

[59] Fee, *The First Epistle*, 355.
[60] Danker et al., *A Greek-English Lexicon*, 549.
[61] Fee, *The First Epistle*, 355.
[62] S. Scott Bartchy, "Paul did not teach 'Stay in Slavery': The Mistranslation of κλῆσις in 1 Corinthians," A Paper presented to the Combined Session of the African-American Hermeneutics and Paul and Politics Sections of the Society of Biblical Literature (2008), 2; shared with the written permission of the author.
[63] Elliott, *Liberating Paul*, 35.

to imagine that their slaves had been *called to be slaves*. This could not have been Paul's view, though many a slave master in America during the dark centuries of slavery here tried to claim that view for him.

So then, the real question regards whether they were called to follow Christ while *still in* slavery, or was their slavery to be their past story now *in Christ*? To be sure, slave masters in the early 18th and 19th centuries of American history never wanted their slaves to think that "real freedom" was their calling. Paul has a different idea. What is most interesting in this context is that while Paul might on occasion have called himself a "slave of Christ", for others he commended being slaves to one another in a communal context of love.[64] On the other hand, he had not the slightest problem with ascribing slave status to Jesus as we see in Philippians 2:5–7. "Let the same mind be in you that was in Christ Jesus, who, though he was in the form of God did not regard equality with God as something to be exploited, but emptied himself taking the form of a slave…"

Paul wasn't asking for those called to be in Christ to be slaves of Christ, but rather Paul held out the ethical vision of mutual service toward one another. Even when he used the phrase "slave of Christ" in 1 Cor 9:19 he really seemed to be pointing toward his ministry of service to all. When we look back at 1 Corinthians 7 in its entirety, we realize that at every point Paul was emphasizing consideration for *one-another*: wife for her husband, the husband for the wife. One might be circumcised and one uncircumcised, but both were called. To those enslaved, though, Paul invoked the concept of freedom, but it was in the context of their *calling* in Christ *into* a community that was different.

A picture of *ekklēsia* comes to us with the concluding chapter of Romans, where Paul mentions so many people by their names, and in some instances, the important role they were playing or had played in his life. What a mixture of names it is. Two thirds of those mentioned have Greek names indicating an immigrant status. Thirteen of the many named have something definite said about them (i.e., something that is story-related), and nine of them

---

[64] Paul did, however, mention that the freedom to be known would come "through love" as they became "slaves of one another" (Gal 5:13).

bear names pointing to a slave origin.[65] In Romans we see evidence of slaves participating in active ways in the life of shared ministry with Paul. In 1 Corinthians we see that one of the questions addressed to Paul, alongside questions about marriage, celibacy, and women participating in worship, was at least one question about the status of slaves inside the community called *ekklēsia*. The structure of the argument, however, has a strange twist.

In 1 Corinthians 7 when Paul addressed questions about marriage, all his comments were addressed sequentially to the man, and then the woman. Then he addressed the unmarried and those who were married. There was a question about divorce, and the pattern broke some, as he allowed an exception for a woman divorced by her pagan husband. Just prior to the passage about slavery, Paul was addressing those men who either were or were not circumcised. Overall, the advice suggests relationships not of dominance of one over the other, but of mutual responsibility. He was addressing adults expected to be in free stable relationships.

What if the question about the status of slaves inside *ekklēsia* came from the slaves themselves? As Amos Jones Jr. notes, verse 7:20 simply states that "all persons (slaves included) were to remain in the situation they were in when they were called by God, a calling that beckoned people to come out of the Corinthian world and into the *ekklēsia*."[66] Leaving that pagan world behind, meant a whole new kind of freedom for everyone—as well as serious responsibilities of mutual obligation and respect. Paul was not simply addressing slaves when he wrote, "For freedom Christ has set us free. Stand firm, therefore, and do not submit again to a yoke of slavery" (Gal. 5:1). It was his story in Christ. Don't go backwards, Paul, told the Galatians.

What we find in Paul is an explosive comment not directed at a single slave like Onesimus but to *any* slave inside the community of Christ. "For whoever was called in the Lord as a slave is a free person belonging to the Lord, just as whoever was free when called is a slave of Christ. You were bought with the price; do not become slaves of human masters" (1 Cor 7:22–23). But many were slaves of human masters. What were they to do?

---

[65] Jewett. *Romans*, 953.
[66] Jones, *Paul's Message of Freedom*, 53.

We've labored a bit over this text, but that is because in the history of the church it was sometimes thought Paul was talking about a kind of slavery to sin. Not so! As Amos Jones Jr. framed it this passage "breaks the slave away from all social and political obligations."[67] Richard Horsley makes an important contribution to this more emancipatory way of reading this text with his critique of 1 Cor. 7:21 as it appears in the NRSV version. "Were you a slave when called? Do not be concerned about it. Even if you can gain your freedom, make use of your present condition now more than ever." Horsley suggests that the phrase "Even if" should be "But if."[68] The verse would read "But if (indeed) you can gain your freedom do so now." But was there a way they could be free?

What may have been missing, but which was Paul's intent, according to Callahan was the practice of *ecclesial manumission*.[69] There is evidence in the early centuries of the church that some communities paid for the freedom of slaves who belonged to their community. Bartchy mentioned three early Christian writings in which there was evidence of faith communities which "did purchase the freedom of slaves who were sisters and brothers in Christ."[70]

There is more to this, however, than what might have been random situations in which slaves were fortunate to have their freedom given. According to Callahan, for communities shaped in an ethic following Christ crucified, Paul was advocating three practices: *manumission, mutualism, and morality*.[71] Throughout his travels and letters Pauline communities are connected to one another and to their brothers and sisters in the "churches in Judea that are in Christ" (Gal. 1:22). What they share is freedom found in Christ. It wasn't a "do your own thing" freedom, however. It was a calling in Christ to be free of the destructive world of injustice and violence and be bound to one another in mutual love and

---

[67] Jones, *Paul's Message of Freedom*, 57.
[68] Horsley, *1 Corinthians*, 103.
[69] Allen Dwight Callahan, "Paul, *Ekklēsia*, and Emancipation in Corinth," in *Paul and Politics: Ekklēsia, Israel, Imperium, Interpretation*, ed. Richard A. Horsley (Harrisburg: Trinity International Press, 2000), 220.
[70] Bartchy, "Paul Did Not Teach," 100.
[71] Callahan, "Paul, *Ekklēsia*, and Emancipation," 218.

service. Memories of the past might remain, but the calling was into a new creation.

Excursus. 10.2 Reservations about Paul's Commitment to Freeing Slaves
The title of this excursus may seem out of place with the preceding discussion and my final concluding thoughts, but there are some doubts about Paul that have kept me awake at night. Some of these concerns are raised by Jennifer Glancy.[72] In the seven undisputed letters Paul never *condemns* the institution of slavery as it was practiced in his world. "Paul seems to have been indifferent to the circumstances of church members who were slaves (and to the circumstances of prostituted slaves who might have wanted to join the church). In other contexts, he was often blunt in his disapproval, but he never cited slave-holding as a moral wrong."[73] This is an indictment we must treat with all seriousness.

Paul in the strongest possible terms condemned any man in the Jesus Messiah community from visiting a prostitute. (1 Cor 6:15-18a) Yet Sheila Briggs came to what I consider to be a sad conclusion with this comment: "There is no Pauline or New Testament passage that addresses the vulnerability of slaves to sexual exploitation or physical torture.[74] Glancy concludes, based on this passage, that there was no way for a prostitute to belong to the Corinthian assembly. Paul's silence about sexually exploited slaves must have meant that they were excluded, or he may have known it happened and didn't consider it a moral issue.[75] We may find it hard to comprehend what Paul's world was like, but it was a world where the sexual use of slaves was common. It was such a part of the Greco-Roman world that it was not debated in terms of morality, but simply was a fact of life. As much as I might wish that the rights of slaves with regard to their bodies mattered in the

---

[72] See the Bibliography for her writings.
[73] Jennifer Glancy, *Slavery as Moral Problem: In the Early Church and Today* (Minneapolis: Fortress Press, 2011), 50.
[74] Sheila Briggs, "Paul on Bondage and Freedom in Imperial Roman Society" in *Paul and Politics: Ekklēsia, Israel, Imperium, Interpretation,* ed. Richard A. Horsley (Harrisburg: Trinity Press International, 2000), 117.
[75] Glancy wrote, "Paul may have believed that the forced sexual activity of slaves was beyond moral judgment," Jennifer Glancy, "Obstacles to Slaves' Participation in the Corinthian Church," *Journal of Biblical Literature* 117, no 3 (1998): 481-501.

earliest documents of the Christian movement the evidence is not there.

We are working with a limited amount of evidence regarding what appears to be Paul's silence on a most troubling issue. The passages we have looked at, however, (from the letter to Philemon and chapter 7 of 1 Corinthians) at least, give us some hope that Paul really meant what he said in Galatians 3:28 that there "is no longer Jew or Greek, there is no longer slave or free, there is no longer male and female." There was also the continuing theme of freedom that Paul expressed in nearly all his letters. Perhaps, most importantly, we have the example he offered. The title of the fifth chapter of this book, "Paul Lost in the Crowd", was my way of suggesting the possibility that no one would have noticed Paul arriving in any city on one of his many travels. He was one of the many who worked with their hands, and often worked side by side with those who were slaves. Paul clearly challenged the presumptions of importance in the patronal world of the elite and refused to be part of it. In Christ, he would consider himself a slave. Maybe he was speaking out against slavery by sharing their life and embracing slaves as equal members of *ekklēsia*

We keep finding ourselves wondering about questions and details from Paul's life that cannot be proved. Was he really a Roman citizen? Was he born in Tarsus? The list can go on. Acts is our only source for these details. There was a mention by Jerome (347-420 CE) that Paul's family had been prisoners of war taken from Galilee to Tarsus. There Paul's father became a citizen. Knowing that this detail is more apocryphal in nature, Callahan still wondered if Paul might have been conscious of a family story tracing back to slavery. Callahan wondered if he "shared the deracinated, servile ancestry of his addressees?"[76] Perhaps it was such a memory that led Paul to declare, "For you were called to freedom, brothers and sisters" (Gal. 5:13).

We know from the Pastoral Epistles that in the end, and for many centuries that followed, the message of freedom was sadly and violently compromised. Freedom's story still needs to be acted on, often from below, by those whose freedom is most endangered. The vision of freedom is there, though, in our story of Christ, embedded as we have seen in the Jewish story, and there

---

[76] Callahan, "Paul, *Ekklēsia*, and Emancipation," 223.

in the midst of some dim but flickering candles from those early assemblies Paul knew as *ekklēsia*.

Chapter 11
Paul in a Troubled World

"I am in Birmingham, because injustice is here... Just as the Apostle Paul left his little village of Tarsus and heard and carried the gospel of Jesus Christ to practically every hamlet and city of the Greco-Roman world, I too am compelled to carry the gospel of freedom beyond my particular hometown.
Like Paul, I must constantly respond to the Macedonian call for aid."[1]

"All things on earth with one accord,
like those in heaven, shall call you Lord."[2]

"And as the last, indelible reminder that Jesus was born and died in human shame and weakness, the three-day interment of his body made certain that the Church's proclamation of his Lordship and divinity, far from a mythical accommodation to alien culture,
is a scandalous and revolutionary dissent from *every* culture then and now."[3]

"The crucifixion of Jesus is, after all, one of the most unequivocally political events recorded in the New Testament."[4]

---

[1] King, Martin Luther. The Letter from Birmingham Jail, http://okra.stanford.edu/transcription/document_images/undecided/630416-019.pdf

[2] "Creator of the Stars of Night," 9th Century Latin hymn, 1982 Hymnal, New York, The Church Hymnal Corporation, Hymn #60.

[3] Lewis, Alan E., *Between Cross and Resurrection: A Theology of Holy Saturday* (Grand Rapids: William B. Eerdmans, 2001), 112.

[4] Neil Elliott, 1997, "The Anti-Imperial Message of the Cross," in *Paul and Empire: Religion and Power in Roman Imperial Society*, ed. Richard A. Horsley (Harrisburg: Trinity Press International, 1997), 167.

11.1 Introduction

Paul's relationship with the early followers in Corinth was troubled by the lack of unity and the arrogance of some leaders who did not share Paul's understanding of the gospel. He claimed to be their father and as such addressed the many questions they had for him. Thankfully there were many other issues and questions that he addressed. In doing so we see deeper into his heart and soul.

The second part of this chapter concentrates on Paul's expected visit to a community he did not start. In Romans Paul acknowledged his principle of never doing missionary work where other apostles worked (Rom 15:20). Up to this point only communities he founded received letters from him. But one of Paul's ultimate goals was to take the Gospel to Spain, which we will examine in Chapter 13. He would pass through Rome on his way there. And he was asking for their assistance with his next venture. Paul wasn't the only one who traveled a great deal. Even if he had not been to Rome before, he had, as we can discover in Romans 16, a great many friends living there. They would have told stories about Paul. Now with this letter they would actually hear him.

What we find in Romans are detailed, comprehensive, and rather involved arguments explaining the Gospel of Jesus Messiah using the Hebraic scriptures with references to Adam and Abraham, along with the prophets and psalms. Paul could assume a literate audience in the sense they knew scripture, not from reading but from hearing. There were Jewish believers belonging to those assemblies, and there were followers from many other ethnicities. Paul presumed they knew his references to scripture as much as those were raised up in the Judean faith.

Paul also had to know the socio-economic make-up of these small communities. He would have learned that from those like Prisca and Aquila who met Paul perhaps in Ephesus. By now they were back in Rome. This chapter will spell out what living was like for those housed in dangerous tenements. They came from the most marginalized part of Rome's population. They also lived through a series of Roman emperors who in the time of Paul rarely evidenced moderation and morality in their personal lives. It is in light of the immorality and injustice so visible in Rome in the first century that we can read Paul's letter to the Romans. First, however, we begin with a troubled apostle who emerges in his Corinthian correspondence.

11.2 Was Paul a failed pastor?

The title of this section derives from a book about clergy failure: *Fail: Finding Hope and Grace in the Midst of Ministry Failure*. The author J. R. Briggs offers a grim statistic to start his book, namely that "fifteen hundred pastors abandon their pastoral vocation every month because of either burnout or contention in their congregations"[5] Conflict and disagreements in a religious community are not new, and they certainly existed in Paul's time as we see in his letters. We can be grateful for some of those issues because they led Paul to write to those communities.

Was Paul a failed pastor in the eyes of some in Corinth? It may seem a strange question to ask in light of his status as a saint with his own holy day. (June 29th) The charges made against Paul appearing in a later section of 2 Corinthians 10-13, would seem to preclude such an honor for him. Further on in this chapter, we will consider this segment in some depth as it helps us first see Paul's deep concerns with a congregation he started. It will also reveal much more about the experiences and trials Paul had in his ministry. And most importantly we will see Paul who embraced his failures!

We will shortly consider Paul's response to one particular leader in Corinth who, if we used today's terminology, wanted to fire Paul. First however, we need to consider the possibility that 2 Corinthians is not a single letter but is actually composed of pieces from other letters sent to Corinth. To be sure there are scholars who see it as a single composite letter. Some presume that all the breaks and discontinuities in the letter (discussed below) are due to Paul's mind wandering off to other issues This is the conclusion of Antoinette Wire who cautioned that "partition theories raise more problems than they solve."[6] Her reference to the somewhat chaotic character of arguments might be called, I believe, *literary bricolage*.

The thesis here is that it was Paul who wrote all of 2 Corinthians, but some scribe finding the various letters, or parts thereof, who saved them (!) and pasted them together, as best as he could.

---

[5] J. R. Briggs, *Finding Hope and Grace in the Midst of Ministry* Failure (Downers Grove, IL: InterVarsity Press, 2014), loc. 75 out of 2931.

[6] Wire, *2 Corinthians*, lvi.

Excursus 11:1 A letter in 5 pieces

Calvin Roetzel offers what I think is the most compelling analysis of the composition of 2 Corinthians. His theory considers the possibility that some faithful follower of Paul was dealing with various tattered and worn-out pieces of Paul's correspondence. In order to save the pieces, they were pasted together lest any be lost. It may be more accurate to say they were re-copied. The reconfiguration of these pieces probably didn't happen in Paul's time, but we know it happened early enough because there have not been discoveries of competing versions of 2 Corinthians to discredit this theory. Roetzel, knowing how pieces of Paul were saved, maintains that this letter may have been one of "Paul's greatest theological achievements, if not his greatest."[7]

Imagine that we have taken 2 Corinthians and cut up various chapters and parts of some chapters. They are lying on the table. Some logic about timing and subject matter must support our reconstruction. Following Professor Roetzel[8] as our guide, A, B, C, D, and E identify the order in which they were written.

Letter A. 2 Cor 8. This is a letter carried by Titus and "the brothers" in which Paul seeks help in completing the collection he wishes to take to Jerusalem. Some may have been questioning this enterprise. Paul defends himself and his co-workers.

Letter B. 2 Cor. 2:14–7:4 (minus 6:14–7:1[9]). In a section laden with amazing examples and metaphors, Paul defends and explains his apostolic ministry.

Letter C. 2 Cor 10:1-13:10. This is the so-called *"Letter of Tears.* Most likely Titus carried it to Corinth. Sometime later Titus brought Paul news from Corinth reporting on their "longing, mourning, [and] zeal" they were expressing for Paul" (2 Cor. 7:7). Letter C had set the stage for a reconciliation.

---

[7] Calvin Roetzel, 2015. *The Letters of Paul: Conversations in Context* (Louisville: Westminster John Knox Press, 2015). Note: I am leaving it to Biblical theologians to debate which letter is the model for Paul's "greatest theological achievement."

[8] The most recent and expanded analysis of the theory of multiple letters in the Corinthian correspondence is the work of Frank W. Hughes and Robert Jewett, *The Corinthian Correspondence: Redaction, Rhetoric and History* (Lanham, MD: Lexington Books, 2021). It came to my attention in the final stages of this book.

[9] Roetzel says this is an interpolation, placed there by a later scribe. It is unlike Paul, and actually is "more characteristic of Qumran texts." *The Letters of Paul*, 148.

Letter D. 2 Cor 1:1-2:13; 7:5-16; 13:11-13. This is Paul's letter expressing reconciliation and his grateful hope that members of that community would surround the man he had hurt with forgiveness.

Letter E. 2 Cor 9. This is a group letter sent not just to Corinth but to other communities in southern Greece (Achaia) regarding the collection.

Letters A and E will not be considered at this point, though their subject matter known as *Paul's Collection* will be covered in Chapter 13, *Paul's Watch*. Before we find Paul about to be fired, however, we need to turn to recollections of his ministry as an ambassador.

11.3 Paul's challenges in ministry: Letter B (2 Cor 2:14-7:4)

Regarding Letter B (2 Cor 2:14-7:4) it must be noted that in no other letter is Paul so revealing about his understanding of ministry. Here he offers contrasts with those he would not emulate, such as those who were "peddlers of God's word" (2 Cor 2:17). He airs his issues with others who falsified God's word (2 Cor 4:2), as well as those who "boast in outward appearance and not in heart" (2 Cor 5:11). Some of the most treasured things Paul ever wrote are also found here, in part, because he had invested so much of himself into this community. For all the problems he addressed in their formative years, what stands out is his love for them like a parent for their growing children.

Complimenting the Corinthians with lavish praise was the way he addressed them. His friends in Corinth are, he wrote, "a letter of Christ, prepared by us, written not with ink but with the Spirit of the living God, not on tablets of stone but on tablets of human hearts" (2 Cor 3:3). Paul and these new followers of Jesus were sharing a mystical and spiritual sense of unity: "all of us with unveiled faces seeing the glory of the Lord as though reflected in a mirror, are being transformed into the same image from one degree of glory to another; for this comes from the Lord, the Spirit" (2 Cor 3:18).

To be sure there were challenges in his ministry. He remembered times of "great endurance, in afflictions, hardships, calamities, beatings, imprisonments, riots, labors, sleepless nights, hunger" (2 Cor 6:4-5). A section about the spiritual gifts follows, with references to other troubled times. Paul and others had known dishonor and ill repute. There were occasions when they were treated as imposters, as unknown, as punished, as sorrowful, as poor, and as having nothing (2 Cor 6:10). To every one of these misfortunes Paul counters with something positive. Most significantly there are Paul's words calling for all to know the power of reconciliation, particularly in the story of Christ "who has given us the ministry of reconciliation" (2 Cor 5:18). While many might be skeptical if this could really happen Paul, as we will see, would not lose hope. Even within the contentious Corinthian *ekklēsia* there was Paul's belief in unity.

11.4 Paul is slandered: Letter C (2 Cor 10:1-13)

One accusation made against Paul was this: "For they say, 'His letters are weighty and strong, but his bodily presence is weak and his speech contemptible'" (2 Cor 10:10). The text asserts a group voice (i.e., "they say"), but the charge is most likely from a single accuser. According to the standards of the rhetorical world Paul was *not naming* the man responsible for this accusation. "The effect of not-naming is to avoid the possibility of 'rubbing salt into an open wound,' so to speak, by explicitly identifying persons connected with the cause of the strife."[10] Such reluctance to embarrass someone publicly leaves open the possibility for what happened at the end of this affair: reconciliation.

Complaining about Paul's speaking ability may not seem like a serious charge, but it was not the only allegation made against him. Some thought him to be a fool (2 Cor 11:16). The Greek word for *fool* in that accusation was *aphrōn*. This is the kind of fool who is irrational or thoughtless, i.e., not capable of making prudent decisions.

The more serious charge against Paul appears in 2 Cor 12:16-18 where *they say* he was *crafty* and took them in by *deceit*. I am quoting words from the NRSV which seem to be serious charges, but other translations reflect at a deeper level the low esteem in which Paul was held by some. I like what Eugene Peterson did with this passage. Peterson's Paul heard "whiffs of gossip about how my self-support was a front behind which I worked an elaborate scam."[11] The NIV also gets at the root of the issue with Paul's question: "Did I exploit

---

[10] L. L Welborn, *An End to Enmity: Paul and the "Wrongdoer" of Second Corinthians* (Göttingen: Walter de Gruyter, 2011), 225.

[11] Eugene Peterson, *The Message//Remix The Bible in Contemporary Language* (Colorado Springs: Navpress, 2003), 2108.

you through any of the men I sent to you?" (2 Cor 12:17). The NRSV, weakly, has Paul wondering if they thought he had taken advantage of them. What was the basic charge? It had to be that Paul was alleged to have pocketed the collection or was some kind of "confidence trickster."[12] Remember it seems like a group attacking Paul, but as pointed out above it was probably just one person.

There are a few men of importance and maybe wealth — at least in having more than most — named in the Corinthian literature. Paul remembered Gaius and Crispus as two he had baptized (1 Cor 1:14). Was his detractor someone in the household of Stephanos (1 Cor. 1:16)? Was it Apollos, since some claimed that they belonged to him? (1 Cor 1:12) In his book, *An End to Enmity*, Welborn gives consideration to each of these as possible suspects. He concludes that it was Gaius.[13] Though hidden away behind the earlier charges made against Paul, he also was not named as the man who should be forgiven in Letter D. It would be Gaius, Welborn maintains, who should be forgiven by the community: "Forgive and console him, so that he may not be overwhelmed by excessive sorrow" (2 Cor 2:7). They knew who Paul had in mind.

Paul added something surprising to this pastoral advice: "Anyone whom you forgive, I also forgive" (2 Cor 2:10). What is remarkable about this statement is that forgiveness came from Paul. Here it is the injured party, Paul himself, who wrote those marvelous words about reconciliation as a pro-active stance within the Jesus Messiah community (2 Cor 4:11–21). Welborn writes that "Paul's account of God as the one who takes initiative in offering reconciliation would seem to be a *novum* in the theology of antiquity."[14]

By the time Paul wrote to the Romans from Corinth he and Gaius were on good terms again. At the very end of that letter his greetings to all are extended: "Gaius, who is host to me and to the whole church, greets you" (Rom 16:23). I suspect that Gaius was one of the first to hear the letter to the Romans. I can imagine the two of them discussing Paul's plans to travel first to Rome and then to Spain. In addition, the reference to the entire *ekklēsia* in Corinth, suggests that

---

[12] Welborn, *An End to Enmity*, 166, 170.

[13] It is not within the scope of my book to explain how Welborn comes to this conclusion. Like any detective story all I can advise is that even though Welborn's book is a scholarly treatise, it has the feel of a good mystery.

[14] Welborn, *An End to Enmity*, 453.

for all the concerns Paul had regarding their divisions and failure to support the least in their midst, he sees it as a community that has grown up in Christ.

11.5 A Letter of Tears with a Real Purpose

Looking more closely at the *Letter of Tears* (2 Cor 10–13) [Letter C above.] brings Paul into view. In this tightly packed set of chapters, we have the greatest amount of autobiographical material from any of the undisputed letters. It was all for a purpose, but not simply to call out one leader in that community.

Leaping out from the *Letter of Tears,* 2 Cor 10–13 is a list of experiences that could easily lead to many stories and chapters in the book about Paul's life that he never wrote. Instead, Paul was admonishing a community that was forgetting the essentials in the gospel, the foundational story of Jesus crucified. He was interpreting this event for the Corinthians, who seemed to have heard others preaching a *different* gospel. For Paul the gospel never made anyone to be important in the world, but it brought life, hope and identity, to those who had little hope in the world. Paul was laying down the gauntlet at the feet of some puffed-up spiritually elites who embraced a *different* Jesus. A related aspect of this process is that Paul was addressing the critical issue of identity: "Who are *we* who call Jesus our Messiah and our Lord?"

Paul's roots in the Pharisaic world were deep, abiding, and creative. Remember his recitation of his Jewish credentials in the *Letter of Tears*: "Are they Hebrews? So am I. Are they Israelites? So am I. Are they descendants of Abraham? So am I. Are they ministers of Christ?" The last question led Paul to declare: "I am talking like a madman—I am a better one; with far greater labors, far more imprisonments" (2 Cor 11:22-23). All that follows are painful parts of a story we can be sure the super-apostles would have never experienced.

What we need to see for our purposes of letting Paul tell us his story is that it wasn't about success. It reflects not just a verbal commitment to the story of the crucified Messiah but a life faithful to that event. Once-upon-a-time Paul could claim all the credentials needed for status and leadership in his world but knowing Jesus as Messiah led him to discount all that once mattered as "loss because of Christ" (Phil 3:8).

With this brief second look at the *Letter of Tears*, we have an opportunity to examine what it meant to *boast* in the Greco-Roman world. In that world and in ours 2,000 years later those in positions of power not only appreciate praise and gratitude but expect it. Many are not afraid to declare why they deserve those accolades. Even in a process many of us know quite well, such as applying for a new job or some appointment, the rules of the game are to present yourself in the most favorable light possible. It wasn't much different in Paul's world except that the great majority of the population, being either slaves or the working poor, had little to offer that could be regarded as credentials.

While Paul mostly talked about himself in this *Letter of Tears*, we should realize he was also telling us a great deal about those opposed to him who had their own concept of Jesus in mind. They were boasting about their superior knowledge and rhetorical abilities. They had performed signs and wonders. They must have shared stories of their visions and revelations because Paul felt compelled to tell of a vision he had. We also know they looked down on those who worked with their hands and who refused the support of a patron. Their boasting was "androcentric," or measured by "human standards" 2 Cor 10:3. For Paul the only boasting that made sense was "theocentric": "Let the one who boasts, boast in the Lord" (1 Cor 1:31).[15]

Even in that regard, Paul took pains to avoid personal boasting. Paul began his narrative about a revelation of an event that took place fourteen years prior to his writing this portion of 2 Corinthians by declaring: "I know a person in Christ who fourteen years ago was caught up to the third heaven" (2 Cor 12:2). Most scholars believe he was talking about himself. The content of Paul's vision is enigmatic and sparse. (See much more in Chapter 13, "Paul the Mystic.")

---

[15] It is a quote of Jeremiah 9:24.

We need to place these four chapters in a context that reveals more of the purpose behind Paul in his ministry. We also need to know that Paul would not function very well in ministry as it is often defined in our world. Many conceive ministry to be about the cure of souls, especially being with people in their times of need while facing life's profound questions. Sometimes Christian theological talk even sounds like the title of a popular 20th century book, *I'm Ok, You're Ok*. Paul would shake his head. The world as he knew it was not OK. Paul was on a mission, and he was living in what he knew and felt to be apocalyptic times. Paul's ministry was as a prophet, and not as a therapist. We see this at work in this *Letter of Tears*.

In 1 Corinthians 10-13 we can feel a sense of urgency coming from Paul. He turned up the volume in hope that this community might be aware of how critical it was that they see the world for what it was and respond with a renewed dedication to the story the world desperately needed but could not discern for their blindness. Paul lived with a distinct sense of a break in time, which resulted in a bifurcated world with his watchword being "No longer." In the words of J. Louis Martyn, "The present is not a timeless time in which one is encouraged to run away from real life into a dreamy romanticism. It is, on the contrary, the time of the most vigorous struggle (*agōn*) for the extension of God's rectifying justice to the whole world."[16]

The most important thing to remember about this *Letter of Tears* is that it led to reconciliation! Paul acknowledged such with his comment, "For even if I made you sorry with my letter...Now I rejoice, not because you grieved, but because your grief led to repentance" (2 Cor 7:8-9).[17] How did Paul know this? Titus told him what had happened. How did Titus know? Because he *delivered* the *Letter of Tears*. That didn't mean he handed it over, so it could be passed from one person to another to read. Instead, as you will recall from Chapter 8, we assume he *performed* the letter. We are talking about theater that is beyond simple entertainment, but the kind that can cause tears and heartfelt intentions leading to change.

---

[16] J. Louis Martyn, *Theological Issues in the Letters of Paul* (Nashville: Abingdon Press, 1997), 63.

[17] Remember, with the logic of this analysis we are talking about Letter D at this point.

The letter Titus carried to Corinth was most likely delivered from his memory. More to the point, very likely it was *practiced* in the presence of Paul so that Titus could also deliver the *tone* of the letter, not as Titus but *as* Paul. To bring his audience to tears, "he would have needed to implore, cajole, and accuse his listeners with voice, gestures, and emotions."[18] When the reading-performance was done Titus most likely didn't just exit the stage, but stayed with the community to answer their questions. We should note that many of those in Corinth were in the good graces of Paul when he wrote the conclusion to Romans—Paul was staying in the house of Gaius (Rom 16:23)!

11.6 God's Patience with a Troubled World

We're not sure about all the things that kept Paul awake at night, but the expected return of the Messiah, and its delay, certainly were on Paul's mind. In the next to last chapter, we explore this issue of *Paul's Watch*, as I call it, but for now we have Paul on the move. With the letter he sent to the communities of followers of Jesus in Rome, we find Paul taking a detour before setting his eyes on the capital of the Roman Empire. It may have been a world where symbolically all roads led to Rome, but Jerusalem not Rome was the center of Paul's world.

To be sure, a visit to Rome was not just a last-minute idea. Toward the end of Romans, he wrote about his missionary work among the *ethnē*. His strategy meant never building "on someone else's foundation" While he intended to pass through Rome, he was prevented from doing so. He stated something "hindered [me] from coming to you" (Rom 15:29). He added something more about coming to Rome. He was not staying. "For I do hope to see you on my journey and to be sent on by you, once I have enjoyed your company for a while. At present I am going to Jerusalem in a ministry to the saints" (Rom 15:22-25). He was bringing his beloved collection[19] to Jerusalem. This was, after all, an international movement of very small communities all over the empire, connected by the same story of Jesus with a vision of taking it to others.

---

[18] Lee A. Johnson, "Performance in Corinth: Envisioning Paul's Successful 'Letter of Tears'," *Perspectives in Religious Studies* 42, no. 1 (2015): 56.

[19] Covered in Chapter 13.

The letter to Rome was written somewhere between 55 and 58 CE[20] during the early years of the reign of Emperor Nero (54–68 CE). Paul did not know on a personal level the various assemblies of followers meeting in Rome, but he had friends there. Given the size of Rome Paul was mostly like addressing the largest number of Jesus-messiah communities in the Roman Empire located in any one place. The truth of the matter is, however, that these were small, disparate, fragile, and often socially alienated collections of people from poorest of the poor.

The story of the gospel of Jesus in Rome "prior to the 40s is shrouded in mystery."[21] By the time Paul writes Romans there may have been 1400 followers of Jesus Messiah in the *entire* Mediterranean world.[22] Whatever their numbers in Rome, maybe up to 200, they were scattered, in the estimation of Jewett, into eight to ten congregations or assemblies.[23] The most in-depth study of the population dynamics of these early followers in Rome was done by Peter Lampe who concluded that most of these early followers were living in a section of Rome called Trastevere. It was the poorest, most densely crowded, least fire-resistant and most plague-ridden part of Rome at the harbor's edge.[24] At least four of the cells receiving this letter "consisted entirely of the urban underclass, primarily slaves and poor freedmen/women. Lacking a patron who would function as a leader, the pattern of leadership appears to have been egalitarian in tenement churches."[25]

I think it is fair to say that, on the surface level, we see less of Paul's own story in the letter to the Romans than we have found in the other six letters. I am proposing, however, that we can see and hear a more politically minded Paul[26], and a more prophetic Paul, in this letter. What we may also see in Romans, and maybe with more clarity than expected, is Paul's character.

---

[20] Hultgren, *Paul's Letter to the Romans*, 3.

[21] Jewett, *Romans*, 60.

[22] Stark, *The Rise of Christianity*, 7.

[23] Jewett, *Romans*, 62.

[24] Peter Lampe, *From Paul to Valentinus: Christians at Rome in the First Two Centuries* (Minneapolis: Fortress Press, 2003), 50–53.

[25] Jewett, *Romans*, 66. The term *tenement churches* was coined by Jewett.

[26] Neil Elliott writes, "The themes that dominate Romans are *political* topics...." *The Arrogance of the Nations* (Minneapolis: Fortress Press, 2010), 6.

Here is what Paul had to say about *character* in Romans.

> Therefore, since we are justified by faith, we have peace with God through our Lord Jesus Christ, through whom we have obtained access to this grace in which we stand; and we boast in our hope of sharing the glory of God. And not only that, but we also boast in our sufferings, knowing that suffering produces endurance, and endurance produces character, and character produces hope, and hope does not disappoint us, because God's love has been poured into our hearts through the Holy Spirit that has been given to us (Rom 5:1-3).

We have to remember that "boasting" is something Paul saw as a characteristic of the world of privilege. Not all boasting, though, was pernicious. As Robert Jewett succinctly expressed it in regard to Romans 5:1-3, Paul "is able to carry through with his argument that ordinary boasting is disallowed before God."[27] But boasting in what God has done is what produces hope. Maybe the real theme of Romans is Paul's hope for the coming reign of God in which "the creation will be set free from its bondage to decay and will obtain the freedom of the glory of God" (Rom 8:21). As we will see, shortly, Paul was not averse to talking about the reality of evil in a world turned against God. Indeed, it was a world waiting for a new creation!

But what does it mean to suggest that Paul's real character is revealed in this letter? The Greek word for character in Romans 5:4 is *dokimē*. The word is not found in Greek literature prior to Paul's use of it in a few of his letters: 2 Cor 2:9, 13; Phil 2:22, for example.[28] Translating it as character relates it to the idea of someone who has been tested and tried, and thus someone who endures. We see an ordered logic in Paul who linked suffering, endurance, character and hope in this passage. It is clear that Paul was not elevating suffering to be a virtue, but he knew that suffering along with endurance had brought forth faith, hope and confidence. The biblical scholar Arland Hultgren wisely notes, "Since suffering is capable of

---

[27] Jewett, *Romans*, 353.
[28] As a noun, *dokimē* means a test or ordeal (i.e., something that reveals character. As a participle in 1 Peter 1:7 it becomes a "genuineness of faith" which means without an alloy, Danker et al., *A Greek-English Lexicon*, 256.

misinterpretation, the believer's existence that is bound up with faith can be one of hope."[29]

The letter to the Romans was written soon after the seventeen-year-old Nero became the Emperor of Rome after his father Claudius was assassinated.[30] While there were accusations of Nero causing the death of family members (i.e., perhaps, his brother Brittanicus and his mother Agrippina), there are questions as to his complicity. More direct responsibility can be laid at the feet of Nero for the public persecution of Christ-followers in the aftermath of the great fire in Rome in 64 CE.

Even though Paul's letter to the Romans, according to most scholars, was written in the early principate of Nero, I don't think we can necessarily read much of Nero into this letter. Many malicious rumors would eventually be spread abroad about Nero, and he would be remembered, maybe with exaggeration, of going "out of his palace incognito on rapacious nighttime jaunts... The new princeps was turning out to be a lawless teen with no moral compass."[31] Paul didn't need any new information, however, about this latest emperor, for he had more than enough evidence of the degradation and excesses of the rulers of his world. It was not the world God intended. We can see Paul's character emerge in the letter to the Romans when we read the first chapters of Romans as political and social commentary. Paul was writing a series of strong accusations about Roman privilege and any and all of their claims to ethnic superiority, especially in light of the cruelty and disregard for human life evidenced in so many ugly ways.

In particular, Romans is written by the Jewish Paul to "Christian Judeans (*Ioudaioi*) whose manner of loyalty to Jesus does not yet correspond to Paul's *euangelion*."[32] As discussed previously what we

---

[29] Hultgren, *Paul's Letter to the Romans*, 207.

[30] John F. Drinkwater, *Nero: Emperor and Court* (Cambridge: Cambridge University Press, 2019). According to Drinkwater, Nero was not responsible for his death.

[31] James S. Romm, *Dying Every Day: Seneca at the Court of Nero* (New York: Alfred A. Knopf, 2014), 93.

[32] Mason, Steve, *Josephus, Judea, and Christian Origins: Methods and Categories*, (Peabody: Henrickson Publishers, 2009), 303. The word *euangelion* is the singular word translated as "the gospel." Mason, importantly, translates *euangelion* as "The Announcement" noting that as singular good news it is distinctly Pauline." "Paul Without Judaism: Historical Method Over Perspective," in *Paul and Matthew among*

know as Christianity began its life inside the faith of Judeans open to the story of Jesus Messiah. These are the communities in Rome that Paul did not start, and to whom he writes in the aftermath of the crucifixion of Jesus. I am therefore suggesting we read Romans as having a mostly Judean audience of followers of Jesus alongside the political awareness required of those knowing that their faith in Jesus was contrary to expected norms in the Roman world. As Hultgren notes Paul's argument in Romans has 51 quotations from the Septuagint. That's 51 quotations out of a total of 89 in all the letters.[33]

It is highly possible that some of my readers here are not fully familiar with Paul's first three chapters in Romans.[34] If so some may never heard the charges Paul makes against the rulers of his world: "For the wrath of God is revealed (*apokaluptetai*) from heaven against all ungodliness (*asebeian*) and wickedness (*adikian*) of those who by their wickedness (*adikia*) suppress the truth" (Rom.1:18 NRSV). A careful consideration of translating this passage should pull us away from its moralistic overtones so that we can discover the political implications of faith in Jesus Messiah.

The Greek verb translated as "revealed" is *apokaluptetai*. This is an apocalypse, or revelation, which happened in the past. Two more words in the NRSV translation to consider are "ungodliness and wickedness." The Greek words there are *asebeian* and *adikia*, which can be translated as impiety and injustice. In the eyes of Rome impiety[35] was considered "a most heinous crime—the failure to respect deity."[36] Paul was charging the Roman dominated world with the practice of impiety. We can immediately hear Paul congratulating those followers in Thessalonika who had "turned to

---

Jews and Gentiles: Essays in Honor of Terence L. Donaldson (London: T & T Clark, 2021), 26.

[33] Hultgren, *Paul's Letter to the Romans*, 10.

[34] Only Romans 1:1–7 is read on the Fourth Sunday of Advent in Year A from the Revised Common Lectionary. Other readings from chapter 4 and later appear at different times in the three-year cycle. You will not hear about God's wrath if your community uses this lectionary.

[35] The most widely copied sculptural image of Augustus (which Paul must have seen somewhere) depicted him not with a sword, but his toga pulled over his head to emphasize his piety. It was not piety in the eyes of Paul; Neil Elliott and Mark Reasoner, *Documents and Images for the Study of Paul* (Minneapolis: Fortress Press, 2011), 131.

[36] Jewett, *Romans*, 152.

God, from idols, to serve a living and true God" (1 Thess 1:9). They had learned the Ten Commandments, the first of which was to worship no other God, but the God of Israel.

The other word "*adikia*," translated in this reckoning as injustice, is a variant on the all- important word for our reading of Romans which in English lettering is *dikaiosynē*.[37] What we find in most English translations of Romans is that when Paul uses the word *dikaiosynē* it is often rendered as righteousness. Thus, in the verse preceding the one about the wrath of God we find Paul describing the gospel as it comes to the Jew and Greek alike. "For in it the righteousness (*dikaiosynē*) of God is revealed through faith for faith; as it is written, 'The one who is righteous (*dikaios*, i.e., a just man) will live by faith'" (Rom 1:17).[38]

The Greek sense of the word *dikaiosynē* carries some different connotations. It was about justice, namely punishment, or at least giving someone their due. How then did this Greek word for justice end up in our English bibles as righteousness? Some of the credit—or is it dis-credit?—can be laid at the feet of Augustine, some 350 years after Paul. Augustine's bible was in Latin in which the Greek word *dikaiosynē* in its verbal form was *iustificare* ('to justify'), or sometimes as *iustum facere* ('to make righteous').[39] Augustine, with his own guilt-ridden mind focusing on Paul's letters, was a theologian wrestling with the question of how God could justify and thereby declare the unrighteous righteous? The question, of course, became the central question of Luther and the Protestant reformation. In that process the letter to the Romans became Paul's singular theological treatise, divorced from the historical reality in which it was written. That is the direction in which we must turn, knowing that the Greek word *dikaiosynē* had political implications in Paul's world. It remains true for our world as well.

---

[37] The prefix "a" added to a Greek word (i.e., *adikian*) is like adding the word "not" to the suffix. Thus, in English what is "moral" becomes its opposite with the word "amoral." There are many Greek versions of the word "*dikaios*" which refers to a man who is "upright, just, righteous…conforming to the laws of God and man;" Danker et al., *A Greek-English Lexicon*, 246. An unjust person is an *ädikos*.

[38] This is the NRSV translation. Note how different this sounds if "justice" is used rather than "righteousness" when Paul is describing the gospel. "For in it justice of God is revealed through faith for faith; as it is written, 'The one who is just will live by faith'."

[39] Alister E. McGrath, *Iustia Dei: A History of the Christian Doctrine of Justification* (New York: Cambridge University Press, 2005), 20.

The problem that had emerged for Paul involved those followers who had been "turned from idols" to worship Jesus as their Lord and were passing judgment on those followers who also maintained practices of food and calendar appropriate to their Judean heritage (Rom 14:13-23). Paul was addressing what Jewett called a "Gentile majority" that was "discriminating against a Judean minority whom it was claiming to replace."[40] Paul's terms for the two groups were the "strong" and the "weak," with the latter following the *halakhah* of Judaism, which meant cultural practices regarding food and other aspects of daily life.

The truth of the matter, both then and now, is that to follow *halakhah* just in terms of the food requirements required diligence and perseverance. Those who kept those standards were never weak and Paul knew it. Peter Tomson in *Paul and the Jewish Law* suggests that Paul's reference to those keeping dietary restrictions should be understood as the care involved in that practice. They were being *delicate*[41] or careful when it came to food. That is the way, Tomson says, in which to understand the Greek word *astheneō*, which is often translated as *weak*. The main point in all this is that Judean and gentile (all the others, from Judean point of view) should be able to eat together when celebrating together. What we see with Paul's concept of *halakhah* are practices, and sensitivity toward those who are more delicate, with the goal to "love one another with mutual affection; outdo one another in showing honor" (Rom 12:10).

My purpose in the latter part of this chapter has been to capture a picture of Paul's genius in addressing the conflict which had been brought to his attention. The unity of the ekklēsia was at stake. Certainly, beginning with Romans 9 Paul was focused on the seeming failure of the gospel with his own people. In what at times might seem to be a convoluted argument, we find Paul holding up a vision when "all Israel will be saved" (Rom 11:26). The next three chapters (Romans 12-14) are like *halakhah* for all (the *ethnē* as well as Judean followers) who had been baptized.

If we see Paul as writing Romans to solve community issues, we also see him placing the story of the death of Jesus in the context of the history of the Roman empire under the Caesars. He knew who

---

[40] Jewett, *Romans*, 70.
[41] Peter J., Tomson, *Paul and the Jewish Law: Halakha in the Letters of The Apostle to the Gentiles* (Minneapolis: Fortress Press, 1990), 243.

was responsible for the death of Jesus. Yoder puts it this way: "In [Jesus'] death the Powers — in this case the most worthy, weighty representatives of Jewish religion and Roman politics — acted in collusion."[42] Who were these rulers, in Paul's eyes? Speaking of a wisdom only to be found in Christ who was crucified Paul said, 'None of the rulers of this age understood this; for if they had they would not have crucified the Lord (*Kyrios*, singular) of glory'" (1 Cor 2:8). We must never forget that these early followers were not going to be seen as respectable in the eyes of Rome.

To be sure Paul offered some advice regarding the stance to take vis-à-vis the powers-that-be when in the 13th chapter of Romans we read, "Let every person be subject to the governing authorities." It is a passage that has been misused for the most part by governing authorities, who *want* it to mean *that* any questioning of their actions is a violation of a biblical commandment. A former Attorney General of the United States, Jeff Sessions, saw fit to quote from this passage in defending the Trump administration's "zero-tolerance persecution policy" with regard to illegal immigration. Sessions said, "I would cite to you the Apostle Paul and his clear and wise command in Romans 13, to obey the laws of the government because God has ordained them for the purpose of order."[43] I wouldn't advise that we ought to turn to the former Attorney General for advice about a biblical passage. These verses have often been used to silence dissent and to enforce the totalitarian exercise of power in slave-holding America and even to undergird Nazi authority in the previous century.

A few examples from this troubling text may help us understand how Paul cleverly offered advice to those living in Caesar's very shadow about how they might survive as witnesses to Christ while not bring attention to themselves. From what we know about Paul's politics, we need to read this letter as a kind of "hidden transcript of resistance," which can be understood as the way those most oppressed in an "off-stage" context can be critical of those in power. There is a place in which sub-ordinate people have a "realm of

---

[42] John Yoder, *The Politics of Jesus:* Vicit Agnus Noster, 2nd ed. (Grand Rapids: William. B. Eerdmans Publishing Company 1994), 145.

[43] https://www.washingtonpost.com/news/acts-of-faith/wp/2018/06/14/jeff-sessions-points-to-the-bible-in-defense-of-separating-immigrant-families/(accessed on 8/23/2022).

relative discursive freedom, in a privileged site for nonhegemonic, contrapuntal, dissident, subversive discourse."[44] Speaking truth to power, even in what Scott calls a "hidden transcript" (one that the oppressed can read) always bears risk. We need to see that even when Paul seemingly affirmed the power of Caesar, he was not saying the authorities were ordained by God. Neil Elliott also observes that in the first century C.E. there was evidence that the status of Judeans was not secure in Rome. Some of their leaders, had been forced into exile under Claudius. The political dispossession of Judeans was a recent memory.[45] One of the historical ironies regarding Romans 13 is that it was quoted so often by those who were about to be martyred in the next few centuries.

Nevertheless, Paul expected some kind of public witness on the part of followers of Jesus. There is the phrase that the authorities "were instituted by God" (Rom 13:1). No matter how many authorities through the ages have twisted that phrase to justify despotic rule, it did not mean they were ordained.[46]

This passage from Romans 13:4 is an example of a "hidden transcript." In reference to a "governing authority" the passage is: "But if you do what is wrong, you should be afraid, for the authority does not bear the sword in vain! It is the servant of God to execute (*edikos*) wrath on the wrongdoer." NRSV. What is significant is that the Greek word *edikos* meant executive vengeance or avenging a wrong. This was the way justice was understood and enacted in Rome. It was what we call retributive justice.[47] Its primary symbol was the cross.

Imperial iconography meant that Rome's power was always visible. The Roman arches in Gaul would be a constant reminder of what it meant to be conquered and subdued by Roman armies. ". . . in the iconography on the Augustan triumphal arches in Gaul [southern France today] bound male and female barbarian captives are portrayed in abject humiliation. They stand or kneel, chained by the neck to a trophy tree, with arms pinioned behind their backs, and

---

[44] James C. Scott, *Domination and the Arts of Resistance: Hidden Transcripts* (New Haven: Yale University Press, 1990), 25.
[45] Elliott, *Liberating Paul*, 221.
[46] Yoder, *The Politics of Jesus*, 201.
[47] Gordon Zerbe, "From Retributive Justice to Restorative Justice," *Direction* 44, no. 1 (Spring 2015): 57.

their weapons, armor and tunics displayed on the tree."[48] That Roman soldier holding his sword next to the sorrowful woman representing the defeat of Judea in 70CE remains a symbol of military might over the powerless. (Chapter 6 "Paul Lost in the Crowd.)

Neil Elliott understands the advice in Romans 13:1-7 as a form "of an ad hoc survival strategy in an impossible situation." He adds that, "in effect, Paul declares: 'The empire is as dangerous as it has ever been. Nothing has changed. Exercise caution.'"[49]

The message of the preceding chapter is also important. It was a call to live in a distinct way so that others could see what life in Christ looked like. Contrasted to the vertical world of privilege and political power over others was Paul's vision of harmony that included the least in the world. Consider Romans 12:3 as a clear example: "For by the grace given to me I say to everyone among you not to think of yourself more highly than you ought to think...." Paul evokes an image of a community as a body with many parts and functions. The poetry of this passage flows into an ethic as true today as it was 2,000 years ago: "Let love be genuine; hate what is evil, hold fast to what is good; love one another with mutual affection; outdo one another in showing honor" (Rom 12:9-10).

The ethical advice continued in a way that clearly echoes the teaching of Jesus. Have we not returned to the Sermon on the Mount in Luke with these passages from Romans? "Bless those who persecute you; bless and do not curse them . . . Do not repay evil for evil . . . never avenge yourselves. . . . if your enemies are hungry, feed them; if they are thirsty, give them something to drink" (Rom 12:14-20). "There is little doubt that in all these cases Paul is demonstrating his intimate familiarity with Jesus' dominical teaching."[50]

---

[48] James R. Harrison, "Paul's "Indebtedness" to the Barbarian (Rom 1:14) in Latin West Perspective," *Novum Testamentum* 55 (2013): 328-29.

[49] Neal Elliott, "Strategies of Resistance and Hidden Transcripts in the Pauline Communities," in *Hidden Transcripts and the Arts of Resistance*, ed. Richard A. Horsley (Atlanta: Society of Biblical Literature, 2004) 121.

[50] James, R. Harrison, "The 'Clemency' of Nero and Paul's Language of 'Mercy' in Romans—Paul's Reconfiguration of Imperial Values in the Mid-Fifties Rome," in *Justice, Mercy, and Well-Being: Interdisciplinary Perspectives*, eds. Peter G. Bolt and James R. Harrison. (Eugene: Wipf and Stock, 2020), 211.

We need to regard Jesus' vision of the "kingdom of God" and Paul's use of the term "*ekklesia,*" as overt political concepts of a shared equalitarianism in the Roman world of oppression and domination. When Paul was discussing different spiritual gifts being expressed in the worship of the Corinthian assemblies, he was ascribing gifts to all, even though they were diverse in their character and function (1 Cor. 12:1-10). The gifts mattered, but much less so, in the context of all who belonged to the one body. "In 12:1-10 he shows that the body of Christ is a pluralistic and egalitarian entity. Within it, unity and diversity stand in dialectical relationship and all of the members have equal rights and responsibilities.

The kinds of relationships Paul calls for in a world that centers itself through baptism in the story of Christ crucified should not let them be instrumental in gaining power *over* others. Instead, in the words of Davina Lopez, "the 'truth of the gospel' (Gal 2:14) requires the different groups of the defeated to connect with one another in the same space without duplicating vertical hierarchical domination. This is the task of new creation ushered in by mother Paul."[51] Thus, Paul ends Romans with ethical instructions to welcome one another as they have been welcomed by Christ (Rom 15:7).

Those who were formerly outside the story of God, enmeshed in a world in sin, were to know that "God proves his love for us in that while we still were sinners Christ died for us" (Rom 5:8). Paul's vision boiled down to real justice for those in Christ. More than once, of course, Paul acknowledged how those following Christ would live and act in ways contrary to the ways of Caesar's world. Paul could never equate the Jewish concept of *dikaiosynē* with Caesar's concept of justice. Much of what should concern us, and would be true of Paul as well, is the *injustice* we see in the lives of refugees, asylum seekers, and all who are marginalized. The term "miscarriage of justice" is as much in evidence in our world as it was 2,000 years ago for Paul.

Traditionally, as we've said, the Greek word *dikiaosyne* in English has become either justice or righteousness. Translators have probably had extensive arguments among themselves over which is the right word to use. Ever since Augustine, however, we have seen

---

[51] Davina Lopez, *Apostle to the Conquered* (Minneapolis: Fortress Press, 2008), 147-48.

Christian theology become ever more soteriological[52] in its focus. It is as if the goal of Christianity is to be saved. Concentration has been on the choices individuals make with regard to faith and practice. That is *not* how to read Paul. He called for ethical living to be sure, but not as a road to God's grace. If we had a French bible, we would find the word for righteousness is *doiture* (virtue), while the word translating *dikaiosynē* is justice.

What we have with Paul in his mission work is a historian, a preacher, and a language teacher, who knew the vision of Jesus and what the world looks like when it becomes the kingdom of God.

Excursus 11.2: Belonging to ekklēsia meant learning the language

We have no first-person accounts of people having met Paul, but my supposition is that many must have walked away, shaking their heads, at this crazy man working and talking about a man once dead who is alive. But if they stayed around for the evening meal, they would have been invited to share what was being served. (We have to remember that in 1 Corinthians Paul assumed that outsiders were welcomed in worship (1 Cor 14:23).) In the life of those early communities the meal was called "The *Agape.*" Jewett notes that the article "the" is used in a distinctive way in Romans 13:10, but it is a little detail often lost in many a translation. The NRSV translates Romans 13:10 "Love does no wrong to a neighbor; therefore, love is the fulfilling of the law.[53]" Jewett's translation of this verse is more of a literal translation: "The *agape* does no evil to the neighbor; therefore, the *agape* is law's fulfillment."[54] It was not just any love that was in evidence in this meal, but as Jewett points out, the specific character of a meal binding people together who lived in the tenements of Rome. It was inside these meals and their gatherings that they welcomed others as their neighbors in Christ, and where the Judean traditions were taught in reference to the story of Jesus

---

[52] The general meaning is the theological study of doctrines of salvation. We may often encounter the question in some parts of the Christian world, "Are you saved?" That is a *soteriological* question.

[53] What is also wrong with this translation is that the Greek doesn't say "the law." There is no definite article there.

[54] Jewett, *Romans*, 804; italics added.

Messiah. They came not just to any meal, but to the *agape*.[55] Language matters.

The historical theologian George Lindbeck made a significant contribution to academic theology with his publication of *The Nature of Doctrine* in 1984. Bruce Marshall introduced Lindbeck's work as the call "to understand Christianity as [a] unique cultural-linguistic system, rooted in the life and practice of a particular community, and governed by its own rules."[56] Lindbeck said, "just as an individual becomes human by learning a language, so here she begins to become a new creature through hearing and interiorizing the language that speaks of Christ."[57] What all this means in relationship to Paul's ministry is that everyone coming to faith in Jesus Messiah were claiming a communal identity in the practices of baptism and the *Agape* feast. It was fellowship that included knowing not just the stories about Jesus[58] but the world of stories Jesus knew rooted in the God of Abraham, Isaac, and Jacob.

Paul was writing to small assemblies of Jews and others from different ethnicities. The latter especially were learning a new language.[59] Judeans participating also had challenges because there were many cultural and theological reasons to resist what Paul had concluded about Jesus. Equally true in its own way, those coming from more of a pagan background in the polytheistic Greek and Roman world were challenged by the singularity of God in Paul's preaching and its particularity in terms of its roots in that strange land called Judea. The fact that all or nearly all his recipients were being drawn into a Jewish way of thinking about Jesus Messiah

---

[55] Note the same construction is found in Gal 5:13 where this translation is possible "...but through *the agape* (the meal) become slaves to one another."

[56] George A. Lindbeck, *The Nature of Doctrine: Religion and Theology in a Postliberal Age* (Louisville: Westminster John Knox Press, 2009), xi. The quote is from the Preface by Bruce D. Marshall.

[57] Lindbeck, *The Nature of Doctrine*, 48.

[58] Michael Thompson writes about the stories of Jesus that Paul must have learned while living in Antioch, the city from which it is supposed that the formation of the first collection of the earliest sayings of Jesus emerged in *Clothed in Christ: The Example and Teaching of Jesus in Romans 12.1–15.13* (Eugene: Wipf and Stock, 2011), 65.

[59] Stanley Hauerwas, "Making Sense of Paul Holmer," *Wilderness Wanderings: Probing Twentieth Century Theology and Philosophy,* (Boulder: Westview Press, 1997). 1997), 145. He was quoting the phrase "to become 'religious' is, in part, a matter of learning a new language" which comes from a quote of Paul Homer in *Theology and the Scientific Study of Religion* (Minneapolis, T.S. Dennison, 1961), 163.

makes the concept of learning a new language important for our understanding of what Paul was doing in his letters.

11.7 Welcome one another

Perhaps the single and most important passage in the entire letter is Romans 15:7. "Welcome one another, therefore, just as Christ has welcomed you, for the glory of God." To paraphrase Robert Jewett it meant accepting each other into full fellowship, putting an end to the hostile competition so evident in their world, and admitting the basic legitimacy of the other side.[60] Paul's call for acceptance of one another wasn't simply a matter of giving in on principles, but it was calling for a kind of unconditional love. Paul's faith also included the mercy and forgiveness of God — ideas clearly not current in the Roman world. There was a philosopher, though, in that world from the Cynic tradition who did try to influence the teenage Nero to act with some mercy in his new role as emperor.

A document titled *De Clementia* written by Nero's philosopher-advisor Seneca was a gift for the seventeen-year-old new emperor to help his reign restore Rome to greatness. "Seneca showed that he was still restraining the young emperor, keeping him off Caligula's path. It would be Seneca's humane principles, here superimposed onto Nero by rhetorical sleight of hand, that would guide the regime."[61] Seneca had advised Nero to cautiously exercise power with clemency or mercy. But mercy or clemency did not mean forgiveness, as it did for Paul. It meant some kind of measured response to the wrongs which were done while holding violence in check. And it certainly didn't apply to the whole human race.

Our world is not so different, in that we live with the expectation that debts must be paid. This means that when there are questions of justice, an economic level of analysis applied. Some kind of accounting, some kind of restitution must balance the scales as it were. But with the kind of mercy or justice representing the spirit of Jesus and the soul of Paul there is a kind of *excess* of mercy. Consequently, it resists imposing economic equations on the matter. The philosopher Caputo has noted regarding the return of the

---

[60] Robert Jewett, *Christian Tolerance: Paul's Message to the Modern Church* (Philadelphia: Wesminster Press, 1982,) 29.

[61] James S. Romm, *Dying Every Day*, (New York: A. Knopf Doubleday Publishing Group, 2014), 90.

prodigal son in the parable in Luke 15:11-32 that the father did not try to have his son pay back his inheritance. There wasn't any computation of what was owed.[62] "When the son returned home, this father did not seek to determine the right measure of punishment that would redress the offense and repair his wounded dignity. He did not look to settle the accounts, but rather set aside all such calculation for the excess of love he bore his son! So, he threw a party that bent the nose of the older son out of joint..." [63]

If the party seems beyond reason, we also have the mystical side of Paul to consider. That's next.

---

[62] Robert Jewett discussed Rom 13:8 where Paul wrote "Owe no one anything except to love one another." His advice was "to avoid dependency relations, except for radical dependency as a slave of Christ;" *Romans*, 806.

[63] John Caputo, *What Would Jesus Deconstruct? (The Church and Postmodern Culture): The Good News of Postmodernism for the Church*, (Grand Rapids: Baker Publishing Group, 2007), 74.

Chapter 12
Paul the Mystic

> Poverty of spirit becomes a doorway to an encounter with God and to immersion in transcendence.[1]

> Paul is the only Jewish mystic to report his own personal, identifiably confessional mystical experiences in the 1500 years that separate Ezekiel from the rise of Kabbalah.[2]

> Whoever takes away the mystical element from Paul, the man of antiquity, sins against the Pauline word.[3]

I don't know to what extent this chapter poses some challenges for my readers, but it is about experiences that are often beyond words. To write about the mystical side of life almost seems wrong. Mysticism isn't meant be brought up into the clear light of day. It is there for us to see, but maybe not to comprehend, yet to know and not be able to explain and to hear without being able to put it into words.

I hope this brief story from the actor John Lithgow serves as a door into this chapter. In an introduction to his book *Poet's Corner: The One-and-Only Poetry Book for the Whole Family*, Lithgow tells the story of going to a fund-raising event for an organization educating autistic children. He was asked to recite a few poems related to this topic with all its struggles and challenges. The poems, he writes, "began to cut closer to the bone," concluding with one written by "a twenty-two-year-old woman writing with heart-breaking clarity about her own autism. By the time I finished, everyone in the hall was in tears, myself included." Adding to this experience Lithgow

---

[1] Johann B. Metz, *Poverty of Spirit* (New York: Paulist Press), 46–47.
[2] Segal, *Paul the Convert*, 51-2.
[3] Adolf Diessmann, *Paul: A Study in Social and Religious History* (New York: Harper and Brothers Publishers, 1927), 80.

said he "could sense electricity in the air."[4] That's what this chapter is about, and that metaphor helps to explain, if it is even possible, what it meant for people to claim that their identity was "in Christ."

We are still seeking to let Paul tell us who he is in these seven letters, but now we must go with him into a reality in which words would fail him. That wasn't the case with the various ideas, personal challenges, and ecclesiastical conflicts he often faced. If, as we've explored earlier, he retraced the steps of Abraham, we have seen how his mission was focused on the place of *ethnē* in the life of this Judean sect remembering Jesus. With regard to the cultural expectations that compromised the freedom of women and slaves, we've seen Paul speaking in bold ways in his world. We've seen him come clearer into focus in terms of some of the misplaced assumptions about him especially in regard to marriage and to what some have considered to be a prudish Paul. Truly, though, we traditionally see Paul in a "mirror dimly" (1 Cor 13:12). In this chapter we have a few of Paul's accounts looking through that mirror.

More often than not, these letters bring us close to the faith of Paul, or a kind of faith in action, with its focus on what Paul experienced. Please note, we are not considering Paul having had a singular experience of God, which we tend to do if the story of Paul's conversion from Acts is the main example of mysticism in Paul's life. His seven letters tell a different story—about different aspects of Paul's mysticism.

It will be a critical part of imagining on our part to realize that what bound these fragile communities together was not so much what they *believed* (in the sense of being able to explain their faith), but what they *experienced* together in the context of the foundational story they learned from Paul. Sustaining these communities is what James D. G. Dunn termed "something like a mystical sense of the divine presence of Christ within and without, establishing and sustaining the individual in relation to God. Likewise, we can hardly avoid speaking of the community which understood itself not only from the gospel which called it into existence, but also from the

---

[4] John Lithgow, *The Poet's Corner: The One-and-Only Poetry Book for the Whole Family* (New York: Grand Central Publishing, 2007), xix.

shared experience of Christ, which bonded them as one."[5] What they experienced was often beyond words.

As we consider the mystical side of Paul he is not the professor, but one more like a confessor referring to spiritual things he saw and heard. It is difficult, however, to define what a mystic is, but Evelyn Underhill had this observation: "The visionary is a mystic when his vision mediates to him an actuality beyond the reach of the senses. The philosopher is a mystic when he passes beyond thought to the pure apprehension of truth. The active man is a mystic when he knows his actions to be a part of a greater activity."[6]

It's not hard to recognize that Paul's mystic side has been, if not disregarded in much of Christian history, at the very least marginalized. Discussion of this topic must, by necessity, involve a few conversational partners with grounding in deeper spiritual experiences. We need a context to comprehend the more luminous and deeper mysteries of the holy, as this is what we find in Paul's letters. One partner in helping us understand mysticism is the English mystic Evelyn Underhill (1875-1940). Her book *Christian Mysticism* is considered a classic.

In this book Underhill covers an amazing historical array of mystics not just from Christianity, but also within Judaism, Islam, Hinduism, and Buddhism. While there are references in her writing to Paul, she did not number him among the community of mystics. I realized in writing this chapter, consequently, that Paul should not be considered as *one* among the great company of mystics, but simply as one with mysticism as an essential part of his story and that of his friends in Christ. One place where Underhill's insights did pertain to Paul, however, was her discussion of mystics as a "race of adventurers…who have transcended the 'sense world' in order to live on high levels of the spiritual life."[7]

The other aspect so prominent in the stories of mystics through the ages involves the many who renounced the comforts and privileges in this world to devote themselves to a more contemplative life and practice. To be sure, we've seen Paul leaving the world of privilege behind him, but we don't necessarily see him

---

[5] James D.G. Dunn, *The Theology of Paul the Apostle* (Grand Rapids: William B. Eerdmans Publishing Company, 1998), 401.

[6] Evelyn Underhill, *Practical Mysticism* (Columbus, OH: Ariel Press, 1942), 28.

[7] Evelyn Underhill, *Mysticism: A Study in Nature and Development of Spiritual Consciousness* (New York: E. P. Dutton and Compnay Inc. Publishers, 1948), 35.

as a contemplative. In his life he had opportunities to be alone with his thought, his prayers, and his God. He went to the desert—to Arabia. He traveled long distances. Wherever he went he brought a faith pointing beyond the politics and economics of his day. He seemed to sense that something was missing, but the time was short. The call was to wait and watch and hope. Paul spoke of living in the time of God's "divine forbearance" (Rom 3:25) which meant looking in the present time (Rom 3:26, *kairo*) for God's justice (*diakiosynē*). The evidence for this wasn't in the news of the day, but in the faith of God's people.

Underhill's emphasis on mysticism probably meant she was less attentive to the news of the day in the smoky noisy world of industrial England than the life of the mind and spirit. Many of us also wonder about our own adaptability to a world that seems one-dimensional with a focus on products, manufacturing, and the consumer culture. We live in the world of making and selling things. And those who labor for us in service industries, meat plants, and all other dangerous occupations may still fit the image of those described in the poem "The Grandeur of God" by Gerard Manly Hopkins. The poet wonders why "men did not reck his [God's] rod."[8] That is to say, if I may relate this to Paul, Hopkins was echoing the concerns in the first two chapters of Romans describing a world ruled by sin. Hopkins' poem describes the grimy world known to many working in English factories and mines in the 19th century:

> Generations have trod, have trod, have trod
> And all is seared with trade; bleared, smeared with toil;
> And wears man's smudge and shares man's smell: the soil
> Is bare now, nor can foot feel, being shod.[9]

Paul, by our reckoning, actually knew from his life as a tradesman what it meant to "wear man's smudge and share man's smell." To live in that world, at least for many, meant facing harsh realities of day-to-day existence, that had long ago left behind what Charles Taylor described as the "enchanted world."[10] To the poet's dismay, with feet shod they could not even feel the earth beneath them.

---

[8] One way to interpret this line is see that the verb "reck" is short for *reckon*. In others words, "Why can't people realize who God is, and accept God's rule?"

[9] Gerard Manly Hopkins, *The Poems of Gerard Manly Hopkins* (New York: Oxford University Press, 1967), 66.

[10] Taylor, *A Secular Age*, 25–6

Philosopher Charles Taylor's monumental book, *A Secular Age*, describes the distance we have traveled from the world Paul knew. Taylor's argument is that humans once lived in a Cosmos awash with God (albeit by many different names and practices) but have come to a time where at least in the circles of academic and intellectual life the basic presumption is one of *unbelief*.[11] We have moved far past the pre-modern world where people lived in the context of "spirits, demons, and moral forces."[12] Identity in that world was shaped by family and tribe in the context of mysterious spirits and forces. Echoes of this world, however, reverberate through scripture, if we have a heart and mind to hear those words. All of scripture from Torah, the historical accounts, the psalms, the prophets, and the wisdom literature were rooted in a kind of truth that did not need to be factual or verifiable by scientific proof.

We are the heirs of a process of *disenchantment*, according to Taylor. A large part of the cause could be ascribed to the Reformation of the 16th century. The magic of the sacraments was stripped away and became "purely symbolic," while the challenges to the papacy and the hierarchical authority of the church were transferred to the scripture in printed bibles making it possible for *anyone* to read and interpret the holy word in their own language.[13] The logical conclusion is what Taylor called "The Great Disembedding." It meant that "Disenchantment, Reform, and ... personal religion went together.... society itself comes to be reconceived as made up of individuals."[14] What thereby becomes secular time has led us to a rational world in which we have expelled mystery.[15]

What we will see more clearly is that Paul and those he addressed were not living in our less imaginative secular age, but in a world of dreams, omens, prophecy, and myths expressed in poetry, songs, ecstasy, riddles, and visions. These were not the preserve of certain designated holy people, but accessible to all within the communal life of storytelling, singing, and rituals.

---

[11] Charles Taylor, *A Secular Age* (Cambridge: The Belknap Press of Harvard University Press, 2007), 13.
[12] Taylor, *A Secular Age*, 26.
[13] Taylor, *A Secular Age*, 75.
[14] Taylor, *A Secular Age*, 146.
[15] Taylor, *A Secular Age*, 80.

Our focus on the mysticism connected to Jesus Messiah assemblies needs to be framed in the context of the first century Judaism that involved not simply the more intellectual midrash that characterized Judaism in the centuries following the destruction of the temple. The truth in Jewish history is that mysticism, which was at times shoved off to sides or was not always visible, nonetheless persisted through the centuries since.

We find ourselves, instead, in a highly individualistic world where doubt runs rampant, and spiritual people tend to be quiet about what they know and believe. As Amos Wilder points out, "Religious communication generally must overcome a long addiction to the discursive, the rationalistic, and the prosaic."[16] When Wilder talks about "religious communication" he was not thinking about what might be found in books of theology. The quote comes from his book with the title *Theopoetic: Theology and the Religious Imagination*. Appropriately, this book is without an index, which means it is not about facts, dates, geography, or people and places. Nowhere in the book is there even a definition of the word *theopoetic* per se. References abound though to dreams, mysteries, myths, stories, songs, and ritual. To be sure all these elements also abound in holy scripture and were the fertile soil for Paul's imagination. We have to be careful here, however, for when our microscopic eyes try to analyze and abstract mystery from Holy Scripture, this can lead to a wooden kind of biblical criticism that, according to Wilder, tries "to turn such books as Daniel or Revelation into blueprints."[17] That isn't my goal in describing Paul the mystic, because what he describes and helps us see, even if we cannot fully comprehend it, is the vibrant and deeply felt faith that bewildered the high and mighty in the early days of the Jesus Messiah movement. Wilder brilliantly captures that paradox in this sentence: "The empire did not know what to do with this clandestine movement whose dreams were more universal and contagious than those of the Sibyls and the oracles of Virgil himself."[18]

When we look at God's presence with Paul's scriptural eyes dictating how he sees the world and God's *spirit of God* at work we need the sense of stepping on holy ground. Perhaps we even remove

---

[16] Wilder, *Theopoetic*, 1.
[17] Wilder, *Theopoetic*, 49.
[18] Wilder, *Theopoetic*, 30.

our shoes and find ourselves ready to kneel. To be sure we are talking about Paul's theology, but lest any of my readers think theology has to be a dry boring topic, listen to Wilder's description: "Another name for theology is divinity, and divine wisdom has always been thought of as imparted by the Spirit to those 'in the Spirit.'"[19] This is where we find Paul and those who received his epistles. Indeed, we should consider ourselves in that company, for even now, 2000 years later, we can call ourselves the recipients of his letters. To the degree that it is possible to *hear* Paul's voice (recall Chapter 8: "Paul Found in Letters Heard) we are seeking to encounter the *spirit of God* as present in his letters. If we take the advice of Hoskyns and Davey, we should not look be looking for Paul's theological system, but rather to understand how "...he was struggling to express a mystical experience, and to answer the needs of the early church in terms of it."[20]

12.1 The mystical background in which we discover Paul's mysticism.

Acts gives us a dramatic story of Paul's call with God striking and blinding Paul as he headed to Damascus to persecute followers of Jesus Messiah. A few scholars[21] think that Paul alludes to this event in 2 Corinthians when he mentioned those who saw the gospel veiled. "In their case the god of this world has blinded the minds of the unbelievers, to keep them from seeing the light of the gospel..." (2 Cor 4:4). More in line with what we have been considering is to read the whole of scripture with its accounts and metaphors of light and darkness, along with blindness and seeing. Paul's bible included burning bushes[22] and the glory of the Lord that was removed from the temple. Perhaps most memorable of all the divine epiphanies Paul would have known was the story of Elisha on the Mountain of God — a site perhaps seen by Paul when he was in Arabia. There on that mountain the prophet experienced a strong wind, strong

---

[19] Wilder, *Theopoetic*, 57.
[20] Edwin Hoskyns and Noel Davey, *The Riddle of the New Testament* (London: Faber and Faber Limited 1963), 155.
[21] i.e., Karen Armstrong, *St. Paul*. She titles her second chapter "Damascus." She never doubts the historical accuracy of the story in Acts.
[22] See Antoinette Wire, *2 Corinthians*, 79. In her discussion of this verse she explored the "...Israelite literary circles present...(Sophia/Wisdom) as a female companion or personification of God characterized by light."

enough to break rocks. God was not in it. Neither was God in the earthquake or the fire that followed. But God was in the "sheer silence" that followed. (1 Kings 19:11–18). Paul, as did Elisha, would wait for God to speak. I'm not sure it was on a mountain but he clearly had time in the desert of Arabia.

Paul's call to know Jesus Messiah changed the course of his life, but not as the director of a movie about Paul might like it to be. Paul would never have conceived the more modern, and certainly Hollywood-modified interpretations of his call. While "the modern apocalyptic imagination is preoccupied with the collapse of civilization,"[23] we shall find Paul's declaration one of contrast, affirming a hope that nothing "will be able to separate us from the love of God in Christ Jesus our Lord" (Rom 8:39). The word *apocalypse* in Paul's world can carry with it the more profound connotation of "the disclosure of supernatural persons or secrets."[24] Looking at the background of Paul's mysticism requires us to place his visionary account in the context of other scriptures that are properly understood to be *apocalyptic,* such as, Ezekiel, Isaiah 6, Daniel, I Enoch, and various texts connected to Qumran.

Another word that matters to Paul's mysticism is eschatology. The root word of *eschatology* is *eschatos*, a Greek word meaning *last*. Technically the word *eschatology* simply means the study of last things. Please don't think this means the end of the world. The term makes sense, however, for someone like Paul rooted in a historical consciousness. He was living in the midst of a world that seemed out of touch with its divine origins. Apocalyptic literature was floating in Paul's head, along with the psalms and prophets. God's divine plan was there, but also hidden in a world where injustice and brutal existence was so visible. The book of Daniel is one example of this type of literature which involved a "single-minded preoccupation with suffering, martyrdom, and eschatological vindication."[25]

Our focus on the mysticism connected to Jesus Messiah assemblies needs to be situated in the context of Judaism. It is important to pause for a moment, however, because there was no

---

[23] Amos N. Wilder, *Jesus' Parables and the War of Myths: Essays on Imagination in the Scriptures,* Edited with a preface by James Breech (Philadelphia: Fortress Press, 1982), 8.

[24] Christopher Rowland, *Christian Origins: An Account of the Setting and Character of the most Important Messianic Sect of Judaism* (London: SPCK, 1989), 56.

[25] Rowland, *Christian Origins*, 59.

Judaism in the time of Paul. I've alluded to this before, but this is a place for this to be emphasized. There was an ethnic identity of being a Judean, but Judaism, as a distinct religion did not exist. As Steve Mason puts it regarding Paul, "The path he chose, including his posture toward the laws of Moses and ancestral custom, needs to be understood for itself, not as certifying his membership in a system constructed by modern scholarship or late antique Christians."[26]

Even though studies of early Jewish mysticism involve a number of scholarly disputes, there is little doubt, especially from the evidence of the Dead Sea Scrolls, that mysticism was in the air in the centuries preceding the birth of Jesus. The post-exilic period was awash with expectations regarding God's messiah. In scholarly circles a particular branch of this mystic thought is called Merkavah[27] Judaism. *Merkabah* is the Hebrew name for *chariot*. Its roots are in Ezekiel—though the word *Merkabah* isn't there. The prophecy begins with a fantastic description of a four-wheeled vehicle (i.e., a *Merkabah*) carried by four partly-human and partly-animal creatures bringing that vehicle and its prophet to what he vaguely described as "the appearance of the likeness of the glory of the Lord" (Ezek 1:28). He could not actually see the *glory* (the *kavod*[28]) of God but described what he saw in vague terms. Words always seem to come up short in these visions.

Two other texts are central to the early Jewish mystical tradition. One is the account of Isaiah 6:1-4 where the vision took the prophet into divine glory where he encountered and heard voices and creatures praising God. The other text is the book of Enoch, a non-canonical text dated somewhere between 300-200 BCE, well-known to both Jews and Christians in the formative centuries of the common era. Enoch includes the account of an ascension to the third heaven, with descriptive images that seem to have been modeled on

---

[26] Mason, "Paul Without Judaism," 26.

[27] Scholars spell this word *Merkabah* or *Merkavah* depending on the transliteration of the Hebrew word. The spelling "*Merkabah*" is more frequently encountered.

[28] There are two words in Hebrew which in English are often translated as *glory*. The word "*kavod*" (sometimes is spelled *kabhod*) is more frequent in the Hebrew bible. It means "glory" and is similar to a Hebrew word meaning "heavy." It describes God's greatness and power. The other word is *Shekhina* which appears in rabbinic literature and Aramaic bibles as the word for God's presence. Beginning with Ezekiel it was God's presence that was missing in the rebuilt second temple. See below on God's absent presence. See Raphael Patai, "The Shekhina," *Journal of Religion* 44, no. 4 (1964): 275-88.

the temple in Jerusalem.[29] In the literature of Merkabah mystical experiences there are far more accounts of a sevenfold process of steps to the highest heaven, but the "third heaven" accounts are older. Reaching the third heaven is what Paul recorded.

What we have with these visions from Ezekiel, Isaiah, Daniel, Enoch, and finally from Paul, are experiences that emerged from "altered states of consciousness," from "ecstasy or paranormal consciousness."[30] Recognition of these experiences as part and parcel of the essential story of Paul will come as something of a lightning bolt to those more accustomed to a Paul who seems more like a theologian with a PhD. That bias has led major parts of the Christian world to distrust any aspects of worship that reflect enthusiasm. Although he admitted to being able to speak in tongues, for example, there are scholars who read that he was denigrating this aspect of worship. Interpreting Paul as one opposed to all religious ecstasy, Colleen Shantz, for example, added, "In the case of tongues, Paul's relative ranking of *uninterpreted* glossolalia *in the assembly* is transformed into a comprehensive denigration of ecstatic speech."[31] That wasn't the case at all. He simply wanted outsiders to understand what was happening in worship.

Though visionary experiences may be delusional, medically induced or caused by addictive substances, we find with Evelyn Underhill something authentic and disciplined in the lives of true mystics. Certainly, *authentic* and *disciplined* apply in Paul's case. There is a level of rationality, and we might add hesitancy, in the accounts of religious mysticism regarding "perception of transcendent reality and presence of God. Hence the monoideism of the mystic is rational, whilst that of the hysteric patient is invariably irrational."[32] Underhill also talked about how many mystics evidence "...a vital and creative power, a constructive logic, and extended scale of realization—in a word, a genius—which is in truth

---

[29] C. R. A. Morray-Jones, "The Jewish Mystical Background of Paul's Apostolate. Part One: The Jewish Sources," *Harvard Theological Review* 86, no. 2 (1993): 204.

[30] Segal, *Paul the Convert*, 52.

[31] Colleen Shantz, *Paul in Ecstasy: The Neurobiology of the Apostle's Life and Thought* (New York: Cambridge University Press, 2009), 45, italics in original; Giovanni Bazzana strongly disagrees declaring "Paul does not chastise . . . the practice of glossolalia." In fact, Paul may have invented the word *glossolalia.*" *Having the Spirit of Christ: Spirit Possession and Exorcism in the Early Christ Groups* (New Haven: Yale University Press, 2000), 189-92.

[32] Underhill, *Mysticism*, 60.

their essential quality."[33] Other shared characteristics are accounts of self-renunciation and a lack of great health. In 2 Corinthians (6:4-10; 11:24-32) Paul expresses an amazing response to a whole set of afflictions that could easily lead many of us into depression, bitterness, or anger, but not Paul. "We are treated as imposters, and yet are true; as unknown and yet are well known; as dying, and see — we are alive; as punished, and yet not killed; as sorrowful, yet always rejoicing; as poor, yet making many rich; as having nothing, and yet possessing everything" (2 Cor 6:8-10). These are not the words of a madman smoking bad weed, or dreams from a poet fantasizing about another world that just might be around the corner.

12.2 Paul's Account of God's Apocalypse

While we are at a distance of 2,000 years of history from what Paul saw and knew, we also have original texts in a language and time far removed from us. And we are dealing with a poet and a seer, caught up in heaven, who "heard things that are not be told, that no mortal is permitted to repeat" (2 Cor 12:4) There is something authentic in Paul's account, and yet something is missing. How are we to make sense of Paul's narrative, the one with missing words — the words he cannot speak! (2 Cor 12:4)? That question is addressed in the observation of the historian Walter Benjamin who wrote an essay titled "The Task of the Translator." Benjamin, contrasting the functions of a poet and that of a translator, says, "The intention of the poet is spontaneous, primary, graphic; that of the translator is derivative, ultimate, ideational."[34] We are the ones who translate Paul, while his voice is that of a mystic poet living with Christ.

We can't know if Paul was near or far sighted, but my guess is that with the visions that shaped his call he was as far-sighted as any prophet or poet. His opening to the Galatians relates an early vision that changed Paul's focus. What we have here is a transcendental experience of Paul. It did not, as he repeated, have a human source!

---

[33] Underhill, *Mysticism*, 62.

[34] Walter Benjamin, "The Task of the Translator," in *Walter Benjamin Illuminations: Essays and Reflections*, ed. Hannah Arendt (New York: Houghton Mifflin, Harcourt, 2019), 18.

> For I want you to know, brothers and sisters, that the gospel that was proclaimed by me is <u>not of human origin;</u> for I did <u>not receive</u> it from a human source, *nor was I taught* it, but I received it through <u>a revelation</u> of Jesus Christ. You have heard, no doubt, of my earlier life in Judaism. I was violently persecuting the church of God and was trying to destroy it. I advanced in Judaism beyond many among my people of the same age, for I was far more zealous for the traditions of my ancestors. But when God, who had <u>set me apart</u> before I was born and <u>called me</u> through his grace, was pleased to <u>reveal</u> his Son to me, so that I might proclaim him among the Gentiles, I <u>did not confer with any human being, nor did I go up to Jerusalem</u> to those who were already apostles before me, but I went away at once into Arabia, and afterwards I returned to Damascus (Gal 1:11-17).

The underlined phrases are the clues to Paul's spiritual experiences. He was not passing on some experience or teaching that he received from others. There were those in Galatia (and others later in Corinth) who called Paul's credentials as an apostle into question. My assumption is that what Paul wrote in this letter was not just meant to serve as his credentials, but it also expressed what may have been inexpressible. What we have in Galatians may have been a more frequent introduction that he made.

I know from my own ministry, in a number of different churches, how I usually began with stories about my own sense of call to ministry. I never framed my sense of call, however, as one like the prophet Jeremiah, but that's exactly what Paul said. The book of Jeremiah begins as well with the story of his call. "Before I formed you in the womb I knew you, and before you were born I consecrated you; I appointed you a prophet to the nations (*ethnē*)" (Jer 1:5.) Indeed, Paul echoes Jeremiah in Gal 1:15 when he introduces himself: "But when God, who had set me apart, before I was born..." Being called and formed in the womb is the way Isaiah 49:1–6 begins. The prophecy concludes: "I will give you as a light to the nations (*ethnē*), that my salvation may reach to the end of the earth." I wouldn't be surprised if Paul's calling card had that verse on it. (We will explore Paul's vision of going to "the end of the earth" in our next chapter.)

12.3 The community of the sanctified

When it comes to understanding the language of being *sanctified in Christ Jesus*, the real challenge is to comprehend what it meant to say that these early followers, with all their faults and differences, were essentially being made *holy persons*. The language Paul used to describe all the workings of the *Spirit* or the *Holy Spirit*, namely to be *sanctified*, was inscribed in the very lives of those in his communities.[35] This wasn't an intellectual idea in the category of a *belief* about something. It was experienced. It was at work in lives that were changed and in those who kept their faith in the face of persecution.

I'm not sure if it's possible to build a linguistic or experiential bridge back to Paul's world, but I admit that's what I am trying to do. It has been a little easier to use historical material and social issues in the previous chapters. The topic of Paul's mysticism and spirit present in communities of his followers is harder to express. A quote from the philosopher Hans Georg Gadamer, known for his work on the way we understand one another (i.e., *hermeneutics*) is appropriate: "*A hermeneutically trained mind must be, from the start, sensitive to the text's quality of newness.*"[36] It is the word *newness* that adds insight and may help open our eyes. Something was happening in those communities who were addressed in Paul's letters. Remarkably, even with all the troubles Paul addressed in the first letter to the Corinthians, Paul saw them as "sanctified in Christ" (1 Cor 1:2). His love (*agape*) is to be with all them (1 Cor 16:24). So many of them had started off as "not wise," "not powerful," or of "noble birth," but all had found "life in Christ" (1 Cor. 1:26, 30).

Speaking of *something unique* we have to accord Chapter 13 of 1 Corinthians a preeminent position in what was new and amazing in the life of these early followers of Jesus. Think of all the conditional "If" declarations that open this passage: "If I speak in the tongues of mortals and angels...if I have prophetic powers...if I have all

---

[35] Giovanni Bazzanna notes that Paul did not use the definite article "the" in connection to *Spirit* or *Holy Spirit*. Later copyists seem to have added it in places. What mattered for Paul was the Christ *pneuma* (spirit); *Having the Spirit of Christ*, 176.

[36] Anthony C. Thistleton, *The Two Horizons: New Testament Hermeneutics and Philosophical Description with Special Reference to Heidegger, Bultmann, Gadamer, and Wittgenstein* (Grand Rapids: William B. Eerdmans Publishing Company, 1980), 305.

faith…if I give away all my possessions…If I hand over my body." These conditional statements hark back to the 8th century prophets of the Bible knowing just how distorted God's people had become. Every one of these "if" passages speak to communal practices reflecting the world in disarray, where there is nothing if there is not love. God's new world was not a world of honors, degrees, and better titles and chairs at the table for a privileged few. It is grounded in *agape*, what Ruden called a "selfless love that people can feel for enemies or strangers. It is utterly impractical and makes no sense, but it is real."[37] Unity and reconciliation is what this newness in Messiah Jesus is all about.

The section of 1 Cor 12-14 ends with Paul's crescendo of energy coming first from prophetic voices in worship, and then in the ecstatic utterance of incomprehensible words (*glossolalia*) that would be meaningless to a stranger. These were gifts to be cherished only if they led to the "building up of the church" (1 Cor 14:12). Paul himself, with little modesty as was characteristic from time to time, declared that he was able "to speak in tongues more than all of you" (1 Cor 14:18). But Paul went on to condemn the overuse of tongues in public worship going so far as to say, "Brothers and sisters, do not be children in your thinking; rather, be infants in evil, but in thinking be adults" (1 Cor 14:20).

From the way Paul addressed issues of worship in Corinth we know that quiet contemplation wasn't part of their common life, or if it existed it wasn't a problem that Paul addressed. Front and center in saying that "Jesus is Lord (*Kyrios*)" was the Holy Spirit. Then in Paul's ingenious way he gave speaking parts to many parts of the body.[38] It is almost like all the body parts were on stage, or rather some of the body parts were trying to be in the spotlight, while other parts were out of sight or offstage. Paul wanted a unified body of believers, respect for the weaker members, just as there was respect for the weaker parts of one's body.

Once more we are trying to have a picture of Paul on his knees and not with pen in hand. We must keep in our minds what Paul repeated from what had to be an early hymn of praise when he wrote to the Philippians. Speaking of God who highly exalted Messiah Jesus, he was given the name "that is above every name, so that at

---

[37] Ruden, *Paul Among the People*, 171.
[38] See 1 Cor 12:14-26. Those who speaking parts include a foot, an ear, and an eye!

the name of Jesus every knee should bend, in heaven and on earth, and under the earth" (Phil 2:9-10). Wilder would call this a theopoetic image, but more than an image, it was a call to imitate.

12.4 Paul's descriptions of mystical encounters.

Our examination of Paul has hopefully led us to consider the many different ways he alluded to his mystical experiences. One comes in a rhetorical flourish in which Paul was defending his credentials as an apostle. Chapter 9 of 1 Corinthians begins: "Am I not free? Am I not an apostle? Have I not seen the Lord? Are you not my work in the Lord?" To all those rhetorical questions the answer would be found in heads nodding "Yes! Of course!" Those who had heard Paul before most likely heard of some of his experiences of a transcendental nature.

Paul's declaration of "having seen the Lord" must be put into context. His is the first written eye-witness report, as Paul's letters preceded the earliest gospel Mark by at least fifteen years. Mark's gospel contains no eye-witness accounts of the resurrection. The witness was the empty grave. (Mark 16.6)[39] Another single line reference to Paul's experience of the Lord, or in this case to the Risen Messiah is found in 1 Cor.15:3-11, where Paul tells his recipients what they already know, which was his teaching about those who were witnesses to the resurrection. Paul was the final witness. "Last of all, as to one untimely born, he also appeared to me." There is no description of what he saw. It just a simple affirmation of what he knew to be true.

Ironically Paul speaks of the resurrection in a totally different way in Philippians. There he writes that he "wants to know Christ and the power of resurrection and the sharing of his sufferings by becoming like him in his death" (Phil 3:10). Two verses later Paul declared, not what he lacked, but what had happened to him: "Christ Jesus has made me his own" (Phil 3:12).

The verbal description *"made me"* translates the Greek word *katalambano*. It can mean to seize, win, attain, make one's own.

Something of the drama may be lost by thinking of the phrase "made me his own" as an action in the past and completed. In that sense the phrase could be a snapshot of Paul at a particular moment.

---

[39] Note that there are two other endings of Mark, titled the Shorter Ending and the Longer ending. These are not considered part of Mark's original gospel.

The moment, however, references his entire past (thus his past credentials) and the future (the goal he has not achieved). Paul could have been thinking of a long list of past experiences, including those he listed as credentials from his past. None of that mattered. What he recalled was simply that Christ had seized him. That may be as close as we will ever get to the Damascus road story from Acts. And in reality, in writing from that prison cell, Paul was not looking backwards but "only straining forward to what lies ahead" (Phil 3:13).

The theologian Nicholas Lash has said about the experience of being found by God: "To... speak of God finding us has the merit of respecting the primacy of grace, whereas to speak is if we had found God is not only Pelagian[40] but, by encouraging us to suppose that, having 'found' him, we now have only to 'hang on to' him, it reduces the 'God' whom we have found to a 'possession' that we have acquired — and this is just another form of idolatry."[41] Regarding Paul's claim that the Lord had taken a hold of him, or had "grasped him, arrested him," Lash remarks that there is something very personal about these experiences of God, which "require us to acknowledge ourselves not merely produced but addressed, not merely made but loved."[42]

Paul's distinctive understanding is also evident in various comments he made about things he learned from the Lord. A most significant vision, if that is what it was, is found in Paul's comments about a celebration of the Lord's Supper when the rich were getting drunk and eating well, before the poorer members arrived. Paul refused to commend them for this practice. And he added this: "For I received from the Lord what I also handed on to you, that the Lord Jesus on the night when he was betrayed[43] took a loaf of bread..." (1

---

[40] Pelagius (355–420 CE) emphasized free will, in contrast to Augustinian ideas focused on original sin and a corrupt human nature. With ideas on ways to earn salvation, Pelagius expected a kind of perfectionist life leading to eternity; Diarmaid MacCulloch, *Christianity: The First Three Thousand Years* (New York: Viking Press, 2010), 306–8.

[41] Nicholas Lash, *Theology on the Way to Emmaus* (Eugene: Wipf & Stock 1986) 11.

[42] Nicholas Lash, *Easter in Ordinary: Reflections on Human Experience and the Knowledge of God* (Notre Dame: Notre Dame Press 1986), 276.

[43] The Greek word there is *paradideto*. The root word is *Paradidomai* which means "to hand over." It can also mean "to commend," and with regard to traditions what is "passed on." Using the phrase" was betrayed" (NRSV) always invokes the face

Cor. 11:23). Remember, Paul never mentioned in his first visit with Peter what they discussed. It may or may not have included this revelation. If Peter had told Paul about the last supper, we would expect a different account at this point in 1 Corinthians. All we can presume is that these were words that came to Paul and have, subsequently, been at the heart of the eucharistic worship that has been central throughout Christian history and practice. It was what Paul "received from the Lord."

Mystical language also flows through many parts of Paul's letters. When Paul recalled the creation story in 2 Corinthians 4:6 it became a mysticism he shares with his recipients. "For it is God who said, "Let light shine out of darkness," who has shone in our hearts, to give the light of the knowledge of the glory of God in the face of Jesus Christ." When a man says a "light shone in his heart." it is light-years from a transcendent distant God described with theological words like "omnipotence." The philosopher Jack Caputo noted that this puts us "back in a theology of the One with all the power to reward and punish. This one you anger at your peril."[44] Paul, however, knew God *only* in terms of Christ crucified and God shining in his heart. It sounds like mystical language.

Paul concluded his discussion of mystical experiences by this enigmatic reference to something he called both a "thorn in the flesh, *and* "a messenger from Satan to torment me" (2 Cor 12:7-9). Throughout the ages scholars have proposed innumerable theories about that "thorn." The word means "stake." Whatever it was it hurt. Most presume it was some physical malady. Knox, on the other hand, is certain it was not a physical illness, because that would mean Paul was a *sickly* kind of man. Nobody with a sickly frame would have endured the kinds of trials and travels and Paul did. "Surely that long list of labors, exposures, deprivations, and dangers hardly suggested an invalid! The evidence on the whole supports the description from the author of *The Acts of Paul* that Paul was: "of vigorous physique."[45] Were they one and the same thing or two

---

of Judas. The better translation is just to say, "on the night he was handed over." This is just my bias.

[44] Jack Caputo, *Hoping Against Hope: Confessions of a Postmodern Pilgrim* (Minneapolis: Fortress Press, 2015), 107

[45] Knox, *Chapters in a Life*, 77. Note: *The Acts of Paul* was a second century account. It was part of the remembered Paul tradition in the early church. Scholars do not look on it as a reliable source.

different, but similar, realities for Paul? Moreover, what was that "thorn in the flesh?"

We should not be surprised if Paul felt hindered by Satan. He was extremely mindful of the reality of evil as can be seen in his letters. It isn't as if every letter has numerous references to Satan, but, as John Anderson puts it, "though the explicit references to (the) Satan are few, given the apocalyptic basis of much of Paul's thinking, there is an implicit presence on almost every page."[46] Earlier in the Letter of Tears Paul stated that "Satan disguises himself as an angel of light" (2 Cor 11:14). Paul's final words of encouragement in Romans have this promise: "The God of Peace will shortly crush Satan under your feet" (Rom 16:20) We would err if we simply ignored Paul's consciousness of evil personified in the name of Satan. "One cannot diminish the role of (the) Satan in the thought of Paul. For him the universe was to be seen as engaged in a titanic struggle between the forces of good and evil."[47]

We have to wonder if Paul would agree with the mystic Malaval who observed that not all accounts of spiritual rapture can be ascribed to God. Indeed, some come, "...by the force of a heated imagination which vividly apprehends a sensible object, or by the artifice of the Devil"[48] We have only to recall the stories of the temptation of Jesus by the Devil to realize how much this imaginative apprehension was ingrained in a Judean world view that both Jesus and Paul shared.

Paul's attitude toward mysticism is revealed by this phrase "even considering the exceptional character of the revelations" (2 Cor 12:7). Notice that they were *revelations*. Plural! It wasn't just a single one-time event. This accords with the earlier statement of Paul's regarding his "visions and revelations of the Lord" (2 Cor 12:1) Paul wasn't the only one to mention this aspect of his life for there is evidence this was in the memory of Paul as recorded by the author of Acts.

In spite of the historical unreliability of Acts, I recognize its value to us as part of our canon, and certainly as a witness to the early followers of Jesus Messiah in the Roman world. Certainly, we can

---

[46] John T. Anderson, "The Body of Satan According to Paul," *Proceedings* 13 (1993): 103.

[47] Anderson, "The Body of Satan," 103.

[48] Underhill, *Mysticism*, 361.

credit Acts as giving us *stories* of Paul *remembered*. Acts, in the decades after Paul ascribed to Paul various visions and revelations. For example, there was a time when traveling through Phyrygia and Galacia, Paul along with his companions, had been "...forbidden by the Holy Spirit to speak the word in Asia" (Acts 16:6).

Another report in Acts involved the voice of the Lord. Paul had baptized Crispus, a synagogue official and his household. Then in a dream Paul was told he had no reason to be afraid to speak, for there were many in Corinth who were God's people. (Acts 18: 9-10) Also supporting the mystic side of Paul was his address to the elders from Ephesus. He stated that he was "a captive to the Holy Spirit." He did not know what would happen to him when he arrived in Jerusalem, "except that the Holy Spirit testifies to me in every city that imprisonment and persecutions are waiting for me" (Acts 20:22-23). Thus Acts remembered a Paul who had dreams and visions. You would think the author would have reported Paul's ascent into heaven if he had that story. Thankfully, Paul did.

12.5 Paul's heavenly ascent

A key part of discovering Paul has led us to discuss the many occasions he was defending his call to be an apostle. The author of Acts seemed to have doubts about calling Paul an Apostle, but his pen seemed to slip at one point. In two verses[49] Paul and Barnabas were called apostles, though in the rest of the account the author did not see Paul as equal to the other apostles, namely as a disciple of Jesus.

Paul has a more expansive view of apostles. In addition to those Acts recognized, Paul saw Andronicus and Juia as "apostles before him" (Rom 16:7) and he saw some claiming to be apostles in regard to the Corinthian community. Paul said he was "not in the least inferior to these super-apostles" (2 Cor 11:5) who had followed him into the Corinthian community with their assertions of spiritual superiority over Paul. Those who kept finding fault with Paul, for example, those who provoked the "Letter of Tears," found themselves receiving an extremely sharp rebuke. And it worked!

What I didn't cover in the earlier section was the way the "Letter of Tears" was concluded. The list of hardships and Paul boasting of his weakness was not the conclusion. Paul switched gears and

---

[49] Acts 14: 4, 14

testified to something that he may have shared for the first time ever in a letter, or maybe even in a public event. Paul couched the story in the veneer of the third person singular pronoun: "I know a person in Christ who fourteen years ago was caught up to the third heaven" (2 Cor 12:2). With that introduction we have something unique about Paul in the world of ancient Judean literature, as noted by Segal: "In fact, he is the only early Jewish mystic and apocalyptist whose personal, confessional writing has come down to us."[50]

Though Paul lived in the Roman world of the first century in the Common Era, with his mystical experiences we need to back up a number of centuries to enter the world of Post-Exilic Israel following the Babylonian captivity. The temple in Jerusalem had been rebuilt but it was not the same as before. The prophet Ezekiel is our guide to what was missing, as well as to a mystic tradition in which we find Paul.

Ezekiel's other-worldly description included that four-wheeled chariot taking the prophet to a place which allowed him to see what "was the appearance of the likeness of the glory of the Lord." What he saw in his vision would be what could not be found in the re-built temple in Jerusalem. Nine chapters following the ascent of the chariot Ezekiel 10 begins with the title "God's glory leaves Jerusalem."[51] The reason for God's presence abandoning the temple is explained in Ezekiel 12. There were 25 wicked counselors at the gates of the city, resulting in a terrible judgment falling upon Israel.

The departure of God's glory from the temple meant that God's covenant was broken. God had declared to Noah in Genesis 9:1–17, following the flood, that this new covenant was everlasting.[52] But now, for Ezekiel, the covenant had been broken. In this Second Temple part of Israel's history, divine wisdom then became the province of "a special elect in the literature of the period..."[53] Paul's experience of Paradise placed him in their company.

Paul stood in the mystical tradition kept alive ever since the temple had been rebuilt. As a Pharisee he was grounded in *Merkabah mysticism*. In those four hundred years separating Paul from the

---

[50] Segal, *Paul the Convert*, 34.
[51] In the NRSV version.
[52] Grant Macaskill, *Union with Christ in the New Testament* (Oxford: Oxford University Press, 2013), 105. He explained this is the called the Noachic Covenant, and it wasn't just for all humanity, but for "all life."
[53] Macaskill, *Union with Christ*, 114.

rebuilding of the second century there were "visionaries in the pre-Christian era, and particularly in the first two centuries of the Christian era who sought to repeat the experience of the *Merkavah*."[54] According to Gershom Scholem, the pre-eminent scholar of Jewish mysticism, this early flourishing of mysticism was rooted in the practices and teachings of the Pharisees and the Essenes, both of which harbored apocalyptic tendencies.[55]

While it is not germane to our discussion of Paul, what is interesting about mysticism within Judaism is the way it continued and developed in Western and Eastern Europe in the Middle Ages and into the contemporary world. There is a history of many mystics with various accounts of spiritual encounters with the divine with the reports from their disciples and students. Just as the record of Christian mystics continued through the centuries, the same happened within Judaism. Movements like the Spanish Kabbalists and the German Hasidics[56] abound with stories written about those mystics, but rare is an autobiographical account such as we find with Paul.

Paul opens his account of this divine encounter bringing him to a third heaven as if it was not his story to tell. Thus, it began, "I know a person in Christ..." (2 Cor 12:2) All the scholars that I have read, however, believe it *was his* spiritual journey. It seems, though, as if he was telling it for the first time with this letter. Why? It could have been brought to Paul's mind by the things the "so-called" super apostles were declaring about their spiritual gifts. We must bear in mind that the recipients of this letter had to know from Paul's way of talking about Christ that a kind mystical theology was natural to him. Paul, the dry boring theologian? Never. Paul visiting the third heaven? That they could imagine.

Evelyn Underhill would understand this mystical encounter of Paul as fitting for a vast number of mystics she had studied. She wrote about mystics who enter a fully transcendental world, so different and unlike this world. There the mystic faces what she called a "huge disparity between...unspeakable experience" and language. Whoever hears such an account is probably filled with

---

[54] Gershom Scholem, *On the Mystical Shape of the Godhead: Basic Concepts in the Kabbalh* (New York: Schoken Books, 1991), 20.
[55] Gershom Scholem, *Kabbalah* (New York: Dorset Press 1987), 10.
[56] Scholem, *Kabbalah*, 81.

more bewilderment than understanding.[57] Paul claimed that he could not remember if he was in or out of his body. The experience wasn't so much about seeing, but rather hearing "things that are not be told, that no mortal is permitted to repeat" (2 Cor 12:3-4).

What were the Corinthians to make of this story? At one point the New Testament scholar John Ashton wondered if there wasn't something in Paul comparable to a tribal shaman, but then partially discounted that possibility since "Shamans are not missionaries and their authority is restricted."[58] Nonetheless Ashton suggested the comparison because Paul's very being "could be torn apart and reconstituted as a new person at the time he was established in his calling."[59] Ashton, furthermore—in a difference from what I am saying—was convinced that the Damascus road experience recorded in Acts, was the decisive event in Paul's conversion. "…it was indeed Paul's Damascus road experience, perceived as a transformation of all his previous values, that colored the whole of his subsequent life."[60]

By the time Paul wrote to the Galatians, once more defending his title as an apostle, he discussed it as a call rooted in a time before he was born, but then revealed to him. It certainly wasn't the last time he heard or saw something connected to a divine revelation. Given the context in which Paul was speaking of "visions and revelations" (2 Cor. 12:1)—all plural—he chose from what was by now a longer mystical journey with Christ to share in this *Letter of Tears* the time he was caught up into Paradise. From singular memorable divine encounters, there was also something much deeper with Paul on a daily basis, and that was found in his most frequently used two-worded sense of his self-identification. If you wanted to know where he lived, it was *in Christ*.

12.6 In Christ

Ever since the Reformation, according the historian Brad Gregory, those of us whom he calls "Westerners" are now living in the "Kingdom of Whatever."[61] We live in the world of personal

---

[57] Underhill, *Mysticism*, 76.
[58] John Ashton, *The Religion of Paul the Apostle* (New Haven: Yale University Press, 2000), 29.
[59] Ashton, *The Religion of Paul the Apostle*, 122.
[60] Ashton, *The Religion of the Apostle Paul*, 116.
[61] Brad Gregory, *The Unintended Revolution*, 112.

choice. Individual preference rules decision making. "Be your own person. Do your own thing." The advertising world leads the way in this world. Once more, Paul would be appalled.

We are also part of a process that Talal Asad has called "a historical project whose aim is the increasing triumph of individual autonomy." The major question asked in this context is "what should human beings do to realize their freedom, empower themselves and choose pleasure." The goal is "to become more powerful so that disempowerment — suffering — can be overcome."[62] Paul could not begin to live with this mindset, because, as he said, his life wasn't even his own anymore: "and it is no longer I who live, but it is Christ who lives in me" (Gal 2:20). The "historic project" for Paul was to create spirit-filled communities where Christ lived in all, .

To understand Paul's visceral language of being *located* in Christ, we can thank Albert Schweitzer, who identified in Paul a "Christ-centered mysticism." He did not mean by *mysticism*, however, what I have emphasized in this chapter. "Schweitzer's mysticism is curiously cerebral....and at the beginning of his final chapter when he calls Paul the patron saint of *thought* in Christianity."[63]

What Schweitzer did that rings true today within a rather large collection of Pauline scholars is to contest the claim stemming from the Reformation that "justification by faith" was the center of Paul's theology. Vanhoozer comments on Schweitzer's declaration that something else was far more important to Paul: Schweitzer downsized justification to the status of a "subsidiary crater" on planet Paul, lying within the "main crater" of his understanding of union with Christ."[64] Such a declaration did not settle well within many Protestant circles in the 1930s, but Schweitzer's insight was a crack in the door that led to a more balanced consideration of the way Christian scholars have looked far more positively at Judaism, and as seen here with a deeper appreciation of Paul's roots in the

---

[62] Talal Asad, *Formations*, 71.

[63] John Ashton, *The Religion of Paul*, 44. Reference is to Albert Schweitzer, *The Mysticism of Paul the Apostle* (London: Adam and Charles Black, 1953). Emphasis in the quote is mine.

[64] Kevin J. Vanhoozer, "'From "Blessed in Christ' to "'Being in Christ' The State of Union and the Place of Participation in Paul's Discourse, New Testament Exegesis, and Systematic Theology Today," in *"In Christ" in Paul*, ed. Michael J. Thate, et. al. (Tübingen: Mohr Siebeck, 2014), 5-6.

Hebraic testament. The other positive side of Schweitzer's contribution was to emphasize the "corporate dimension to being in Christ."[65]

The argument here continues to be that the concept of being "in Christ" is not connected to the evangelical question, "Are you saved?" The operational assumption behind that inquiry is that being saved is a choice to be made by each person.[66] That is a premise hard to find in Paul because he was nearly always referring to the communal dimensions of this movement reaching the nations to bring them the fulfillment of Christ crucified. His work for reconciliation preceded his ministry. "All this is from God, who reconciled us to himself through Christ, and has given us the ministry of reconciliation; that is, in Christ God was reconciling the world to himself, not counting their trespasses against them, and then trusting the message of reconciliation to us" (2 Cor 5:18-19).

More than once I have suggested that Paul's story begins with his revocation of status. It had to be a stunning story to witness for those who knew Paul as a proud Pharisee when he aligned himself with the most vulnerable in his world. To be sure certain people seem to gain a kind of saintliness in this world for such a trajectory. We can think of Albert Schweitzer and Mother Teresa in that regard. What sets Paul apart, though, has a great deal to do with his reluctance to claim this as his story alone. Paul's *in-Christ mysticism* isn't just about *his* experience of God, but the experience of God *in community.*

What we find in nearly all of Paul's references to the work of the Spirit of Christ in the midst of the common life of the *ekklēsia* is a life of mutual obligation and service unlike what they had known previously. Robert Jewett expressed it this way: "The regulative principal for Christian family members is the Spirit of Christ, which redefines all social obligations, at times with considerable cost and pain."[67] To understand Paul's concept of those "social obligations," we can take a phrase from Romans as an example of what is different for those *in Christ.* "

---

[65] Kevin Vanhoozer, "From 'Blessed in Christ'," 5-6.

[66] Talal Asad notes that we are the inheritors of "a view that neatly historicizes and secularizes the Reformation doctrine that correct belief must be more highly valued than correct practice." *Genealogies of Religion: Discipline and Reasons of Power in Christianity and Islam* (Baltimore: The Johns Hopkins Press, 1993), 58.

[67] Jewett, *Romans*, 493.

> So then, Brothers and sisters, we are debtors, not to the flesh, to live according to the flesh –for if you live according to flesh, you will die; but if by the Spirit you put to death the deeds of the body, you will live. For all who are led by the Spirit of God are children of God (Rom 8:12-14).

Paul's emphasis on the work of the Spirit, which is the Spirit of Christ (Rom. 8:9–11) is what animates not only Paul but all who have become the children of God. The all-pervasive work of the Spirit is what shapes their collective life. Clearly in focus is the contrast between *flesh (sarx)* and *Spirit (pneuma)*. As Dale Martin points out there is a radical dualism at work in Paul's mind when it comes to these two realities. Twice in the same passage Paul connected the work of *flesh (sarx)* as equal to death (Rom 8:6 and 8:12-14). Martin writes that for Paul "the overwhelming bulk of his references to *sarx* place it in the category of "this world" in its opposition to the plan of God."[68] When it comes to Paul's negative thinking about the word "flesh" we err, however, if we think Paul is some kind of ascetic refusing all the joys of living in the physical world. More to the point is the weakness and corruptibility even unto death implied with *sarx*.

There is another Greek word to consider with regard to the Spirit-filled life of the Jesus-Messiah communities. That is the word for body — *sōma* in Greek. It occurs more than 50 times in Paul's letters. As one example, Paul devoted most of 1 Corinthians 12 to the image of the metaphor of the human body, to emphasize the respect due to the weaker, or lesser members of any body — including the members of *ekklēsia*! Body, for Paul, is not so much about the physical body, but more about "the embodiment of the person. In this sense *sōma* is a relational concept. It denotes the person embodied in a particular environment."[69] Paul's use of the terms *sōma* and *pneuma*, as the ingredients to the unity of Jesus Messiah people is evident in this key passage from 1 Corinthians, "For in one spirit *(pneuma)* we were baptized into one body *(soma)* — Jews or Greeks, slaves or free — and we were made to drink of one Spirit *(pneuma)*" (12:13) Dunn also focuses on the corporate dimension of Paul's understanding of *sōma*. Body in 1 Corinthians 12:17-27 is "a

---

[68] Martin, *The Corinthian Body*, 172.
[69] Dunn, *The Theology of Paul*, 56.

model of human cooperation and interrelationships."[70] Among all the different ways in which Paul referred to *pneuma* what was central for him was the *community* that was formed and shaped by the spirit of Christ.

The primary meaning of *pneuma*[71] in my favorite Greek-English lexicon is "blowing, breathing."[72] The second definition is "breath, spirit, soul." It is such a critical word in scripture that this lexicon devotes five pages to just this one word! The word is pervasive in Paul's letters, except for Philemon where it appears just once in the final verse: "The grace of the Lord Jesus Christ be with your spirit" (Phlm 25) We find in Paul examples where the Spirit is a singular expression of God's presence (Rom 8:4), but we also find it is the Spirit of Christ that is present. (Rom. 8:9) Sometimes it is the Spirit of God. (Rom 8:9) Whatever it is called it had to be part of the air they were sharing.

Paul expressed this principle in Romans, as well as in Galatians. There we can find Paul admonishing that community to avoid using "their freedom as an opportunity for self-indulgence, but through love[73] become slaves to one another" (Gal 5:13). The Greek word for "one another" is *allēlon*.[74] According to Bridgett Kahl it comes from two Greek words *allos-allos* which literally would translate as *other-other*. This term appears seven times in the last two chapters of Galatians, and it means having "the re-organization of community in a non-hierarchical, non-antagonistic, non-exclusive way of horizontal mutuality and solidarity, as non-competition, non-combat, non-consumption of the other..."[75] Inside this community is where the Spirit of Christ dwells.

"*To be or not to be* in Christ was, for Paul, the only question—new, urgent, and ever relevant...Paul identified with Christ to the point

---

[70] Dunn, *The Theology of Paul*, 59.

[71] *Pneuma* in Hebrew is *ruach*. Genesis 1:2 in the NRSV speaks of the wind (*ruach*) of God that swept over the face of the waters.

[72] Danker et al., *A Greek-English Lexicon*, 832.

[73] In the Greek it is "but through the love (*the agape*) become slaves to one another." It may be a reference to the agape feast that was a core part of the communal life of early Jesus Messiah people. Note the reference to the meal in Chapter 11.4 with regard to the same phrase "the love" or "the agape" used twice in Romans 13:10.

[74] This word is also discussed briefly at the end of the *Excursus 10.1. Paul's Message of Freedom* above.

[75] Kahl, *Galatians Re-Imagined*, 269–70.

of viewing his own story as overlapping with that of Jesus: "I have been crucified with Christ" (Gal 2:19)."[76] Thus, Vanhooser, the author of that quote, concludes that Paul and his followers were *located in Christ*. Neither geographical location nor ethnicity mattered to Paul. The relationship to Christ was the source of their identity. Paul emphasized that when he proclaimed that he was "unknown by sight to the churches (*ekklēsia*) of Judea that are *in Christ*" (Gal 1:22, my emphasis).

So, what is the function of the Spirit of Christ in reference to communities who were responsible for what Paul called *the ministry of the Spirit*. On the surface it seems a somewhat odd expression, but it has a specific role to play in the formation of the communities founded by Paul which he refers to as "our letter." It wasn't an epistle written with ink, but with the Spirit of the Living God. This is the passage:

> You yourselves are our letter, written on our hearts, to be known and read by all; and you show that you are a letter (*epistle*) of Christ, prepared by us, written (*eggegrammenē*) not with ink but with the Spirit (*pneuma*) of the living God, not on tablets of stone but on tablets of human hearts (2 Cor 3:2-3).

Richard Hays thinks it is better to understand that this is a letter "*inscribed on our hearts.*"[77] That translation helps us see the connection with the prophecy of Jeremiah. On a day to come God would make a covenant with the house of Israel and the house of Judah that would be written on their hearts. They wouldn't even need to teach one another about God because all people, from the least to the greatest, would know the Lord. (Paraphrase of Jer 31:31-34). The same passage appears in Paul's admonitions to the Corinthians concerning the words Jesus offered at the Last Supper: "Taking the cup Jesus said, "This cup is the new covenant in my blood."

This is about a *ministry of the spirit*, and what was critical for Paul was the ministry of belonging to *ekklēsia*. Paul's understanding of the new covenant in the words of Hays meant that it "…is marked and attested by God's writing on hearts, not in script: the ministry of the new covenant is attested by the formation of communities whose

---

[76] Vanhoozer, From "Blessed in Christ,' 3 (Italics in original)
[77] Hays, *Echoes of Scripture*, 130.

lives, transformed by the Holy Spirit, bear undeniable witness to the truth of God's work in their midst."[78] It wasn't a debating society. Earlier in this chapter I discussed the idea that God's glory was not to be found in the temple. (Section 12.1) According to Paul the glory missing in the temple was reflected "in a mirror" in which the members of the Jesus Messiah community were sharing an image (*eikona*) reflecting God's glory that came from the Lord, the Spirit. (2 Cor 3:18). Notice that Paul ends this verse with reference to "the Lord" he immediately adds the word *pneumatos* (i.e., Spirit).

There is a phenomenon in the scientific world that bears the name *atmospheric electricity*. On normal days with sunny skies and mild breezes we don't even notice this reality. But imagine an incoming thunderstorm with a rush of wind and thundering clouds, and the boom of lightening striking the ground near us; we awake to take cover. The unseen becomes instantly felt. As this chapter began I used a phrase from the actor John Lithgow about a poetry reading when he said he "could sense electricity in the air." This metaphor helps us understand what Paul knew about "being in Christ." It's not simply one belief from a world of other beliefs. This, for Paul, was a phrase marking lives that had been changed with the awareness that those *in Christ* would never seek to return to their past. The phrase *"in Christ"* was in the air his friends breathed. The passage in 2 Corinthians 5:17 is a case in point: "So if anyone is in Christ, there is a new creation: everything old has passed away; see, everything has become new!"[79]

What we find with the many references to being "in Christ" is what Wikenhauser called "a mysterious and vital union…to things and powers which derive from this union or which presuppose it."[80] To be "in Christ" involved power and transformation. Paul wrote, "I can do all things through him who strengthens me" (Phil 4:13). The conclusion to Romans 8 rivals that of the ending notes of the greatest of symphonies. Paul named all the realities of the world: death, life, angels, rulers, things present, things to come, powers, height, depth and concluded "…nor nothing else in all creation will

---

[78] Hays, *Echoes of Scripture*, 149-50.

[79] A longer explanation of this verse was found in Chapter 7.2 In that section I offered the translation of N. T. Wright which I like best because it honors a verse without a verb: *"If anyone in Messiah, new creation!"*

[80] Alfred Wikenhauser, *Pauline Mysticism: Christ in the Mystical Teaching of Paul* (New York: Herder and Herder: 1960), 25-6.

be able to separate us from the love of God in Christ Jesus our Lord" (Rom 8:39). To be "in Christ" was the entire composition meant for the whole world.

There was a real sense that Christ was present in their midst. It didn't necessarily mean that it happened overnight. Paul believed that it had to be accomplished in a birthing process. He says in Galatians 4:19: "My Little children, for whom I am again in the pain of childbirth until Christ is formed in you…" Why would Paul use that birthing image for those who had been baptized in Christ? In a very real sense, the Teachers who had followed Paul into the Galatian communities had "in effect reversed the birth process. It has put the birth of the Galatians in question, throwing Paul back into anxious labor."[81]

Christ was *formed* in Galatia, and then Paul could call them, corporately, to be *re-formed*. It was to be a process of separating from conformity to the world, and finding themselves in a world where there was "neither Jew nor Greek, there is no longer slave or free, there is no longer male and female, for all of you are one *in* Christ Jesus" (Gal 3:28).

Such a community had what Paul called a "sharing in the Spirit" (Philippians 2:1) — from the Greek word *koinonia* which meant an "association, communion, fellowship, close relationship."[82] The verb form of this word was *koinoneo*. It means to have a share in something. Most interesting is that in the older Greek sources *koinoneo* could mean being initiated into one of the Greek mystery rites. The verb wasn't used, though, in this passage from Philippians.

The noun used in Philippians was *koinonia pneumatos: Spirit fellowship*. In Philemon Paul used the word *koinonia* but linked it to the faith (*pistis*) of Philemon. Thus, "I pray that the sharing of your faith[83] may become effective" (Phil 6, NRSV). Once more the NRSV translation used the word "sharing" for what was a *fellowship*. Why is this important? It is more than simply sharing the salt and pepper at the dinner table. This word *koinonia* refers to a strong energetic

---

[81] Martyn, *Galatians*, 429

[82] Danker et al., *A Greek-English Lexicon*, 552–53.

[83] The Greek usually translated faith is *pistis*. According to Gordon Zerbe it should be translated as loyalty faith, or trusting faith. As he points out it is way beyond "a mental conviction." Gordon Zerve, *Retributive to Restorative Justice*, 44-5.

bond. As N. T. Wright puts it, "It is an energizing principle. It is meant to produce the full reality of which it speaks."[84]

This bond with others, in a community commended to "welcome …one another as Christ has welcomed you" (Rom 15:7) meant seeing each other in the context of belonging to one family. Paul spoke of his separation from his friends in Thessalonica and said of their separation it was like "we were made orphans by being separated from you." Then in Romans when Paul offers greetings to so many, the phrase "in Christ" was the defining part of his relationship with Prisca and Aquila and so many others. Particularly notable was Paul's recognition of the apostles Andronicus and Junia, said to be "prominent among the apostles, *and* they were *in Christ* before me" (Rom 16:7).

Being *in Christ* also entailed living in expectation of the return of the Messiah, his *Parousia*. We turn to that topic in the next chapter. Typical for Paul was his advice to the Thessalonians that in light of the day of the Lord which would come like a thief in the night, we who wait would not be surprised. Then Paul concluded this counsel writing, "…whether we are awake or asleep we may live with him. Therefore encourage one another and build up each other, as indeed you are doing" (1 Thess 5:10-11). Paul was also saying, "Wait and watch with me."

---

[84] Wright, *Faithfulness*, 17.

Chapter 13
Paul's Watch

> Paul stood astride the line between Judaism and paganism, between Jewish covenantal eschatology and Roman imperial eschatology, between Christian and Augustan utopian visons, each announcing not just the imminent advent of the Golden Age, but proclaiming that it has already begun.[1]

> The time is out of joint—O cursèd spite
> That ever I was born to set it right!
> Nay, come, let's go together.[2]

> Now concerning the times and the seasons, brothers and sisters (1 Thess 5:1).

> The Christ event changes everything, including time.[3]

Paul never wore a watch, but he was watching, or as we must also say he was "on watch." These opening comments are not there just to play with words, but to help us address a critical part of Paul's story in a very real politically charged world seemingly in great disarray. All of us pay attention to the clock while watching the time so we won't be late for something important to us. We also watch the *times*, as it refers to the events and developments happening in the world around us. But do we watch with expectancy or fear? Do we watch out of the corner of the eye, or wishing we had eyes in the back of our heads? Do we watch as if looking into a dense dark fog? All of these questions are posed in the context of trying to fathom Paul's understanding of the "times and the seasons" (1 Thess 5:1). Following that generic reference Paul then spoke of a specific day which was to come:

---

[1] Crosson, John Dominic and Jonathan Reed, *In Search of Paul: How Jesus's Apostle Opposed Rome's Empire with God's Kingdom* (San Francisco: Harper Collins, 2004), 129.

[2] William Shakespeare *Hamlet* Act. 1, Scene 5, 186-190.

[3] Athanastos Despostis, "Reconsidering the Pauline Conception of Time," *Journal for the Study of Paul and His Letters* 8, nos. 1-2 (2019): 38.

> For you yourselves know very well that the day of Lord will come like a thief in the night (1 Thess 5:2).

The words may sound awesome and threatening, but we have to realize as I wrote in the last chapter that Paul had a troubled view of his world. In one respect he was something like Hamlet who had learned some things from his father's ghost. The quote at the start of this chapter comes from Shakespeare's play Hamlet. Things were not right in Demark, and Hamlet's lament was that he was somehow called to "set it right." Both Paul and Hamlet faced a world where "The time is out of joint." The comparison with Paul ends there, however. Paul never seemed to complain about his mission even when it involved danger or trial, though as we shall see he could ask for prayers because of a well-grounded fear with regard to the collection he planned to take to Jerusalem.

What is critical to this account is that Paul wasn't expecting the world to end in a sudden kind of cosmic disaster. Standing so close to the day Christ was crucified Paul and his friends were living with what Despotis has called ""shortened" eschatological time that began with the coming of Christ and remains until the parousia."[4] It continues to be present in the practice of many churches as seen in the Christian liturgical calendar and the season of Advent with its time of expectation and watching.

Thus, in this chapter we explore Paul's understanding of the expected return of the Messiah. More than that, however, we need to see Paul planning a trip to Jerusalem to deliver a collection, and then a new missionary enterprise taking him to Spain. The letter to the Romans is something like Paul's last will and testament,[5] but only from the perspective of Paul's future plans, and not in the aftermath of his hopes and dreams. The failure that may have marked some sleepless nights for Paul is the sad reality he confronted at the end. Paul feared rejection of the vision of a world gathered together inside the Jewish story of God without any ethnic exclusions. Nonetheless, he hoped and prayed that he would see such a world.

You might think the clock was ticking for Paul, but what is most interesting is that he wasn't, as near as we can tell, running out of

---

[4] Despostis, "Reconsidering the Pauline Conception of Time," 37.
[5] Dieter Georgi, *Remembering the Poor: The History of Paul's Collection for Jerusalem* (Nashville: Abingdon Press, 1965), 127.

time. We must consider, of course, that his first letter to the Thessalonians and his last letter (Romans) seem to have Paul telling time in different ways. That first letter of his, 1 Thessalonians, has a tone of urgency and expectation, while Romans coming maybe ten or more years later,[6] offers us a more leisurely Paul.

As already noted, but critical to finding Paul, is recognizing his deep conviction that something decisive happened with the crucifixion of Jesus. It was the critical moment in *all* time. As noted above, in a strange sense time was shortened. It is a difficult concept for many of us who live in a world where time stretches forward into a distance we call *eternity*. That wasn't a word in Paul's vocabulary. For him "the appointed time has grown short." Such a declaration made to us, perhaps by an oncologist in the midst of receiving the latest news about a cancer diagnosis would mean we had better get our affairs in order. "Time that has grown short" in a chronological sense means we don't have many days or weeks left to live.

Paul had two Greeks words for time. The word *chronos* meant time according to the hours of the day or what is called chronological time. It could also mean *considerable time* or *a long time*.[7] It is used in the previously quoted phrase "times (*chronon*) and seasons (*kairon*)." Ask someone what time it is? If they say "It's 7:32 pm," that is *chronological* time. If they say, "I think it is about time to think of about what I'll do next," they are reflecting the Greek idea of *kairos* time.[8]

Kairos could be used to describe a happy or a difficult time. It could be translated as "seasons." It wasn't about any precise date, but an experience. The same word could be used in the context of "the right proper, favorable time."[9] Particularly important for understanding Paul's apocalyptic expectations and the *parousia* (i.e., return) of the Messiah, *kairos* is often used in the eschatological Biblical passages referring to *"the last times"* and *"before the end-time and judgment*.[10]

---

[6] It is maybe almost a 20-year difference in time if Douglas Campbell is right about 1 Thessalonians possibly being dated as early as 40 CE; *Framing Paul*, 154.

[7] Danker et al., *A Greek-English Lexicon*, 1092.

[8] Note that *chronon* and *kairon* are plural. Paul more often used the singular *Kairos* when discussing time.

[9] Danker et al., *A Greek-English Lexicon*, 497.

[10] Danker et al., *A Greek-English Lexicon*, 497.

What may be something of an enigma is that Paul in the context of *kairos* wasn't running around the world trying to save as many as possible. Actually, being in a hurry is what characterizes life in terms of chronological time. That doesn't describe Paul. Consider his travel plans in Romans. He wasn't in a hurry. He lived and traveled in a deliberate, but certainly purposeful, measured pace. From the moment of God's *apocalypse* Paul saw the signs of the divine action at work in his world, expecting that Messiah would usher in a new age. But time had already changed. In fact, this new world, this new creation had already started. "Creation," Paul declared "waits with eager longing for the revealing of its children" (Rom 8:19). Paul and Jesus Messiah assemblies were living in *Messianic time*.

How are we to understand *Messianic time?* It certainly can't be understood as the way things simply evolve over time, because the underlying presupposition is of an *interruption* in time. The philosopher Agamben described it as "a moment of immanence, or, if one prefers, a zone of absolute indiscernibility between immanence and transcendence, between this world and the future world."[11] That's a rather dense description, but it reflects the difficulty in this unusual but critical concept. I have been alluding to this concept throughout this book whenever I mentioned Paul's choosing to live alongside the least in the world leading to his life shaped by Christ crucified. His original vocation was no more. It had been revoked. Thus, in Agamben's words, "*The messianic vocation is the revocation of every vocation.*"[12] We must remember that Paul in light of God's *apocalypse* lived his life in the shadow of the cross. He didn't just wake up one morning to think it was something worth considering. This mystical Paul had experiences of God that took him down, not just one notch, but to the place where his life and the story of Christ brought him alongside the least in his world. What is also most clear in light of our considerations of how Paul told time is that he had a most unusual mission with his focus on bringing the gospel (*euangelion*, the Announcement) to the nations or to use the term favored by Paula Fredriksen, to the pagans. It wasn't Paul's Judaism that was revoked, but rather how Paul's life was opened up in a way that he fully embraced.

---

[11] Agamben, *The Time that Remains*, 25.
[12] Agamben, *The Time that Remains*, 23, italics in original.

The concept of wasting time may have never crossed Paul's mind, but in the aftermath of his call to know Jesus Messiah, he sensed that time "had grown short." In giving advice regarding marriage and divorce in 1 Corinthians 7 Paul said, "I mean, brothers and sisters, the appointed time has grown short" (1 Cor 7:29). It wasn't a time for people to complicate their lives. Remember that Paul also saw that for some it was important to marry, even if it wasn't something he wanted for himself. There is much more to consider, however, how the very concept that time, namely chronological time, could in some way be abridged, and so it was for those living in messianic time.

We are also not to think about the coming of Christ—the *parousia*—as a future event. Agamben notes that the word simply means *presence*. It is not, according to Agamben, the second coming of Christ. It is not about adding onto something that is lacking or lost. The word itself contains the Greek word *ousia,* and that means substance or being. Paul in using this terms knows the presence of Christ and claims that the community knows it as well. It correlates to what I noted in the previous chapter with the phrase *in Christ*. The Messiah who arrived and who will arrive again is also present—indeed very present (i.e., *par* plus *ousia*). Thus, *parousia* in Paul's world is the convergence of *chronos and kairos,* or as Agamben suggests, using a phrase by Walter Benjamin it is "the small door through which the Messiah enters."[13]

13.1 Apocalyptic thought in the first century CE

The first task in terms of understanding the apocalyptic mindset of Paul is to realize he didn't invent the concept. It was in the air for all Judeans. They were breathing apocalyptic or eschatological air at least for the past 400 years. That sense of time was there whenever they reflected on the faithfulness of the God of Israel, especially in light of the times when they wandered away from their promises. It even had started when Moses was on the mountain to receive the Ten Commandments, while the people below danced around a golden calf made from all their jewelry. (Exodus 32:1-35)

As noted in the previous chapter, following the rebuilding of the temple in Jerusalem the one thing that was missing was God's *shekhinah,* or presence. God was not dwelling in the temple. "But one

---

[13] Agamben, *The Time That Remains*, 70-71.

of the fascinating features of the second-Temple Jewish world, the world that emerged following the rebuilding of Jerusalem and the Temple, is that nowhere are we told that YHWH and his glory have at last returned. Indeed, we are told the opposite."[14] Paul, without directly acknowledging this curious reality of God's glory *in absentia*, speaks, nonetheless, of a "ministry of the Spirit come in glory" (2 Cor 3:8). It is a *diakonia pneumatikos*[15] – Greek for a spirit-filled diaconal ministry – for all in the reconciling work of God's glory that prepares us for "an eternal weight of glory beyond all measure" (2 Cor 4:17). All are to be taken up into the light of God's glory.

Sometimes scholars talk about Paul living in what has been called an "already-not yet" kind of time. It is a way of pointing to what God has done that is consequential and telling, and what is yet to come. The "already" is about a kind of end that marks the end of one age and the strange uncertain time ushering in a new age. Zielger reflected on the apocalyptic thinking of both Jesus and Paul that "...bespeaks a salvation whose advent involves an unanticipated divine action that marks a radical break with what has gone before, its overturning, its revolution, its displacement."[16] Thus from 1 Thessalonians through to Romans Paul continued to evoke the idea that the end, or the second coming of the Messiah, was in sight, indeed as noted earlier, actually present in some strange way. But that was all he could say. It wasn't about a specific day. Unlike the Millenarianists of Christian history, whether in the coming of the year 1000, or 2000, or some other date, Paul never picked a date. He wouldn't say when that day would come, but only told the Thessalonians it would come like a thief in the night.[17] A much less ominous understanding of what is yet to come is found in Romans where Paul spoke of a new creation waiting "with eager longing for the revealing of the children of God" (Rom 8:19).

---

[14] Wright, *Faithfulness*, 189.

[15] John Koenig, "The Knowing of Glory and its Consequences (2 Corinthians 3-5)" in *Studies in Paul and John: In Honor of J Louis Martyn*, eds. Robert T. Fortna and Beverly R. Gaventa (Nashville, TN: Abington Press, 1990), 165.

[16] Philip G. Ziegler, "Some Remarks on Apocalyptic in Modern Christian Theology" in *Paul and the Apocalyptic Imagination: An Introduction*, ed. Ben C. Blackwell et al. (Minneapolis: Fortress Press, 2016), 212.

[17] 1 Thessalonians 5:2. This phrase also appeared in Matthew 24.43 as part of an expanded apocalyptic prophecy from Jesus. Did Paul know of that prophecy? There's no way to answer that question except to see the similarity in both passages.

It is knowledge itself that is challenged by Paul's apocalyptic mindset. The old way of knowing in a world where a few were able to able to exercise dominance was overturned in the event of the cross. Paul very clearly in the early chapters of 1 Corinthians let the understanding of the cross be the dividing line between the powerful and the weak, the wise and the foolish. Paul declared that in their midst, "I decided to know nothing among you except Jesus Christ, and him crucified" (1 Cor 2:2). The new way of knowing, according to Martyn, was with the Spirit (*pneuma*) given by God.[18]

Paul's expectation about the day of the Lord, as a time of fulfillment to be expected and welcomed, could also be framed as a day of judgment. In its more popularized narrative of apocalyptic thinking in our media-saturated world the last day is a day or wrath and destruction. Judgment, for Paul though, did not mean a destructive blowing up of the world. Paul saw God's judgment connected to the wickedness so evident in the Roman world portrayed in chapter 2 of Romans. There would come, he wrote, a day of judgment when "according to my gospel, God, through Jesus Christ, will judge the secret thoughts of all" (Rom 2:16). Paul's mysticism had to overlap with his apocalyptic watch.

Lest that thought of the God who judges the secrets of all be considered something to fear, consider the Collect for Purity that opens the celebration of the Holy Eucharist according to the Book of Common Prayer as used in Episcopal churches. "Almighty God, to you all hearts are open, all desires are known, and from you no secrets are hid: Cleanse the thoughts of our hearts by the inspiration of the Holy Spirit, that we may perfectly love you, and worthily magnify your holy Name; through Christ our Lord,"[19] It is *not* a scary prayer to start worship. And it draws on that verse from Romans.

Moltmann also understands Paul references to the coming judgment of God in a more favorable light. It is not even so much as a moment in time, but the occasion when the fulfillment of reconciliation happens. As Moltmann so eloquently wrote, "It is only in Christ's Parousia that "'all the tears will be wiped away.'" It

---

[18] Louis Martyn, *Theological Issues in the Letters of Paul* (Nashville: Abingdon Press, 1997), 107.

[19] *The Book of Common Prayer* (New York: The Seabury Press, 1977), 355.

is only in Christ's parousia that Israel will be redeemed, and this 'unredeemed world' created anew."[20]

Even more relevant for our discussion of judgment are a series of quotes from Hosea and Isaiah that form the heart of Paul's argument in Romans 9 where he is discussing the fate of his fellow Judeans. The chapter begins with Paul's lament that his own people haven't seemed to respond to the gospel as he expected. The whole chapter is composed using pieces from the Hebraic story of God. As Paul turns to the ancient prophecies the emphasis concerning God's grace is that those who were once rejected have been reclaimed. Israel will be redeemed and there will be a faithful remnant. Theodore Jennings in his translation and commentary on Romans noted that the only way to read chapter nine is to do so alongside Karl Barth. What Jennings learned from Barth is that "…the divine NO, however severe and unrelenting, has no other aim than that it serve the manifestation of the divine YES." He concludes that thought, saying, "…judgment has no other meaning than that all be saved."[21]

Paul wasn't rushing around the world trying to warn everyone of a judgment to come. And he did not seem compelled to follow a contemporary strategy particular to evangelical Christianity in our world which is "to grow the church." Paul's mind was on geography not numbers. Romans concludes with Paul's discussing his hopes for the collection he was taking to Jerusalem along with some fears and concerns. It wasn't time that he was worried about, however. He also sought the help of those in Rome with his plans to take the Gospel to Spain. All these plans and adventures clearly meant time was *not* running out for Paul. As Agamben states Paul was living in *the time that remains*. And so do we.

13.2 The collection to take to Jerusalem

As Paul concluded his first letter to the Corinthians he wrote, "Now concerning the collection for the saints; you should follow the directions I gave to the churches (*ekklēsia*) of Galatia" (1 Cor 16:1). What we have with Paul's collection is a dream of his mentioned in four of the seven undisputed letters — 1 &2 Corinthians, Philippians, and Romans. Taking that collection to Jerusalem was also connected

---

[20] Moltmann, *The Way of Jesus Christ*, 319.
[21] Jennings, *Outlaw Justice*, 150.

to his passion to see all the people of every nation welcomed into the Hebraic story of God. But Paul knew of those who would even kill to prevent that from happening. The fears of Paul seem justified based on the account in Acts which describes Paul's last visit to the holy city. The rejection of the collection that Paul feared (discussed herein) might actually have happened. (See Acts 21:7 to the end).

To this point Acts has not been the template used for finding Paul, but it may help us see Paul at the end of his ministry. He had his detractors as seen in 1 and 2 Corinthians and Galatians. Opposition to Paul is also part of the entire narrative of Acts with many accounts of Paul first preaching in a synagogue and then having the Jews reject his message.

According to Acts the rumors about Paul that circulated in the streets of Jerusalem were that Paul no longer respected or followed the traditions of Israel. A crowd seized him in the temple on the second day and they shouted "This is the man who is teaching everyone everywhere against our people, our law, and this place; more than that, he has actually brought Greeks into the temple and has defiled this holy place" (Acts 21:28). The entire story in Acts involved the arrest of Paul whose life was saved only because he was sent to the Roman provincial governor in Caesarea and then to Rome. He was still alive under house arrest in the last scene in Acts. There was just one thing missing in the Acts narrative of Paul coming to Jerusalem: *nothing* was said about the collection. It is never mentioned in this account. Yet it was so much a part of Paul's purpose in coming when we read his own words near the end of Romans. We know from other letters the deep theological significance the collection had for Paul.

The collection bore great corporate symbolism and significance as it derived from the various ethnic communities where Paul preached and founded Jesus communities. Jerusalem was to be seen as the new center of the world. How would they get there? With their gifts! But Paul worried. Would their gifts be received and welcomed? As Paul set his sights on Judea and the Holy City he asked for their prayers: "I appeal to you...to join me in earnest prayers to God on my behalf, that I may be rescued from the unbelievers in Judea, and that my ministry (*diakonia*) to Jerusalem may be acceptable to the saints" (Rom 15:30–31). He was truly worried, but not about the dangers of travel, or it seems the threat of robbery, but simply by *how* this gift would be received. Paul saw "very real dangers" and he knew of those who opposed "the cross-cultural reconciliation that Paul...placed at the center of the gospel."[22] For a long time, of course, Paul was aware that his ministry was not fully endorsed by the leaders of the Jesus Messiah community in Jerusalem.

What was the *source* of the idea for the collection? Did it begin with Peter and James and what they asked of Paul at their conference which Paul recorded in Galatians? Paul's second visit to Jerusalem took place 14 years after the previous one. (Gal. 2:1) It thus took place in the late 40's of the first century following what seem to be some lost years for how we account for Paul. We can presume that some of the time was spent in Damascus and then by his own account in Syria and Cilicia. (Gal 1:21) In Paul's time these two areas were combined into a single Roman Province. Most of its wealth was in its coastal cities, while the mountainous area to the East was home to barbarians.[23] The same cities are cited in Acts 15.23, which is the only mention of a letter in all of Acts. It wasn't written by Paul. Sent by the elders in Jerusalem, it was a letter of commendation for Paul, Barnabas, and Silas[24] as they traveled to Syria and Cilicia.

The Jerusalem council, as the matter is often called, is not exactly the same in terms of its details when we compare Galatians (Paul's version) and Acts 15:1–35. The emphasis in Acts was that the elders approved of missionary work among "those Gentiles who are turning to God" (Acts 15:19). The requirement expected by the elders, in their letter, meant following Jewish practices: abstaining "from things polluted by idols and from fornication and from whatever has been strangled and from blood" (Acts. 15:20). Paul told a different story.

Paul's more autobiographical account in Galatians describes the leadership in Jerusalem entrusting Paul "with the gospel for the uncircumcised, just as Peter had been entrusted with the gospel for circumcised" (Gal. 2:8). Nothing was said by Paul regarding idolatry, fornication, or dietary laws. Instead, "They asked only one

---

[22] Jewett, *Romans*, 935.
[23] Elias J Bickerman, "Syria and Cilicia," *The American Journal of Philology* 68, no. 4 (1947): 355.
[24] There was also a man with the name of Judas who was to deliver the message "by word of mouth" (Acts 15:27). Obviously, this wasn't the Judas who belonged with the 12 disciples of Jesus.

thing, that we remember the poor which was actually what I was eager to do" (Gal 2:10).

The collection mattered a great deal to Paul. Was it simply to help the poor in Jerusalem, however? A colleague of mine, knowing about my research, said she didn't like Paul because Paul showed no concern for the poor. Gerd Longnecker addressed the same matter with regard to the question "Did Paul have "an under-developed sense of concern for the poor"?[25] Indeed, you will not find Paul directly pointing out the desperate needs of the vast numbers of people who lived at the subsistence level. He never started a "war on poverty." What he did, however, was make an agreement with the Jerusalem leaders "to remember the poor."

By the time we come to his writing about the collection it was described as a gift for the saints in Jerusalem or what he called a "sharing (*koinonia*) in this ministry (*diakonias*) to the saints" (1 Cor 8:4, 9:1; Rom 15:25). Paul's language here mattered a great deal. Verbrugge and Krell offered an extended comment on the significance of Paul's words:

> These words describe uniquely Christian acts of service to others. It became a term denoting loving action for brother or sister and neighbor, which in turn is derived from divine love; it also describes the outworking of *koinōnia*, fellowship. Through using this word group, Paul is encouraging the believers in Corinth to a life of Christian service, one aspect of which is to share their resources with the impoverished Jewish Christians in Jerusalem.[26]

Even though that analysis referred to those impoverished in Jerusalem, the major emphasis for Paul was a debt of gratitude to those in the holy land where Christ was crucified. The added factor is that we are talking about Paul's Judean heritage with its pervasive concern for the poor, the widow, and the orphans. As just one example among many, we find this from Psalm 82:3-4: "Defend the poor and fatherless; do justice to the afflicted and needy. Deliver the poor and needy; free them from the hand of the wicked." A great many similar passages ranging from Exodus and Deuteronomy through all the prophets and the psalms express the same sentiment.

---

[25] Longernecker, *Remember the Poor*, 138.
[26] Verlyn D. Verbrugge and Keith R. Krell, *Paul and Money* (Grand Rapids: Zondervan, 2015), 176.

This is what formed, shaped, and grounded Paul in compassion. To that he easily added the example of Christ. "For you know the generous act of our Lord Jesus Christ, that though he was rich, yet for your sakes became poor, so that by his poverty you might become rich" (2 Cor 9:9).

Paul's comments linking generosity to God meant that whatever we give away to others is also a "loan" to God.[27] "Whoever is kind to the poor lends to the Lord, and will be repaid in full" (Prov 19:17). It may have made sense in the Judean world, but it certainly was strange in the Greco-Roman world, where gifts always involved an element of reciprocity.

Reciprocity was at the heart of the patron-client system that shaped nearly all relationships in the Greco-Roman world. There were two forms of patronage which shaped the political and social world.[28] The first form was *political patronage*. It meant that the Roman emperor was the patron over all others. With his outward promises of peace brought about by subjecting Rome's enemies, all were to be grateful to the emperor.

The other form of patronage was *personal patronage*. This involved an unequal relationship with the patron holding social, economic, or political power, and various clients who benefited from their service and obligation to their patron. Those who attached themselves to a patron offered services that could enhance the social status of the one they served. It was a relationship involving reciprocity (albeit one-sided), personal and often lasting for a long time but always asymmetrical.[29] There were also implicit hierarchical assumptions of moral obligation. "Obligation was first extended to country and parents, then to children and family, and, last, to kinsmen."[30]

Paul's ethic was entirely different, as we can see in the way he regards the collection as generosity for those who cannot return the gift, namely "the poor among the saints in Jerusalem" (Rom 15:26).

---

[27] Nathan Eubank, "Justice Endures Forever: Paul's Grammar of Generosity," *Journal for the Study of Paul and His Letters* 5, no. 2 (2015): 172.

[28] See Verbrugge and Krell, *Paul and Money*, 81–85 for an extended discussion of these terms.

[29] Richard P. Saller, *Personal Patronage under the Early Empire* (Cambridge: Cambridge University Press, 1982), 1.

[30] James Harrison, "Paul's 'Indebtedness' to the Barbarian (Rom 1:14) In Latin West Perspective," *Novum Testamentum* 55 (2013): 347.

As for those who were asked to participate in this collection their reward was not defined as a monetary one, but as something that "overflows with many thanksgivings to God." Essentially Paul was *upending* the Roman reciprocity system measured in social, political, and personal power to emerge into a communal life of mutual service where there is what Barclay called a "new communal life, oriented to God through Christ in service and worship."[31] Paul in writing to the Romans seemed particularly adept at contrasting the way of Christ with the presumptions of superiority that so characterized Roman claims. Most surprising of all, in the context of Roman iconography in its sculpture and arches proclaiming victory over its enemies, Paul said in the opening of Romans that he was indebted to Greek and barbarians alike. (Rom 1:14) All were the children of Abraham and were covered by God's impartiality. As Harrison—interprets it, "Christ's dependents, including the barbarians, experience the reversal of dishonor through their acquisition of Christ's imputed righteousness."[32] The barbarians who were portrayed as humiliated and defeated on those temple arches actually, in Christ, become "more than conquerors" (Rom. 8:37) and "could now stand without accusation before God."[33] Those from that larger world—in Jewish eyes, the *ethnē*—would come with Paul to bring the collection to the saints in Jerusalem.

The so-called "saints" were, if Acts is right about the way things ended for Paul, hardly gracious receivers of this collection. Deiter Georgi is one scholar who assumes that Paul walked right into the wrath of those Jews who saw him as one "contemptuous of the Torah."[34] Was there a way out for Paul? Curiously, Paul pays a ransom for four destitute Nazirites but had to go to the temple to be purified. (Acts 21:23-26). If that happened, it had to be extremely humiliating for Paul who emphasized freedom from such regulations for those from the nations following Jesus Messiah. As Giorgio notes, the irony might have been that the collection had been used to pay for cultic services.[35] The other tragedy would have been the failure of the prophetic dreams that might have been part of

---

[31] John M. G. Barclay, *Paul and the Gift* (Grand Rapids: Eerdmans, 2015), 510.
[32] Harrison, "Paul's 'Indebtedness'," 343-34.
[33] Harrison, "Paul's 'Indebtedness'," 344.
[34] Georgi, *Remembering the Poor*, 125.
[35] Georgi, *Remembering the Poor*, 125.

Paul's vision for this gift, but there is not a clear consensus about that in the literature.

Even if Paul's vision didn't materialize as he hoped, Giorgio points out, "There is no indication in Paul's letters that the apostle conceptualized the collection as a fulfillment of the eschatological pilgrims to Zion by Gentiles depicted in some Old Testament and early Jewish texts."[36] Nevertheless there may have been in the end some lasting memory in the early centuries of Christianity that might testify to the vision of Paul with regard to the collection. But it was more than a memory for *such concern for the poor* was still part of the ethical life of Christian communities 400 years later. In 362 the emperor Julian tried to institute a campaign to launch pagan charities that would outdo those of the Christians. It failed. Julian wrote, "The impious Galileans [i.e Christians] support not only their poor, but ours as well, everywhere one can see that our people lack aid from us."[37]

Downs described the collection as "an act of corporate worship"[38] which "symbolized the unity of Jews and Gentiles under the one gospel of Jesus Christ."[39] That is the unity that may have been *rejected* when Paul and those from various nations came with their gifts. Paul's lasting witness in Romans is the vision of unity with God who shows no partiality. (Rom 2:11) We're not able to say that Christianity represents that unity, but Paul's vision will haunt us until it happens.

David Downs noted an observation by the historian Peter Brown that into the fourth and fifth centuries of the common era a new virtue was visibly present in the world. It was a time when "being a 'lover of the poor" became a public virtue."[40] The bishops were charged to remember the poor, and it is still asked of those about to

---

[36] David J. Downs, "The Offering of the Gentiles' in Romans 15.16," *Journal for the Study of the New Testament* 29, no. 2 (2006): 161; see also David J. Downs, *The Offering of the Gentiles: Paul's Collection for Jerusalem in its Chronological, Cultural, and Cultic Context* (Grand Rapids: Eerdmans, 2008).

[37] Rodney Stark, *The Rise of Christianity: How the Obscure, Marginal Jesus Movement Became the Dominant Religious Force in the Western World in a Few Centuries* (New York: Harper Collins, 1996), 83–84.

[38] Downs, "The Offering of the Gentiles' in Romans 15.16," 160.

[39] Downs, "The Offering of the Gentiles' in Romans 15.16," 161.

[40] Peter Brown, *Povery and Leadership in the Later Roman Empire: The Menahem Stern Jerusalem Lectures* (Hanover and London: University of New England Press, 2002), 1; as quoted in Downs, *The Offering of the Gentiles*, 165.

be made bishops in the Episcopal church: "Will you be merciful to all, show compassion to the poor and strangers, and defend those who have no helper?" The response: "I will, for the sake of Christ Jesus."[41]

13.3 On to Spain.

Why Spain? It is not a question we can easily answer. We don't even know where in Spain Paul intended to go, and, as we will see, the choices could make a difference, especially in terms of language and culture. We know from what Paul said in Romans that he would need some funds to support this venture. We can take as a reasonable guess that Phoebe, who seemed to have some wealth, might have been called on to help raise the money he would need. She had been his benefactor (Rom 16:2) and would be asking her peers perhaps to assist.

There are at least two ideas to consider about Paul's choice of Spain. Some scholars think that Paul has in mind a number of passages in the bible he had in his head about Tarshish as the end of the world. There were at least 25 references to Tarshish in his bible,[42] including two references in the story of Jonah fleeing from God to hide out in this place in the fictional end of the world. It wasn't just a fiction. Tarshish was a city perhaps founded by the Phoenicians.[43] In the words of Nanos it was "the uttermost end of the earth, the biblical Tarshish, to which he will bring the light of the nations, as Isaiah foretold."[44] Most important is the passage at the end of Isaiah mentioning Tarshish[45] as one of the far-off places that will send survivors to come to Jerusalem all of whom will bring grain offerings. (Isa 66:18-21)

---

[41] *Book of Common Prayer*, 518.

[42] https://en.wikipedia.org/wiki/Tarshish

[43] Barry J. Beitzel, "Was There a Joint Nautical Venture on the Mediterranean Sea by Tyrian Phoenicians and Early Israelites?" *Bulletin of the American Schools of Oriental Research* 360 (Nov. 2010): 37-66; see also David Griffiths, "Augustus and the Roman Provinces on Iberia," (PhD, diss. The University of Liverpool, 2013), 56. We should also note that the Roman historian Strabo reported elements of Phoenician culture that continued into his time to be found in Hispania.

[44] Mark D. Nanos, "The Jewish Context of the Gentile Audience in Paul's Letter to the Romans," in *Reading Romans Within Judaism: Collected Essays of Mark D. Nanos*, vol. 2, ed. Mark D. Nanos (Eugene, Wipf and Stock, 2018), loc. 1714 of 9136, Kindle.

[45] Tarshish is the *first* city in that list (Isa 60:9; 66:19).

Even though Spain in the imagination of some of the prophets was a far-away place it was actually part of the trade that went on for centuries, especially with regard to the Phoenicians sailing the Mediterranean. Its importance for Paul is connected to the history of Rome with regard to Spain, as well as its geographical location. At the same time only in Romans do we hear about Paul's plan to take the gospel to Spain. It is here, however, that we discover how Paul's sense of geography was connected to his vision of his ministry and the coming day of the Lord.

Excursus 13.1 Recalling Paul's travels

Our journey with Paul began with the focus on his trip to Arabia. In Chapter 2 we considered if there was some connection to Abraham's journey involved in Paul's decision to wander far to the South away from Damascus. Traveling through that desert, maybe in the company of Nabataean traders with their camels loaded with treasures, Paul may have passed through Haran where Abraham and Sarah were buried. Their tombs are sacred in both Jewish and Islamic communities of faith. My guess is that Paul found his way to Petra the capital of the Nabatean King Aretas IV, and that while there he said or did things that made him a marked man. N. T. Wright even wonders if Paul made a visit to Mount Horeb, or Mount Sinai as it is also known?[46] It is an interesting proposal.

What pertains to Paul's travels that will take him to Jerusalem, Rome, and Spain is the scope of this picture. Paul will have been in the desert far to the South of Jerusalem, and then will have traveled north and east into Syria and Antioch, before turning toward the northwest where he would be in Antioch, Ephesus, Corinth, Athens, and then to Macedonia which would bring him to Philippi and Thessalonica. In Paul's own words he said, "so that from Jerusalem and as far around as Illyricum I have fully proclaimed the good news of Christ" (Rom 15:19). Had he reached the coast of Illyricum he would find it a very short journey across the Adriatic sea to Rome. As Roger Aus noted regarding this map in Paul's mind as well as what was to be found in Isaiah with its mention of Tarshish, "The general direction, east to west, thus corresponds to a combination of

---

[46] Wright, *Faithfulness*, 152–59.

those nations found in Isaiah 66.19, Tarshish being equated with Spain."[47]

Paul has no other place in mind other than the one where he believed the gospel has *not* reached and that is Spain. It is probably far more than a coincidence that it matches with the vision of Isaiah. Much more was at work, though, with Paul's eyes on Spain. It had been significant for Augustus, and now Paul would bring his gospel—the only one that was true!—to the land where Augustus had proclaimed his gospel. This is where the letter of Romans helps us to see Paul offering a gospel so contrary to the prevailing myths about Rome.

13.4 Only one gospel could be true

A theme running throughout Romans is that the Gospel is what is meant to bring Jew and those from all tribes and nations together. In *Christian Tolerance* the author Robert Jewett makes the case that maybe the most important verse in Romans is "Welcome one another, therefore, just as Christ has welcomed you, for the glory of God" (Rom 15:7).[48] Words of welcome seem so common place and unoffensive, but Paul meant to bring together those who were opposites: "I am a debtor both to Greeks and to barbarians, both to the wise and the foolish" (Rom. 1:14).

Paul's strange idea of being a debtor to both Greeks and barbarians could have been a reflection on Roman domination of Spain, which had finally been achieved by the later years of the Emperor Augustus when both Paul and Jesus were born. We may bemoan how some of the military conflicts of our time seem to be endless, but we have nothing that compares with Rome's conflict with Carthage and the Punic Wars which began in 264 BCE and only came to some kind of settled conclusion around 16 BCE.

It was in the year 26 BCE that Octavian was given the name Augustus which meant *august* or *exalted one*.[49] That name change inverts what I suspect happened to Paul, for Octavian received a name that enhanced his reputation. One becomes the *exalted one*

---

[47] Roger D. Aus, "Paul's Travel Plans to Spain and the 'Full Number of the Gentiles' of Rom XI 25," *Novum Testamentum* 21, fasc. 3 (July 1979): 241.

[48] Jewett, *Romans*, 982. This one verse is cited 15 times in the book. It's far more than any other verse.

[49] Beard, *SPQR*, 354 writes that "revered one" is a good translation of Augustus.

while the other is known for the second part of his life as *small*. It wouldn't be surprising if Augustus in his retinue of slaves had one called Paulus.

In a fascinating Ph.D. dissertation David Griffiths examines Augustus' part in finally subduing the most northern provinces of Iberia—in modern day Portugal—and channeling their economic resources to Rome. Octavian emerged as the victor from the civil wars that marked the end of the first century BCE. With his power growing he turned his eyes to the rebellious tribes in Spain. When the Roman Senate finally made him the sole ruler of the Roman Empire, the almost 700 years history of the old Republic became in the words of Beard "an increasingly distant memory."[50] A new story was about to be inscribed in stone that would encapsulate all the glory Augustus had brought to their empire.

In the year 27BCE Augustus was authorized by the Roman Senate to be responsible for "the unsettled parts of the Empire which required military defense."[51] Spain was among those many provinces. Augustus, experienced in numerous military campaigns, turned his eyes to the unsettled northern parts of Spain with its undefeated barbarian tribes. In 27 BCE Augustus led the war against those tribes, and two years later he declared his victory in Spain. It wasn't a complete victory. It would take years for the Roman legions under the command of others to finally subdue them in what Griffiths described as a "bitter and protracted warfare against a determined guerilla enemy."[52]

Paul's determination to take the gospel to Spain must have been connected to his obligation to *both* Greeks and barbarians (Rom 1:14).[53] In the mindset of Rome the Spanish were *barbarians* with all the negative attributes possible. David Griffiths wrote that Iberians ... showed "no hint of civility or the diversity of Spanish society and culture. Almost every reference to them is imbued with an overtly negative value: warlike, animalistic and feral, they are ... drinkers of horse blood...brigands...unsavory and promiscuous ..."[54] One

---

[50] Beard, *SPQR*, 333.
[51] A. H. M. Jones, *Augustus*, 46.
[52] Griffiths, "Augustus and the Roman Provinces," 8.
[53] Often Paul referred to Greeks, meaning "all non-Jewish people within the so-called civilized world," Fee, *The First Epistle to the Corinthians*, 539; Here Paul is making a reference to the *civilized world (i.e Greeks)* and *all the rest* (i.e., barbarians).
[54] Griffiths, "Augustus and the Roman Provinces," 41

ancient writer described the Cantabrians as "the pinnacle of barbarism...brushing their teeth in urine, subordinating reason to their physical desires."[55]

Once they were finally and brutally subdued, with many captured as slaves, Rome depicted its victory and their defeat on its coins. Augustus would have known about a coin from the time of Caesar's victory over Pompeius in 46 BCE that shows an iconic representation of defeated barbarians: a captive woman with a bare breast, arms bound in rope, head down. She has been identified as Hispania. According to Griffith "This is *Hispania capta, Hispania devicta.*"[56]

Clearly Paul knew the iconographic representations of barbarians as they were pervasive in ancient Greek cities and throughout all the temples and arches the Romans built. Did Paul also know that in the aftermath of Roman subjugation of its most warlike tribes, the imperial cult was also spreading throughout the northern part of Spain and meant to be a visual reminder to all about the power of Rome and the honor due to the emperor? No emperor ever felt remorse for going to war against barbarian tribes, and that was clearly true for Augustus.

In the final year of his life Augustus composed a eulogy listing all the accomplishments in his long term as emperor. He was 76 years old and would die on August 19th in the year 14 C.E. The list was called the *Res Gestae,* which in the legal world simply means "things done." This included all the military accomplishments of Augustus inscribed on stone in both Latin and Greek throughout the Empire so that Paul may have seen it. The *Res Gestae* was a public transcript, an affirmation of the power, superiority, and dominance of the emperor who "perfectly embodied the qualities of honor, clemency, justice and piety."[57]

In *Res Gestae* there is no mention of reciprocal justice or real mercy. It made clear that death and enslavement were to be expected for those who resisted the authority of the Emperor and of Rome. Paul's letter to the Romans is a dramatic contrast, one in which "Paul

---

[55] Griffiths, "Augustus and the Roman Provinces," 53.
[56] Griffiths, "Augustus and the Roman Provinces," 222.
[57] Elliott, *The Arrogance of the Nations,* 72.

wishes to reverse the imbalance of honor and insist on the impartial mercy of God that treats each group alike."[58]

Paul had an interesting policy for deciding where to take the gospel next: "Thus, I make it my ambition to proclaim the good news, not where Christ has already been named, so that I do not build on someone else's foundation" (Rom 15:20). Paul, who began Romans saying he had an obligation to barbarians, made the stunning declaration at the end that his intention was to take the gospel to Spain.

In what I think is a stroke of genius Robert Jewett suggests that all of Romans was written by Paul with the Spanish mission in view.[59] Once we get to the end of the letter we find Paul carefully laying out his plans to come to Rome, but not to stay there. It may have meant that the communities founded by Paul were well established and no longer needed his attention.

Paul began his letter by saying he hoped to preach the gospel (*euangelion*, singular) to them when he arrived. He was doing more than simply writing a letter of introduction. If he was going to receive their support for his Spanish mission they "needed to know what Paul taught and how he understood his own mission."[60] Paul, moreover, needed to insist on unity and mutual respect for one another; he called for all baptized to "welcome one another, therefore, just as Christ has welcomed you" (Rom 15:7). That summons applied to all Judeans believing in Jesus Messiah and all from any other part of the world, the *ethnē*.[61] Paul's mission to the pagan world, inviting them to know and love Jesus Messiah, was simply "the inclusion of the previously excluded."[62] For, "Everyone (*pas*) who calls on the name of the Lord shall be saved" (Rom 10:13; see also Joel 2:32). This is the message Paul would take to Spain.

As he contemplated going to Spain we have to wonder if he was aware that there really were no Jewish communities there—not even

---

[58] Jewett, *Romans*, 89.

[59] Jewett, *Romans*, 79.

[60] Nils A. Dahl, *Studies in Paul: Theology for the Early Christian Mission* (Eugene: Wipf and Stock Publishers, 1977), 77.

[61] Gaston makes an interesting comment on this with regard to Paul's focus on reaching those people outside of Judea. Rather than thinking that Paul's main theological focus is "justification by faith," Gaston says it is "the justification of the legitimacy of his apostleship to and gospel for the Gentiles," *Paul and the Torah*, 57.

[62] Gaston *Paul and the Torah*, 116.

in the more Romanized provinces to the South where many Italians also lived. Even though a far greater number of Jews were living throughout the Roman Empire than in Judea, it turns out that Rome was "effectively the western limit of the Diaspora at that time."[63] Not until the 3rd century CE according to Bowers is there evidence of Jewish settlements in Spain.[64]

Another reality facing Paul is that there were only three small pockets of Greek-speaking communities settled in Spain. Though Roman armies had been in and out of Spain for more than 200 years, you could only find Latin spoken in its major cities. According to Jewett the four main languages in Spain were "the Indo-European languages, the Iberian, the Punic languages, and a wide range of primitive languages of obscure origin."[65] Around the city of Cadiz, a port city with over 3,000 years of history, "the Phoenician language was still in use."[66] Kathy Ehrensperger supplies another list of the languages Paul would have had to learn in order to proclaim the Gospel in Spain: Celtiberian, Lusitanian, South Lusitanian, and Iberian-Punic.[67]

Paul would definitely be dealing with barbarians, in the most basic definition: those who could not speak Greek or Latin.[68] According to Jewett, "Spaniards were viewed as Barbarians par excellence because so large a proportion continued to resist Roman rule, to rebel with frightening frequency, to refuse to speak Latin or use the Roman names for their cities, streams, or mountains."[69]

In her work on Paul as someone who is both bi-lingual and bi-cultural, Ehrensperger points out that Paul comes from a barbaric

---

[63] W. P. Bowers, "Jewish Communities in Spain in the Time of Paul the Apostle," *The Journal of Theological Studies* 16, no. 1 (1975): 402.

[64] Bowers, "Jewish Communities," 400. We have to wonder about the claim Josephus made that there "was not a single nation to which our [Judean] customs have not spread." A little hyperbole most likely; Ehrensperger, *Paul at the Crossroads*, 127.

[65] Jewett, *Romans*, 76

[66] Jewett, *Romans*, 76.

[67] Ehrensperger, *Paul at the Crossroads*, 72.

[68] Robert Jewett, "Response, Exegetical Support from Romans and Other Letters," in *Paul and Politics: Ekklēsia, Israel, Imperium, Interpretation*, ed. Richard A. Horsley (Harrisburg: Trinity Press International, 2000), 63, quoting Hans Windisch, "barbarous," *The Theological Dictionary of the New Testament*, vol. 1 (Grand Rapids: Eerdmans Publishing Company, 1964), 5478.

[69] Jewett, "Response, Exegetical Support,"63.

people — the Judeans. [70] In Roman eyes the province of Judea, in the first century hardly seemed pacified under Roman control. Paul knew how Romans saw him and his people. Paul knew that Roman legions stationed in Judea were a constant reminder that it was a subjugated nation. Judean faith was in the eyes of Seneca "the religion of a defeated people (*vici*)."[71] Judean people, moreover, were not citizens of the Roman empire. Contrary to a Paul who may have saved his life by claiming Roman citizenship in Acts 22:25 , what we see in Romans is a Paul seeking to take the gospel to the victims of Roman violence and subjugation. Paul would be going to those most recently defeated.

In her remarkable book *Galatians Re-Imagined* Bridgett Kahl helps us see the connection between Galatians living in the Eastern Roman province of Galatia and the Gallic tribes of what we know as Europe, whose ethnic heritage connected them to centuries of various Celtic tribes in Europe and Greece and Asia Minor.[72] There was an abiding "myth of the Galatians as prototypical enemies and barbarians."[73] Paul may have been the very first to feel indebted to them as he made his plans to go to Spain.

Paul had to be considering where he would find those *most in need* of his message. There were just three tribes on the Western side of the peninsula that had remained free for over 200 years. They were portrayed as almost impossible to subjugate so totally were they opposed to civilization. Suicide rather than capture was preferred with "mothers killing their own children before committing suicide, and the men, who habitually carry poison should the need for suicide arise, singing their hymn of victory even as they are crucified." This was a report from the historian Strabo.[74]

When the last independent tribes in Hispania were finally subdued, they wore the shame of utter defeat. It seems possible that when Paul said he intended to take the gospel to Spain that these were the *barbarians* he had in mind. The three tribes in the Northwest

---

[70] Ehrensperger, *Paul at the Crossroads*, 108.

[71] Elliott, *The Arrogance of Nations*, 135.

[72] Adrian Goldsworthy explains that the Galatians in Paul's time had settled in part of Central Anatolia (i.e., Modern Turkey) for three centuries. Three different Celtic tribes were there; *Pax Romana: War, Peace and Conquest in the Roman World* (New Haven: Yale University Press, 2016), 48.

[73] Kahl, *Galatians Re-Imagined*, 63.

[74] Griffiths, "Augustus and the Roman Provinces," 54.

of Spain which for over 200 years had asserted their freedom from the control of Rome were utterly humiliated about 30 years before Paul was born. Who would be most receptive to a gospel message that included them in the story of God? Perhaps those most recently crushed, defeated, and enslaved by Rome.

But what if Paul was coming to them as a Roman citizen? The question about Paul's citizenship always lurks around the corners whenever people consider his story, especially when using Acts. We can argue that it could never have been Paul the Roman citizen coming to the remnants of those defeated tribes. How could they even begin to trust one who had the protection and privileges of Roman citizenship. Paul may have been canny enough to invoke the notion of citizenship when the success of his ministry was at stake (per Acts 22:25), but we know from his motives for going to Spain, that Paul was on the side of those who could never claim such a status—those who were lucky to still be alive and under the heavy hand of Roman taxation. We can put to rest the idea that Paul was a citizen

Did he make it to Spain? Clement of Rome (born about 35 CE) wrote what is called *1 Clement* most likely in the early part of the second century. There is some overlap consequently with the stories of Paul and what Clement knew about him. He reports in this document that Paul made it to Rome. From 1 Clement we have the following:

> Having become a preacher in the East and in the West [Paul] received the noble renown of his faith Having taught righteousness in the whole world. Having reached the limits of the West[75] and having witnessed before the governing authorities thus he departed from the world and was received up into the holy place"[76]

Another early 2nd century document, *The Acts of Peter*, also maintains that Paul made it to Spain, and then back to Rome where he died. If the author of Acts even knew about Paul's intention to travel to Spain, the issue is totally absent from that account.

What matters is that Paul was making *plans* to go to Spain. That simple fact from the letter to the Romans establishes how significant

---

[75] Clement was writing from Rome and looking West when this was written.
[76] http://www.earlychristianwritings.com/text/1clement-lightfoot.html (1 Clement 5:5-6).

a mission to Spain was in terms of Paul's claims about the gospel itself. His wasn't a gospel for some kind of inner spiritual renewal, but it was actually a bold political vision, a direct challenge to those claiming to rule the world.

Two historical figures must come to the fore in our understanding of what was at stake with Paul's last letter: Augustus and Paul.

The first, Augustus, set his sights on Spain in 25 BCE. The second, Paul, set his sights on Spain around 58 CE.

Reaching Spain meant each man was making a huge statement with universal consequences.

One proclaimed the gospel of the divine Caesar and the other the gospel of the divine Christ.[77]

One came bearing a sword, the other carrying a pen.

One expected his image to be worshipped in every city in the Empire. He could never have imagined a day would come when groups comprised of barbarians and citizens would together worship one crucified by Rome. The other wrote, "May I never boast of anything except the cross of our Lord Jesus Christ, by which the world has been crucified to me, and I to the world" (Gal. 6:14).

One expected to be known as divine. The other would never call any Caesar his Lord. He would only know Christ crucified.

This chapter began with an opening scene from Hamlet. Something was rotten in Denmark. We have seen that something was rotten in Rome in the first century. Hamlet responded to his reality with a lament. For Paul, to go to Spain, it was an *opportunity* to take the gospel of Jesus Messiah to those most recently subjugated, enslaved, and falling under Rome's oppressive taxation. Many others through the centuries and still to this day follow Paul's example. Thankfully in our world there are amazing stories of those who despair in the search for justice and dignity, but who yet still find hope in Paul. This is the Paul who is found over and over again!

---

[77] John Dominic Crossan and Jonathan L. Reed, *In Search of Paul: How Jesus's Apostle Opposed Rome's Empire with God's Kingdom: A New Vision of Paul's Words and World* (San Francisco: Harper San Francisco, 2004), 12 (Not an exact quote).

Chapter 14
Paul and the Kingdom to Come

> "There it's only the fight to recover what has been lost
> And found and lost again and again: and now, under conditions
> That seem unpropitious."
> -T. S. Eliot[1]

The quote about recovering what has been lost comes from T.S. Elliot. It is an extended poem in four parts titled "Four Quartets." The second part, "East Coker" offers the pessimism of an old man considering the end of his life. It may seem like a dismal quote, and that spirit marks much of T. S. Elliot at times. There is, however, a way to read this poem in a better light if we simply change the last word to "propitious." There have been *propitious* times in the history of Christianity when Paul has been discovered to be extremely relevant. To be sure Paul has been found over and over again, but not always in the same clothes. I would maintain that we are in a most propitious time in which to find Paul. He is not lost—never has been, really, though, as you know by now, he was lost in a number of early church accounts that sadly have caused so much pain, even to this day.

Paula Fredriksen notes that he has been "the deeschatalogical Paul of Acts, the bureaucratic Paul of the Pastoral Epistles, and the philosophical Paul of Ephesians and Acts."[2] Adopted by Augustine many have assumed ever since that Paul had a guilty conscience.[3] Luther picked up that theme. From the time of the Pastoral Epistles to this very day in many faith communities Paul's words (*but not his words!*) prohibit women from leading in worship and participating as leaders in decision making. Tragically for slaves in the Americas Paul was adopted by slave owners to justify—if it can be called

---

[1] T. S Eliot, *T.S. Eliot: Collected Poems 1909-1962* (New York: Harcourt Brace Jovanovich, 1991), 189.

[2] Fredriksen, *From Jesus to Christ*, 171.

[3] Wright, *Faithfulness*, 747. John Caputo called Augustine a "universalist", but more specifically "the author of a theory of universal condemnation;" *St. Paul among the Philosophers*, 18.

that — the subjugation of Africans, treating them as less than human — of all things only 3/5ths equal to those with the right to vote when the American Constitution was adopted.

Perhaps more relevant to the church in the 21st century is the "legacy of a cognitive-doctrinal Paul [which] still monopolizes New Testament scholarship whenever it interprets Paul in terms of dogmatic topics or in terms of a fixed doctrinal core."[4] Many an eye may roll when it is announced in a worship service of another reading from one of Paul's letters. Some parent may have the child next to them whisper "Boring!" At least Linus, in a Peanut comic from long ago, had a more ironic take on the matter of reading his letters.

> Linus comes home from Church School and meets Charlie Brown.
> "Where have you been?" Charlie Brown asks.
> "Church school. We've been studying the letters of the Apostle Paul," Linus answers.
> "That should be interesting."
> "It is – although I must admit it makes me feel a little guilty."
> "Why?"
> Linus replies: "I always feel like I'm reading someone else's mail!"[5]

Linus may have been right, but Paul never wrote personal letters. They were public and as I am sure happened at least with those written from prison, they had most likely been read by a censor before they were carried away. Unlike most public readings of Paul's letters in worship today, in his time they were *events* in the life of the community. What we can never know is how they were received, except our analysis of 2 Corinthians showed Paul in the midst of a serious conflict that led to reconciliation. There his letter writing mattered.

Where we stand today is that Paul's letters continue to be read, and understood in some most surprising ways. Consider, for example the work of Elsa Tamez who looks at the doctrine

---

[4] Beker, *Heirs of Paul*, 22.
[5] Trobisch, *Paul's Letter Collection*, 48. Credit is given to Jeffrey H. Loria, *What's It All About Charlie Brown? Peanuts Kids Look at American Today* (Greenwich, CT: Faucett Publications, 1968).

"Justification by Faith from a Latin American Perspective". That is the subtitle of her book *The Amnesty of Grace*. The Paul that Tamez finds was "a traveler, rubbing shoulders constantly with other travelers of every sort: sailors, slaves on the way to be sold, fugitive slaves, traders, teachers, and soldiers among others."[6] She also emphasizes as I have done in this book Paul's experiences in prison, and his sharing the life of those who lived from day to day. Paul, she declares, lived in "an inverted society, [where] judgment favors the unjust and condemns the innocent."[7] What Paul affirmed in the Messiah was "the solidarity of God with humankind, to the point of taking on their humanity, and even more specifically, the humanity of the poor, who in Paul's day were the principal victims of sin."[8] The singular word "sin" stands for the structural oppression of all who are excluded and marginalized, but in the understanding of *justification* offered by Tamez they are "worthy historical subjects re-created for life, with the power to transform their history..."[9]

Paul was also frequently used on both sides of the issue of slavery as it affected the earliest settlements in America, and as it continues to plague the lives of minorities in terms of issues of justice, poverty, education, and economic opportunities. In the chapter "Paul Slave of Christ," I discussed the troubling texts, mostly from the Pastoral Epistles, but also in 1 Corinthians 7:21 and Philemon, which may have supported, or seem to, the institution of slavery. Many of those texts were used by Southern slave masters, and white clergy to preach that slavery was part of God's design. I noted in that chapter that a number of African American theologians and pastors have had trouble with the Paul who seemingly did not oppose slavery. You may remember the story of Howard Thurman who vividly remembered the words of his grandmother who vowed to never read the parts of the bible where Paul wrote about slavery. Yet, a great many in slavery, and those in the years after the Civil War living under the heavy burden of Jim Crow segregation actually embraced Paul as the apostle who opposed slavery. That is the story told by Lisa Bowens in *African American Readings of Paul: Reception,*

---

[6] Tamez, "Author's Introduction," 48.
[7] Tamez, "Author's Introduction," 101.
[8] Tamez, "Author's Introduction," 114.
[9] Tamez, "Author's Introduction," 165.

Resistance, and Transformation.[10] Long before I even thought of writing this book, there were so many fighting the evils of slavery and racism in America who turned to Paul. Their voices need to be heard in light of what I hope is also a new way of hearing Paul.

The American War for Independence, grounded in the desire for freedom, did not mean freedom for all. A few slaves though, like Lemuel Haynes (1753-1833) were able to fight with "the Minutemen and served in the Continental army."[11] He had been freed from being an indentured servant when the revolution started. After the war he studied Latin and Greek and by 1785 was the "first black to be ordained to any religious organization."[12] One of the passages that American slaveowners used from the Bible to justify enslaving black people went back to the curse Noah laid on his son Ham (Gen 9:2-27). Haynes read that this curse was "eradicated by Christ's advent."[13] Equally important was his reading of 1 Cor 7:21 which he interpreted to mean "if there is any hope of attaining it [freedom], use all Lawful measures to attain it."[14] In addition Haynes quoted from Acts 17:26, which became a central text for all who saw the evils of American slavery. We can find words in Acts which help us find Paul. Preaching in the marketplace of Athens Paul said "[God] hath made of one blood all nations of men for to dwell on the all the face of the earth…" (Acts 17:26)[15] Haynes read the King James Bible which is unique among English translations in the use of the phrase "one blood" in that verse. A number of African American interpreters call this interpretation the "one-blood doctrine." It was used over and over in the literature opposing American slavery.

Zilpha Elaw (born in 1790) was a "renowned early black woman preacher"[16] who wrote "Oh! That men would outgrow their nursery prejudices and learn that *'God hath made of one blood all the nations of men that dwell upon the face of the earth.'*" She went on to emphasize

---

[10] Lisa M. Bowens, *African American Readings of Paul: Reception, Resistance, and Transformation* (Grand Rapids: Eerdmans, 2020).

[11] Bowens, *African American Readings of Paul*, 49.

[12] Bowens, *African American Readings of Paul*, 49.

[13] Bowens, *African American Readings of Paul*, 52

[14] Bowens, *African American Readings of Paul*, 52.

[15] Note: the word "blood" is not in the Greek text. Literally it is "he made of one every nation of men to dwell." The NRSV version reads "From one ancestor he made all nations." The Wycliff bible is the closest to the KJV: "and made of one all the kind of men [for] to inhabit on all the face of the earth."

[16] Bowens, *African American Readings of Paul*, 83.

that the Spirit fell on both Jews and Gentiles. Thus, Bowens writes that Elaw saw all people as "one."[17]

The story of Daniel Payne (1811-1893) is remarkable. He was born to free Christian parents in South Carolina and would spend his life encouraging African Americans to share his love of learning. When the General Assembly in South Carolina passed a law forbidding the education of slave or free people of color, he closed the school he had started there. He opened one up North. His "separation" from that dream he wrote "was the bitter product of unjust, cruel, and blasphemous laws — cruel and unjust to a defenseless race, blasphemous of that God who *of one blood did make all the nations of the earth.*"[18]

The book by Bowens is filled with so many examples of courageous black preachers, teachers, and theologians who could discover that Paul was the apostle for the freedom they so longed for. Especially significant is the role that Paul played in the life and ministry of Martin Luther King Jr., who saw himself "as a modern-day Paul who carries the gospel around the world."[19] The model for his *Letter from the Birmingham Jail?* Philippians! It was also a prison letter. King could read in Paul with his emphasis on our "bodies as a living sacrifice, holy, acceptable unto God" (Rom 12:1), the endorsement of non-violence as the tactic to turn the hearts of the cruel enforcers of Jim Crow segregation to realize the moral injustice in that systematic oppression of people of color. Paul's emphasis on love in 1 Corinthians 13, was Kings way of understanding Paul's words about showing us a "more excellent way" (1 Cor 12:31). That was the phrase Paul used to introduce that famous chapter with the title "The Gift of Love" (NRSV). We are also reminded by Bowens how Martin Luther King Jr. saw a "Paul who learned to stand tall and without despairing amid the disappointments in life."[20] I agree. Paul may have been short, but he could stand tall to be a witness for justice and mercy to all those who did not know this in their lives of oppression and subjugation.

There is just one final question to ask which I posed in the opening of the book. What about the word "church?" Or better yet,

---

[17] Bowens, *African American Readings of Paul*, 96.
[18] Bowens, *African American Readings of Paul*, 218.
[19] Bowens, *African American Readings of Paul*, 247.
[20] Bowens, *African American Readings of Paul*, 259

not just the word, but how we live and breathe *church* in the life of those who call Jesus Messiah? In the introduction I explained that I would use the Greek word *ekklēsia* so that we would not think of particular buildings or organized worship communities we associate with the word church in reference to those receiving Paul's letters. But I also place myself in the company of people who love the word *church*.

In my case I was blessed in a long pastoral ministry to serve a great many communities known as churches. My memories are of all the people—the good times, and the times of stress and challenge. I also welcomed them on Sundays as "church" which I learned from a colleague I once had. Like him I happily started many a worship service on a Sunday morning with the greeting, "Good morning Church!" In my mind we only used that term because it was about us being together to start a worship service and to continue the ministry that bound us all together. Do we who follow Jesus Messiah have a politics? Indeed, we do, and from Stanley Hauerwas we learn its name is *Church!*[21]

What must be challenged over and over is the lie for someone to say they are a Christian, but they don't go to church. To follow Jesus means to engage with others in an unlikely assembly with those who kneel, share the Eucharist, and who are continually reminded through reading scripture and reflections on it that we do not own our lives, but have been given life and a call to serve one another. The weekly embarrassment, and certainly contrary to the vision of Paul, is that we mark ourselves off from one another with our denominational differences, and most cruelly with bars to participation from outsiders keeping them from the table, or other parts of our common life. Every church must ask itself if it has truly been reaching out to all its neighbors and to welcome them to the story of God as Paul knew it.

What we know from Paul's letters is that the story of God beginning with creation, extended through the call of Abraham, father of all in the world, and culminating in the death and resurrection of Jesus, was meant to reach all the world. To those without hope for their lives, without the agency to change their circumstances, came this message of peace and justice along with a

---

[21] Hauerwas and Pinches, *Christians among the Virtues*, xi.

welcome to a community that promised a vision of a kingdom to come. We still have that prayer.

Bibliography

Adams, Edward. *The Earliest Christian Meeting Places: Almost Exclusively Houses?* London: Bloomsbury T & T Clark, 2013.

Adelmann, Rachel. "'My Father Was a Wandering Aramean...': The Ethical Legacy of Our Origins in Exile (Parashat Ki Tavo, Deuteronomy 26:1–29:8)," *Huffington Post*, Dec. 7, 2016. Found at: https://www.huffpost.com/entry/my-father-was-a-wandering-aramean-the-ethical_b_57e1e98de4b05d3737be5099.

Agamben, Giorgio. *The Time That Remains: A Commentary on the Letter to the Romans*. Stanford, CA: Stanford University Press, 2005.

———. "The Remnants of Auschwitz," in *The Omnibus Homo Sacer*. 761–880. Stanford, CA: Stanford University Press, 2017, 2017.

Anderson, John T. "The Body of Satan According to Paul" *Proceedings* 13 (1993): 103-112.

Armstrong, Karen. *St. Paul: The Apostle We Love to Hate*. Boston: New Harvest, 2016.

Arndt, William F. and F. Wilbur Gingrich. *A Greek-English Lexicon of the New Testament and Other Early Christian Literature*, 2nd ed. Chicago: The University of Chicago Press, 1958.

Asad, Talal. *Genealogies of Religion: Discipline and Reasons of Power in Christianity and Islam*. Baltimore, MD: The Johns Hopkins University Press, 1993.

———. *Formations of the Secular: Christianity, Islam, Modernity*. Stanford CA: Stanford University Press. 2003.

Ascough, Richard S. *Paul's Macedonian Associations: The Social Context of Philippians and 1 Thessalonians*. Tübingen: J. C. B. Mohr, 2003.

Ashton, John. *The Religion of Paul the Apostle*. New Haven: Yale University Press, 2000.

Assman, Jan. *Religion and Cultural Memory: Ten Studies*. Stanford: Stanford University Press, 2006.

———. *Cultural Memory and Early Civilization: Writing, Remembrances, and Political Imagination*. New York: Cambridge University Press, 2011.

Aus, Roger D. "Paul's Travel Plans to Spain and the "Full Number of the Gentles" of Rom. XI 25." *Novum Testamentum* 21, Fasc. 3 (July 1979): 231–62.

Bailey, Kenneth. *Poet and Peasant and Through Peasant Eyes: A Literary-Cultural Approach to the Parables in Luke*, vol 2. Grand Rapids: Eerdman's, 1976.

_____. *Paul Through Mediterranean Eyes: Cultural Studies in 1 Corinthians*. Downers Grove: IVP Academic, 2011.

Barclay, John M.G "Offensive and uncanny": Jesus and Paul on the Caustic Grace of God" *in Jesus and Paul Reconnected: Fresh Pathways into an Old Debate* edited by Todd D. Still, 1–17. Grand Rapids: Eerdman's, 2007.

_____. *Paul and the Gift*. Grand Rapids: Eerdman's, 2015.

Barrier, Jeremy W. *The Acts of Paul and Thecla: A Critical Introduction and Commentary*. Tübingen: Mohr Siebeck, 2009.

Bateman, Elizabeth. "Hair and the Artifice of Roman Female Adornment," *American Journal of Archeology*, 105, no. 1 (Jan 2001): 1–25.

Bartchy, S. Scott.. *First-Century Slavery and 1 Corinthians 7:21*. Eugene: Wipf and Stock Publishers, 2003.

Bazzana, Giovanni B. *Having the Spirit of Christ: Spirit Possession and Exorcism in the Early Christ Groups*. New Haven: Yale University Press, 2000

Beard, Mary. SPQR: *A History of Rome*. New York: Liveright Publishing Corp., 2015.

Becker, Eve-Marie. *Paul on Humility*. Translated by Wayne Coppins. Waco, TX: Baylor University Press, 2020.

Beker, J. C. *Heirs of Paul: Their Legacy in the New Testament and The Church Today*. Grand Rapids: Wm B. Eerdman's, 1991.

Beitzel, Barry J. "Was There a Joint Nautical Venture on the Mediterranean Sea by Tyrian Phoenicians and Early Israelites?" *Bulletin of the American Schools of Oriental Research* 360 (November 2010): 37–66.

Benjamin, Walter. "The Task of the Translator." In *Illuminations*. Edited by Hannah Arendt, 11–25. Boston: Mariner Books, 1955.

Betz, Hans Dieter. *Galatians: A Commentary on Paul's Letter to the Churches of Galatia*. Philadelphia: Fortress Press, 1979.

Bickerman, Elias J. "*Syria and Cilicia*" *The American Journal of Philology* 68, no. 4, (1947): 353–62.

Benjamin, Walter. "The Task of the Translator." In *Illuminations*, edited by Hannah Arendt, 11–25. Translated by Harry Zohn. Boston: Mariner Books, 2021.

Bird, Michael F. ""One Who Will Arise to Rule Over the Nations": Paul's Letter to the Romans and the Roman Empire." In *Jesus is Lord Caesar is Not: Evaluating Empire in New Testament Studies*, edited by Scot McKnight and Joseph B. Modica, 146–65. Downers Grove: IVP Academic, 2010.

Bird, Michael F. *An Anomalous Jews: Paul Among Jews, Greeks, and Romans*. Grand Rapids: Eerdman's, 2016.

Bockmuehl, Marcus. *Seeing the Word: Refocusing New Testament Study*. Grand Rapids: Baker Academic, 2006

———. "Peter between Jesus and Paul: The 'Third Quest' and the 'New Perspective' on the First Disciple." In *Jesus and Paul Reconnected: Fresh Pathways into an Old Debate*, edited by Todd D. Still, 67–102. Grand Rapids: William B Eerdman's Publishing Company, 2007.

Borg, Marcus and John Dominic Crossan. *The First Paul: Reclaiming the Radical Visionary Behind the Church's Conservative Icon*. New York: Harper Collins Publishers, 2009.

Bount, Brian K., Cain Hope Felder, Clarice J. Martin, and Emerson B. Powery eds. *True to Our Native Land: An African American New Testament Commentary*. Minneapolis: Fortress Press, 2007.

Bowens, Lisa M. *African American Readings of Paul: Reception, Resistance, and Transformation*. Grand Rapids: Eerdman's, 2020.

Bowers, W. P. "Jewish Communities in Spain in the Time of Paul", *The Journal of Theological Studies*, 26, no. 2 (October 1975): 395–402.

Boyarin, Daniel. *A Radical Jew: Paul and the Politics of Identity*. Berkley: University of California Press, 1994.

———. *Border Lines: The Partition of Judaeo-Christianity*. Philadelphia: University of Pennsylvania Press, 2004.

Bowerstock, G.W., *Roman Arabia*. Cambridge: Harvard University Press, 1983.

Bozarth-Campbell, Alla. *The Word's Body: An Incarnational Aesthetic of Interpretation*. Tuscaloosa: University of Alabama Press, 1979.

Bradley, Keith R. *Slavery and Society at Rome*. New York: Cambridge University Press, 1994.

———. *Slaves and Masters in the Roman Empire: A Study in Social Control*. New York: Oxford University Press, 1987.

Briggs, J. R. *Fail: Finding Hope and Grace in the Midst of Ministry Failure*. Downers Grove: InterVarsity Press, 2014.

Briggs, Sheila, "Paul on Bondage and Freedom in Imperial Roman Society" in *Paul and Politics: Ekklesia, Israel, Imperium, Interpretation*, edited by Richard A. Horsley, 110-23. Harrisburg: Trinity Press International, 2000.

Bristow, John. *What Paul Really Said about Women: An Apostle's Liberating Views on Equality in Marriage, Leadership, and Love*. San Francisco: Harper & Row, 1988.

Brown, Alexandra K. "The Gospel Takes Place in Weakness: Paul's Theology of Power-in-Weakness in 2 Corinthians," *Interpretation* 52, no. 3 (1998): 271-85.

Brown, Peter. *Poverty and Leadership in the Later Roman Empire: The Menahem Stern Jerusalem Lectures*. Hanover and London: University of New England Press, 2002.

Bryant, K. E. Edwin. *Paul and the Rise of the Slave: Death and Resurrection of the Oppressed in the Epistle to the Romans*. Boston: Brill, 2016.

Callahan, Allen Dwight. "Brother Saul: An Ambivalent Witness to Freedom." *Semeia*, 83-84, (1997): 235-50.

_____. *Embassy of Onesimus: The Letter of Paul to Philemon*. Valley Forge: Trinity Press International, 1997.

_____. "Paul, *Ekklesia*, and Emancipation in Corinth," in *Paul and Politics: Ekklesia, Israel, Imperium, Interpretation*, edited by Richard A. Horsley, 216-23. Harrisburg: Trinity International Press, 2000.

_____. *The Talking Book: African Americans and the Bible*. New Haven: Yale University Press, 2006.

Campbell, Charles L. *1 Corinthians*. Louisville: Westminster John Knox Press, 2018.

Campbell, Douglas A. "An Anchor for Pauline Chronology: Paul's Flight from the Ethnarch of King Aretas :2 Corinthians 11:32-33" *Journal of Biblical Literature* 121/2, (2002): 279-302.

_____. *The Deliverance of God: An Apocalyptic Rereading of Justification in Paul*. Grand Rapids, Wm B. Eerdmans Publishing, 2009.

_____. *Framing Paul: An Epistolary Biography*. Grand Rapids: William B. Eerdman's Company, 2014.

_____*Paul: An Apostle's Journey*. Grand Rapids: Wm. B. Eerdmans Publishing Company, 2018.

Caputo, John D. *The Weakness of God: A Theology of the Event*. Bloomington: Indiana University Press, 2006.

———. "Beyond Sovereignty: Many Nations Under the Weakness of God." *Soundings* 84, no. 1/2 (2006): 21–35.

———. *St. Paul among the Philosophers*. Bloomington: Indiana University Press, 2009.

———. *The Insistence of God: A Theology of Perhaps*. Bloomington: Indiana University Press, 2013.

———. "A Prayer for the Impossible: A Catechumen's Guide to Deconstruction." In *The Essential Caputo*, edited by Keith Olthuis, 369–89. Bloomington: Indiana University Press, 2018.

Castelli, Elizabeth A. "Paul on Women and Gender," in *Women and Christian Origins*. Edited by Ross Sheppard Kraemer and Mary Rose D'Angelo, 221–235. New York: Oxford University Press, 1999.

Cervin, Richard S. "A Note Regarding the Name 'Junia(s)' in Romans 16.7." *New Testament Studies* 40 (1994): 464-70.

Chapple, Allan. "Getting Romans to the Right Romans: Phoebe and the Delivery of Paul's Letter," *Tyndale Bulletin* 62.2 (2011): 195-214

Collins, Raymond. *The Birth of the New Testament: The Origin and Development of the First Christian Generation*. New York: Crossroad, 1993.

Cone, James H. *The Cross and the Lynching Tree*. Maryknoll: Orbis Books, 2011.

Crites, Stephen. "The Narrative Quality of Experience." In *Why Narrative? Readings in Narrative Theology,"* edited by Stanley Hauerwas and L. Gregory Jones, 65–88. Eugene: Wipf and Stock Publishers, 1997.

Crossan, John Dominic and Jonathan L. Reed. *In Search of Paul: How Jesus's Apostle Opposed Rome's Empire with God's Kingdom*. San Francisco: Harper, 2004.

———. *Render unto Caesar: The Struggle Over Christ and Culture in the New Testament*. New York: Harper Collins Publishers, 2022.

Dahl, Nils A. *Studies in Paul: Theology for the Early Christian Mission*. Eugene: Wipf and Stock Publishers, 1977.

Danker, Frederick William. *A Greek-English Lexicon of the New Testament and other Early Christian Literature*. Chicago: The University of Chicago Press, 2001.

Despotis, Athanasios. "Reconsidering the Pauline Conception of Time," *Journal for the Study of Paul and His Letters* 8, no. 1-2 (2019): 20–42.

Dewey, Arthur J. "A Re-Hearing of Romans 10:1-15." *Semeia* 65 (1994): 109–27.
Dewey. Arthur J., Roy W. Hoover, Lane C. McGaughy, and Daryl D. Schmidt, eds. *The Authentic Letters of Paul: A New Reading of Paul's Rhetoric and Meaning.* Salem: Polebridge Press, 2010.
Dewey, Joanna. "Textuality in an Oral Culture," *Semeia* 65 (1994): 37–65.
Diessmann, Adolf. *Paul: A Study in Social and Religious History.* New York: Harper and Brothers Publisher, 1927.
Dorff, Elliot N. 2015. "Borowitz on Halakhah, Aggadah, and Ethics." *Journal of Jewish Ethics* 1, no.1 (2015): 59–76.
Downs, David J. "The Offering of the Gentiles in Romans 15–16," *Journal for the Study of the New Testament* 29, no. 2 (2006): 173–86.
_____. *The Offering of the Gentiles: Paul's Collection for Jerusalem in its Chronological, Cultural, and Cultic Contexts.* Grand Rapids: Eerdman's Publishing Co, 2008.
Drinkwater, John F. *Nero: Emperor and Court.* Cambridge: Cambridge University Press, 2019.
Dunn, James D. G. *The Theology of Paul the Apostle.* Grand Rapids: Eerdman's Publishing Company, 1998.
Dunnett, Walter. *The Book of Acts.* Grand Rapid: Baker Book House, 1981.
Eastman, Susan. *Recovering Paul's Mother Tongue: Language and Theology in Galatians.* Grand Rapids: Eerdman's Publishing Company, 2007.
Ehrensperger, Kathy. *That We May Be Mutually Encouraged: Feminism and the New Perspective in Pauline Studies.* London: T & T Clark, 2004.
_____. *Paul and the Dynamics of Power: Communication and Interaction in the Early Christ-Movement.* London: T & T Clark, 2009.
_____. "Speaking Greek Under Rome: Paul the Power of Language and the Language of Power," *Neotestamentica* 46, no 1 (2012): 9–28.
_____. *Paul at the Crossroads of Cultures: Theologizing in the Space Between.* London: Bloomsbury T & T Clark, 2013.
_____. "The Question(s) of Gender: Relocating Paul in Relation to Judaism." In *Paul within Judaism: Restoring the First-Century Context to the Apostle,* edited by Mark D. Nanos and Magnus Zetterholm, 245–76. Minneapolis: Fortress Press, 2015.
Eisenbaum, Pamela. "Paul, Polemics, and the Problem of Essentialism,' *Biblical Interpretation* 13, no 3 (2005): 224–38.

———. *Paul was Not a Christian: The Original Message of a Misunderstood Apostle*. New York: Harper Collins, 2009.

Elliott, Neal. "The Anti-Imperial Message of the Cross." In *Paul and Empire: Religion and Power in Roman Imperial Society*, edited by Richard A. Horsley, 167–83. Harrisburg: Trinity Press International, 1997.

———. *The Rhetoric of Romans; Argumentative Constraint and Argument and Paul's Dialogue with Judaism*. Nashville: Augsburg Publishing, 2000.

———. "Strategies of Resistance and Hidden Transcripts in the Pauline Communities." In *Hidden Transcripts and the Arts of Resistance*, edited by Richard A. Horsley, 97–122. Semeia Studies 48. Atlanta: Society of Biblical Literature, 2004.

———. *Liberating Paul: The Justice of God and the Politics of the Apostle*. Minneapolis: Fortress Press, 2006.

———. "The Apostle Paul and Empire." In *In the Shadow of Empire: Reclaiming the Bible as a History of Faithful Resistance*, edited by Richard A. Horsley, 97–116. Louisville: Westminster John Knox Press, 2008.

———. *The Arrogance of the Nations*. Minneapolis, MN: Fortress Press, 2010.

Elliott, Neil and Mark Reasoner. *Documents and Images for the Study of Paul*. Minneapolis: Fortress Press, 2011.

Ellis, E. Earle. 1991. "The End of the Earth (Acts 1:8)."*Bulletin for Biblical Research* 1 (1991): 123–32.

Eisenbaum, Pamela. *Paul Was Not a Christian: The Original Message of a Misunderstood Apostle*. New York: Harper Collins Publishers, 2009.

Ensor, Jonathan B. *Paul and the Corinthians: Leadership, Ordeals, and the Politics of Displacement*. London: T and T Clark, 2022.

Episcopal Church. *The Book of Common Prayer*. New York: Seabury Press, 1977.

Eubank, Nathan. "Justice Endures Forever: Paul's Grammar of Generosity." *Journal for the Study of Paul and His Letters* 5, no. 2 (2015): 169–87.

Eyl, Jennifer. *Signs, Wonders, and Gifts: Divination in the Letters of Paul*. New York: Oxford University Press, 2019.

Fee, Gordon D. *The First Epistle to the Corinthians: Revised Edition*. Grand Rapid: Eerdman's, 2014.

Fiorenza, Elizabeth Schüssler. "Missionaries, Apostles, Coworkers: Romans 16 and the Reconstruction of Women's Early Christian History." *Word and World* 6, no. 4 (1986): 420–33.

———. *But She Said: Feminist Practices of Biblical Interpretation*. Boston: Beason Press, 1992.

———. *In Memory of Her: A Feminist Theological Reconstruction of Christian Origins*. New York: Crossroad, 1994.

Frankopan, Peter. *The Silk Roads: A New History of the World*. New York: Alfred A. Knopf, 2016.

Fredriksen, Paula. *From Jesus to Christ: The Origins of the New Testament Images of Jesus*. New Haven: Yale University Press, 1988.

———. "The Question of Worship: Gods, Pagans, and the Redemption of Israel." In *The Question of Worship: Gods, Pagans, and the Redemption of Israel*, edited by Mark D. Nanos and Magnus Zetterholm, 175-201. Minneapolis: Fortress Press, 2015.

———. *Paul, The Pagan's Apostle*. New Haven: Yale University Press, 2017.

———. *When Christians Were Jews: The First Generation*. New Haven: Yale University Press, 2018.

Frei, Hans. "Apologetics, Criticism, and the Loss of Narrative Interpretation." In *Why Narrative: Readings in Narrative Theology*, edited by. Stanley Hauerwas and L. Gregory Jones, 45–64. Eugene: Wipf and Stock Publishers, 1997.

Friesen, Steven J. "Poverty in Pauline Studies: Beyond the So-called New Consensus." *Journal for the Study of the New Testament* 263 (2004): 323-61.

———. "Injustice or God's Will: Explanations of Poverty in Proto-Christian Communities." In *Christian History: A People's History of Christianity*, edited by Richard A. Horsley, 240–60. Minneapolis, Fortress Press, 2005.

Gager, John G. 1982. "Shall We Marry Our Enemies? Sociology and the New Testament." *Interpretation* 36, no. 3 (1982): 256–65.

———. *Reinventing Paul*. New York: Oxford University Press, 2000.

———. *The Jewish Lives of the Apostle Paul: Who Made Early Christianity?* New York; Columbia University Press, 2015.

Garroway, Joshua D. *The Beginning of the Gospel: Paul, Philippi and the Origins of Christianity*. Cham: Palgrave Macmillion, 2018.

Gaston, Lloyd. *Paul and the Torah*. Vancouver: University of British Columbia Press, 1987.

Gaventa, Beverly Roberts. "The Overthrown Enemy: Luke's Portrait of Paul." *Society of Biblical Literature Seminar Papers 1985*, 439-49. Atlanta: Scholars Press, 1985.

―――. *Our Mother St. Paul*. Louisville: Westminster John Knox Press, 2007.

Gench, Francis Taylor. *Encountering God in Tyrannical Texts: Reflections on Paul, Women, and the Authority of Scripture*. Louisville: Westminster John Knox Press, 2015.

Georgi, Dieter. *Remembering the Poor: The History of Paul's Collection for Jerusalem*. Nashville: Abingdon Press, 1965.

―――. *Theocracy: In Paul's Praxis and Theology*. Minneapolis: Fortress Press, 1991.

Glancy, Jennifer A. "Obstacles to Slaves' Participation in the Corinthian Church," *Journal of Biblical Literature* 117, no. 3 (1998): 481-501.

―――. *Slavery as Moral Problem: In the Early Church and Today*. Minneapolis: Fortress Press, 2011.

―――. *Slavery in Early Christianity*. Minneapolis: Fortress Press, 2013.

―――. "The Sexual Use of Slaves: A Response to Kyle Harper on Jewish and Christian Porneia." *Journal of Biblical Literature*, 134, no. 1 (2015): 215-29.

Goldsworthy, Adrian. *Pax Romana: War, Peace and Conquest in the Roman World*. New Haven: Yale University Press. 2016.

Gooder, Paula. *Only the Third Heaven? 2 Corinthians 12.1-10 and Heavenly Ascent*. Library of New Testament Studies 313. London: T & T Clark, 2006.

Gordon, Richard. 1997. "The Veil of Power." In *Paul and Empire: Religion and Power in Roman Imperial Society,* edited by Richard A. Horsley, 127-37. Harrisburg: Trinity Press International, 1997.

Goldsworthy, Adrian. *Pax Romana: War, Peace an Conquest in the Roman World*. New Haven: Yale University Press, 2016.

Gray, Paul. *Paul as a Problem in History and Culture: The Apostle and His Critics Through the Centuries*. Grand Rapids: Baker Academic, 2016.

Gorman, Michael J. *Cruciformity: Paul's Narrative Spirituality of the Cross*. Grand Rapids: Eerdman's Publishing, 2001.

Gregory, Brad, *The Unintended Revolution: How a Religious Revolution Secularized Society*. Cambridge: The Belknap Press of Harvard University Press, 2012.

Griffiths, David. "Augustus and the Roman Provinces on Iberia." PhD diss., The University of Liverpool, 2013.

Haenchen, Ernst. *The Acts of the Apostles: A Commentary.* Philadelphia: The Westminster Press, 1971.

Hardy, Barbara. *Tellers and Listeners: The Narrative Imagination.* London: The Athlone Press, 1975.

Harink, Douglas. *Paul Among the Postliberals: Pauline Theology Beyond Christendom and Modernity.* Grand Rapids: Brazos Press, 2003.

Harrill, J. Albert, *Slaves in the New Testament: Literary, Social and Moral Dimensions.* Minneapolis: Fortress Press, 2006.

_____. "Slavery and Inhumanity: Keith Bradley's Legacy on Slavery in New Testament Studies." *Biblical Interpretation*m 21, no 4-5 (2013): 506-19.

Harrison, James R. "More than conquerors" (Rom 8:37): Paul's Gospel and Augustan Triumphal Arches of the Greek East and the Latin West." *Buried History* 47 (2011): 3-20.

_____. "Paul's "Indebtedness" to the Barbarian (Rom 1:14) in Latin West Perspective." *Novum Testamentum* 55 (2013): 311-48.

_____. "Augustan Rome and the body of Christ: a comparison of the "Res Gestae" and Paul's Letter to the Romans." *Harvard Theological Review* 106, no 1(2013): 1-36.

_____. "The "Clemency" of Nero and Paul's Language of "Mercy" in Romans—Paul's Reconfiguration of Imperial Values in the Mid-Fifties Rome." In *Justice, Mercy, and Well-Being: Interdisciplinary Perspectives,* edited by Peter G. Bolt and James R. Harrison, 193-222. Eugene: Wipf and Stock 2020.

Hauerwas, Stanley. *Christian Existence Today: Essays on Church, World, and Living In-Between.* Durham: The Labyrinth Press, 1988.

_____. "The Church as God's New Language." In *Christian Existence Today: Essays on Church, World and Living In Between,* 47-65. Durham: The Labyrinth Press, 1988.

_____. "How to Go on When You Know You Are Going to Be Misunderstood, or How Paul Homer Ruined My Life or Making Sense of Paul Holmer." In *Wilderness Wanderings: Probing Twentieth Century Theology and Philosophy,* 143-52. Boulder: Westview Press, 1997.

_____. *With the Grain of the Universe: The Church's Witness and Natural Theology.* Grand Rapids: Brazos Press, 2001.

Hauerwas, Stanley and L. Gregory Jones, eds. *Why Narrative: Readings in Narrative Theology.* Eugene: Wipf and Stock Publishers, 1997.

Hauerwas, Stanley and Charles Pinches. *Christians among the Virtues: Theological Conversations with Ancient and Modern Ethics.* Notre Dame: Notre Dame Press, 1997.

Hauerwas, Stanley and William Willimon. *Where Resident Aliens Live.* Nashville: Abingdon Press, 1996.

Hawkins, Faith Kirkham. "Does Paul Make a Difference." In *A Feminist Companion to Paul,* edited by Amy Jill Levine with Marianne Blickenstaff, 169-82. New York: T & T Clark International, 2004.

Hay, David M. "Pauline Theology After Paul." In *Pauline Theology: Vol. IV. Looking Back, Pressing On,"* edited by by E. Elizabeth Johnson and David M. Hay, 181-98. Atlanta: Scholars Press. 1997.

Hays, Richard B. 1983. *The Faith of Jesus Christ: The Narrative Substructure of Galatians 3:1-4:11.* Downers Grove: InterVarsity Press.

_____. "Christology and Ethics in Galatians: The Law of Christ," The *Catholic Biblical Quarterly* 49 (1987): 268-90.

_____. *Echoes of Scripture in the Letters of Paul.* New Haven: Yale University Press, 1989.

_____. *The Moral Vision of the New Testament: Community, Cross, New Creation.* New York: Harper Collins, 1996.

_____. 1997. *First Corinthians.* Louisville: Westminster John Knox Press.

_____. *The Conversion of the Imagination: Paul as Interpreter of Israel's Scripture.* Grand Rapids: Eerdman's, 2005.

Hengel, Martin. "Paul in Arabia," *Bulletin for Biblical Research* 12.1 (2002): 47-66.

Hobsbawm, Eric. *On History.* New York, The New Press, 1997.

Hock, Ronald F. "Paul's Tentmaking and the Problem of His Social Class." *Journal of Biblical Literature* 97, no. 4 (1978): 555-64.

Hodge, Caroline Johnson. "Apostle to the Gentiles: Constructions of Paul's Identity." *Biblical Interpretation* 13, no 3 (2005): 270-88.

_____. The Question of Identity: Gentiles as Gentiles—but also Not—in Pauline Communities." in *Paul Within Judaism: Restoring the First-Century Context to the Apostle.* eds. Mark D. Nanos and Magnus Zetterholm, 153-73. Minneapolis: Fortress Press, 2015.

Hogan, Pauline Nigh. "Paul and Women in Second-Century Christianity." In *Paul and the Second Century,* edited by Michael J. Bird and Joseph R. Dodson, 226-43. New York: T&T Clark, 2009.

Hopkins, Gerard Manly. *The Poems of Gerard Manly Hopkins"*. New York: Oxford University Press, 1967.

Hopkins, Keith. *A World Full of Gods: Pagans, Jews, and Christians in the Roman Empire*. London: Weidenfield and Nicolson, 1999.

Horrell, David. G. "Paul's Narratives or Substructure? The Significance of 'Paul's Story'." In *Narrative Dynamics in Paul: A Critical Assessment*, edited by Bruce W. Longenecker, 15771. Louisville: Westminster John Knox Press, 2002.

_____. *Solidarity and Difference: A Contemporary Reading of Paul's Ethics*. New York: Bloomsbury T & T Clark, 2016.

Horsley, Richard A., "General Introduction." In *Paul and Empire: Religion and Power in Roman Imperial Society*, edited by Richard A. Horsley, 1-8. Harrisburg: Trinity Press International, 1997.

_____. "Introduction: Paul's Counter-Imperial Gospel." In *Paul and Empire: Religion and Power in Roman Imperial Society*, edited by Richard A. Horsley, 140-47. Harrisburg: Trinity Press International, 1997.

_____. "Building an Alternative Society: Introduction." In *Paul and Empire: Religion and Power in Roman Imperial Society*, edited by Richard A. Horsley, 205-214. Harrisburg: Trinity Press International, 1997.

_____. "I Corinthians: A Case Study of Paul's Assembly as an Alternative Society." In *Paul and Empire: Religion and Power in Roman Imperial Society*, edited by Richard A. Horsley, 242-52. Harrisburg, PA: Trinity Press International, 1997.

_____. *1 Corinthians*. Nashville, TN: Abingdon Press, 1998.

_____. "Paul and Slavery: A Critical Alternative to Recent Readings." *Semeia* 83-84 (1998): 152-200

_____. "The Slave Systems of Classical Antiquity and Their Reluctant Recognition by Modern Scholars." *Semeia* 83-84 (1998): 19-66.

_____, ed. *Paul and Politics: Ekklesia, Israel, Imperium, Interpretation*. Harrisburg: Trinity International Press, 2000.

_____. *Hearing the Whole Story: The Politics of Plot in Mark's Gospel*. Louisville: Westminster John Knox Press, 2001.

_____. *Text and Tradition in Performance and Writing*. Eugene, OR: Cascade Books, Kindle edition, 2013.

_____. *Jesus and the Politics of Roman Palestine*. Columbia: University of South Carolina Press, 2014.

Horsley, Richard A. and Neil Asher Silverman, *The Message and the Kingdom: How Jesus and Paul Ignited a Revolution and Transformed the Ancient World*. New York: Penguin Putnam, 1997.

Hoskyns, Edwin and Noel Davey. *The Riddle of the New Testament*. London: Faber and Faber Limited, 1963.

Hultgren, Arland J. "On Translating and Interpreting Galatians 1:13." *Bible Translator* 26 (1975): 146-48.

_____. "Paul's Pre-Christian Persecutions of the Church: Their Purpose, Locale, and Nature." *Journal of Biblical Literature* 95 (1976) 97-111.

_____. *Paul's Letter to the Romans: A Commentary*. Grand Rapids: Wm. B. Eeerdman's Publishing, 2011

Hutton, Patrick H. *History as an Art of Memory*. Hanover: University of Vermont, 1993.

Jennings, W. Theodore, Jr. *Reading Derrida / Thinking Paul*. Stanford: Stanford University Press, 2006.

_____. *Transforming Atonement: A Political Theology of the Cross*. Minneapolis: Fortress Press, 2009.

_____. *Outlaw Justice: The Messianic Politics of Paul*. Stanford: Stanford University Press, 2013.

Jewett, Robert. *Christian Tolerance: Paul's Message to the Modern Church*. Philadelphia: Westminster Press, 1982.

_____. *Romans: A Commentary*. Hermeneia. Minneapolis: Fortress Press, 2007.

Johnson, Lee A. "Performance in Corinth: Envisioning Paul's Successful "Letter of Tears." *Perspectives in Religious Studies* 42, no. 1 (2015): 43-59.

Jones, A. H. M. *Augustus*. New York: W.W. Norton & Company, 1970.

Jones, Amos Jr. *Paul's Message of Freedom: What Does it Mean to the Black Church?* Valley Forge: Judson Press, 1984.

Judge, E. A. *Social Distinctives of the Christians in the First Century: Pivotal Essays by E. A. Judge*, edited by David M. Scholer. Peabody: Hendrickson Publishers Inc, 2008.

Kahl, Bridget. "Acts of the Apostles: Pro(to)-Imperial Script and Hidden Transcript." In *In the Shadow of the Empire*, edited by Richard A. Horsley, 137-56. Louisville: Westminster John Knox Press, 2008.

_____. *Galatians Re-Imagined: Reading with the Eyes of the Vanquished*. Minneapolis: Fortress Press.

Kallenberg, Brad J. "The Gospel Truth of Relativism." *Scottish Journal of Reality* 53, no. 2 (2000): 177–211.

———. *Live to Tell: Evangelism for a Postmodern Age*. Grand Rapids: Brazos Press, 2002.

Kasemann, Ernst. *Perspectives on Paul*. Minneapolis: Fortress Press, 1971.

Keck, Leander E. "Paul as Thinker." *Interpretation* 47, no. 1 (1983):27–38.

Kelber, Werner H. "Jesus and Tradition: Words in Time, Words in Space." *Semeia* 64 (1994): 139–67.

Kerr, Fergus. *Theology After Wittgenstein*. London: Society for Promoting Christian Knowledge, 1997.

Kim, Yung Suk. *Christ's Body in Corinth: The Politics of a Metaphor*. Minneapolis: Fortress Press, 2008.

Kirk, J.R. *Jesus I Have Loved, by Paul? A Narrative Approach to the Problem of Pauline Christianity*. Grand Rapids: Baker Academic, 2012.

Kirk, Alexander N. *The Departure of an Apostle: Paul's Death Anticipated and Remembered*. Tübingen Germany: Mohr Siebeck, 2015.

Kittridge, Cynthia Briggs. *Community Authority: The Rhetoric of Obedience in the Pauline Tradition*. Harrisburg: Trinity Press International, 1998.

———. "Rethinking Authorship in the Letters of Paul: Elizabeth Schüssler Fiorenza's Model of Pauline Theology." In *Walk in the Ways of Wisdom: Essays in Honor of Elizabeth Schüssler Fiorenza*," edited by Shelly Matthews, Cynthia Briggs Kittridge and Melanie Johnson-DeBaufre, 297–317. Harrisburg: Trinity Press International, 2003.

Knox, John. *Philemon Among the Letters of Paul: A New View of its Place and Importance*. Knox, NY: Abingdon Press, 1959.

———. "Chapters in a Life of Paul—A Response to Robert Jewett and Gerd Leudemann." In *Colloquy on New Testament Studies: A Time for Reappraisal and Fresh Approaches*, edited by Bruce Corley, 339–64. Macon GA: Mercer University Press, 1983.

———. *Chapters in a Life of Paul*. Macon: Mercer University Press, 1987.

———. "On the Pauline Chronology: Buck-Taylor Hurd Revisited." In *Studies in Paul and John: In Honor of J Louis Martyn*, edited by Robert T. Fortna and Beverly R. Gaventa, 258–74. Nashville: Abington Press, 1990.

Kochenash, Michael. "Better Call Paul "Saul": Literary Models and a Lukan Innovation." *Journal of Biblical Literature* 138, no. 2 (2019): 433-49.

Koenig, John. "The Knowing of Glory and its Consequences (2 Corinthians 3-5)." In *Studies in Paul and John: In Honor of J Louis Martyn,* edited by Robert T. Fortna and Beverly R. Gaventa, 158-69. Nashville: Abington Press, 1990.

Krauss, Samuel. "The Jewish Rite of Covering the Head," *Hebrew Union College Annual* 19 (1945-1946): 121-46.

LaGrand, James. "Proliferation of the "Gentile" in the New Revised Standard Version." *Biblical Research* 41 (1996.): 77-87.

Lake, Kirsopp. *The Earlier Epistles of St. Paul: Their Motive and Origin.* London: Rivingtons, 1919.

Lampe, Peter.. *From Paul to Valentinus: Christians at Rome in the First Two Centuries.* Minneapolis: Fortress Press, 2003.

Laquer, Thomas. *Making Sex: Body and Gender from the Greeks to Freud.* Cambridge: Harvard University Press, 1990.

Lash, Nicholas.. *Theology on the Way to Emmaus.* Eugene, OR: Wipf & Stock, 1986.

_____. *Easter in Ordinary: Reflections on Human Experience and the Knowledge of God.* Notre Dame: Notre Dame Press, 1986.

Last, Richard. "*Ekklesia* outside the Septuagint and the *Demos*: The Title of Graeco-Roman Associations and Christ-Follower Groups." *Journal of Biblical Literature* 137, no 4 (2018) 959-80.

Lewis, Allan E. *Between Cross and Resurrection: A Theology of Holy Saturday.* Grand Rapids: Eerdman's, 2001.

Lewis, Robert Bryan. *Paul's Spirit of Adoption in its Roman Imperial Context.* New York: Bloomsbury T & T Clark, 2016.

Lieu, Judith M. "The Battle for Paul in the Second Century." *Irish Theological Quarterly* 75, no. 1 (2009): 1-12.

Lindbeck, George A. *The Nature of Doctrine: Religion and Theology in a Postliberal Age.* Louisville: Westminster John Knox Press, 2009.

Lithgow, John. *The Poet's Corner: The One-and-Only Poetry Book for the Whole Family.* New York: Grand Central Publishing, 2007.

Longenecker, Bruce W. "Sharing in their Spiritual Blessings? The Stories of Israel in Galatians and Romans" In *Narrative Dynamics in Paul: A Critical Assessment,* edited by Bruce Longenecker, 58-84. Louisville: Westminster John Knox Press, 2002.

_____. *Remember the Poor: Paul, Poverty and the Greco-Roman World.* Grand Rapids: Wm. B. Eerdmans Publishing Company, 2010.

Lopez, Davina C. "Paul, Gender and Gender Paradigms." *Union Seminary Quarterly Review* 50, no 3-4 (2005): 92–106.

_____. *Apostle to the Conquered: Reimaging Paul's Mission.* Minneapolis: Fortress Press, 2008.

Lindbeck, George A. *The Nature of Doctrine: Religion and Theology in a Postliberal Age.* Louisville: Westminster John Knox Press, 2009.

Lüdemann, Gerd. *Paul, Apostle to the Gentiles: Studies in Chronology.* Philadelphia: Fortress Press, 1984.

_____. *Opposition to Paul in Jewish Christianity.* Philadelphia: Fortress Press, 1989.

Lyons, George. *Pauline Autobiography: Toward a New Understanding.* Atlanta: Scholars Press, 1985.

Macaskill, Grant. *Union with Christ in the New Testament.* Oxford: Oxford University Press, 2013.

MacCulloch, Diarmaid. *Christianity: The First Three Thousand Years.* New York: Viking Press, 2010.

MacDonald, Dennis R. *The Legend and the Apostle: The Battle for Paul in Story and Canon.* Philadelphia: The Westminster Press, 1983.

_____. *There is No Male and Female: The Fate of a Dominical Saying in Paul and Gnosticism.* Philadelphia: Fortress Press, 1987.

MacDonald, Margaret Y. *Early Christian Women and Pagan Opinion: The Power of the Hysterical Woman.* Cambridge: Cambridge University Press, 1996.

_____. "Reading Real Women Through the Undisputed Letters of Paul." In *Women and Christian Origins*, edited by Ross Shepherd Kraemer and Mary Rose D'Angelo, 199-220. New York: Oxford University Press, 1999.

MacIntyre, Alasdair. *Three Rival Versions of Moral Enquiry: Encyclopedia, Genealogy, and Tradition.* Notre Dame: University of Notre Dame Press, 1990.

_____. "The Virtues, the Unity of a Human Life, and the Concept of a Tradition." In *Readings in Narrative Theology: Why Narrative?* edited by Stanley Hauerwas and L. Gregory Jones, 89–112. Eugene: Wipf and Stock, 1997.

_____. *After Virtue: A Study in Moral Theory.* Notre Dame, IN; University of Notre Dame Press, 3rd ed, 2007.

Malina, Bruce J. and Jerome H. Neyrey. *Portraits of Paul: An Archeology of Ancient Personality.* Louisville, Kentucky: Westminster John Knox Press, 1996.

Marchal, Joseph A. "The Usefulness of Onesimus: The Sexual Use of Slaves and Paul's Letter to Philemon," *Journal of Biblical Literature*, 130, no. 4 (2011): 749-70.

Marguerat, Daniel. *Paul in Acts and Paul in His Letters*. Tubingen, Germany: Mohr Siebeck, 2013.

Marshall, Bruce. "Introduction: *The Nature of Doctrine* after 25 Years." In *The Nature of Doctrine: Religion and Theology in a Post Liberal Age*, edited by George A. Lindbeck, vii-xxvii. Louisville: Westminster John Knox Press, 2009.

Martin, Clarice J. ""Somebody Done Hoodoo'd the Hoodoo Man": Language, Power, Resistance, and the Effective History of Pauline Texts in American Slavery." *Semeia* 83-84 (1998): 203-35.

Martin, Dale B. *Slavery as Salvation: The Metaphor of Slavery in Pauline Christianity*. New Haven: Yale University Press, 1990.

———. *The Corinthian Body*. New Haven: Yale University Press, 1995.

Martyn, J. Louis. *Galatians: A New Translation with Introduction and Commentary*. New Haven: Yale University Press, 1997.

———. *Theological Issues in the Letters of Paul*. Nashville: Abingdon Press, 1997.

———. "The Apocalyptic Gospel in Galatians." *Interpretation* 54, no. 3 (2000): 246-66.

Mason, Steve. "Jews, Judeans, Judaizing, Judaism: Problems of Categorization in Ancient History" *Journal for the Study of Judaism* 38 (2007): 457-512.

———. *Josephus, Judea, and Christian Origins: Methods and Categories*, Peabody: Henrickson Publishers, 2009.

———. "Paul Without Judaism: Historical Method over Perspective." In *Paul and Matthew Among Jews and Gentiles*, ed. Ronald Charles, 9-40. London: Bloomsbury T & T Clark, 2021.

Mattern, Susan P. *Rome and the Enemy: Imperial Strategy in the Principate*. Berkley: University of California Press, 1999.

McClendon Jr., James Wm. *Systematic Theology: Ethics*. Nashville: Abingdon Press, 1986.

McDonough, Sean. "Small Change: Saul to Paul Again." *Journal of Biblical Literature* 125 no 2 (2006): 390-91.

McGrath, Alister E. *Iustitia Dei: A History of the Christian Doctrine of Justification*, 3rd ed. Cambridge: Cambridge University Press, 2005.

McKnight, Scott. *The Letter to Philemon.*, Grand Rapids: William. B. Eerdmans Publishing Company, 2017.

McNeel, Jennifer Houston. "Feeding with Milk: Paul's Nursing Metaphors in Context." *Review and Expositor* 111 2013): 561-75.

Meeks, Wayne A. "The Christian Proteus." In *The Writings of St. Paul*, edited by Wayne A. Meeks, 435-44. New York: W.W. Norton & Company, 1972.

Meggitt, Justin J. *Paul, Poverty, and Survival*. Edinburgh: T & T Clark, 1998.

_____. "Taking the Emperor's Clothes Seriously: The New Testament and the Roman Emperor." In *The Quest for Wisdom: Essays in Honour of Philip Budd*, edited by C. Joynes, 143-70. Cambridge: Orchard Academic, 2002.

Metz, Johannes B. *Poverty of Spirit*. New York: Paulist Press, 1968.

Meyer, Paul W. "Pauline Theology: A Proposal for a Pause in Its Pursuit." In *Pauline Theology. Vol. 7, Looking Back, Pressing On*, edited by E. Elizabeth Johnson and David M. Hay, 140-60. Atlanta: Scholars Press, 1997.

_____. *The Word in This World: Essays in New Testament Exegesis and Theology*. Louisville: John Knox Press, 2004.

Miller, J. David. 2009. "Translating Paul's Words About Women." *Stone-Campbell Journal* 12 (2009): 61-71.

Mitchell, Margaret M. *Paul and the Rhetoric of Reconciliation: An Exegetical Investigation of the Language and Composition of 1 Corinthians*. Louisville: Westminster/John Knox Press, 1991.

_____. "Virgins, Widows, and Wives: The Women of 1 Corinthians 7." n *A Feminist Companion to Paul*, edited by Amy-Jill Levine with Marianne Blickenstaff, 148-68. New York: T & T Clark International, 2004.

Milbank, John. *Theology and Social Theory: Beyond Secular Reason*. Malden: Blackwell Publishing, 2006.

Miller, Colin D. *The Practice of the Body of Christ: Human Agency in Pauline Theology after MacIntyre*." Cambridge: James Clarke & Co, 2014.

Minor, Mitzi. *2 Corinthians*. Macon: Smyth and Helwys Publishing, 2009.

Moltmann, Jurgen. *The Way of Jesus Christ*. Minneapolis: Fortress Press, 1999.

Morley, Neville. "The Poor in the City of Rome." In *Poverty in the Roman World*, edited by Margaret Atkins and Robin Osborne, 21-39. New York: Cambridge University Press, 2006.

Morray-Jones, C. R. A. "The Jewish Mystical Background of Paul's Apostolate. Part One: The Jewish Sources." *Harvard Theological Review* 86, no. 2 (1993): 177-217.

_____. "Paradise Revisted (2 Cor 12:1-12): The Jewish Mystical Background of Paul's Apostalate. Part 2: Paul's Heavenly Ascent and Its Significance." *Harvard Theological Review* 86, no. 3 (1993): 265-92.

Mount, Christopher. "1 Corinthians 11:3-16: Spirit Possession and Authority in a Non-Pauline Interpolation." *Journal of Biblical Literature* 124. no.2 (2005), 313-40.

Murphy-O'Conner, Jerome. *Paul His Story*. New York: Oxford University Press, 2004.

_____. *Paul A History*. New York: Oxford University Press, 2006.

Nanos, Mark D. *The Mystery of Romans: The Jewish Context of Paul's Letter*. Minneapolis: Fortress Press, 1996.

_____. "The Jewish Context of the Gentile Audience Addressed in Paul's Letter to the Romans." *The Catholic Biblical Quarterly* 61 no. 2 (1999): 283-304.

_____. *The Irony of Galatians*. Minneapolis: Fortress Press, 2002.

_____. "The Question of Conceptualization: Qualifying Paul's Position on Circumcision in Dialogue with Josephus's Advisors to King Izates." In *Paul Within Judaism: Restoring the First-Century Context to the Apostle*, edited by Mark D. Nanos and Magnus Zetterholm, 105-52. Minneapolis: Fortress Press, 2015.

_____. "How Could Paul Accuse Peter of "Living Ethné-ishly" in Antioch (Gal 2:11-21): If Peter Was Eating according to Jewish Dietary Norms?" *Journal for the Study of Paul and His Letters* 6, no. 2 (2016): 199-223.

_____. "The Myth of the "Law-Free" Paul Standing between Christians and Jews," in *Reading Paul Within Judaism: Collected Essays of Mark Nanos*, vol 1, loc. 2252 of 5769, 3429 of 5769. Eugene: Cascade Books (Kindle Reader).

Nanos, Mark D. and Magnus Zetterholm, eds. *Paul Within Judaism: Restoring the First-Century Context to the Apostle*. Minneapolis: Fortress Press, 2015.

Newbigin, Leslie. *The Open Secret: An Introduction to the Theology of Mission*. Grand Rapids: Eerdman's's Publishing Company, 1995.

Neyrey, Jerome H. *Paul In Other Words: A Cultural Reading of His Letters*. Louisville KY: Westminster John Knox Press, 1990.

Novenson, Matthew V. *Paul: Then and Now*. Grand Rapids: Eerdman's Publishing, 2022.

Odell-Scott, David. W. "Let Women Speak Church: An Egalitarian Interpretation of 1 Cor. 14:33b-36." *Biblical Theology Bulletin* 13, no. 3 (1983): 90-3.

_____. "In Defense of an Egalitarian Interpretation of First Corinthians 14:34-36: A reply to Murphy O'Connor's Critique." *Biblical Theology Bulletin* 17, no 3 (1987) 100-3.

_____. *Paul's Critique of Theocracy: A/Theocracy in Corinthians and Galatians,* New York: T & T Clark, 2003.

Ong, Walter. "Text as Interpretation: Mark and After." *Semeia,* 39 (1987): 7-26.

Osiek, Carolyn and Margaret Y. MacDonald, with Janet H. Tulloch. *A Woman's Place: House Churches in Earliest Christianity.* Minneapolis: Fortress Press, 2006.

Padgett, Alan. "Paul on Women in the Church: The Contradiction of Coiffeur in 1 Corinthians 11:2-16." *Journal for the Study of the New Testament* 6 no. 2 (1984): 69-86.

Patel, Raphael. "The Shakhina." *Journal of Religion* 44, no. 4 (Oct. 1960): 275-288.

Patterson, Orlando, *Slavery and Social Death: A Comparative Study.* Cambridge: Harvard University Press, 1982.

Patterson, Stephen J. *The Forgotten Creed: Christianity's Original Struggle Against Bigotry, Slavery and Sexism.* New York: Oxford University Press, 2018.

Pervo, Richard I. *The Mystery of Acts: Unraveling Its Story.* Santa Rosa: Polebridge Press, 2008.

_____. *Luke's Story of Paul.* Minneapolis: Fortress Press, 2009

_____. "Acts in the Suburbs of the Apologists." In *Contemporary Studies in Acts,* edited by Thomas E. Phillips, 29-46. Macon: Mercer University Press, 2009.

_____. *Acts: A Commentary.* Minneapolis: Fortress Press, 2009

_____. *The Making of Paul: Constructions of the Apostle in Early Christainity.* Minneapolis: Fortress Press, 2010.

J. B Phillips. *Letters to Young Churches: A Translation of the New Testament Epistles.* New York: The Macmillan Company, 1954.

Phillips, Thomas E. *Paul, His Letters and Acts.* Grand Rapids: Baker Publishing Company, 2009.

_____. "Prophets, Priests, and Godfearing Readers: The Priestly and Prophetic Tradtions in Luke-Acts." In *Contemporary Studies in Acts,* edited by Thomas E. Phillips, 222-39. Macon: Mercer University Press, 2009.

_____. "When did Paul become a Christian?" In *Christian Origins and the New Testament in Greco-Roman Context*, edited by Margaret Froelich, Michael Kochenash, and Thomas E. Phillips, 180-201. Claremont, CA: Claremont Press.

Polaski, Sandra Hock. *A Feminist Introduction to Paul*. St. Louis: Chalice Press, 2005.

Powery, Emerson B. "'Rise Up, Ye Women': Harriet Jacobs and the Bible." *Postscripts* 5, no. 2 (2009): 171-84.

Ramsey, W. M. *St. Paul The Traveler: And the Roman Citizen*. New York: G. P. Putnam, 1904.

Richardson, Neil. *Paul for Today: New Perspectives on a Controversial Apostle*. London: Methodist Church House, 2008.

Robbins, Vernon. "Oral, Rhetorical and Literary Cultures." *Semeia*, 65 (1994): 75-91.

Robinson, Brian J. *Being Subordinate Men: Paul's Rhetoric of Gender and Power in 1 Corinthians*. London: Lexington Books, 2019.

Roetzel, Calvin J. *Paul: The Man and the Myth*. Minneapolis: Fortress Press, 1999.

_____. *The Letters of Paul: Conversations in Context*. Louisville: Westminster John Knox Press, 2015.

Roland, Christopher, *Christian Origins: An Account of the Setting and Character of the Most Important Messianic Sect of Judaism*, London: SPCK, 1989.

Rowling, J. K. *Harry Potter and the Sorcerer's Stone*. New York: Scholastic Press, 1998.

Ruden, Sarah. *Paul Among the People: The Apostle Reinterpreted and Reimagined in His Own Time*. New York: Image Books, 2010.

Runesson, Anders. "The Question of Terminology: The Architecture of Contemporary Discussions on Paul." In *Paul within Judaism: Restoring the First-Century Context to the Apostle*, edited by Mark D. Nanos and Magnus Zetterholm, 53-77. Minneapolis: Fortress Press, 2015.

Sachs, Jonathan. *The Great Partnership: God, Science and the Search for Meeting*. London: Hodder and Stoughton, 2011.

Saller, Richard P. *Personal Patronage under the Early Empire*. Cambridge: Cambridge University Press, 1982.

Sanders, E. P. *Paul, the Law, and the Jewish People*. Minneapolis: Fortress Press, 1983.

_____. *Comparing Judaism and Christianity: Common Judaism, Paul, and the Inner and Outer in Ancient Religion*. Minneapolis: Fortress Press, 2016.

Schellenberg, Ryan. *Abject Joy: Paul Prison, and the Art of Making Do.* New York: Oxford University Press, 2021.

Scholem, Gershom. *Kabblah.* New York: Dorset Press, 1987.

———. *On the Mystical Shape of the Godhead: Basic Concepts in the Kabbalh.* New York: Schoken Books, 1991.

Scott, Bernard Brandon, "Blowing in the Wind: A Response." *Semeia,* 65 (1994): 181–91.

———. *The Real Paul: Recovering His Radical Challenge.* Salem: Polebridge Press, 2015.

Scott, James C. *Domination and the Arts of Resistance: Hidden Transcripts.* New Haven: Yale University Press, 1990.

Sechrest, Love L. *A Former Jew: Paul and the Dialectics of Race.* New York: T&T Clark, 2009.

Segal, Alan F. *Paul the Convert: The Apostolate and Apostasy of Saul the Pharisee.* New Haven: Yale University Press, 1990.

Seneca. *Seneca's Letters from a Stoic.* Mineola, NY: Dover Publications, 2016.

Schantz, Colleen *Paul in Ecstasy: The Neurobiology of the Apostle's Life and Thought.* New York: Cambridge University Press, 2009.

Smart, James B. trans. *Revolutionary Theology in the Making: Bart-Thurneysen Correspondence, 1914–1925.* Richmond: John Knox Press, 1964.

Smith, Dennis E. and Joseph B Tyson. *Acts and Christian Beginnings: The Acts Seminar Report.* Salem: Polebridge Press, 2013.

Solnit, Rebecca. *The Faraway Nearby.* New York: Penguin Books, 2013.

Stark, Rodney. *The Rise of Christianity: How the Obscure, Marginal Jesus Movement Became the Dominant Religious Force in the Western World in a Few Centuries.* New York: Harper Collins Publishers, 1996.

Stendahl, Krister, "The Apostle Paul and the Introspective Conscience of the West." *Harvard Theological Review* 56, no. 3 (1963): 199–215.

———. *Paul Among Jews and Gentiles and Other Essays.* Philadelphia: Fortress Press, 1976.

Stowers, Stanley K. 1984. "Social Status, Public Speaking and Private Teaching: The Circumstances of Paul's Preaching Activity." *Novum Testamentum* 26 no. 1 (1984): 59-82.

———. *A Re-Reading of Romans: Justice, Jews and Gentiles.* New Haven:

Yale University Press, 1994.

———. *Letter-Writing in Greco-Roman Antiquity*. Philadelphia: Westminster Press, 1986.

Sumney, Jerry L. "Paul's 'Weakness': An Integral Part of His Conception of Aposleship." *Journal for the Study of the New Testament* 52 (1993): 71–91.

Swancutt, Diana M. "Still Before Sexuality—"Greek" Androgyny, the Roman Imperial Politics of Masculinity and the Roman Invention of the Tribas." In *Mapping Gender in Ancient Religious Discourses*, edited by Todd Penner and Caroline Vander Stichele, 11–62. Boston: Brill, 2006.

Tamez, Elizabeth. "Author's Introduction to Philippians." In *Philippians, Colossians, Philemon*, edited by Elsa Tamez, Cynthia Kittridge, Claire Colombo, and Alicia J.Batten, 1–36. Collegeville: Liturgical Press, 2016.

Taylor, Charles. 1994. "The Politics of Recognition." In *Muticuluralism: Examining the Politics of Recognition*, edited by Amy Guttmann, 25–73. Princeton: Princeton University Press, 1994.

———. *A Secular Age*. Cambridge: The Belknap Press of Harvard University Press, 2007.

Taylor, Justin. "The Ethnarch of King Aretas at Damascus: A Note of 2 Cor. 11.32-33." *Revue Biblique* 99 (1992): 718–28.

Taylor, Justin. "Why Were the Disciples First Called 'Christians' at Antioch?" *Revue Biblique* 101 (1994): 75–94.

Theissen, Gerd. *The Social Setting of Pauline Christianity: Essays on Corinth*. Philadelphia: Fortress Press, 1982.

———. "Social Conflicts in the Corinthian Community: Further Remarks on J.J. Meggitt, *Paul, Poverty and Survival*." *Journal for the Study of the New Testament* 25 (2003): 371–91.

Thompson, Michael B. *Clothed with Christ: The Example and Teaching of Jesus in Romans 12.1-15.13*. Eugene: Wipf and Stock, 2011.

Thorley, John. "Junia, A Woman Apostle," *Novum Testamentum* 38 no. 1 (1996): 18–29.

Thurman, Howard, *With Heart and Hand: The Autobiography of Howard Thurman*. New York: Houghton Mifflin Harcourt Publishing Company, 1979.

———. *Jesus and the Disinherited*. Boston: Beacon Press, 2012.

Tomson, Peter J., *Paul and the Jewish Law: Halakha in the Letters of The Apostle to the Gentiles,* Minneapolis: Fortress Press, 1990.

Toole, David. *Waiting for God in Sarajevo: Theological Reflections on*

Nihilism, Tragedy and Apocalypse. Boulder: Westview Press, 1988.

Trobisch, David. *Paul's Letter Collection: Tracing the Origins*. Minneapolis: Augsburg Fortress, 1994.

Tyson, Joseph B. "The Problem of the Jewish Rejection in Acts." In *Luke-Acts and the Jewish People: Eight Critical Perspectives*, edited by Joseph B. Tyson, 124-137. Nashville: Augsburg Publishing, 1988.

———. "Acts and the Apostles: Issues of Leadership in the Second Century." Perspectives in Religious Studies 43, no. 4 (2016.): 385-98.

Underhill, Evelyn. *Mysticism: A Study in Nature and Development of Spiritual Consciousness*. New York: E. P. Dutton and Company Inc. Publishers, 1948.

———. *Practical Mysticism*. Columbus, OH: Ariel Press, 1942.

Vanhoozer, Kevin J. "From 'Blessed in Christ' to 'Being in Christ': The State of Union and the Place of Participation in Paul's Discourse, New Testament Exegesis, and Systematic Theology Today." In *"In Christ" in Paul*, edited by Michael J. Thate, Kevin J. VanHoozer, and Constantine R. Campbell, 3-36. Tübingen: Mohr Siebeck, 2014.

Vassas, Claudine & Anne Stevens. "Presences of the Feminine within Judaism," *Clio, Women Gender, History* 44 (2016): 220-28.

Volf, Miroslav. *Exclusion and Embrace: A Theological Exploration of Identity, Otherness, and Reconciliation*. Nashville: Abingdon Press, 1996.

Walker, Jr., W. O. "The Letters of Paul as Sources for Acts." In *Acts and Christian Beginnings: The Acts Seminar Report*, edited by Dennis E. Smith and Joseph B. Tyson, 116-17. Salem: Polebridge Press, 2013.

Wallace, James Buchanan. *Snatched into Paradise: Paul's Heavenly Journey in the Context of Early Christian Experience*. Berlin: De Gruyter, 2011).

Wansink, Craig S. *Chained in Christ: The Experience and Rhetoric of Paul's Imprisonments*. Sheffield: Sheffield Academic Press, 1996.

Welborn, L.L. *Paul, the Fool of Christ: A Study of 1 Corinthians 1-4 in the Comic-Philosophic Tradition*. New York: T & T Clark Publishing, 2005.

_____. "Paul's Caricature of his Chief Rival as a Pompous Parasite in 2 Corinthians 11.20." *Journal for the Study of the New Testament* 32, no. 1 (2009): 39–56.

_____. *An End to Enmity: Paul and the "Wrongdoer" of Second Corinthians*. Göttingen: Walter de Gruyter GmbH & Co, 2011.

Westfall, Cynthia Long. *Paul and Gender: Reclaiming the Apostle's Vision for Men and Women in Christ*. Grand Rapids: Baker Academic, 2016.

White, Benjamin L. *Remembering Paul: Ancient and Modern Contests over the Image of the Apostle*. New York: Oxford University Press, 2014.

Wikenhauser, Alfred. *Pauline Mysticism: Christ in the Mystical Teaching of Paul*. New York: Herder and Herder, 1960.

Williams, Margaret. "The Use of Alternative Names by Diaspora Jews In Graeco-Roman Antiquity." *Journal for the Study of Judaism* 38 (2007): 307–26.

Williams, Rowan. *Why Study the Past?: The Quest for the Historical Church*. Grand Rapids: Eerdman's, 2005.

Wickenhauser, Alfred. *Pauline Mysticism: Christ in the Mystical Teaching of Paul*. New York: Herder and Herder, 1960.

Wilder, Amos. *Otherworldliness and the New Testament*. Chicago: S.C.M. Book Club, 1955.

_____. *Early Christian Rhetoric: The Language of the Gospel*. Cambridge: Harvard University Press, 1971.

_____. *Theopoetic: Theology and the Religious Imagination*. Lima, Ohio: Academic Renewal Press, 1976.

_____. *Jesus' Parables and the War of Myths: Essays on Imagination in the Scriptures*, Philadelphia: Fortress Press, 1982.

_____. "Story and Story World," *Interpretation* 37, no. 4 1983): 353–64.

_____. *Theopoetic: Theology and the Religious Imagination*. Lima, Ohio: Academic Renewal Press, 2001.

Wilder, Terry L. "Phoebe, the Letter-Carrier of Romans, and the Impact of Her Role on Biblical Theology." *Southwestern Journal of Theology* 56, no 1 (2013): 43–51.

Williams, Demetrius. "The Acts of the Apostles." In *True to our Native Land*, edited by Brian K. Blount, Cain Hope Felder, Clarice J. Martin, and Emerson B. Powery, 213–48. Minneapolis: Fortress Press, 2007.

Willis, Wendell, "Paul's Downward Mobility." *Journal for the Study of Paul and His Letters* 5 (2015):109–27.

Willitts, Joel, 2016. "Paul the Rabbi of Messianic Judaism: Reading the Antioch Incident within Judaism as an Irreducibility Story," *Journal for the Study of Paul and His Letters*, 6 no. 2 2016): 225–47.

Wills, Gary. *What Paul Meant*. New York: Viking, 2006.

Wilson, Brittany E. *Refigurations of Masculinity in Luke-Acts*. Oxford: Oxford University Press, 2015.

Winter, Sara C., "Methodological Observations on a New Interpretation of Paul's Letter to Philemon." *Union Seminary Quarterly Review* 39 no. 3 (1984): 203–12.

Wire, Antoinette Clark. *The Corinthian Women Prophets: A Reconstruction through Paul's Rhetoric*. Minneapolis: Fortress Press, 1990.

_____. *2 Corinthians*. Collegeville, MN: Liturgical Press, 2019.

Woolf, Greg. 2006. "Writing Poverty in Rome." In *Poverty in the Roman World*, edited by Margaret Atkins and Robin Osborner, 83–99. New York: Cambridge University Press, 2006.

Wright, N. T. "Christ in You, The Hope of Glory (Colossians 1.27): Eschatology in St Paul." In *Pauline Perspectives: Essays on Paul, 1978 – 2013*, edited by N. T. Wright, 379–91. Minneapolis: Fortress Press, 2013.

_____. *Pauline Perspectives: Essays on Paul, 1978-2013*. Minneapolis: Fortress Press, 2013.

_____. *Paul and The Faithfulness of God*. Minneapolis: Fortress Press, 2013.

_____. *Paul and His Recent Interpreters: Some Contemporary Debates*. Minneapolis: Fortress Press, 2015.

_____. *Paul: A Biography*. San Francisco: Harper One, 2018.

Yoder, John Howard. "The Apostle's Apology Revisited." In *The New Way of Jesus: Essays Presented to Howard Charles*, edited by William Klassen, 115–134. Newton, KS: Faith and Life Press, 1980.

_____. "Ethics and Eschatology." *Ex Auditu*, 6, (1990): 119-128.

_____. *The Politics of Jesus: Vicit Agnus Noster*. Grand Rapids, MI: Wm. B. Eerdmans Publishing. (Second edition), 1994.

_____. "Meaning After Babble." *Journal of Religious Ethics* 24, no. 1 (1996): 125–39.

Zerbe, Gordon. "The One and the Many, the Part and the All: Unity and Diversity in the Messiah's Body Politic." *Vision: A Journal of Church and Theology* 11, no. 1 (2010): 77-90.

_____. "From Retributive Justice to Restorative Justice." *Direction* 44, no. 1 (2015): 43-58.

_____. *Citizenship: Paul on Peace and Politics*. Winnipeg: CMU Press, 2018.

Zetterholm, Magnus. *Approaches to Paul: A Student's Guide to Recent Scholarship*. Minneapolis: Fortress Press, 2009.

_____. "Paul within Judaism: The State of the Questions." In *Paul within Judaism: Restoring the First-Century Context to the Apostle*, edited by Mark D. Nanos and Magnus Zetterholm, 31–51. Minneapolis: Fortress Press, 2015.

Ziegler, Philip G. "Some Remarks on Apocalyptic in Modern Christian Theology." In *Paul and the Apocalyptic Imagination: An Introduction*, edited by Ben C. Blackwell, John K. Goodrich, and Jason Maston, 199-218. Minneapolis: Fortress Press, 2016.

Zuck, Roy B. "The Jews, Modern Israel, and the New Supercessionism." *Bibliotheca Sacra* 168 (2011): 487.

Index to Authors

Adams, Edward, 99
Adelman, Rachel, 202
Agamben, Giorgio, 57–59, 73, 84, 122, 278, 280
Anderson, John T., 262
Armstrong, Karen, 114, 251
Asad, Talal, 126, 267
Ascough, Richard, 131
Ashton, John, 39, 266
Assmann, Jan, 134
Aus, Roger D., 290–91

Bailey, Kenneth, 90, 104–5, 133, 173, 176–77, 183
Barclay, John M. G., 40, 287
Bateman, Elizabeth, 172
Bartchy, S. Scott, 211, 214
Bazzana, Giovanni, 254, 257
Beard, Mary, 76, 89, 171, 291–92
Becker, Eve-Marie, 93
Beker, J.C., 15, 17, 301
Beitzel, Barry J., 289
Benjamin, Walter, 255, 279
Betz, Hans Dieter, 42, 48
Bickerman, Elias J., 284
Bird, Michael F., 50–51, 113–114, 118–19, 185
Borg, Marcus, 204–5
Bowens, Lisa M., 201, 210, 301–3
Boyarin, Daniel, 117–20
Bowersock, G. W., 31, 43, 48–50
Bozarth-Campbell, Alla, 140–42, 145–46
Bradley, Keith R., 198–99, 200, 204
Briggs, J. R., 221
Briggs, Sheila, 215
Bristow, John, 157, 173, 183, 189
Bryant, K. E. Edwin, 199, 201

Callahan, Allen Dwight, 201, 204, 214, 216
Campbell, Douglas A., vii, 28, 32, 47, 50–51, 160, 277
Caputo, Jack, 123, 128, 130–31, 242–43, 261, 299
Castelli, Elizabeth A., 190
Cervo, Richard, 3
Chapple, Allan, 144
Collins, Raymond, 155
Cone, James H., 198
Crites, Stephen, 70
Crossan, John Dominic, 7, 54, 204–5, 298

Dahl, Nils A., 294
Danker, William, 36, 76, 93, 127, 162, 179, 185, 211, 231, 234, 270, 273, 277
Davey, Noel, 251
Despostis, Athanasious, 275–76
Dewey, Arthur J., 140
Dewey, Joanna, 146, 153
Deissmann, Adolf, 40, 88, 245
Dorff, Elliot N., 113
Downs, David J., 288
Drinkwater, John F., 232
Dunn, James D., 12, 246–47, 269–70
Dunnett, Walter, vii

Eastman, Susan, 104, 165
Ehrensperger, Kathy, 15, 43, 121–22, 148, 157, 159, 295–96
Eisenbaum, Pamela, 1, 35, 40, 55–56, 110–11, 115, 118
Elliott, Neil, vii, 24, 54, 113, 171, 211, 219, 230, 233, 237–38, 293, 296, 299
Eubank, Nathan, 286

Fee, Gordon, 173, 184–86, 211, 292
Fiorenza, Elizabeth Schüssler, 72, 163, 180, 182
Frankopan, Peter, 43
Fredriksen, Paula, 34, 42, 70, 113, 118, 278, 299
Frei, Hans, 69
Friesen, Steven, 102–3

Gager, John G., 54, 89, 116, 121
Garroway, Joshua D., 46
Gaston, Lloyd, 294
Gaventa, Beverly, 72, 155, 157, 163, 166–68, 280
Gench, Francis Taylor, 162–63, 182–83
Georgi, Dieter, 276, 287
Glancy, Jennifer A., 197–98, 204, 215
Goldsworthy, Adrian, 296
Gordon, Richard, 35, 171
Gray, Patrick, 12, 29
Gorman, Michael J., 60
Gregory, Brad, 125, 266
Griffiths, David, 289, 290–93, 296

Haenchen, Ernst, 26, 54
Hardy, Barbara, 69
Harink, Douglas, 45
Harrill, J. Albert, 199, 207
Harrison, James R., 238, 286–87
Hauerwas, Stanley, 69–70, 109, 241, 304
Hawkins, Faith Kirkham, 175
Hays, Richard B., 58, 70, 84, 117, 172, 271–72
Hengel, Martin, 43
Hobsbawm, Eric, 27, 191
Hopkins, Gerard Manly, 248
Horrell, David G., 2, 87
Horsley, Richard A., 26, 34–35, 42, 47, 95, 132, 140–41, 159, 176, 194, 205, 214–15, 219, 238, 295
Hoskyns, Arland J., 251
Hultgren, Arland, ix, 33, 37, 136, 230–33

Jennings, W. Theodore Jr., 75, 114, 194, 282
Jewett, Robert, 89, 97–98, 136, 140, 153–54, 207, 213, 222, 230–31, 233, 235, 240, 242–43, 268, 284, 291, 294–95
Johnson, Lee A., 229
Jones, A. H. M., 290
Jones, Amos Jr., 193, 201, 209–10, 213–14
Jones, L. Gregory, 69–70
Judge, E. A., 161

Kahl, Bridget, 36–37, 54, 97, 203, 270, 296
Kim, Yung Suk, 186
King, Martin Luther, 125, 196, 201, 219, 303
Kirk, J. R., 125–26, 196
Kittridge, Cynthia Briggs, 130, 180
Knox, John, 1, 3, 16, 18, 33, 261
Kochenash, Michael, 56
Koenig, John, 280
Krauss, Samuel, 171

Lake, Kirsopp, 39–40
Lampe, Peter, 230
Laqueur, Thomas, 158
Lash, Nicholas, 260
Lewis, Allan E., 219
Lewis, Robert Bryan, 48, 75, 191
Lieu, Judith M., 159–60
Lindbeck, George A., 241
Lithgow, John, 245–46, 272
Longenecker, Bruce W., 87
Lopez, Davina C., 81, 95–96, 192, 239
Lüdemann, Gerd, 1
Lyons, George, ix, 17

Macaskill, Grant, 262
MacCulloch, Diarmaid, 83, 127
MacDonald, Dennis, 8, 15–16, 139, 169, 172, 184–85
MacDonald, Margaret Y., 166
MacIntyre, Alasdair, 70–71, 73–74, 126
Malina, Bruce J., 50, 106–7
Marchal, Joseph A., 205
Marguerat, Daniel, 172
Marshall, Bruce D., 239
Martin, Clarice Jr., 199
Martin, Dale B., 77, 159, 173, 191, 195, 200, 269
Martyn, J. Louis, 41, 228, 273, 280–81

Mason, Steve, 38, 110, 128, 232, 253
Mattern, Susan P., 47
McGrath, Alister E., 234
McNeel, Jennifer Houston, 168
Meeks, Wayne A., 29
Meggitt, Justin J., 89, 97, 99–100, 104
Metz, Johannes B, 245
Miller, Colin D, 126
Miller, J. David, 178
Mitchell, Margaret M., 77–78, 129, 189
Moltmann, Jürgen, 126–27, 165, 281–82
Morley, Neville, 102
Morray-Jones, C. R. A., 254
Mount, Christopher, 176
Murphy-O'Connor, Jerome, 174, 186

Nanos, Mark D., 27, 70, 111, 116, 119, 157, 159, 289
Newbigin, Leslie, 69, 123
Neyrey, Jerome H. 106–7

Odell-Scott, David, 170, 176, 179, 186–87
Ong, Walter, 141
Osiek, Carolyn, ix, 163, 166

Padgett, Alan, 170, 176, 179
Patterson, Orlando, 197, 199–200, 205
Pervo, Richard I., vii, 11, 28
Phillips, J. B., 177
Phillips, Thomas E., vii, 51, 83
Polaski, Sandra Hock, 163, 173, 189–190, 192

Reasoner, Mark, 233
Robbins, Vernon, 90–91
Robinson, Brian, J., 161, 174–75
Roetzel, Calvin J., 53, 222
Ruden, Sarah, 172–73, 188, 190–91, 258
Runesson, Anders, 27

Saller, Richard P., 286
Sanders, E. P., 112
Scholem, Gershom, 265
Scott, Bernard Brandon, 23, 25, 152
Scott James C., 237

Secrest, Love. L L., 115
Segal, Alan F., 31, 82, 118, 245, 254, 264
Silverman, Neil Asher, 47
Smith, Dennis E., 6, 7, 26, 55, 83–84
Solnit, Rebecca, 21, 53
Stark, Rodney, 98, 100–1, 132, 230, 288
Stendahl, Krister, 31, 76–77, 81–82, 153
Stowers, Stanley K., 105, 146, 149–52
Sumney, Jerry L., 125, 161
Swancutt, Diana M., 163

Tamez. Elizabeth, 1, 18, 131, 163, 300–1
Taylor, Charles, 72, 79–80, 248–49
Taylor, Justin, 51
Theissen, Gerd, 88–89, 98–99
Thompson, Michael B., 241
Thorley, John, 3
Thurman, Howard, 139, 196–97, 301
Tomson, Peter, 235
Toole, David, 79
Trobisch, David, 7, 300
Tyson, Joseph B, 6–7, 26, 55, 83–84, 112

Underhill, Evelyn, 247–48, 254-555, 262, 265–66

Vanhoozer, Kevin J., 267–68, 271
Volf, Miroslav, 72–73, 160–61

Walker, William O. Jr., 7, 55
Wansink, Craig S, 205–6
Welborn, L. L., 58, 91, 105, 124, 149, 224–25
Westfall, Cynthia Long, 157, 163, 174, 177
White, Benjamin, 9–11, 28, 54, 82, 106
Williams, Margaret, 59
Williams, Rowan, 132
Wilder, Amos, 71, 202, 250–52, 259
Willis, Wendell, 92
Wilson, Brittany E., 139, 158–59, 163, 192
Winter, Sara C., 206, 208–9

Wire, Antoinette Clark, 161–62, 179–80, 182, 185, 221, 251
Wright, N.T., 11, 26, 30, 36, 41, 78, 83, 109, 121, 128, 161, 203–4, 272, 274, 280, 290, 299

Yoder, John Howard, 79, 236–37

Ziegler, Philip G., 280
Zerbe, Gordon, 17, 237, 273